232, 240, 242
tian feng [heavenly wind]

Reinforce/challenge culture.
139, 140, 141 (symbolism), 142 ff, 147, 184
189, 141, 195, 201, 208, 210, 213, 220, 222
Lao Tsu - Dao
divination   p. 101, 102, 148, 129, 131, 137

CONFUCIUS, THE BUDDHA, AND CHRIST

CONFUCIUS, THE BUDDHA, AND CHRIST

A History of the Gospel in Chinese

Ralph R. Covell

Wipf & Stock
PUBLISHERS
Eugene, Oregon

Wipf and Stock Publishers
199 West 8th Avenue, Suite 3
Eugene, Oregon 97401

Confucius, the Buddha, and Christ
A History of the Gospel in Chinese
By Covell, Ralph R.
Copyright©1986 by Covell, Ralph R.
ISBN: 1-59244-533-0
Publication date 1/20/2004
Previously published by Orbis Books, 1986

In memory of my colleague,
James Edwin Cummings,
who lived and preached the Gospel in Chinese
among the people of Taiwan for thirty years

Contents

Preface to the Series   xi

Preface   xiii

Chapter 1
The Many Faces of Christianity   1
    Christianity through the Ages   1
    Failed Strategies in China   3
    Peoples of China   4
    The Chinese Mind   7
    Indigenization of the Christian Faith   14
    Principles of Indigenization   17

Chapter 2
Jesus and the Lotus—The Nestorian Faith   20
    Origins of the Nestorian Church   20
    The Nestorian Gospel   24
    Evaluation of the Nestorian Gospel   31

Chapter 3
Christ the Scholar—The Jesuit Approach   36
    Christianity under the Mongols   36
    The Jesuits Come to China   39
    Jesuit Writings   44
    Chinese Converts   57
    Problems Facing the Jesuits   59

Chapter 4
The Gospel of Power—The Protestant Approach   68
    Missions and Power before the Protestant Period   68
    Protestant Attitudes to Catholic Missions   69
    A Wall of Light around China   70
    Bolder Efforts to Penetrate China   73
    The Opium War and Its Consequences   81

Chapter 5
East Meets West—Chinese Natural Theology and Western Common Sense 85
    Protestant Bible Controversy   85
    Oral Communication of the Gospel in Chinese   90
    Protestant Missionary Literature   91
    Catholic Literature   114
    The Gospel according to Chinese Converts   115
    Ancestral Rites and the Gospel   117

Chapter 6
The *Dao* and The *Logos*   **122**
    Disparagement of Buddhism   122
    Buddhism as a Preparation for Christianity   123
    Buddhism as the Gospel in Chinese   125
    Friends of the *Dao*   128

Chapter 7
Buddhism in China—The Contextualization of a Foreign Faith   **133**
    Massive Borrowing   136
    The Way of Accommodation   140
    Resistance and Adaptation   141
    Domestication and Appropriation of Buddhism   145
    Success Where Others Failed   147

Chapter 8
New Deities and Demons—Taiping Christianity   **150**
    Taiping Origins   151
    The Taiping Constitution   154
    Sources of Taiping Ideology   155
    The Taiping Gospel in Chinese   157
    Weaknesses of Taiping Christianity   168
    Evaluation of the Taiping Gospel in Chinese   170
    The Chinese Content of the Taiping Gospel   173
    Missionary Evaluation of the Taipings   174
    "Not Once in a Thousand Years"   180

Chapter 9
The Gospels of Pietism and Revolution—The Daoist and Confucian
        Contexts   **182**
    The Context for Change, 1860–1949   182
    The Gospel of Confucian Activism   187
    The Gospel of Daoist Mysticism   195
    Catholic Responses   202
    No Integral, Integrated Gospel for the Times   204

Chapter 10
The Gospel about China 206
    Chinese Pictograms   206
    Modern Neo-Confucianism   208
    The Potential for Hyphenated Christianity   209
    Chinese Theologies   211
    The Theological Meaning of "New China"   213

Chapter 11
Jesus and Mao in the New China—The Chinese Gospel
        in a Marxist Setting 224
    The Churches in China, 1949–1985   225
    The Gospel in Chinese under Communism   231

Chapter 12
Rejection of the Gospel in Chinese 248
    The Failure of All Efforts   248
    An Anti-Christian Tradition   249
    The Gospel of Power   250
    Future Prospects   252

Notes 255

Bibliography 263

Index 271

Preface to the Series

The purpose of the ASM Series is to publish, without regard for disciplinary need, national, or denominational boundaries, scholarly works of high quality and wide interest on missiological themes from the entire spectrum of scholarly pursuits, e.g., theology, history, anthropology, sociology, linguistics, health, education, art, political science, economics, and development, to articulate but a partial list. Always the focus will be on Christian mission.

By "mission" in this context is meant a cross-cultural passage over the boundary between faith in Jesus Christ and its absence. In this understanding of mission, the basic functions of Christian proclamation, dialogue, witness, service, fellowship, worship, and nurture are of special concern. How does the transition from one cultural context to another influence the shape and interaction of these dynamic functions?

Missiologists know that they need the other disciplines. And other disciplines, we dare to suggest, need missiology, perhaps more than they sometimes realize. Neither the insider's nor the outsider's view is complete in itself. The world Christian mission has through two millennia amassed a rich and well-documented body of experience to share with other disciplines.

Interaction will be the hallmark of this Series. It desires to be a channel for talking to one another instead of about one another. Secular scholars and church-related missiologists have too long engaged in a sterile venting of feelings about one another, often lacking in full evidence. Ignorance of and indifference to one another's work has been no less harmful to good scholarship.

The promotion of scholarly dialogue among missiologists may, at times, involve the publication of views and positions that other missiologists cannot accept, and with which members of the Editorial Committee do not agree. The manuscripts published reflect the opinions of their authors and are not meant to represent the position of the American Society of Missiology or the Editorial Committee of the ASM Series.

We express our warm thanks to various agencies whose financial contributions enabled leaders of vision in the ASM to launch this new venture. The future of the ASM series will, we feel sure, fully justify their confidence and support.

William J. Danker, Chairperson,
ASM Series Editorial Committee

xi

Preface

The gospel message has been in China for nearly fourteen hundred years. Unfortunately, China has not often really been "in" the gospel. The Christian proclamation has been transplanted with minimal relationship to its Chinese environment. Little differentiated it from what was preached in Nairobi, New York, or New Delhi.

Predictably, then, until very recently, the Christian message in China has been viewed as "foreign"—the "religion from across the seas." When a Chinese embraced the faith, unbelievers sarcastically remarked, "one more Christian, one less Chinese." To become a Christian meant to forsake one's roots.

This kind of predicament baffles North American, Latin American, and European Christians. For them, religious faith has strengthened their ties to their country. They have become more patriotic, prouder to be citizens. Whatever hassle they have had at the time of their conversion has not included being accused of espousing a foreign faith or of being unpatriotic.

Missionaries and Chinese Christians have tended either to ignore the epithet "foreign faith" or to dismiss it lightly. First, they claimed, for those who believe, the Christian message has not been foreign. As with believers everywhere, the gospel has met their deepest needs.

This argument would hold water only if, previous to 1949, more than one percent of the vast Chinese population had been Christian.

The gospel is to be brought to unbelievers, but the impact of its foreignness kept most Chinese from receiving it.

Another way that missionaries and Chinese believers have sought to lessen the force of the foreignness objection was to go on the attack. God's message, they claimed, must always be foreign in a dark world of sinful, human beings. Should it not also be viewed as foreign in China?

But why, then, do North Americans, Latin Americans, and Europeans, among whom are also many benighted human beings, not see the gospel as foreign? Only too obviously, the gospel on these continents has had a hand-and-glove relationship with the culture. Indeed, more recent critics of Western Christianity have accused the Christian message of being overacculturated to a sinful environment.

A denial of plain facts is the third way some missionaries have dealt with the foreign quality of Christianity in China. They point out that, at least since the mid-1800s, Christian missionaries have sought to establish an indigenous church in China. Such a church, classically defined as self-supporting, self-propagating, self-governing, can hardly be thought of as "foreign."

Except that it has been! To the extent that the church has realized the "three selves," its indigenization has been in form only. The exterior structures of church life—the style of some buildings, some of the hymnody and lyrics, the seating arrangement of congregations—have taken on a Chinese flavor. But the shape and authority of the gospel message itself has remained foreign.

This leads to the final argument that missionaries have used to dismiss the "foreign religion" label of Christianity. To what extent can the gospel message be indigenized? Do we not here have a "given," the heavenly deposition of divine truth? Can it be changed chameleonlike to fit different contexts?

Here we must be careful to distinguish the inspired, authoritative record of God's revelation—the written word of God—from our feeble, culture-bound efforts to organize it into a theological system that speaks to human needs. A Chinese theology need not be any more anomalous than a North American or European theology. More about this later.

The gospel has not in every instance been viewed as foreign in China. One day I had just returned home with a missionary colleague after a few days of evangelistic preaching in a small cluster of villages in far western China. An elderly Chinese pastor greeted me warmly. Finding out where I had been, he pointedly asked, "Do you think that the first time the gospel is preached in an area it ought to be done by a foreigner? Would it not be better to wait for some Chinese evangelists to be trained to do such a job?" While I was struggling for an answer to this forthright question, he continued with an illustration. He related how he had been preaching in an area some distance away during the previous week. In the course of his preaching, he told a story that included a reference to some American and English believers. After his sermon, an elderly Chinese woman came up to him and inquired, "Pastor Wei, do you mean to tell us that American and English people also believe in Jesus?" Then, with a twinkle in his eye, he pressed home his point to me. "We want believers in China to think of the gospel as uniquely their own and to be surprised when they learn that foreigners also know about it."

This is but one small example of many efforts, often on a very large scale, to put China into the gospel—to bring the Christian faith and Chinese culture together. The purpose of this book is to analyze the more notable examples of this attempt. My hope is that this will provide insights to help the Christian church understand the Chinese mind and Chinese society, and enable it to meet the spiritual needs of mainland and diaspora Chinese. I shall not go deeply into Chinese history, although the past obviously cannot be neglected. The long history of China was the particular context in which words and action were concretely applied. This book does not deal primarily with the sociology, religions, and cultures of China, even though these are closely intertwined with the proclamation of the Christian faith. Neither is it a book on Christian missions or on the Chinese church, except as these embody the message that was believed. The focus is on the shape and nature of the message that has been preached in China—the gospel in Chinese. It is an intellectual history, a history of Christian ideas in Chinese garb.

The gospel in Chinese is not just words and concepts, although they will receive primary attention. It also includes the "paramessage," those symbolic signals of gospel messengers that spoke more loudly than their words. I shall consider issues to which the message was directed, the persons in whom it was embodied, and the institutions through which it was expressed.

A number of interrelated questions have directed the research. What was the role of scripture? What place did Jesus occupy? What was the nature of the worshiping communities that developed? How did Christians view God? How was the purpose of the Christian life demonstrated or articulated? What was the path of conversion? What specific issues or obstacles were addressed by believers?

In the course of this investigation it will be imperative to study another set of foreign ideas, imported from India—Buddhism. They were ultimately sinicized and accepted as Chinese. Why was this not the case with Christianity?

A word about footnoting. A work of this nature, although hardly definitive, depends heavily on the research of others. To record all the sources, however, would weary all but the most academic and serve no practical purpose. For these reasons I document only the most important points in the research and ask the indulgence of those readers who may be dissatisfied.

In general, I follow the pinyin system of romanizing Chinese expressions, except in those instances where specific names or words are more widely recognized in some older orthography. Occasionally, at the first occurrence of a phrase, I use the pinyin spelling followed by the more usual spelling in parentheses. Examples would be: Beijing (Peking), Nanjing (Nanking), Taibei (Taipei), *dao (tao), I: Jing (I Ching)*. I have included Chinese pictograms where they might be of service to those who have some understanding of Chinese.

CONFUCIUS, THE BUDDHA,
AND CHRIST

CHAPTER ONE

The Many Faces of Christianity

CHRISTIANITY THROUGH THE AGES

An imaginative writer has posed an interesting scenario: a long-living space visitor who returns to earth periodically over a span of two thousand years to investigate the status of Christianity. He first attends a meeting of Jerusalem Christians in 37 A.D. Several things about their faith and practice stand out: they meet in the Jewish temple on the Sabbath; they circumcise their male children; they offer animal sacrifices and observe many of the traditional Jewish ritual practices; they love the Old Testament law; they have a strong sense of community and family life. Very Jewish in all their appearances, they are, in fact, viewed as a Jewish sect, but they worship and follow the messiah Jesus.

The nameless space visitor makes his next descent to planet earth nearly three hundred years later to attend the Council of Nicea. He notes that no Jews are present at this gathering and that most of the council members are rather hostile to Jews. Certainly, they would never accept the idea of animal sacrifices. All of them men, they adhere to a traditional celibacy. They work on the seventh day of the week and reserve Sunday, the first day, for their weekly worship. They love the Old Testament, but they spend even more time in study of the New Testament. In common with those Christians whom he had met much earlier in Jerusalem, these church leaders also worship the messiah. Now, however, the title "messiah" has become the name of the savior—"Christ." Their understanding of the Christian faith is very theological and metaphysical, causing them to debate endlessly over the importance of one letter in the Greek alphabet; should it be homo-ousios or homoi-ousios?

The planetary traveler waits another three hundred years before he attends a meeting of monks along the coast of Ireland in 650. He observes with some horror that many of these devoted believers are standing in ice water up to their necks as they recite the Psalms. Some are praying with their arms extended in the form of a cross. One penitent monk has just received six strokes of a lash because, following a very simple meal, he had not said "amen" loud enough. Some of the monks regularly sat in dark caves and meditated on passages from the Bible. All these observances were related to their deep desire to be holy. When they talked about their faith, however, it sounded very nearly like what he had heard at Nicea three hundred years earlier.

The space visitor delayed his next visit for 1200 years, not coming to earth again until about 1840. He found himself in the midst of a very exciting gathering of British Christians in Exeter Hall, London. They were meeting specifically to commission several missionaries to go to Africa and Asia. Their concern was not only to send bibles to distant heathen lands, but also to export cotton seeds to help raise the living standards of Africans and Asians. They were politically active. One item on their agenda this particular evening was to write and sign a petition demanding that their government exert itself to stop the slave trade in the West Indies and Africa. The Bible was very prominent in their meeting; it was quoted extensively and the songs they sang were based on it. The creed adopted at Nicea was accepted by them without any reservations. Like the Irish monks over a millennium earlier, they also talked of holiness. They did not, however, believe it had anything to do with standing in ice water, meditating in caves, or living an austere life. In fact, they appeared to be well-off, obviously well-fed, and smartly dressed. The space visitor was very impressed with their enthusiasm and dedication.

His last visit to view the status of Christianity came in 1980 in Lagos, Nigeria. He observed that the Christians formed a procession as they were going to church. They wore white robes, and danced and chanted in the streets. They called themselves Cherubim and Seraphim. All carried bibles and prayer books. As part of their worship service they recited the Nicene Creed. During much of their church service they talked about revelations and miraculous healings given them by God. They did not say anything that related to the political and social life of Nigeria. They were not at all interested in the precise theological relationship between the Holy Spirit and the Son of God. They were, however, very concerned about the power of God—how they could get it and use it in their everyday lives.

As our space visitor returned home he was puzzled. His visits had not been random; he had tried on each occasion to find a truly representative type of Christianity. Each expression of the Christian faith would have been widely accepted as "normative" at the time of his visit. And yet profound differences existed among the groups he had seen, so much so, in fact, that had they all come together at one place and time, they might have denied that the others were truly Christian.

Not that there were not similarities among the groups. With all of their differences, there were some common elements. Each group believed that the sacred scriptures were in some sense authoritative for its faith, worship, and practice. All but the initial group in Jerusalem gave some type of assent to the creed developed at Nicea. They all believed in and worshiped the triune God, although they differed in the precise way they formulated this belief. Each group, apart from the first, called itself Christian.

Also apparent to the space traveler were the historical connections among these five groups. Those early Jerusalem Christians brought the gospel to the Greek churches represented at Nicea. They, in turn, were a prominent element in the development of the vital Celtic Christianity found in Ireland in the seventh century. The missionary expansion of the Celtic faith to Europe ultimately led to the faith demonstrated at Exeter Hall. And because these missionary groups in London sent missionaries to Africa, there were African Christians to dance in the streets of Lagos, Nigeria [Walls, 39–43].

What would have happened if our legendary, long-living space traveler had used some of his spare time to visit China? What would he have thought of the Nestorian centers of worship, decorated with the cross and lotus, in the fabulous city of Changan during the Tang dynasty (626–910 A.D.)? Or of the latinized Franciscan churches during the time when the followers of Genghis Khan ruled China (1279–1368 A.D.)? How would he have evaluated, in the Middle Kingdom (1582–1724), the practice of ancient Chinese ancestral rites in churches founded by the Society of Jesus? Which one of these expressions of the Chinese church was "authentic"? Would he have called the Taiping believers "Christian"? Would he have found, in the last analysis, that the same continuities were there among the many differences? Was there that same submission to scripture, that same commitment to a basic credal formulation, that same worship of the triune God, and that sense of being within the historical stream of world Christianity?

For the purposes of this book, an even more important question emerges: Would the "dress" of this Christianity be as significantly different from the representative types of the Christian faith that the space visitor examined as these types were from each other? Or to put it another way, Was the faith in China ever indigenized to the extent that it was in Jerusalem, Nicea, Ireland, England and Nigeria? Or did the Christian faith in the Middle Kingdom never really take on a Chinese garb?

FAILED STRATEGIES IN CHINA

We know little about the mission theory that informed the work of the church in China during the Tang and Yuan dynasties. Later, in the sixteenth and seventeenth centuries, the Jesuits adopted a specific strategy, derived in part, at least, from the experience of Francis Xavier in India and of Aleosandri Valignano in Japan. Unfortunately, the opposition of later Catholic missionary orders aborted this process, making any long-term assessment difficult. Many Protestant missionaries, among them John Nevius and Roland Allen, were concerned that the church be authentically Chinese and biblical, but their thinking seldom went beyond peripheral matters—a kind of "structural indigeneity." Chinese Christian thinkers, particularly after the revolution of 1911, began to develop an embryonic Chinese theology, but Chinese cultural identity was too much in flux for any positive results to emerge.

Where pioneering efforts were made at certain times and by a select few to give serious thought to what we today might call indigenization or contextualization, the verdict of contemporary or later colleagues was often harshly critical. The rank and file of both Catholic and Protestant missionary bodies were all too ready to label anything radically different as syncretistic and a betrayal of the gospel.

Unfortunately, whether Christian messengers attempted to present a Chinese gospel or one uncritically imported from a distant land, the results were virtually the same. The response to the Christian faith in China was always minimal, and the church never constituted more than a fraction of one percent of the national population. The Chinese masses never perceived that the biblical message really addressed their deepest needs.

Where must the blame be placed for this unhappy result? Have the Chinese basically been a nonreligious people, too humanistic or materialistic to accept transcendental values? Did superstitious and idolatrous practices, as many early missionaries claimed, blind the Chinese to the truth of Christianity? Or is God the reason? Did God exclude the Chinese from the elect because of the grievous way they may have transgressed divine laws (see Romans 1:18–32)? Or does the fault lie with those who proclaimed the message? Were they insensitive to the Chinese context, unwilling to search for the key that would open the Chinese mind and heart? Or did their sense of urgency lead them to use, without further thought, keys that had worked elsewhere? Or, even more erroneously, did it lead them to assume there was a master key that would open doors in every culture?

The concern of this book is to follow the trail of those who have looked for the key of faith in China. In fact, however, the search has been for many keys. Chinese culture is not monolithic, homogeneous. Rather it is a mosaic of cultures—a variety of "people groups." These various groups, in the past and at present, are distinguishable in terms of racial, linguistic, social, economic, political, geographical, and religious factors.

PEOPLES OF CHINA

The vast majority of Chinese nationals live in the eastern half of the country, in the fertile basins of the Yangtze, Yellow, and Hsi rivers. All but five percent of them are Han Chinese, unified in their writing system, but speaking several major versions of Chinese. The other five percent of the population of China comprises at least fifty-five minority groups, largely of Mongoloid stock, but of diverse linguistic and cultural traits. Although these groups are scattered all over China, they tend to be concentrated more in the western portion of the country. Included here are Tibeto-Burmese peoples (Tibetans and many hill groups such as the Yi peoples of Sichuan and Yunnan), Tai-speaking lowland peoples, and the Miao-Yao tribal groups.

The remainder of the five percent is made up of largely three major groups: the Altaic family, which includes Mongols, Turkic peoples, and Tungusic groups; the Indo-European Tadzhiks found in southwest Xinjiang; and the Mon-Khmer of Austroasiatic stock. With each of these racial differences there are linguistic distinctions. Even within the major languages of the majority Han peoples there are innumerable dialectical differences, which can impede mutual understanding.

China is slightly larger than the United States, crisscrossed by mountain ranges, large rivers, and countless valleys. Separated from each other by these many physical barriers, the populace developed countless thousands of dialects, proverbially stated by the Chinese as "every three *li* [about a mile and a half] a difference in language."

The population of China can also be analyzed in terms of social and economic units. Such stratifications have always been present, and their needs and response to the Christian message have not been the same. In socio-economic terms, present-day China can be schematized as follows:

1) GOVERNMENT AUTHORITIES
   the cadre or government officials
   the military forces
   public security personnel
2) URBAN GROUPINGS
   A. *intelligentsia groups*
      science and technology professionals
      artists and writers
      high-level intelligentsia
      middle-school teachers and staff
      primary-school teachers and staff
      performing artists and support workers
      medical personnel
      coaches and athletes
   B. *industrial groups*
      industrial workers
   C. *service groups*
      public service workers
      sales clerks
   D. *student groups*
      primary-school students
      middle-school students
      university students
   E. *home related groups*
      housewives
      individual producers
      retired persons
      preschool children
   F. *nonconformists*
      unemployed youth

            political prisoners
            dissidents
3) RURAL GROUPINGS
        "commercial crop" farmers
        food grain farmers
        fishing workers
        hunters
        shepherds and livestock farmers
        the "lost generation" (students sent to the countryside)
        the elderly
        children[1]

Every period of Chinese history has had some comparable groupings, and the Christian effort made during each period had a unique, although not exclusive, focus on particular groups. The Nestorian emphasis was apparently on the many foreign groups that had gone to China for trade and diplomatic purposes during the Tang dynasty. The same may have been true during the reign of the Mongols over China in the thirteenth and fourteenth centuries. The Society of Jesus first directed its attention to the official and gentry classes, although eventually it claimed many converts in rural areas. The Protestant missionary effort, theoretically, was directed toward all groups, although the most notable impact was made on lower-class rural groups. Many Protestant missionaries, however, were concerned, as were the earlier Jesuits, with the needs of the upper classes. They used literature, education, special lectures, and scientific data to reach them [Covell, *Martin*, 220–21].

The presence, then, of a variety of "people groups" in China stymied the effort to find "the one key" that would invariably open the door of Chinese minds and hearts to the Christian message. There are many Chinese "minds," and it is both precarious and naive to assume cultural uniformity. However, compared with many regions of the world with a much more restricted geographical area, Han China is *relatively* homogeneous. Sinologues have traced the roots of this homogeneity to several unique features of Chinese life.[2] A unified script, understandable throughout China by all literate persons regardless of their thousands of dialectical differences, has been a tremendous stimulus to cultural identity as a single people. This stimulated the development of a common cultural tradition, often called Confucianism, available both to the literate gentry class, by reason of civil service examinations, and also to the illiterate commoner through popular media such as drama, proverbs, and story telling. An accepted core of tradition, the "big story," was generally available to all Han Chinese, and this helped to level the "smaller stories" unique only to particular social groups and specific occupations.

The accessibility of this common tradition to all levels and groups of persons was also made possible because within China there never were inflexible distinctions between bureaucrat and commoner. A type of feudalism was in effect during most periods of Chinese history, but it was a far cry—despite

Chinese communist rhetoric about many obvious inequities—from the fixed, immobile system of European feudalism. Even the lowest commoners were able to move into a higher class and change their social status, for both themselves and their families.

The ability of the major Chinese religions—Confucianism, Daoism, and Buddhism—to coexist without eliminating one another by bloody conflict contributed to the stability of this common tradition. Not that there were not conflicts and the ascendancy of one or the other for shorter or longer periods of time. But all three systems continued to exist, and all contributed immeasurably in very similar ways to the life of both lower and upper classes. Unlike religious systems in other parts of the world, these nonexclusive religions complemented one another in contributing to the Chinese mind.

Finally, the Chinese social system of polygyny that allowed local women from the very lowest classes to become second and third wives within aristocratic families produced a crosspollination of ideas and values. A large measure of intermingling occurred among the various social levels, again enhancing the common cultural tradition.

THE CHINESE MIND

What are the essential elements of this common Han Chinese tradition with which proclaimers of the Christian Gospel have had to come to terms over the centuries? Of course there have been differences during various historical periods, but these variations usually stayed within the parameters of the larger unity.

A Religious People

To many observers the Chinese have always been a religious people. By this I mean that for lower and upper classes alike there has been a concern for human interrelationships with superhuman supernatural powers.[3] This strong tendency to live according to transcendental concepts antedates Confucius and his more "down-to-earth" humanism. In the ancient classics a dominant idea was "heaven," a personified, supreme governing force in the universe, determining human fate and nature. Heaven rewarded and punished human beings in accord with fairly well-defined moral norms. By the time of Confucius and Mencius, this concept had become secularized and viewed as a more mechanistic type of power, although the personal emphasis continued in popular teaching.

Whether viewed as a personal being or an impersonal power, the will of heaven *(ming)* was decisive in determining all human events. Particularly was this true for the emperor, who was responsible for mediating the will of heaven for all China. Well before the time of Confucius, a technical concept developed of the "mandate of heaven," by which old, decadent dynasties were overthrown and new, more vibrant ones were brought into power. A Han Confucian scholar, Dung Zhungshu, developed this view into a highly schematized system. Human welfare and the success or demise of the empire depended on harmonious relationships between heaven, humankind (the emperor in particular), and earth. Favorable or unfavorable portents in the physical universe—abundant harvests, adequate rainfall, good weather, eclipses, floods, drought, earthquakes, the position of the stars and planets—revealed the favor or disfavor of heaven and indicated corrective measures that the emperor and his followers must take. Heaven spoke every day through nature, and the emperor's ability to respond indicated how long he would continue to have the favor of the people and enjoy the "mandate of heaven."

With heaven so prominent in human affairs, human beings must make special efforts to "learn their fate." Divination, one of the most prominent means of doing this, is a significant theme in all of the five Chinese classics, particularly in the *I Jing (I Ching)*. Tradition records that even Confucius was greatly preoccupied with the subject of divination, using his copy of the *I Jing* so often that he broke its binding three times.

But those who wanted to know their fate would not be content with divination or the *I Jing*. About two centuries after the death of Confucius the first systematic use began to be made of the ideas of yin and yang, the *taiji*, and the five elements.

In ancient Chinese thinking all objects were classified as being yin (negative) or yang (positive). Yin is female, yang is male. Bright elements such as the color red, the sun, fire, and light are yang. Dark elements such as the color black, water, the color blue, the earth, and the moon are yin. These two elements, derived it was believed from an ultimate principle called *taiji*, when combined with the five elements of wood, fire, earth, metal, and water could produce formulas for interpreting all of life and its mysteries. C.K. Yang explains:

> By assigning moral significance to each of the factors of Yin and Yang and the Five Elements, it was possible to work up a frame of reference by which to interpret the intentions behind the phenomena of the supernatural forces in the sky, the earth, the seasons, the crops, the governing of the state, the rise and fall of a dynasty, life and death, health and sickness, poverty and prosperity, divination, palm reading and physiognomy, astrology, chronomancy, and geomancy. From the activities of the sun and the moon to the intimate deeds of the individual's private life, all may be interpreted by this theory of Yin-Yang and the Five Elements; it deeply penetrated the minds of the common men as well as those of most Confucianists ["Functional Relationship," 276].

The practice of many types of sacrifice, an aspect of Chinese life very deeply rooted in Confucianism, is another indication of the religious nature of the Chinese mind. Endorsed, if not promoted, by Confucius, Mencius, and later thinkers, sacrifice has traditionally had diverse meanings for the masses and for the intellectual elites. The common person viewed sacrifice as a means to solicit the protection and blessing of the unseen spirit world. The concept of propitiation had always been present to a greater or lesser degree. The scholar, professing ignorance about the spirit world, accepted sacrificial acts as a merely "human practice," finding its greatest value as a means of promoting social values.

Sacrifice, of course, is a basic aspect of ancestral rites. Again, the common person and the "superior person" saw it as having different functions. The former believed that it provided for the continued welfare of the deceased, and sought by all means to be protected from any of the dead person's evil intentions toward the living. The committed Confucian found the ancestral cult useful "to cultivate kinship values like filial piety, family loyalty, and continuity of the family lineage [Yang, "Functional Relationship," 278].

Although Confucianism would appear to be largely a rationalistic system with primary emphasis on ethics, over the years it came to terms with the more specifically religious elements that circumscribe the total life of the common person. Confucian thought, had it not been flexible enough to accommodate itself to the practices of the masses, would never have been able to occupy the role it did as official arbiter of the Chinese social and political order.

This adaptability made it possible for institutional religion in China to put its stamp of approval upon and reinforce the ethical values of Confucianism. The interpenetration of Confucian thought and Chinese religious ideas and practices is complex and difficult for the outsider to grasp. C.K Yang is particularly helpful in differentiating between what he calls "diffused and specialized religions":

A diffused religion is organizationally diffused in secular institutions, such as ancestor worship in the family, worship of Heaven in the state, and the worship of patron gods in guilds. A specialized religion, on the other hand, has an independent status and organization to serve specifically religious functions, though it may perform many derivative functions also. Buddhism, Taoism, *feng-shui*, and other forms of professionalized magic and animism, like sorcery and divination, belong to this type ["Functional Relationships," 279].

The diffused religions had no unique ethical system. They adhered to the values of Confucianism. In a similar way, Buddhism and Daoism, examples of Yang's "specialized religions," were valued by the common people not so much because they represented an alternative system of ethical values, but because they provided a kind of magical guidance for everyday life. Confucianism, Daoism, Buddhism, and the many diffused religions of China interpenetrated both on the religious and ethical level in such an intimate way that most Chinese were at a loss to analyze their own precise belief system. They could worship a Daoist deity one day and a Buddhist god the next day, along with other gods and spirits. Priests in temples could not explain to visitors whether the temple was Daoist, Buddhist, or Confucianist. It really made no difference.

The Chinese, like human beings everywhere, were reaching out for any handle that would enable them to deal with suffering, quirks of fate, meaninglessness, evil, ignorance, death, and the possibility of life beyond death.

Benevolent Humanism

The Chinese mind, along with its strong religious tendency, is very earthy and close to the soil. Nature is important. Works of art often show a family life of leisure, with rural scenes of relaxation filled with herb gatherers, recluses, and wood cutters. The poverty of the masses, limited good land, poor development of resources and the need to "eat bitterness" in unrelenting work helped to produce these emphases. The Daoist stress on identity with the *dao* of nature as an escape from the rather rigid social conventions of Confucianism, particularly as found in the more urban areas, was another contributing factor. And Confucianism itself focuses upon the family and is skeptical of anything otherworldly.

Very closely related to this "earth-ness," in fact growing out of it, is a benevolent Chinese humanism. The Chinese have always placed primary emphasis on human interests and human relationships. They tend toward a basic goal— to enjoy simplicity, to develop a happy family life, and to promote harmonious social relationships by all means. This is humanism at its best.

The Chinese humanistic tendency has manifested itself in a variety of ways. Personal relationships are more important than anything else. Within institutions, persons are considered to be more important than are the systems or mechanisms so esteemed in the West. Government, as a system, does not work well; only a "personal government by gentlemen" will meet with success. The really important relationships, five in number, are those between: an emperor or prince and his minister; a father and his son; a husband and his wife; an older and a younger brother; a teacher and his pupil.

The character trait most in demand in all these relationships is *ren*, often translated "benevolence." The Chinese pictogram for it is made up of two symbols, one for person and the other for number two. By *ren* or benevolence is meant an attitude of harmony and goodness that is to prevail between two persons. If they cultivate this virtue, both of them will attain to the status of a sage or superior person. Between such persons one-on-one relationships will be prioritized and will be extended to family, neighborhood, village, district, nation, and world, leading to an era of peace and prosperity.

The Chinese humanistic spirit has always had a high ethical ideal. The five virtues of benevolence *(ren)*, righteousness, propriety, knowledge, and sincerity expressed not only the epitome of the superior person, but also the qualities that make for correct relationships among the population as a whole. Expressed in many homey parables, these moral ideals could be found written on strips of paper attached to doorposts and lintels, and in other public places. Although not always practiced in everyday life, they were so much a part of the national spirit that they would be acknowledged immediately by virtually anyone when reminded of them. The Chinese have always been a highly moral people.

For the Chinese, life is made beautiful by harmonious relationships among all groups of persons. Harmony is the measure of all things. This has led to what outsiders have often viewed as an excessive politeness. But within the Chinese context, "no one will blame you if your politeness is excessive," as a well-known proverb put it. Politeness has been viewed as much more important than candor, direct speech, and critical analysis. For most North Americans and Europeans, truth is correspondence to fact, to reality. For the Chinese truth is that which will promote harmony. Harmony goes beyond correspondence to so-called objective reality; it encompasses correspondence to human reality. This emphasis on the human dimension of every situation, sometimes with a seeming neglect of "facts," has caused many foreigners erroneously to accuse the Chinese of lying, of distorting the truth. In the late nineteenth century, a noted missionary, thoroughly fed up with this judgmental attitude, answered such charges in an article entitled "A Nation of Liars?" [Headland, 161–69].

A young missionary, recently arrived in northern China, went with a medical missionary friend of his to the morning staff meeting at the mission hospital. The meeting was unusual in that most of the Chinese staff present stood up to give a word of praise for the work of a particular Chinese doctor, also in the room. When the meeting was ended, the young missionary asked his friend for an explanation of what had transpired. To his amazement, the doctor replied, "They were firing Dr.   ." The uninitiated outsider might respond, "What deceit!" But there was no intention to deceive and no deceit. Everyone in the room, except the missionary doctor's newly-arrived friend, knew exactly what was going on. All the communicative clues were there. It was the Chinese way of dealing publicly with an objective fact—the incompetency of the man being dismissed—*and* the human reality in a way that would not create disharmony.

Chinese humanism also expresses itself in what Lin Yu-tang has called the "spirit of play," a fondness for recreational activities like dancing, acrobatics, and sports. The closeness of the Chinese to nature enables them to celebrate life even in the midst of the most distressing realities. A certain resiliency enables them to live life to the full amid circumstances that would embitter most others. Lin Yu-tang expressed it well: "Taoism is the playing mood of the Chinese people, even as Confucianism is their working mood" [*My Country*, 117].

The Middle Path

Many observers have noted that the Chinese are characterized by common sense, a reasonable, pragmatic spirit, a tendency to choose the middle path rather than go to extremes. They do not commonly engage in theoretical speculation nor do they philosophize on the metaphysical. They think in synthetic, concrete terms, always ready to illustrate their thoughts with appropriate proverbs. Lin Yu-tang claims that the Chinese depend on intuition for solving all of the mysteries of life, utilizing the same "sixth sense that makes many a woman believe a thing because it is so" [*My Country*, 80–81].

With the Chinese, truth cannot be proved logically, only grasped experientially. This type of intuition comes from common sense, not logical reasoning processes. The emphasis is on the whole, not the parts; on the fullness of reality more than on reason. Evolving from the oneness of the human spirit with nature and reality, it produces a type of mystical identification with the *dao*. The Chinese mind tends strongly toward synthesis rather than analysis, seeking always to find complements and to correlate rather than to polarize. Paradoxical thinking poses no problems for the Chinese. They can embrace, at one extreme, Confucianism, which stresses activity, success, a hierarchy of inequality (labeled "feudalism" by the present government of China), many rules, social mores, and decorum and, at the other extreme, Daoism, which emphasizes nonactivity, a return to nature, and living spontaneously without concern for the conventions of social life. They can worship all the deities of Buddhism and animistic Daoism, even as they use Confucian proverbs to profess ignorance and disinterest about the reality of the spiritual world. Logical contradictions, posed in classic Aristotelian formulas, do not bother them.

Common sense leads the Chinese rather naturally to take the middle path that avoids extremes, the balanced path, broad and all-inclusive in its viewpoint. Some have criticized this for bringing on repressed emotions and a passive inscrutability that is always hiding its true feelings. One observer comments:

> The Chinese express their feelings along patterned lines just as other peoples do. Part of that pattern, it is true, calls for reserve, self-control, poise and balance; again, however, the circumstances may result, through sheer force of feeling or social patterns, in an extreme display of emotions. The sufferings and hardships of the race have, through the development of patience, conservatism and fatalism, added the powers making for control. But the vivacity, humor, sadness . . . joy, pain, fear, and anger which work within the Chinese are not buried beneath an unreadable stolidity of countenance [Workman, "The Chinese Mind," 82–83].

Three Basic Cognitive Approaches to Reality

The basic characteristics of the Chinese thinking process is summarized by F.H. Smith in Diagram 1, which contrasts Western, Chinese, and Indian cognitive approaches to reality [from Hesselgrave, 209]. In each case all the same elements are present: concepts, concrete relationships, and psychical experience. The difference is in the priority assigned to them (indicated by the center-to-periphery order) and in the balance among them. Within each culture, of course, there will always be individuals who are atypical or marginal to the dominant emphasis.

Diagram 1

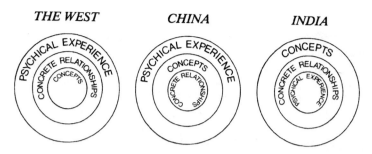

THE WEST   CHINA   INDIA

Unfortunately, the Christian churches in China often founded their strategies on those relatively few individuals who responded to the Christian message. In many instances, christianized Chinese were marginalized from their fellow nationals by their relationships with foreigners, with even their thought patterns taking on Western contours. This disqualified them from being bridges back to their own society.

Ethnic Culturalism

Although the Chinese have always professed to believe that "there is one family under heaven and all within the four seas are brothers," the pyramid of humanity had but one apex—the Imperial Son of Heaven. The supreme heresy for the Chinese was not departure from the traditions of Confucius, although this was serious, or belief in many gods, but acceptance of any ruler other than the Chinese emperor or recognition of any culture other than Chinese culture. After all, China was the "middle kingdom," and, as Ricci was to find out to his dismay when he brought his first European map to Peking, the "middle kingdom" had to be literally at the center of the world.

Those within the circle of Chinese life and society were the "culturally saved" [Bloodworth, 344]; those on the fringes, near and far, were benighted barbarians whose reason for coming to China could only be to pay respect and to learn. Nothing of worth could be brought in from outside.

The Chinese, then, have been very proud of their culture and its attainments. Overseas Chinese, although having no particular loyalty to the Chinese political state, have carried the light of their culture with them and have resisted cultural absorption by other countries. Northern invaders repeatedly conquered portions of China, but, in Dennis Bloodworth's noted phrase, have been absorbed by China the way "stomach juices will treat a steak." Chinese culture with its all-embracing appetite has always prevailed. And this, of course, has been a prime obstacle for the Christian faith—an exclusive, religious doctrine confronting an unbending, exclusive culture.

Theological Thinkers

It is important to realize that the Chinese think "theologically." Among modern scholars, Julia Ching, a noted Catholic sinologist, has noted "the great resemblance between Confucian teaching and the traditional Catholic doctrine of a *natural moral law*—that which is based on human nature itself, the law written in men's hearts" [Ching, "Confucianism," 14]. Human nature has been a prime agenda for Chinese philosophers, or Confucian theologians as we might call them.

According to this frame of reference, heaven has endowed all human beings with a common nature, resulting in a natural equality among them all. And they have been given a conscience, enabling them to distinguish moral good and evil. Benevolence *(ren)* is a universal virtue; all human beings are to practice it. To what extent, however, can human beings achieve, by nature alone, the high ideal of benevolence and the ultimate goal of a society characterized by harmonious personal relationships?

This question has led to endless debates, to which nearly every participant made some contribution. How is human nature to be understood? Is it good, with evil being a "perversion of the natural"? Is the human tendency toward good a consequence of the environment or of moral education? What is the relationship of the emperor to the development of human nature? Or is human nature basically evil, requiring strict laws to restrain its immoral inclinations? If human nature is good, is it merely potentially good or are certain virtues—humanity, righteousness, propriety, wisdom—already present? Obviously, here was fertile ground for missionaries to make contact with the Chinese mind.

Specialized Religions

I have said little specifically about the "specialized religions" of China. Its three major religions—Confucianism, Daoism, and Buddhism—have been essential ingredients in the making of the Chinese mind. They have contributed, however, not so much because of their character as "organized" religions, but because their various strands have been worked into an interfaith collage that has swallowed up their original roots and identity. It is less important to know that something is Daoist, or Buddhist, or Confucianist than it is to know that this is indeed the way the Chinese think and feel. As we encounter the problems of incarnating the Christian message in a particular historical period, I shall elaborate on the specific religious context at that time.

INDIGENIZATION OF THE CHRISTIAN FAITH

Now that some of the essential conceptual elements of the Han Chinese context have been identified, it remains to explain more precisely what is meant by the "gospel in Chinese." The key principle is to be found in the biblical phrase, "and the Word became flesh and dwelled among us" (John 1:14). The eternal Logos, forever one with the Father, fully participated in a specific culture in order that God's truth might be known and God's way followed. This was no theophany, the fleeting revelation of the divine mystery. Nor did the human element pertain to the order of mere appearance. God entered personally into Jewish life, thought, society, and culture. Jesus Christ, fully God, was fully Jewish in all the particular realities of Jewish culture. No one among his peers ever accused him of being Gentile or in any sense foreign to the life of his day.

The term "incarnation" as a theological concept to define the Christian's relationship to the world is coming into its own again.[4] Writers have more commonly used "indigenization" or "contextualization" to express identification with or accommodation to a target culture. Indigenization, the more classic and traditional term, may be defined as the church relating itself to the worldview, values, beliefs, and behavior of a receptor culture at those points where this culture is not in essential conflict with the gospel, in order to communicate God's truth and establish a worshiping community.

Many current writers, particularly those who identify themselves as evangelical, virtually equate the word "contextualization" with "indigenization." It is merely a new, somewhat more sophisticated "in" term. Undoubtedly, the basic factors of indigenization would be included in contextualization. Contextualization, as used here, means that the gospel addresses itself to those broader issues of the social, economic, and political context within a receptor culture. Not concerned merely to relate the Christian faith to a narrow spectrum of culture as it once existed in a more static world, it is a broader, more dynamic, more "now-related" kind of expression. Its aim is not so much to accommodate itself to a specific culture as to change that culture to conform to the demands of the gospel. Liberation theology as articulated by Latin American thinkers is one of the best examples of a contextualized theology.

Issues of indigenization and contextualization have been addressed by many recent consultations. One of the most important was the Willowbank Consultation on the Gospel and Culture held at Willowbank, Bermuda, January 1978. What were some of the ways in which this gathering tried to deal with this important question from the standpoint of sacred scripture?

Old Testament Precedents

One undisputed conclusion reached at Willowbank was that "the biblical writers made critical use of whatever cultural material was available to them for the expression of their message."[5] Scholars have studied the biblical creation account in great detail to determine how it was related to *Enuma Elish,* the Babylonian creation epic. Concluding that this well-known epic was a part of the cultural context in which God's creative activity was revealed, S. Ananda Kumar has noted that the biblical writer "eliminated, adapted and transformed" the material available to him that it might become the "vocabulary of the divine speech."[6]

The Genesis account, in the first place, rejected any evidence of polytheistic idolatry: it was incompatible with God's character. Secondly, certain elements from the epic, such as references to darkness and chaos, are retained in the biblical record: they could serve as a backdrop to highlight God's power to produce order and create light. Finally, it is Yahweh, not some mythological deity, who conquers Leviathan or Rahab, the anticreation sea monster. God's power and character could be understood at that time only in terms of the prevailing worldview of its intended readers, not in terms of data unfamiliar to them. The Babylonian creation epic provided a useful framework for communication, but no content for divine revelation.[7]

The Willowbank report further observes:

> The form of God's "covenant" with his people resembles the ancient Hittite Suzerain's "treaty" with his vassals. The writers also made incidental use of the conceptual imagery [of] the "three-tiered" universe, though they did not thereby affirm pre-Copernican cosmology. We do something similar when we talk about the sun "rising" and "setting" [p. 7].

Not all cultural materials available to Old Testament writers were given a stamp of approval when included in the biblical account. The prohibition recorded in Exodus 23:19, "you shall not boil a kid in its mother's milk," is an example of the rejection of a Canaanite practice. The Ras Shamra Tablet, discovered in the 1930s at ancient Ugarit, indicates that "the practice of boiling a young goat or sheep in its mother's milk was an idolatrous, polytheistic Canaanite fertility ritual, with strong elements of cult magic" [Kumar, "Culture," 56]. Such practices, debased and nonredemptive, could only be rejected. Kumar points out:

> Syncretism, though often used purely in its negative connotation, is capable of a positive sense. When we study the Holy Scriptures against their cultural, religious and theological background, the fact of syncretism in this good sense becomes evident. The whole process from beginning to end is a theocentric cultural contextualization. It is a process enlightened, guided, controlled and sanctified by God himself, as the Israelite theologians were struggling with the framework and content of the cultures in which they lived, to make God's Word indigenous and theologically relevant to their own situation ["Culture," 54].

New Testament Precedents

The same process of making "critical use of whatever cultural material was available to them" was used by New Testament writers. In addressing the heresy of Gnosticism in the Colossian church, Paul used the very phraseology of gnostic writers to express the glory and grandeur of Jesus Christ.

What else could he have done if the message were to have any relevance?

In giving, on Mars Hill, his apologetic for the gospel, Paul quotes two phrases from Greek poetry that, in their original context, can refer only to Zeus, the chief god in the Greek pantheon.[8] The Apostle John's use of the term "logos," with all its wide range of meaning in both Semitic and Greek sources, to express the reality of Jesus Christ was certainly a dangerous tactic! To communicate Christ in a relevant way is never safe! But the whole purpose of his gospel is to use the person of Christ to interpret the meaning of *logos*. This explicit educational process removes much of the danger of syncretism.

As messengers of the Christian gospel moved from the Semitic to the Hellenic world, new, or at least alternative, terms were needed, and others were given an expanded meaning. Jesus' favorite self-designation, "Son of Man," appropriate within the Jewish context to refer to his messianic person and work, is replaced by "Son of God," much more understandable as the Christian message moves into a Greek environment. The phrase "kingdom of God" of the synoptic gospels does not appear nearly as much in the Gospel of John as does the equivalent expression "eternal life." C.H. Dodd has pointed out:

> John . . . has deliberately and expressly transposed the Christian Gospel from eschatological categories derived from Judaism to mystical categories derived from Greek thought—whether derived directly from Greek sources or from Hellenistic Judaism is a question beside the point ["Hellenism," 126].

In a similar vein Dodd also observes of Paul's use of the term "law" in Romans 8:

> At this point the word *nomos* passes from the Hebrew to the Greek field of meaning. It is no longer "the law of commandments contained in ordinances," but an inward principle of action, the law written on the heart [ibid., 118].

PRINCIPLES OF INDIGENIZATION

Form and Meaning

From the foregoing examples of how biblical authors made "critical use of whatever cultural material was available to them for the expression of their message," several observations may be made. First, communication consists of both form—the outer shape or expression—and meaning—information or inner content. Although meaning can be expressed only in some form, these two levels must be clearly distinguished. The terms "Son of Man" and "Son of God" are different forms, but the meaning of a supernatural, divine being proceeding directly from the eternal Father is very similar. On the other hand,

Law written on the heart

although the English term "word," in John 1:1, appears to be very similar to the Greek expression *"logos,"* the range of meaning of the latter is much broader than that of the former.

Anyone communicating a meaning from one culture to another must decide: Do I need to change or replace the form in order to get my meaning across, or is the form as communicative in the one culture as in the other? Speakers or writers may communicate *formally* by retaining the original form, in whole or in part, or they may communicate *dynamically,* which means that they seek to find in the receptor culture a form better apt to convey the meaning understood by the source culture.

Some forms are more closely intertwined with the meaning conveyed than are others. Bruce Nicholls has suggested that we need to distinguish between "symbolic" and "conceptual" forms. The former indicates "language that uses analogy of nature, parables and metaphors," and for which it is relatively easy to find functional substitutes in a receptor culture. By conceptual forms, he refers to those that are "ontologically essential to the message because these forms are consistently used throughout Scripture." In this latter category he would include the use of the term "father" for God and presumably an expression such as "lamb of God" to describe the person and mission of Jesus Christ.[9]

The consistent use of a particular form throughout the scriptural record probably indicates that this term and its corresponding content are so wedded in a historical particularity that to sever them would indeed result in the loss of critical meaning. However, to state that any particular form is "ontologically essential" to express a given meaning is quite another thing. The term "father" may indeed best communicate God's unique attributes to us and to many others, but this does not derive from some universal ontological necessity as much as from a sustained cultural experience. In cultures where the maternal uncle performs all postpartum functions and possesses all the attributes that "father" conveys to us, no one can argue "ontological necessity."

Nicholls would find it difficult to argue in this vein if he felt free to use the crosscultural communicative techniques employed by the biblical writers. However, the fact that they were uniquely inspired and that this inspiration included specific cultural forms in a particular culture causes him to deny that we today may follow the "way in which the biblical writers use their own culture . . . as a corresponding model for our contextualizing of theology." This a priori judgment, however, is not sustained by any biblical data. If indeed Nicholls is correct, then all who have engaged in Bible translation, except in a very wooden, formal style, are in error. The Bible may no more be translated than may the Koran! If the only term that can accurately convey the truth of Jesus Christ is the term "Son of God," then all who seek to communicate the gospel to Muslims are condemned to miscommunicate. But if "Son of Man," "Word of God," "Power of God," "Wisdom of God," as well as many other terms growing out of Islamic culture, are legitimate possibilities, relevant communication can occur.

W.A. Visser 't Hooft comes much closer to the mark when he notes that, whatever forms from the traditional culture are used, "they must be converted in the way in which Paul and John converted Greek philosophical and religious concepts." To be successful, this type of "subversive accommodation" needs a heavy dose of Christian elucidation. He illustrates by noting that it is proper to use the term "Tao," with all its qualities of vagueness and elusiveness, for *logos* in translating John's prologue, "but everything depends on the effort made to show that the Logos-Tao is *not* elusive and vague, and that, in his historic incarnate character, Christ is everything but elusive and vague" ["Accommodation," 13–14].

A Plurality of Approaches

The second observation is that communicators of the Christian faith in a crosscultural context may indigenize their message in a number of ways. The Bible is a vast resource book of God's truth from which the communicator must *select* emphases most appropriate for a given culture. Many have observed, for example, that in the Chinese context, where harmonious social relationships have been highly prized, a good beginning point for the gospel proclamation is the doctrine of reconciliation. This appeals far more to the Chinese mind than does the doctrine of justification, which stresses legal and penal aspects of the faith rather than personal relationships.

Another approach to indigenization is to note areas within the receptor culture where there is a specific need for the Christian message. These might include, in almost any culture, fears of the spirit world, poverty, oppressive social structures, suffering, recurrent natural disasters, guilt, moral failure, meaninglessness, quirks of fate, evil, human inadequacy, desires for familial continuity through ancestral rites, and the dread of death. From the very beginning in China and elsewhere, persons have been seeking ways to confront these situations.

Following World War II the pain of defeat hung heavily over Japan— personal pain in the many families where loved ones had died and national pain because of failure in the war effort. What an appropriate time for Kazoh Kitamori to publish his work *The Pain of God*, which spoke directly to the needs of all within society by showing the many places in scripture, particularly in Jeremiah, where God had a painful love (the term *teng-ai* in Chinese and Japanese expresses it far more adequately than the English translation) for his sinning and sinned-against people. To communicate anything is to go beyond mere announcement. Christian messengers can never be satisfied until the gospel is internalized and becomes an integral part of a person's life. To stop short of this may enable someone to mouth pious shibboleths that appear orthodox, but which are still external to personal or group experience. The Christian faith never becomes indigenized until it is applied to the existential needs of a previously non-Christian people.[10]

CHAPTER TWO

Jesus and the Lotus— The Nestorian Faith

Visitors to the British Museum have been puzzled by a religious drawing of a person adorned with conflicting symbols. The cross on the forehead is clearly of Christian origin and has been thought to picture Jesus Christ or one of his followers. But the vesture and other symbols suggest that it is a portrayal of a bodhisattva, a Buddhist savior who postpones nirvana in order to save others. Scholars have speculated that this drawing is a product of the early Tang dynasty when the Christian faith was entering China for the first time and struggling to find a Chinese identity.

These early missionaries came from Iran (Persia) and were called Nestorians. Unlike later missionaries who came to China from the East across large bodies of water, these emissaries crossed the vast expanse of barren deserts in Central Asia to enter China from the West.

ORIGINS OF THE NESTORIAN CHURCH

The name "Nestorian" was a later addition to a church whose members first came into the Tigris-Euphrates valley in strength in the middle of the second century. Spreading through the city-state of Edessa, the faith continued to expand and by 225 A.D. there were more than twenty bishoprics in the Mesopotamian area. Great monastic schools were founded at Edessa and Nisibis to train missionaries for further advances into Persia and Central Asia.

Following the condemnation of Nestorius at the Council of Ephesus in 431—on the ground that he taught a duality of persons, human and divine, in Jesus—his followers gradually migrated to Persia and infiltrated the church there to the extent that by the middle of the fifth century it was largely Nestorian.

Despite what appeared to be early success in winning converts both at home and in missionary outreach, this Eastern Christian community never won over the local populace to the extent that the Western church did in the Roman empire. This was partly because there had not been the same spiritual vacuum in the East that there had been in the West. In fact, under the Sassanid rulers, who in 227 A.D. had succeeded the Parthians, Zoroastrianism was made the state religion, and Christians were a minority. They never had the political or cultural preponderance of the Western church.

Furthermore, Christians were suspect, because the Roman empire, the deadly enemy of the Sassanids, was a "Christian" state. The government could not be sure of the loyalty of Christians.

Despite its small size, this church developed one of the strongest missionary concerns to be found among any group in Christian history. Without political and cultural authority, but equipped with a simple, zealous faith, it penetrated into Armenia, Mesopotamia, and Arabia, and even into much more distant Afghanistan, India, Turkestan, Siberia, and China.

What explains the zealous missionary outreach of this minority church? Its outreach was the work of individuals and small groups relying mainly on the message of the gospel as their means of advance. Before 300 A.D. there had not been much persecution, but after that time there was more pressure from both Zoroastrianism and the government. This produced a lean, hard, committed Christianity braced for the rigors of missionary expansion.

Equally important, "the Eastern church undertook the spreading of the Gospel as its main objective while the Western church was dissipating its energy in excessive concentration on doctrinal discussions" [Syrdal, 72]. Hendrik Kraemer has commented:

> One of the main consequences of this development [doctrinal divisions] was that the self-consciousness of Christianity became preeminently doctrinal, which is not in accordance with the hidden symphony of emphasis in the Biblical message [*Theology*, 43–44].

At this particular time trade routes to the East were open and accessible to merchants and missionaries alike. Historical records indicate that the first Nestorian Christians to reach China (in 578 A.D.) were traders. But missionaries were not far behind. The cloisters they built along commercial routes served as centers from which they engaged in the copying and distributing of literature and in preaching, both in the immediate area and in more distant locales.

Unlike the more affluent missionaries who would come later from overseas, the Nestorian missionaries fitted in well with the local environment and culture:

> They travelled on foot wearing sandals, a staff in their hands, and on their backs a basket filled with copies of Scripture and other religious books. They received gifts—among them some large grants from the rulers of various tribes. They did not keep what they received, except

what could be used directly for the extension of their work. They distributed the rest to those who were poorer [Syrdal, 74].

Arrival in China

Although the first traders were reaching China by the end of the sixth
century, missionaries did not arrive in any strength until 635 A.D. A well-
established tradition tells us that two monks, presumably Nestorian, smuggled
silkworms from China in a hollow bamboo in 551 A.D. and gave them to
Emperor Justinian so that silk could be produced outside China.

When the Nestorian missionaries reached China they recognized that they
had not come to a spiritual vacuum, devoid of a significant religious heritage.
Leonard Outerbridge has commented:

> The ancient religious concepts of China were considerably higher than
> those of our own forefathers before Roman Civilization and Christianity
> made their contribution in the countries of Europe and the British Isles
> [*Lost Churches*, 28].

Confucianism was named after the brilliant teacher Kung Fu Zi who had
sifted and edited ancient classics and applied them, along with his own insights,
to the ethical and political needs of his home state of Lu in the sixth century
before Christ. It had enjoyed a period of ascendancy as a type of state
orthodoxy during the Han dynasty (200 B.C.–220 A.D.) before declining in the
following four hundred years. During this period of anarchy, chaos, and
division within the Chinese empire, religious Daoism, as well as a Neo-Daoist
philosophy, had flourished. Daoist strength was increased and its prestige
enhanced by its intimate ties with Buddhism, the Indian faith that had entered
China in the first century A.D. and reached its zenith in the late Sui and early
Tang dynasties (589–845 A.D.).

Imperial Welcome

When the Nestorian missionary delegation, headed by a bishop, Alopen,
arrived in the world-renowned Chinese capital, Changan, the reigning emperor, Tang Tai Zung, sent his minister of state to the western outposts to meet
it. The emperor's welcome to the foreign emissaries must have been warm and
effusive. A strong patron of learning, particularly of the Confucian classics, he
encouraged the translation of Nestorian manuscripts in the imperial library
next to the imperial palace. He studied the Nestorian teachings and gave orders
for the propagation of the Nestorian faith, himself sponsoring as a personal
project the building in the capital of a monastery where his own official
portrait would hang.

Under Tai Zung, thought by many to be the greatest emperor ever to rule in
China, the empire had spread to embrace in its influence an extensive area

beyond China itself: Manchuria, Mongolia, northern Korea, Tibet, Sinkiang, part of Central Asia, northern India, Tongking, and Annam. Such a wide sphere of control made it easy for visitors to come to China, whether by land or sea, and created an international and cosmopolitan atmosphere in Changan conducive not only to trade but to an open religious atmosphere. Within the border states to which Chinese influence extended, but not in great strength, followers of Manicheism as well as Muslims, Zoroastrians, and Jews, were to be found. The emperor welcomed many of them even to the capital precincts.

Tai Zung's initial interest in reviving Confucianism and reediting its classics broadened to welcome and investigate new knowledge in art, philosophy, literature, and religion originating outside the country. Despite committing himself to Confucian thought and issuing a number of anti-Buddhist edicts, he was happy to welcome back to China the Buddhist monk Xuan Zhuang, with his hundreds of Sanskrit religious books. Tai Zung's broad, liberal spirit opened wide the Chinese door to investigate anything new.

Earlier in his reign, Tai Zung had not felt this way and had said nothing good about several Persian religions that were hoping to gain access to China. His welcome several years later to Syrian Christians, accompanied by an edict of toleration for Christianity, came as a considerable surprise. His growing spirit of cultural toleration, his political penchant to court all allies, and a number of personal tragedies in his own life apparently predisposed him to learn about the new faith from Persia, Nestorianism.

Something of Tai Zung's tolerant spirit, as well as the general way in which the new faith was being talked about, may be seen in the edict of toleration and on the Nestorian tablet:

In the twelfth Cheng-kuan year, in the Autumn in the seventh month, it was decreed saying: The way has no unchanging name, sages have no unchanging method. Teaching is established to suit the land, that all living may be saved. The man of great virtue, A-lo-pen of the land of Ta-ch'in, bringing books and images from afar, has come to offer them at the upper capital. If we carefully examine the meaning of the teaching it is mysterious, wonderful, full of repose. If we look at the fundamental principle it fixes the essentials of production and perfection. In its speech there is no multitude of words; in its principle there is [perfect accomplishment], forgetting the means. It is the salvation of living beings, it is the wealth of men. It is right that it should have free course under the sky. Let the local officers therefore build a Ta-ch'in monastery in the I'ning quarter at the capital with twenty-one men as regular monks. When the virtue of the ancestral Chou failed, the dark rider went up toward the west; now that the way of the great T'ang shines, a brilliant breeze blows toward the east. [11]

The fact that "the way," the Daoist term for the Absolute and the Confucian term for the moral way, "has no constant name" (Saeki translation), that the greatest of teachers, "the sage," has "no constant form" (Saeki translation), and that, in another passage, "(Heaven) caused a suitable religion to be instituted for every religion and clime," gives some idea of the spiritually open climate in the early Tang period.

During its initial period in China, then, Nestorianism benefited greatly from imperial patronage, spreading so successfully that "it had the reputation that 'the faith spread throughout the ten districts' and 'monasteries abound in a hundred cities' " [Lo Hsiang Lin, 1].

Unfortunately for the Nestorians, not all subsequent rulers accorded them the same welcome as did Tang Tai Zung. His son, Gao Zung, although an ardent Buddhist, continued to allow the Nestorians to construct monasteries and to travel widely in China on their itinerant ministries. A short period of persecution occurred under the infamous Dowager Empress Wu Hou and again in 713 A.D., but these periods of suffering were interspersed with times of prosperity when church leaders were able to gain reinforcements from Persia to augment their ranks.

Emperor Wu Zung delivered the death blow to Nestorianism in 845 A.D. with an edict that ordered all monks—Buddhist, Daoist, and Nestorian—to "return to the world." At this time the Nestorian faith, with its hundreds of monasteries, possibly as many as two thousand religious workers, monks, and teachers, and tens of thousands of adherents, lost its foothold in China proper and survived only by being absorbed among some of the tribes on the northern frontier of China.

P. Y. Saeki speculates that most Nestorian Christians became Muslims:

> We take the existence of over twenty-one millions of Mohammedans in China as one of the external evidences which indicate that there must have been a very large body of Nestorians when our Monument was set up in A.D. 781 [*Monument*, 49].

Both Saeki and Timothy Richard, British Baptist missionary who worked in northern China in the late nineteenth century, believe that a large number of Nestorian believers found their way into Jin Dan Jiao, the "religion of the golden pill," one of the most powerful of all the secret societies in northern China.

The continuing survival of Nestorian believers over the next four hundred years, as well as their reappearance in some strength during the Yuan dynasty, is a fascinating story. But it would lead away from our main concern: What was the Nestorian gospel in Chinese during the Tang dynasty?

THE NESTORIAN GOSPEL

Our Sources

Our knowledge of Nestorian doctrines taught in China is limited to a very small number of sources. Of greatest importance is the "Nestorian Monument," erected by the Nestorians in 781 A.D. in Changan, now called Xian. The monument was lost to history until 1625, when it was discovered by workmen excavating a building site. A slab of stone measuring about nine feet by three feet and containing both a Syriac and Chinese text, this monument preserves for us the basic essentials of Nestorianism in China—names of the first missionaries, a summary of the message proclaimed, the outstanding events of the time, and other details of value.

The only other clues of Nestorian existence in the Middle Kingdom come from manuscripts, probably also dating from late in the eighth century, found in the Dunhuang caves in northwestern China. The most famous of these is the "Hymn to the Holy Trinity," which has been identified as a translation of a Syrian version of the Latin "Gloria in Excelsis Deo." There are four other Christian documents in this collection that deserve to be mentioned: *Yi-shen lun* ["concerning one God"], *Xu-ting Mi-shi-so Jing* ["the introduction to the Messiah book"], *Zhi-xuan an-lo Jing* ["the book of the will for ineffable peace"], and *Da-Qing Jing-Jiao Xuan-Yuan zhi-ben Jing* ["the Ta Ch'in illustrious book proclaiming the first cause"]. A few Chinese edicts and fragments from a number of other sources provide additional details of Nestorian history.[12]

Encouraged by Emperor Tai Zung, the first task for the new faith, initially called "Persian religion," and for its leader Alopen, was to translate the "sacred books"—the scriptures and other religioius books brought to China.

An examination of the text of the Nestorian Monument, and of the manuscripts found in Dunhuang, reveals that the Christian pioneers adapted the communication of their faith to the new environment in which they found themselves. It is apparent that they used both Buddhist and Daoist terminology to convey their meaning. Some early Protestant missionaries, among them the noted James Legge, later to be the first professor of Chinese studies at Oxford University, were quick to accuse the missionaries of syncretism, mixing their Christian faith with Buddhism in a compromising fashion. Legge referred to Nestorianism as "swamped by Confucian, Taoist & Buddhist ideas, a certain degenerate nominal Christianity" [Foster, 112]. Others were more generous in their assessment of this first attempt to put the gospel into Chinese. Alexander Wylie, for example, objectively evaluates the evidence for the authenticity of the Monument, commenting that "the Chinese titles and designations of members of the hierarchy used on this tablet are all taken from the Buddhist vocabularies." He further notes that "Alopun, the Nestorian apostle, seems to have enjoyed great favor under both the emperors Tae-tsung and Kaou-tsung, by the latter of whom he was made *Chin kuo ta fa choo* (the conserver of doctrine for the preservation of the state)" [Wylie, "Nestorian Tablet," 62].

As was to have been expected of the new arrivals in China, with little time to adjust to either the language or the culture, the initial translations made in the imperial library were crude and difficult to understand, notwithstanding the kind words of Tai Zung in his edict of toleration. A committee of five translators was responsible for the writing of the Nestorian tablet, although one of them, Adam, often known by his Chinese name Jing-Jing, did most of the work. Well versed both in Chinese literary style and in Chinese religious thought, Adam may well have been a "missionary kid" brought up in China with a Chinese education.

When it comes to judging the tablet as well as the other extant records of the Nestorian missionary effort, we simply do not know enough about the communication process. Who, for example, were the intended readers of the messages found in these records? Chinese? Foreigners? Chinese of a particular elitist background? The masses of the Chinese? How much of this kind of material was used by missionaries in their preaching at various monasteries? Answers to these questions would help us to evaluate the nature of the communication, whether or not the message was syncretistic, as many scholars have charged, and the effectiveness of the communication.

Christian Content

With the historical context of the Nestorian missionary effort in mind, we can now examine what this gospel looked like in the Chinese inscription on the all-important tablet. God is described as "the unchanging in perfect repose [Saeki translates 'true and firm'] before the first and without beginning." How appropriate a description for the unhurried East! Kosuke Koyama has caught something of this active passivity with his catch phrase "three-mile-an-hour God," in his book with that title.

And God is the creator. "He set the original breath in motion and produced the two principles . . . he made and perfected all things; he fashioned and established the first man." The following phrase, "he imparts his mysterious nature to all the sages," is probably derived from the *I-Jing* and expresses the special relationship of great teachers to the creator. "The two principles" undoubtedly refer to God's control over the yin and yang, which, in Chinese thought, were produced by the absolute, the *taiji,* and then became the origin of everything else. The Nestorians clearly communicated the triune nature of God, referring to the "mysterious Person of our Three in One, the true Lord without beginning, A-lo-he."

God created humankind "with goodness and a just temperament . . . free of lust and a puffed up spirit." This accorded well with the Confucian stress on the goodness of human nature. When, by the instigation of Satan, sin came, two things happened: original human goodness was corrupted by pride—"greatness"—and false religions were spawned. From the language used about the content of the false teaching as "being" and "nonbeing," it is probable that Buddhism was the specific target. The setting in which the fall of humankind took place was China: "in consequence of this [Satan's introducing the idea of "being" and "nonbeing" among human beings] three hundred and sixty-five sects followed side by side crossing one another's tracks, vying one with another in weaving the web of religion."

The next section of the tablet introduces Jesus, the Messiah, *Mi-shih-he,* who undid the evil effect of Satan's work. Jesus is described as "the divided Person of our Three in One (*wo san fen shen jing zeng*)." This type of expression appears again in a Nestorian hymn, where it is said that "divided in nature, he entered the world (*fen shen chu dai*)." This uncommon expression probably points to the unique doctrine of the Nestorians, for which reason, in part, their founder, Nestorius, was condemned as a heretic: that Jesus was not one person with two natures, but two separate persons.[13] If this conjecture is correct, it comes as a reminder that, from the very first penetration of Christianity into China, every group of Christians propagated in their missionary outreach the gospel as they understood it. In this same vein, no evidence appears, either in the tablet or in other Nestorian records, of the doctrine espoused by the Western church, but denied by the Nestorians, that Mary is the "mother of God" and consequently worthy of worship.

The tablet records simply the birth of Jesus in Tachin (Syria or Persia), with the magi identified as "Persians" who saw the bright star and came to offer gifts.

Is any significance to be attached to Adam's failure to make more than a few ambiguous references to the cross when speaking of the work of Jesus? In the early part of the tablet God is said to "set out the figure of ten to define the four quarters." The term "cross" in Chinese is literally rendered "the ten-character cross," and Chinese scholars have recognized that this phrase is an allusion to the Christian cross. A similar expression occurs when it is stated that "the figure of ten which is held as a seal lightens the four quarters to unite all without exception." Much more specific is the statement that Jesus "hung up a brilliant sun to take by storm the halls of darkness; the wiles of the devil were then all destroyed." Moule observes:

> The phrase [to hang up the sun] is not unknown to the Buddhists. Thus a building in the ancient monastery of Ling-yin near Hang-chou had as a motto over the door . . . "the sun of wisdom is hung on high." . . . And "to hang up the Buddha sun" is also found in a poem by Kuan-hsiu of the early 10th century [*Christians*, 37].

Xu-ting Mi-shi-so Jing "the introduction to the Messiah book" gives more detail on the value of the Savior's death. After narrating the way in which the various plots against Jesus had failed, mainly because of his large popular following, the author then comments:

> *Mi-shih-he* took his body and gave it to evil men for all living beings to cause the men of the world to know that man's life is like a flickering candle. Offering his life as a substitute to be put to death for the living beings of the present world, *Mi-shih-he* took and gave his own body and was then put to death. . . . When the men saw it like this, though there were yet some who did not believe the teaching of the scriptures that

death and life were both in *Mi-shih-he,* the men in general had belief [in Moule, *Christians,* 64].

The various references to Jesus' death, some factual and adhering closely to the biblical record and others vague allusions employing Buddhist figures of speech, confirm the observation that Nestorians emphasized the cross. Travelers in China in the twelfth and thirteenth centuries pointed out that "in the Mongol period the Nestorian monasteries were known as the monasteries of the cross" [S.K. Lee, 121].

The Nestorian tablet uses several unique phrases to describe the general ministry of Jesus:

He brought to completion the letter of the ancient law of the twenty-four sages;

He founded the new teaching . . . modelling the practice of virtue on right faith;

He laid down the rule of the eight conditions—cleansing from the defilement of sense and perfecting truth [this probably refers to the beatitudes in Matthew's Gospel, but it may be an allusion to the eight-fold path of Buddhism];

He disclosed life and abolished death;

The wiles of the devil were then all destroyed;

He rowed the boat of mercy to go up to the palaces of light; those who have souls were then completely saved. His mighty works thus finished, he ascended at midday to the spiritual sphere.

Xu-ting Mi-shi-so Jing adds several other unique aspects to this list. The purpose of the coming of the Messiah was described, for those who "take [him]," as "to restrain [persons] and guide them all to do good. *Mi-shih-he* then gave the people the way of heaven; for it was the Lord's will to dispose the people in the world not to serve inferior spirits." During his life Jesus "sought whatever people were of evil life and sent them to turn toward the good life and right way."

Emphasis is also put on his ministry of healing:

Then those who were suffering and dying he made live, blind men received eyes, cripples were restored, the sick were healed, those who were tormented by devils were delivered. All the sick came to *Mi-shih-he* to take hold of his *kashaya* and were always restored.

The Xian tablet speaks about salvation in very general terms and always couched in popular Buddhist or Daoist expressions. As a result of what Jesus has done, there is "purging away the dust from human nature and perfecting a character of truth." It is further explained that "he brought life to light and abolished death" by opening the "three constant gates," possibly a Buddhist phrase alluding to the eye, ear, and nose. In other words, believers were totally opened up to God's life and light.[14]

When Jesus had "taken an oar in the vessel of mercy and ascended to the palaces of light above," referring probably to the ascension, "those who have souls were then completely saved." Here again the figure of speech is the Buddhist concept of humankind hopelessly lost in a sea of suffering and sin, and headed for shipwreck. The compassionate Savior, filled with mercy, provides a vessel for salvation. In a sense, then, Jesus is presented as a Buddhist bodhisattva descended from God to save humankind. The means of salvation were the "water and the Spirit of religious baptism," which "wash away vain glory and cleanse one pure and white" [Saeki, 164].[15]

As evident from this section on salvation, the Nestorian message was heavily indebted to Buddhist terminology. At this early period and continuing to the present, the term *jing* has been used for "scripture." *Si,* "temple," was pressed into service for "monastery."

In the more traditional translation of the "Gloria in Excelsis Deo," found in the current *Chinese Hymns of Universal Praise,* Jesus is called the "merciful, joyful Lamb of the everlasting King of Life." A more radical expression was *shi-zun,* a term used by Buddhists to represent Sakyamoni, the Buddha. Innovative and useful as these Buddhist-flavored terms would seem to be, they were never taken up into popular Chinese Christian vocabulary.

The Nestorians also communicated their message by proclaiming the Confucian *dao,* seeking to rescue it from its ambiguity in popular use:

> The Way is broad: its influence universal.
> We are compelled to name and speak it: to preach the Three
> in one.
> The Lord is able to do: the servant is able to tell.
> Set up a grand monument: praise the supreme felicity
> [Moule, *Christians,* 47].

In matters of conduct and lifestyle:

> The faith was said to make for the peace and tranquility of the realm, the prosperity of the living, and the joy of the dead. The virtues extolled were love, mercy, kindness, the placing of all men on an equality, and the relief of suffering—clothing the naked, feeding the hungry and healing the sick [Latourette, *History,* 56].[16]

The priests were simple in their living—they did not amass riches, kept no slaves or servants, fasted, and practiced the "vigil of silence and watchfulness." Summoned by the beating of wooden boards, they gathered for worship and praise, always toward the East, seven times a day, and observed the Eucharist weekly [Moule, *Christians,* 37]. A vital part of each worship service was the offering of prayers for the dead.

Xu-ting Mi-shi-so Jing teaches that loyalty to the state and filial piety are not contrary to Christian doctrine. As Lo Hsiang Lin comments:

> They sought to implement this policy in practical ways. During the first period of persecution under Empress Wu in 693, a Nestorian layman, Abraham, erected a monument outside the gate of the Imperial City to give honor to the Empress. A few years later when An Lushan revolted against the dynasty, an army made up of many Nestorian believers from among the northern tribes played a major part in restoring peace, order and stability. Such a display of patriotism worked greatly to the advantage of Nestorianism during most of the remainder of the eighth century [*Nestorianism*, 2-3].

The Nestorian leaders were sensitive to popular criticism of monastic religion, whether directed toward Christians or Buddhists. It was, of course, easier for them to avoid attack on the question of filial piety and departed ancestors than it was for the Daoists and Confucianists: they had the practice of praying for the dead seven times daily!

Nestorianism and Buddhism

When Nestorianism first arrived in China it was referred to simply as "Persian religion," an ambiguous generic term that lumped it in with Zoroastrianism and Manicheism. When, nearly one hundred years later, the Nestorians changed their name to *jing jiao* (in an older orthography, *king kiao*), meaning "luminous religion" or "religion of light," what motivation was at work?[17] Was it, as Saeki suggests, a clear attempt to separate themselves from the other religions by having a name that both presented Jesus as the light of the world and that in both its Chinese words preserved the 'k' sound in the Greek term for Christ? [*Monument,* 131-32].

Or was the motivation more sinister—to position themselves even closer to Buddhism by accommodating to a particular school of Buddhism very popular at that time? This Buddhist sect, which worshipped Vairocana, believed to be the incarnation of Buddha's law or doctrine, was called the 'great sun religion' because of its sacred book named the 'Great Sun Scripture.' If there were such a connection, however, and this is pure speculation, would it not have been more plausible for the Vairocana sect to have adapted itself to Nestorianism? A small Buddhist group might have gained much from the popularity of contemporaneous Christianity [Holth, 26-27].

In fact, the extent to which Nestorianism influenced Chinese Buddhism and its subsequent effect in both Korea and Japan has long been discussed. No scholars doubt that the Nestorian custom of saying Masses for the dead, a prominent tradition in the ancient Celtic church in Brittany and in the church in Rome, indirectly helped in the development of reverence for departed souls, a prominent practice of both Chinese and Japanese Buddhism. Some writers, among them Karl Reichelt, trace to Nestorian roots the "salvation by grace" doctrine in the "pure land" school of Buddhism. Others find this connection difficult, because emphasis on grace has never been very marked in Eastern Christianity. Timothy Richard has speculated that Asvagosha, the noted Indian Buddhist leader credited with planting the first seeds of Mahayana or northern Buddhism, may have been influenced by pre-Nestorian missionaries in India, possibly as early as the first century, before the Christian faith had reached China. In Richard's view the remarkable Mahayana work *Qi Xin Lun* ["the awakening of faith"] may have originated in India as a result of such a contact. As will be noted later, he felt that this Buddhist work was, in fact, the first authentic "gospel in Chinese," a Christian document in Buddhist regalia.

The early Persian Christians in China have also been credited with two other doctrines that have distinguished Mahayana, the northern branch of Buddhism, from its more conservative southern counterpart, Hinayana: the concrete ideas of heaven and hell rather than the vague idea of nirvana, and a tendency toward theism in the deification of buddhas or bodhisattvas.

Can any definitive word be said about the relationship between Nestorian Christianity and Buddhism? Latourette concludes:

> Whether Buddhism was influenced by Christianity, or Christianity by Buddhism, whether they owe their likenesses to influences common to both or whether these are due to a parallel but unrelated development, is as yet impossible to say. Future archaeological researches may shed light on the question, but at present any connection between the two is entirely unproved [*History*, 49].

EVALUATION OF THE NESTORIAN GOSPEL

In their efforts to accommodate, the Nestorians committed numerous blunders. For example, it would appear from one of the Dunhuang manuscripts (*Xu-ting Mi-shi-so Jing*) that the first of the ten commandments was translated: "(The Lord) first sent all living beings to worship all the Devas and the Buddhas, and for Buddha to endure suffering." This mistake is far more likely a mistranslation—by a foreign missionary with little translation experience and unaided by a Chinese advisor—than an intentional effort to adapt the Christian message. If so, it is similar to a mistake made by Francis Xavier when he used *Deus*, the Latin term for God, in Japan. To the Japanese it sounded like *daiso*, meaning "great lie."

Nestorian efforts to put the "gospel in Chinese" were directed more toward the Buddhist than the Confucian worldview. Why was this so, particularly when these Christians attained their foothold through the help of a Chinese emperor in the process of reviving the Confucian tradition? Would it not have been better to have courted favor of its advocates even more ardently? Yet, on the other hand, nearly any ruler, despite seeming commitment to the Confucian tradition, covered all the bases in concessions to Buddhism. Moreover, many emperors were ardent Buddhists, and in the uncertain shifting of the politico-religious fortunes of the day, the Nestorians could hardly neglect relating to Buddhists, whose popular religious ideas were much more in competition with their own than were the ethical-moral ideals of Confucian thinkers. And once the Nestorians had urged their followers to observe the three great duties—"the first to serve the Lord, the second to serve the Emperor, and the third to serve father and mother"—had they not fulfilled the essence of Confucianism?

Whether or not a form of Christianity exalting the monastic ideal could really serve the emperor as well as a religion emphasizing father and mother was the ultimate question. Wu Zung, the dedicated Confucian emperor, decided not, and his severe persecution of monastic religion in 845 brought an abrupt halt to the impact Nestorianism had been able to exert in China over the previous two hundred years of its existence there.

If Christianity had not exactly failed in its first penetration into the Middle Kingdom, it certainly had not made the same impact that it had made upon the Roman empire. Latourette suggests that there are several reasons for believing that such a potential did indeed exist. The Nestorians experienced only sporadic persecution, an advantage enjoyed by the church in the West only in the post-Constantinian period. Another benefit was that the Chinese state gave the church financial help, a privilege also extended to other religious groups. Although Nestorianism had no power base in Persia that would have inclined the Chinese state to defer to it, there were excellent trade relationships between the two cultures, at least at the time of its entrance into China. The Nestorian faith attracted the allegiance of some influential Chinese, and the faith it represented was advocated by foreigners of high repute. Given these specific advantages, why did not Nestorianism survive the period of persecution and continue as a religious force in China? Different authors have given different answers to this intriguing question.

A common critique of the Nestorian missionary effort in China has been that its leaders depended too heavily on political favor at court. When it waned, they were left in a very vulnerable position. But to a large extent the same criticism could be leveled at the Buddhists, and although they periodically suffered great losses in times of persecution, their faith did not collapse. In China, then and now, not to align with the state in some significant fashion would risk the accusation of fomenting political dissent and revolution.

Unlike later missionaries who came to China with the prestige and influence of world powers behind them, the Nestorians had no power base in Persia. They operated on the same level as did any other religious group, except that they were newcomers and had to start from scratch to establish a network of official connections. They were remarkably successful, to the extent that several emperors may have given serious thought to conversion. Their failure to sustain their movement within China beyond 845 A.D. may be traced in part to a loss of political support, but this alone is not the full explanation.

Latourette conjectures—apparently because of the lack of names of Chinese priests on the Nestorian tablet—that the Nestorian community was largely made up of foreigners, or at least was "dependent upon foreign leadership and support" [*History*, 58]. It would seem, however, that the Nestorians used the same strategy as did the Buddhists, centering their work about monasteries and supporting themselves by large landholdings almost as a state within a state. If the Buddhist success is a reliable measure in this regard, the Nestorians would have needed little continuing financial aid from the home base in Persia. Monasteries served as training centers for the priesthood; if a large number of those being prepared as leaders were not Chinese, would the Nestorians, along with the Buddhists, be accused of lacking devotion to the family and being deficient in filial piety?

The amount of literature translated and written by the Nestorians and their obvious effort to accommodate the faith to Chinese concepts and practices would have been in vain if most adherents were foreign or if there were not a large number of native priests to use the tools put at their disposal.

Nestorianism, it is said, came to China at a time when there was no need for a new faith. Buddhism, on the scene for nearly six hundred years, had supplied that supernatural dimension lacking in Confucianism and was so well established at this point that the Chinese did not sense any further religious needs. Tang Tai Zung, according to this argument, was motivated only politically to find a counterweight to Buddhism as he extended his favor to the new faith. And yet as books were translated, monasteries opened, and itinerant preaching conducted, a sizeable community of believers was established and endured some measure of persecution and suffering before the final blow fell. Does not the continuance of the faith over two hundred years indicate a significant level of commitment?

It could likewise be argued that there was no religious vacuum when Protestant Christianity came to China in the early nineteenth century. Despite its alliance with military and political power, and despite opposition from all sides, the faith took root within a century and a half, and seems to be moving forward now as an indigenous Chinese Christianity. Could not the same thing have happened with Nestorianism?

Another reason often given to explain the demise of Nestorianism in China was that it accommodated itself too successfully to Buddhism—it could no longer be distinguished from the many flourishing Buddhist sects. If it were so like their own religious traditions, why convert? That the Nestorians made strenuous efforts to put the gospel into Chinese cannot be disputed. How may we be sure that this reached the stage of syncretism, with the distinctiveness of Christianity so mixed with Buddhism that its uniqueness was lost? Were any intrinsically erroneous forms used? Was there failure to fill important terms with normative meanings? Did the problem lie with the Nestorian faith itself— its allegedly defective view of Christ as two persons, for example? Did the syncretism occur initially or only later, as the possibility of persecution made identification increasingly more urgent? Was it largely among the rank and file of Christians or among the leaders? The fact that none of these questions can really be answered leaves little hard evidence to sustain a charge of syncretism.

More fuel has been added to the controversy by a number of material artifacts that some feel portray a potentially dangerous symbolism. The Nestorian tablet has carved on it a cross set in clouds and lotus flowers. In 1919 a Buddhist temple near Beijing was excavated. Found in it were inscriptions of biblical verses in Syriac, and the Chinese inscription *shi zi si*—monastery of the cross [Outerbridge, 43].

John Foster, comparing the work of the Nestorians to that of Justin Martyr and of Clement of Alexandria observes that:

> Not only was this missionary [the scribe of the tablet, probably Adam] endeavouring to make Chinese people Christian, he laboured also to make Christianity, in a worthy sense, Chinese. Underneath the strange terminology—strange to us of the west—are quotations from the Bible and ideas which come from the great Fathers of the Church. Borrowing from non-Christian sources is but the eastern counterpart of the debt owed by the Church in the west to Greek philosophy [*Church*, 112].

He comments further that contemporaneous Buddhists hardly felt that Christianity was becoming too much like them. They fiercely opposed the Christians: "Christianity as represented by Adam is called a 'perversion,' 'error,' 'wrong.' Contrasted with Buddhism, it is as the Ching and Wei rivers, one of which was very muddy" [ibid., 113].

Finally, we must consider the matter of logistics and power— equally as important as concepts and ideas in the indigenization of churches. The trailblazing Nestorian emissaries were a subject people—by this time Persia was coming under the domination of Islam—from a very distant country, having little resources, and with small hope that there could be ongoing replacement of personnel from their home base: supply lines were too distant. This may have caused them to seek power alliances in China. It would have given them locally the kind of help they could not have expected from abroad and it would have enabled them, in the lack of a serious religious vacuum, to compete on more equal terms with Buddhism. Undoubtedly, it also pushed them along the path of indigenization.

Whatever the power alignments, whatever the number and nature of the Nestorian community, and whatever the extent of accommodation to Chinese culture, the Nestorians were never able to gain enough of a foothold in China proper to assure their continuation in the midst of storms of persecution. It was, however, the first notable effort to penetrate the Middle Kingdom with the Christian message. It teaches us, among many other things, that the degree of indigenization or nonindigenization is not the only factor that will lead to a viable church. Matters of timing, length of stay, economics, politics, and power are also essential ingredients.

CHAPTER THREE

Christ the Scholar—
The Jesuit Approach

The change was drastic! From long, tattered gray gowns to luxurious dark purple silk robes; from clean-shaven faces and close-cropped hair to full beard and long hair; from walking to being carried in sedan chairs with several retainers to bring along their scholarly paraphernalia; from living wherever rooms were available in the many temples to having a house of their own where visitors would feel welcome to come and admire their many volumes of canon law, exquisitely printed and beautifully covered with gold ornamentation.

CHRISTIANITY UNDER THE MONGOLS

The two Jesuit missionaries, Matteo Ricci and Michele Ruggieri, had wanted to portray themselves and Jesus as Buddhist monks, religious emissaries, to bring a message from the Lord above. Now, because they had learned after a few years that these religious figures were despised in China, they had made a decision of profound consequences: they and Jesus would not be Buddhist monks but Confucian scholars. They would bring learning from the West, would win for themselves respected roles in educating Chinese officials, and would establish the Catholic faith as the "teaching about the Heavenly Lord." The gospel in Chinese was about to become the gospel of the scholar.

How did all this come about? The last time that the Christian faith had existed in any strength in China proper had been in the middle of the ninth century. Ricci and his companion made their radical role change from Buddhist monks to Chinese scholars at the end of the sixteenth century. What had transpired during these more than seven hundred years of transition?

Descendants of the Nestorians who had not been absorbed either into the Muslim faith or Jin Dan Jiao, the secret society in northern China, continued to live out their faith on the northern boundaries of China among the Kerait, Ongut, and Uighur tribes, which were either partially or totally christianized from 600 A.D. until about the year 1000 through efforts by the same Nestorian

36

church that had brought the faith to China. A noted Kerait tribal chief, Unc Khan, possibly was the fabled Prester John who European Christians hoped would stand with them against the invading Muslim hordes.

After being defeated by the Mongol tribes from further north, the Keraits married off some of their princesses to their conquerors, thus providing a continuing Christian influence.

Two of the Uighur Nestorian Christians, Mark and Sauma, were of particular significance. From devoutly religious families and tonsured as monks in Cambaluc (Beijing), they decided in the late 1270s to visit the holy sites of their Nestorian faith. After their arrival in Persia, Mark, through a series of unusual circumstances, was made metropolitan of Cathay and then, only two years later, in Baghdad, he was elevated to the post of patriarch of the entire Nestorian Church. His ability to speak the Mongol language made him a decided asset in a Mongol empire extending from China in the east to the Ukraine in the west.

Arghun Khan, the regional ruler of this empire in Baghdad, wishing to establish an alliance with European monarchs to fight the Muslims, sent Sauma as his personal envoy on a tour of Western capitals in 1287. Visiting religious and political leaders in Constantinople, Naples, Rome, and Paris, Sauma had two primary messages: the Mongols, "virtually a Christian nation," would be worthy allies, and Nestorian Christianity was no different from either the Eastern or Western branches of the Roman faith. The fact that he was received so well in the religious centers of Europe, blessed and blessing wherever he went, is a remarkable testimony to the "normative" nature of Nestorian Christianity, so long cut off from its roots at the sending base.

The contacts that Mark and Sauma made between East and West were only a part of the larger diplomatic, commercial, and religious relationships developing from the West. This was the period of the *pax tatarica* when relationships between Europe and China, disrupted for four centuries, were now restored by an empire with one supreme power ruling from the Black Sea to the Pacific. Giovanni de Piano Carpini and William of Rubruk visited the Mongol capital at Karakorum bearing messages seeking the friendship of the khan, particularly enlisting his support to liberate the Holy Land from the Muslims. They viewed the Nestorian Christians whom they met as seriously deficient in their faith but acknowledged that their religion was, indeed, quite similar to their own. William of Rubruk was bothered most by the Nestorian failure to practice the faith:

He complained that they did not know the language of their sacred books, that they chanted like the ignorant monks of Europe, were usurers, drunkards and polygamists. He said that the bishop came only once in eighty years and that when he made his visit all the male children were ordained priests. The Nestorians were, he declared, worse than the pagans around them [Latourette, *History*, 65].

As a result of the travels of Maffeo and Nicolo Polo in China between 1260 and 1270, the Khubilai Khan extended an invitation through them to the pope that "one hundred teachers of science and religion be sent to instruct the Chinese in the learning and faith of Europe." He probably was not interested in *Ye-likowen*,[18] the Mongol term for Christianity, for itself. He may have wanted, rather, a way to pit it in discussions against Buddhism and Islam. At any rate, Khubilai's request was never honored. A papal interregnum, the difficulty of travel over the long, arduous route, and the uncertainty of what the khan had in mind contributed to this failure by Western missionaries to respond.

The first missionary to China in this period was John of Montecorvino, a Franciscan, who arrived in Cambaluc in 1294, just at the time when Emperor Timur had replaced the recently deceased Khubilai. Within a short time he baptized six thousand Chinese and laid a foundation for the work of the Christian church in Cambaluc and several other cities. A method he used with success was to buy young boys from their non-Christian parents, baptize them, teach them Greek and Latin, and prepare for them numerous other kinds of literature to aid them in serving the church.

John arranged for the New Testament and the Psalter to be translated into the language of the court, but inasmuch as it was a foreign dynasty, the language was probably not Chinese. He was appointed archbishop of Cambaluc in 1307, and the work continued to progress with churches established as far away as Zaitun in southern China. By the time John of Montecorvino died, in 1328, he and his colleagues had seen approximately one-hundred thousand Chinese become adherents of the Roman church in China.

At every turn John's work was hindered by the Nestorians who held high positions at the Mongol court. They accused him of every possible crime, and only by dint of perseverance did he finally establish a church in Cambaluc. He speaks of their opposition:

> a certain body who profess to bear the Christian name but who deviate sadly from the Christian religion, have grown so powerful in these parts that they will not allow a Christian of another ritual to have ever so small a chapel or to publish any doctrine different from their own [Rowbotham, 31].

How different was the gospel preached by the Franciscans from the Nestorian gospel? No records—either from religious personages such as the Franciscan friar Odorico de Pordenone or from others such as Marco Polo—provide any help in answering this question. If the Franciscans of this period were as conservative and inflexible as those who opposed the Jesuits in the seventeenth century in China, the faith they proclaimed in the earlier period would have differed little in form and meaning from what was practiced in Rome. They forsook the Chinese liturgy used by the Nestorians in preference for the Latin which, they felt, better conveyed the truth of their faith.[19] The Mongols were apparently so tolerant of all religious faiths that there was no pressure for the Franciscans to bridge the gulf that divided the culture of East and West.

When the Mongols were replaced by the Chinese Ming dynasty in 1368, the Christian church again passed from the scene. Only this time there were no survivors; it was indeed a "lost" church, and when the Society of Jesus sent emissaries into China about 1600, they found no remnants of either the Persian or the Roman church.

THE JESUITS COME TO CHINA

In the early sixteenth century, representatives of the Christian church were again knocking on the doors of China, coming this time not overland, as in the two earlier initiatives, but by sea around Africa. This very fact was symbolic of a new era in the contact between East and West, an era marked by new geographic discoveries, economic expansion, new efforts to carry the faith worldwide, and rapidly diverging cultural concepts.

The aspect of widely disparate worldviews was the most crucial. Chinese political theory was unique. On earth there was but one central kingdom—China—ruled by the Son of Heaven, the only real link between heaven and earth. This kingdom was the center and standard of all culture and civilization. All other political states were barbaric and uncivilized, except to the extent that they related appropriately to China. This was not "nationalism" as understood by modern political states, but an ethnic "culturalism" that exalted everything Chinese as superior to anything that might come from outside.

The routinized way by which other countries related to China was to bring tribute to Beijing, and rigorously to observe highly prescribed ceremonies acknowledging the superiority of the Celestial Kingdom and the suzerainty of the Chinese emperor. The emissaries who came on these tribute-bearing missions usually conducted some trade and commerce. This economic activity, however, had no independent value of its own, and its occurrence was incidental to the political act of submitting to China. Franke has observed:

> A limited trade could be graciously permitted to the barbarians as a means whereby they could share in the riches and the achievements of China. . . . But permission to trade was always a gracious concession on the part of the Chinese, and for the foreigners to claim the right to trade was unthinkable according to Chinese ideas [*China*, 26].

How different for the Europeans for whom trade and profit were the primary motives for coming to China in the sixteenth century! The first modern sea barbarians to seek trade relationships with China were the Portuguese. Almost everything they did at Canton in 1517 was wrong—firing a cannon salute on their entrance into the port, taking young boys and girls into slavery, arrogantly refusing to make the ceremonial bow appropriate for anyone coming to visit, and impertinently giving a minor dignitary the important task of delivering a letter from the king of Portugal to the Chinese emperor.

The net result of this comedy of errors was the imprisonment and ultimate death of a Portuguese official and his Chinese translator, as well as an imperial order forbidding the Portuguese to trade in Canton. Only forty years later did the Portuguese secure a trading depot on Macao, a small peninsula at the outlet of the Pearl River into the bay of Canton. This base served as the jumping-off place for the next missionary effort into China.

At the very time when the Portuguese were making these ill-fated efforts to establish relationships with China, a new missionary movement was commencing in Europe. One of the Catholic responses to the Protestant Reformation was to organize in 1540 a counterreformation force, the Society of Jesus, which soon became the dominant missionary arm of the church. Stephen Neill expresses it well: "within the next hundred years Jesuits were to lay their bones in almost every country of the known world and on the shores of almost every sea" [*History*, 148]. Its most prominent missioner to the Far East, Francis Xavier, reached India in 1542 and by 1549 had landed in Japan. Believing that the conversion of China was the key to reach Japan, which had borrowed most of the significant aspects of its culture from China, he set in motion the influences that would direct Jesuit attention to the Middle Kingdom. Although a new missionary order and lacking the tradition and experience of the older Franciscans and Dominicans, the Jesuits in Japan had already developed a reputation for accommodating their Christian faith and practice to the host culture. They were to follow the same strategy in putting the gospel into Chinese.

The first Jesuit missionaries, Ricci and Rugierri, obtained permission from the governor-general of Guangdong and Guangxi in 1582 to reside in the city of Zhaoqing, a few miles north of Canton. From there these two intrepid pioneers worked their way by stages to Nanchang and Nanjing, with Ricci finally gaining a permanent residence in Beijing by 1601. Twenty years had been expended just to reach the capital of the country, and for what? A few converts had been made, but the number of Jesuit missionaries in Chinese territory, apart from the base at Macao, was only seven.

Once a beachhead had been established in Beijing, the work developed rapidly. The Jesuits could eventually count some three-hundred thousand Chinese Christians. Progress did not come easily and was interspersed with many difficult times of persecution, more often of a local nature than on a national scale. By 1773, as the culmination of a dispute between the Vatican and Jesuit missionaries in China that had lasted nearly a century and a half, the pope found it necessary to disband the Jesuits. Seventy years later, in 1840, when treaties were signed between China and Western powers, Catholic work in China, although boasting churches and Christians in nearly every province, was in a state of "retarded growth" at best. Without going into all the details of this immensely interesting period, I want to single out specific efforts that the Jesuits made to incarnate the Christian message into Chinese reality. This effort explains both their success and their failure.

Identification with the Scholarly Elite

The gospel that the Jesuits proclaimed in China grew out of their deep understanding of the Chinese people, a viewpoint they could gain only because of their willingness to identify with the scholarly elite thoroughly immersed in the ancient Chinese classics. Rowbotham argues that for Ricci and many others like him the "methods of compromise and conciliation were rather . . . a part of the policy of . . . [the] order than a matter of . . . personal predilection." And the policy adopted by the Jesuits came from their "Renaissance" spirit which caused them to favor "a deep knowledge of, and a sympathy with, the nature of mankind" more than a withdrawal from the world into a kind of "medieval asceticism" [*Missionary*, 63, 65].

To identify with the elite of China meant much more than external dress. The missionaries had to avoid studiously any criticism of Confucius, the patron saint of the literati. In fact, they would come to side with a particular view of Confucius shared by a radical clique within the government. They were careful to observe all the appropriate amenities when visiting with scholars—attitudes and ceremonies considerably at variance with those in use when visiting with less highly placed persons. Ricci and Rugierri needed to be ostentatious in their display of learning in order to meet the expectations of literate and illiterate alike, who felt that letters and science must be of high repute in Europe, and that these men were surely some of the best representatives of that learning.

Everywhere the missionaries went to live, they sought to cultivate friendships with officials and the gentry. In the Chinese system all officials received their positions through civil-service type examinations that demanded mastery of the Confucian classics and paid homage to scholarly attainments. This meant, then, that these officials could engage in scholarly discussions over a wide range of topics.

The scholar ranked at the very top of the Chinese value hierarchy—above the farmer, artisan, and merchant. As the missionaries cultivated this type of person, and as it became apparent that they could offer expertise not only in European learning but in the type of learning valued by the Chinese themselves, many sought to associate with them as students. One notable official by the name of Chiutaiso, son of a noble of the second order of magistrates, came to Ricci at Zhaoqing and petitioned him to be his teacher, presenting him with the appropriate gifts. This man became one of the Jesuits' first converts.

Ricci's reputation as a scholar meant that the Chinese expected him to do some of the types of things that Chinese scholars would do. Once, for example, he was invited to debate with a man who had forsaken his position with the literati and was now in charge of the idols in a temple. In going, along with others, to visit this man, Ricci became involved in a long discussion on the subject of pantheism. He tried to show his interlocutor how he had identified God with the material world. Because it was to be a religious discussion, he started bluntly with the request, "I would like to know what you think of the first principle of heaven and earth and the creator of all things else, whom we call the God of Heaven." Another favorite topic at the frequent debates was human nature: Was it good or was it evil?

On other occasions Ricci would be far more discreet, engaging in much more general discussions, and even the Chinese rather close to him were not always able to discern his motivation. Li Zhowu, a well-known scholar, commented:

> He is an extraordinarily impressive person. His mind is lucid and his appearance is simple. When a company of ten or a dozen people are involved in an argument, and each is defending his own view against the other, he stands at one side and does not allow himself to be provoked into intervening, and to become confused. Amongst all the men I have seen, none can compare to him. All who are either too arrogant or too anxious to please, who either display their own cleverness or are too ignorant and dull, are inferior to him. But I do not know how it is that he came here. I have already been with him three times, and still do not know why he has come here. I would be more than foolish if it were perhaps his wish to alter our doctrine of the Duke of Chou and of Confucius on the basis of his doctrine. I believe that this is not the reason [Franke, *China*, 39].

Science in the Service of Religion

In keeping with their position as scholars, the Jesuits engaged in a number of different activities. Of most immediate practical importance was their ability to use their varied expertise to arouse Chinese attention and interest. Ricci and many of the other Jesuits were adept, for example, in their use of scientific knowledge.

During his residence at Zhaoqing (1583–1589) and later in Nanchang and Nanjing, Ricci found a few interested Chinese with a scholarly bent to whom he taught theories of European science and the construction of simple instruments used in astronomy, such as the horizontal dial, the astrolabe, and the quadrant. His reputation and fame as a scholar preceded him to Beijing, and during the final ten years of his life in the capital of China, he sought to influence the imperial court on such matters as a proper understanding of astronomy and calendar reform [Franke, 53–66].

On a more popular level, Ricci's entering wedge to the emperor's presence was as a repairman of clocks. Two clocks were among the presents that he offered to the Wan Li emperor in Beijing, and when they needed to be repaired—at least four times each year—Ricci was called to do the job. He soon became indispensable to the emperor, who granted him and his colleagues free lodging, a small stipend, and informal sanction to carry on religious work.

Ricci was also an excellent cartographer. His first presentation to Chinese officials in Zhaoqing was not successful: his world map did not portray the "middle kingdom" in the center of the world nor did it occupy nearly enough of the world. Eventually, however, he was able to convince the Chinese that his drawing was accurate and, with some minor modifications, his later maps were highly treasured and circulated to all the provinces.

Later Jesuit missionaries, particularly Adam Schall von Ball and Ferdinand Verbiest, were very competent astronomers and, profiting from the mistakes of Muslim astronomers in the Chinese capital who wrongly prophesied the dates of solar eclipses, gained prominent official positions on the Board of Astronomy. Given the intense Chinese interest in the development of an accurate calendar to select auspicious dates for many events, this type of activity was extremely useful to the Chinese and met a felt need.

During the period of dynastic change when another foreign dynasty, the Manchus, replaced the now decadent Ming rulers, the Jesuits were valuable for their ability to help in the manufacture of cannon, sanctified, presumably, by giving them the names of saints. They served as interpreters between the Chinese and Russians at the drawing up of the Treaty of Nerchinsk in the late 1600s. Useful men, these Jesuits! Even as in other times in Chinese history when rulers used outsiders for their own ends, so it was the case of the Ming and Manchu rulers of China.

If contextualization is related broadly to development, then the Jesuits were early contextualists! No less a scientific authority than Dr. Joseph Needham feels that in most ways the Jesuits aided the development of science in China. However:

> Sometimes they opposed, with false hypotheses, Chinese views which were closer to the scientific truth than those of the Jesuits. Thus, for example, the Jesuits emphatically supported the geocentric Ptolemaic and Aristotelian theory, and opposed the heliocentric doctrine of Copernicus, which was closer to the Chinese movement of the heavenly bodies in infinite space [Franke, 45].

Later critics have accused the Jesuits of deliberately misleading the Chinese by withholding from them more modern views on science developing in early seventeenth-century Europe. Undoubtedly, they were aware of these new trends at their home base, but, as one observer has commented fairly:

> The Western knowledge which Jesuits published in China in late Ming represented the dominant European theories about natural phenomena, even at the moment that there was a movement in Europe away from scholastic natural philosophy [Peterson, "Philosophy," 316].

Jesuit Attitudes

Although in positions of status and privilege in China because of their ability to fill the roles of scholars and teachers, the Jesuits were careful to adopt proper attitudes. They did not refuse, for example, as did many later, arrogant Protestants, to perform the "bowing" ceremony at the proper time. They were prepared to observe the amenities necessary to get into the royal or imperial quarters, and perform such tasks as the teaching of the young Kangxi, the emperor-to-be.

Most important, they even put themselves in the role of ignorant barbarians coming to learn at the source of knowledge, the imperial court. Ricci, for example, presented himself in the following terms:

> Li Ma-tou, your majesty's servant, come from the far west, addresses himself to your Majesty with respect, in order to offer gifts from his country. Your Majesty's servant comes from a far distant land which has never exchanged presents with the middle kingdom. Despite the distance, fame told me of the remarkable teaching and fine institutions with which the imperial court has endowed all its peoples. I desired to share these advantages and live out my life as one of your Majesty's subjects, hoping in return to be of some small use [Cronin, 168–69].

When one reads Protestant literature, particularly from the 1830–1860 period, one sees how remarkably different is the tone of approach. Scholar and barbarian at the same time!

In keeping with their self-perceived role as barbarians, the Jesuits made extensive use of "tribute"—giving gifts on every occasion in accordance with Chinese expectations. If they had not understood the need for giving in order that the Chinese might, in turn, grant them favors (the idea of reciprocity or *bao* in Chinese culture), the Jesuits would never have reached Beijing, nor would they have made any progress in their work once they arrived there.[20]

JESUIT WRITINGS

Ricci saw clearly that writing was a key to the penetration of Chinese culture:

> Literary studies are cultivated to such an extent that there are few people who are not interested in them to some degree. It is also distinctive of the Chinese, that all their religious sects are spread, and their religious doctrines promulgated, by written word, rather than by the spoken word [*China*, 446].

Toward the end of his life he commented that "in China more can be done with books than with words."[21] Clearly then, scholars are expected to write, and Ricci did not disappoint his Chinese admirers.

Tract on Friendship

One of his first efforts was to publish a tract on friendship, a subject of extreme importance and interest to the Chinese for whom friendship and human relationships rank above most other virtues. The format he used was to portray himself as being questioned by the "king" as to what Europeans think about friendship. In this dialogue, which was not very lengthy, the author gathered together from philosophers such as Seneca, the fathers of the church, and other approved writers, the best material to be found on this subject. Organized into one hundred maxims, this small work gained for Ricci the reputation of a scholar and gave to many Chinese a positive view of European values as well.[22]

Of equal importance with what Ricci wrote on this subject was his ability to model the ideal of friendship. His daytime hours were so filled with receiving a constant succession of visitors that even eating was sometimes omitted. Tasks that he would have preferred to do during the day—such as prayer and letter-writing—had to be postponed until nighttime. A modern admirer has commented:

> In point of fact, it might be said that Ricci, after living a life of friendship, died as a martyr to friendship. In the Spring of 1610 imperial examinations were held in Peking for some 3000 scholars. Many of these wanted to come and meet the wise man from the West. Ricci, in addition to his other occupations, received all those he could. His hospitality surely contributed to the deterioration of his already weak health, and ultimately led to his death on May 10th of that year [Malatesta, 88].

Another major effort made by Ricci was a series of twenty-five tracts on "diverse moral questions and on control of the evil propensities of the soul." This kind of publication, referred to by the Chinese as "opinions" or "sentences," was cast in a form familiar to them. In fact, this particular work was compared by some Chinese in a very favorable way to the "Forty-two Paragraphs" issued by a group of idol worshipers.

The True Idea of God

The most important of Ricci's original works was undoubtedly *Tianzhu Shiyi* ["the true idea of God"]. Prepared as a preevangelistic work for non-Christians rather than for converts, this book, which finally was approved in 1603 when its author was fifty-two years old, was an apologetic for the Christian faith and represented nine years of Ricci's confrontation with adherents of those views most opposed to the gospel message. For many of the elite it was the gospel in Chinese for late Ming and early Qing China, because it spoke directly to the contemporary Chinese context.

Its initial impact was to enable a number of influential literati, such as Xu Guanqi and Feng Yingjing, to become Christians during the closing years of the Ming dynasty. Even much later, during the Qing dynasty, the Kangxi Emperor "liked the book so much that it was his constant companion for over a six-month period, after which he gave permission to the missionaries to resume preaching the Gospel at the Imperial Court" [Lau, 94].

Ricci's approach in *Tianzhu Shiyi* depended on several presuppositions. First was the validity of approaching the Chinese mind by way of "natural law." He states in the preface:

> This does not treat of all the mysteries of our holy faith, which need be explained only to catechumens and Christians, but only of certain principles, especially such as can be proved and understood with the light of natural reason. Thus it can be of service both to Christians and to non-Christians and can be understood in those remote regions which our Fathers cannot immediately reach, preparing the way for those other mysteries which depend upon faith and revealed wisdom [in Dunne, 96–97].

Catholic thinking, as seen both in Ricci and in modern sinologues, has leaned heavily on the "natural law philosophy" propounded by Mencius. Paul Sih has isolated several important aspects of Mencius's thinking:

1. Heaven (or, more personally, God) is the supreme ruler over the universe.
2. Heaven has given to all human beings equally the "law of nature."
3. In human nature may be found the embryonic virtues of "love, justice, propriety, and knowledge," which will develop naturally if not hindered by evil external conditions.
4. The norms by which human beings live, causing them to seek good and avoid evil, are not human creations but come from Heaven.
5. This theory may be applied morally, politically, and economically. Human beings may be exhorted to follow a high moral value system because this natural law is engraved on their hearts. The emperor, in order to rule over his kingdom, must be a moral man. His authority proceeds from his benevolence. Lacking reason, justice, and love, he will forfeit the blessing of Heaven, and it then becomes the responsibility of the people to overthrow him. "The recognition that the ultimate test of the validity of authority lies beyond authority itself is essentially a natural law proposition."
6. Finally, a truly benevolent ruler will concern himself for the economic welfare of his people. This will include, according to Mencius, equal distribution of land, the use of public granaries, a system of public schools, and a concern for all the needs of the people. It is according to reason that a ruler should care for his people in this "kingly way" (*wang dao*) and not mistreat the people (*ba dao*) as a tyrant might do.[23]

The concept of natural law in classic Chinese thinkers—Mencius, Confucius—implies that human beings are able to reason from human nature and from the nature of the universe to the existence and nature of God and the kind of moral life pleasing to God.

Ricci's second assumption was that contemporaneous neo-Confucian thought was a perversion of the traditional Confucian legacy dating back to

Mencius, Confucius himself, and even to the ancient and revered sage king Ricci believed that this tradition, with its awareness of a supreme deity, had derived from the teaching of early Jewish missionaries who made their way to China after the flood that covered the earth in the days of Noah. The philosophical system in vogue when Ricci and his compatriots came to China in the early seventeenth century had originated some four hundred years earlier during the late Sung dynasty. The famous Zhuxi and Lu Xiangshan had been its principal exponents.

Representing an extensive accommodation with Buddhist beliefs, this system carried to a logical conclusion tendencies toward secularization that had first emerged in Confucian thought a short time after the death of Confucius. Living as atheists in a materialistic world, its advocates speculated endlessly about the universe and human nature. They exalted philosophy above personal relationships, replaced early monotheism with polytheism, and in their political thinking stressed absolute power rather than the democratic spirit inherent in ancient Chinese thought.

Ricci and many of his Jesuit contemporaries argued that the metaphysics of the day did not really represent Confucius but had been derived from Buddhism. They have not been alone in this contention. H.G. Creel has observed:

> Neo-Confucianism sought to show that Confucianism could offer everything desirable that Buddhism could, and more. Specifically it undertook, first, to match the Buddhist cosmology; second, to explain the world and the Confucian ethics metaphysically; and finally, while doing these things, to justify social and political activity and to vindicate men's right to find happiness in the ordinary pursuits of the normal life [*Chinese Thought*, 166].

A Jesuit contemporary of Ricci who succeeded him at his death in 1610, Nicolo Longobardi, and a Franciscan, Fr. Ste. Marie, could not accept Ricci's conclusions about Chinese "natural theology." Contemporary Chinese philosophy, they claimed, was what Chinese thought had always been. To them any resemblances between Chinese and Christian ideas on the nature of God, the existence and nature of noncorporeal beings and matter, and the immortality of the human soul were purely coincidental.

At stake in this dispute was not only the method missionaries were to use in approaching Chinese culture, but the very nature of the gospel in Chinese. If Ricci was right, then theological and moral truth could be found in the ancient writings of the Chinese, and to accommodate the gospel presentation to the Chinese mentality was legitimate. Moreover, these theological and moral maxims, when clarified, purified, elevated, and supplemented by a more direct biblical revelation, could easily become an integral part of the gospel content.

By the same token, if Longobardi and Ste. Marie were correct—and this was the line adopted by the later Franciscans and Dominicans when they came to China—Christian missionaries dared not accommodate. They had to insist that converts abandon their long-standing intellectual tradition and replace it entirely with the special revelation found in the Christian Bible.

Not restricted to China, this argument also found its way into the European fascination for all things Chinese in the seventeenth and eighteenth centuries. The early missionaries wrote extensively of their experiences in the Middle Kingdom, and many European thinkers, disillusioned by the social and moral decadence of the time and by the impotence of the church and its dogmas to produce viable solutions, were impressed by and tempted to take over in toto Chinese political, religious, moral, educational, and even scientific thought.

A leading sinophile, Gottfried Leibniz, went so far as to propose an exchange of missionaries between Europe and China. He suggested that "Chinese missionaries should be sent to us to teach us the aim and practice of natural theology as we send missionaries to them to instruct them in the revealed religion" [Rowbotham, 252]. Believing firmly that Ricci was right, Leibniz went to great lengths to show that the ancient Chinese texts not only portrayed a "natural theology consonant with Christianity, and thereby worthy of European respect," but also revealed mathematical theories that Europe was only then beginning to discover. He firmly resisted the "anti-accommodationist position" that began to characterize writings of the later Jesuits as well as of the Franciscans and Dominicans [Discourse].

Not that the positions represented by Longobardi and Ricci were the only options. A French Jesuit, Jean-François Foucquet, thought there was a better way. His system, usually called "figurism," led him to try to find Old Testament figures in the Chinese classics, particularly in those that reflected Daoist influence. If Ricci believed that the Chinese classics were secular documents containing natural theology, Foucquet viewed them as religious writings— God's direct revelation to the Chinese, albeit hidden in enigmatic figures [Witek, 144, 332].

What, specifically, was the gospel in Chinese as found in Ricci's *Tianzhu Shiyi*? The form of this treatise is a dialogue between a Chinese Confucian and a Western scholar seeking to understand one another. The first emphasis seen in Ricci's work is that reason, possessed by all persons everywhere, gives them the potential to know God. In his initial section he delineates six arguments that will naturally lead the human mind to believe in God's existence. First, one's conscience, seeking mercy or fearing judgment, causes one to hope in or respect a being in the universe above oneself. Secondly, there must be a living God controlling the universe who accounts for the orderly orbits of the sun, moon, stars, and planets. Thirdly, the instinct of birds, animals, and insects argues to the existence and work of a higher intelligence. In the fourth place Ricci argues that the very existence of a creation that could not create itself points to a supreme creator. His fifth argument points to the order and arrangement found in the universe, in the human body, and in the life of plants, animals, birds, and insects. These things do not happen accidentally any more than an orderly house fit for human occupancy happens without a worker or than a page of written characters can make a poem without a poet and a printer.

Sixthly, the origin and continuation of life presuppose a being who created the first womb, the first egg, or the first seed. Neither chance nor accident can account for the beginnings of life.

In the remainder of this first chapter on God's creation and providence, Ricci introduces several related topics: God is eternal; is one; is unfathomable and limitless; is great beyond anything in the created universe. No mention is made in this section or in the entire book of God as a triune being. The translator's preface to chapter 1 points out that in the latter Ming and early Qing dynasties most Chinese scholars were materialists and either would not be able to comprehend anything Ricci might say about the Trinity or would reject it and him as foolish. Obviously, without the benefit or any reference to revelation, Ricci had to restrict himself to what was humanly knowable.

If human nature can recognize God, why, according to Ricci's gospel, have so many Chinese not done so? The fault lies in the way the religions of China have led them astray and hindered them from recognizing the true "heavenly Lord." He notes that the "emptiness" of Buddhism and the "nothingness" of Daoism are not to be equated with the true God. The most evident reason for this being true is the philosopher's dictum that "that which one does not have he cannot give to another as if he had it" [*Tianzhu Shiyi*, 53, 55].

The argumentation as it is developed in this section, particularly about the way in which "nothingness" and "emptiness" are to be related to God, undoubtedly reflects Ricci's disputations in Nanjing with the Buddhist monk Sanhui, and his rigorous discussion in Beijing with Hunanghui, "brilliant Buddhist scholar and tutor to Zhu Changlo, heir to the throne" [Dunne, 97]. One conclusion that Ricci presses home in this dialogue is that God's lack of material form cannot be used to disprove the existence of God any more than it can be argued that the five moralities do not exist, because they have neither form nor sound [ibid., 56].

Ricci's gentle spirit is revealed in the give and take of this argument. He knows that the Confucian literati despise and look down upon Buddhists and Daoists, but he points out that this is not the Christian way. To use the mind and reason to relate to them, in his opinion, is far better than to hate them or to belittle them. He reminds his readers that they are, after all, children of the heavenly Lord and part of all of the rest of God's creation.

Ricci directs his next argument to the literati, and asserts that the Confucian idea of the absolute (*taiji*) and reason (*li*) have kept the Chinese people from knowing God. To the Confucian claim that the *taiji* is just another term for the supreme being who rules heaven and earth, Ricci observes that he has found no indication in the classics that it was ever worshiped or revered. Nor is *taiji*, he affirms, to be equated with *li* (principle or truth), which is then to be considered God.

In the third section of *Tianzhu Shiyi* Ricci treats of the nature of the human soul—its essential difference from the soul of insects and animals, and its immortality. Following Thomas Aquinas, he describes three levels of soul: the soul of grass and trees that produces life and growth; the soul of insects and animals that enables them to be conscious of the environment about them; and the human soul that, in addition to the soul-like qualities found in plant and animal life, enables human beings to reason and to differentiate truth and error.

He musters several arguments to show that a person's soul is a spiritual substance without shape or form and thus different from the soul of insects and animals. First, the human soul is able to discipline and control the body in view of higher values and is not completely directed by a whim of physical passions and desires. Human beings can apply reason and logic to deal with the contradictory tensions toward good and evil that they find within themselves, a capability that animals do not have.

Secondly, human beings can love or hate nonmaterial values, which indicates that, in contrast with insects or animals, they have a nonmaterial aspect to their nature that is concerned with moral issues. Thirdly, the human mind has the ability to develop abstract concepts, a possibility deriving from the spiritual nature of the soul. Finally, Ricci observes that all persons are able to transcend themselves and view themselves critically.

Ricci next gives his attention to the eternal existence of the individual soul, a doctrine that he calls the foundation for anyone who truly wishes to cultivate a moral life. He advances several arguments to prove that the soul will never perish or die. First, he notes, is the desire of all persons to have a good reputation that will endure after they have died. If the soul is to die, then it would not be able to hear or know of the good works left behind. And he uses an ad hominem argument tailored for his Chinese listeners: Without the continued existence of the soul, what would be the value of ancestral rites?

Secondly, God has built into all persons the desire to preserve and prolong life, which indicates that everyone has an immaterial soul that shall never die. Ricci indicates, in the third place, that present circumstances and situations of humankind on earth do not satisfy the human spirit, thus pointing to a future existence when there shall be full satisfaction. He quotes Augustine, "an ancient Western sage, who once prayed, 'Oh God you have created us for yourself, and our hearts are restless until we find our rest in thee!' "

His fourth reason is a rather strange one. He claims that all persons are fearful of coming close to a dead body, because they are aware of the continued existence of the soul. This, he avers, is not true of insects and animals with their dead, because they have no consciousness of a soul still in existence. His final argument, a rather common one in apologetics, is that the present life does not exhaust the rewards and punishments demanded by the good and evil deeds of the human race. Only an eternity can provide for this possibility.

At this stage in his argument, his Chinese disputant presents the Confucian doctrine that there must be a difference between the fate of the *junzi* (superior person) and the ordinary person. He contends that the soul of the good man who holds the *dao* firmly in his heart will not be destroyed, but that in the case of the evil man who is not concerned with truth, his soul will indeed perish and not continue after death. Ricci seeks to refute this view, not merely by stating that it contradicts scripture but by arguing from the spiritual nature of the soul and the fact that in his previous arguments he has indicated that God has given to it an eternal existence.

In the fourth major section of *Tianzhu Shiyi* Ricci distinguishes between demons and the human soul, and refutes the doctrine of pantheistic monism that confuses God with the created world. In the course of this effort to distinguish between demons and the human soul, he develops both subjects in more detail. He uses several pages to prove that demons do exist, even though their presence may not be tested by sight and other ordinary sensory means. He appeals to ancient texts, traditional rites, and the experience of daily living as evidence. Obviously he was not willing to wish demons away as the product of superstitious Chinese minds!

His next approach is to discuss in a general way what happens to the soul after death. Does it stay in the home near loved ones? Ricci refers to the statement in the Chinese classics that the "superior man" does not fear death; death is merely a return to the "old home" (*ben xiang*). God has ordained that all things in the universe have their proper place—stars and planets in their orbits, grass in the fields, fish in the water, birds in the air. And so it is that after death the place for the soul is to be with "Heaven," who has given the soul to the person. He rejects the possibility, raised by the Chinese disputant, that the soul is really nothing more than the "two breaths—the yin and yang," and that at death dispersion occurs.

Ricci elaborates at some length his contention that the human soul is an integral part of the very being of a person, something that is not true with demons. Although they exist and have an influence upon human life, demons do not belong by nature to any object. And in no way is it possible that the human soul and a demon (or evil spirit) are the same, or that the nature of a person and of objects in the universe, such as wood, gold, stone, and grass, are the same.

From Ricci's viewpoint, the attempt to blur distinctions between the human soul and evil spirits, as well as between the unique nature of humankind and of the nonhuman world, is but the symptom of a larger problem—confusing the creator and the created universe. He traces this error to Lucifer, one of the spiritual beings created by God before the creation of the physical universe, who led a rebellion against God and was, with his cohorts, cast into hell. Ricci affirms that to identify God with creation is as presumptuous as for Chinese commoners to equate themselves with the emperor in Beijing! One is as unthinkable as the other. He points out, moreover, that pantheism finds no support in the Chinese classics.

As he makes his case against the type of pantheism espoused by Buddhist scholars, Ricci affirms several key points: God has created all things out of nothing—*ex nihilo*; God can no more be identified with all things than a human being can be identified with God; God cannot be a part of the created universe, for then God would be smaller than something that God created; God is omnipresent, but is a personal being not to be identified with creation; God is both inside and outside the universe.

Section five of *Tianzhu Shiyi* is entitled "Refutation of the Six Ways of the Metempsychotic Wheel and the Prohibition against Killing Animals, Together with a True Explanation of Fasting." Were such a complex title used today it might suggest that this was primarily a topic for scholarly discussion. On the contrary, the doctrines that Ricci discusses under this title were of utmost importance to rank and file Chinese in their daily living. To understand and relate to these matters was indispensable for preaching the gospel in Chinese during the late Ming and early Qing dynasties.

Ricci points out that the doctrine of transmigration or metempsychosis did not originate in India with Sakyomoni and Buddhism, but with the ancient Greek philosopher Pythagoras, who speculated that a proper punishment for the wicked would be that in a future life they would be changed into a form corresponding to their particular sin. He gives several reasons why the doctrine of transmigration cannot be correct. In present life no one remembers a previous existence. The theory makes no allowance for three different levels of soul (that of plant life, insect and animal life, and human life). It is impossible to interchange the souls of human beings and animals or insects, because there is a difference here of human and animal nature, and consequently of their souls. Would it not be an advantage, rather than a punishment, for the wicked to be changed into an insect or animal, in which form they could, in effect, carry out their wickedness even more easily? Implications of the doctrine, such as the prohibition of the killing of living things, would make it impossible to carry on certain human activities—agriculture, for example.

Ricci explains that God has provided animals for the good of humankind. The fear of harming a friend or relative from a previous existence now living in a changed form is no reason for not killing and eating animals. He opposes fasting based on this fear, but makes a case for religious fasting of the type practiced widely by Catholics. He affirms that it has value in helping persons to repent of and forsake their sins, as well as in promoting a moral life. He elaborates on several forms of fasting that he has learned of in various places in the world and gives some advice on suiting the form and nature of fasting to the age and health of the person engaged in it.

In section six of *Tianzhu Shiyi* Ricci summarizes his presentation. He has appealed to the Chinese classics and natural reason to argue for the existence of a Supreme Being and for the immortality of the human soul. Now the question arises, "What happens to this soul after death? Where is its final resting place?" A related question is, "If there is a place of rewards called heaven and a place of punishment called hell on what basis does the human soul go to either place?"

In dealing with these eschatological themes Ricci stresses several issues. First, he makes clear that human beings, unlike the rest of creation, have the freedom to do good and to avoid evil. This does not happen automatically; only by the use of reason will persons overcome their "beastly" tendencies. A person's desire to do good, he claims, proceeds from three levels of motivation:

to go to heaven and escape hell; to "pay back" God for the gift of grace; and, most commendably, to desire to do the will of God.

He offers proofs for the existence of heaven and hell. Only a place of complete blessing and happiness can satisfy human longing. God would not put such a longing in human hearts if there were no way to satisfy it. The rewards and punishments of the present life are not sufficient; only the existence of a heaven and hell can do justice to the impartial judgment of God. To these "logical" arguments Ricci adds an appeal from the ancient Chinese classics. The *junzi* (superior person) must believe in the existence of these final resting places; those who disbelieve reveal that they are not superior persons.

Ricci states that he cannot give a detailed description of either heaven or hell, but that its happiness and misery, respectively, are both everlasting. In this section, as in one or two previous ones, he makes obvious and overt references to scripture—almost to the point of exact quotations—without indicating book, chapter, and verse.

In the seventh section of his work Ricci discusses human nature, a topic of perennial interest to Chinese philosophers. First of all, he reviews what various sages since the time of Mencius have contributed to this discussion. For Ricci, and presumably his church, a person's nature at the moment of birth is like a piece of white paper on which either good or evil may be written. God has given all persons *liang shan*, conscience, a type of rudimentary morality for which they receive no credit or merit. Conscience is the feeling of fear that a child may have if it sees it is about to fall into a ditch. Animals and evil persons also possess conscience. To be distinguished from this is *dexin*, the morality that persons learn to practice when, by using reason, they refuse to follow their sensuous desires. When human beings contact their environment, their five senses first process data into their inner beings where memory and reason sift it, and then it becomes their free option to follow or refuse good and evil.

The highest good that human beings achieve is to love the heavenly Lord above all else and their neighbors as themselves. Although not intrinsically evil, human nature is very weak and easily swayed, which explains why so many Chinese scholars are unable to attain their ideals. Only trust in God and God's gracious providence can provide help for this weakness. At this point Ricci specifically points out that Buddhism and Daoism, with their many errors and images, cannot solve the dilemma of the human race, nor, as some apparently were suggesting, will any combination of the three religions of China. Only the one correct doctrine of the heavenly Lord gives a truth sufficiently deep and secure to meet human needs. Ricci's Chinese listener expresses great satisfaction that his presentation of the truth has caused him to awaken from his former stupor.

With his listener then ready to believe, Ricci goes into a bit more detail about the Catholic church. He deals particularly with the matter of celibacy, in direct conflict with the Chinese tenet of filial piety that to have no offspring is the worst violation of morality.

In response to his Chinese colleague's questions, Ricci lists eight reasons, not always sharply differentiated, to explain why it is that Catholic priests are celibate: (1) Marriage involves raising and providing for a family, which, of necessity, involves a concern for sufficient financial resources. (2) Sexual concerns and desires blunt a person's wisdom, whereas celibacy removes the "dust" from one's heart and eyes. (3) The vows of poverty and celibacy symbolize the teaching of the church with respect to the problems of greed and sexual passion. (4) Celibacy enables priests to concentrate on their principal task. (5) Celibacy enables preachers of the gospel to be strong for the task of spreading the truth in every country. (6) Human activities are so often on the same plane as those of the animal world, whereas voluntary celibacy expresses the fact that the "dao" is something that demands our highest sacrifice. (7) The work of the Jesuits is not restricted to one geographic area and celibacy gives them freedom to work everywhere. (8) Although marriage is lawful and only deviant sex is displeasing to God, those who for the sake of religion remain celibate are nearer to God, who has no sexual desires.

When asked about the unfilial nature of celibacy, Ricci replies that this allegation was not made by Confucius, but by Mencius; Confucius never said that not having children was evil. Moreover, when Mencius made the statement China did not have the population it needed. That need, Ricci affirms, no longer exists.

Western sages, Ricci notes, have not judged the failure to have children an unfilial act but have given attention rather to three other matters: to cause one's parents to sin; to kill a relative; and to strip parents of their property. He concludes that the worst offenses against filial piety are to disobey the heavenly Lord, the great father of humankind, and to disobey the emperor and the head of the home.

As he touches upon the heavenly Lord's universal fatherhood, Ricci, for the first time, goes into more detail on creation. He indicates that although the human race was created perfect, it disobeyed God's command, causing all of creation to rebel against it. As a result, the root of human nature has been corrupted and now has "shortcomings." Though this corruption has become habitual, a person may recover by turning from evil and pursuing good.

In a few short lines he goes on to explain that God, in great love, sent Jesus to be the Savior. Ricci gives a short outline of his life. Most notable is the fact that no account is given of the crucifixion and resurrection, two doctrines that would probably have been as difficult to understand and accept as the triune nature of God. He describes some of Jesus' many miracles, proving that he was the heavenly Lord come to earth. These works went beyond any that the great saints of the church were able to do in his name.

It is well to remember that *Tianzhu Shiyi* is largely preevangelistic in nature. Possibly the most notable of Ricci's converts in Beijing, a scholar by the name of Xu Guangqi (Paul Hsü), indicates that the purpose of the book was to "do away with Buddha and to complete the law of the literati." Ricci does not use the catechetical-type material appropriate for those already with a foundation in their understanding of the faith. Nothing is said about believing in Jesus;

only one short sentence speaks about accepting scripture, being baptized, and entering the church. Only a passing statement, this remark would hardly give a reader any idea of what was involved in such a step.

Ricci's masterpiece was widely read by Chinese mandarins in the several editions in which it was published over the years. For multitudes of Chinese officials it was indeed the gospel in Chinese. Cronin has commented on it:

> This book contained the fruits of Ricci's discussions with such friends as the Ministers of Civil Appointments and of War, with the Censor at Nanking, and with the geographer Li Chih-tsao. Appealing in every case to principles acceptable to most Chinese or to their ancient and authoritative texts, in matter, approach and style a triumph of adaptation, bearing witness to his love and understanding of the Chinese, the book probed beneath all the inessential differences, obvious and subtle, between East and West, to proclaim their unity as men made by the same God. As a climate of thought in which Christianity would be most likely to flourish, it advocated a return to the purity of ancient religious thought, stripped of the atheist accretions imparted by Chu Hsi. No appeal could have been better attuned to a people in love with the past. The graduates came to view the new doctrine not as an abhorrent novelty but as the crowning of their noblest traditions while for Chinese Christians and those drawn to Christianity, Ricci's work provided an invaluable summary of apologetic [*Wise Man*, 210].

How may we summarize Ricci's attempt to present the gospel in Chinese for his day? First, he clearly positioned himself with ancient Confucian thought against Buddhism, Daoism, and the contemporary neo-Confucianism. Secondly, he showed that the humanistic perspective of even traditional Confucianism needed to be balanced, supplemented, and corrected by the transcendental dimension. With these modifications, however, the original Confucian ethics had universal relevance and could become a part of the Christian gospel in Chinese.[24] Thirdly, his approach reflected the scholastic philosophy of the day in which he lived. His teaching often appeared to be argumentative, confrontational, and apologetic; great emphasis was placed on "out thinking" the other person. One critic has observed:

> [His approach] reflects a Scholasticism of the later Middle Ages which tended to look upon life as having two distinct phases, the two connected by the moment of death. There is no mention of penetration and transformation of our life in this world by eternal life [Lau, 98].

Not only did this method lead him to put truth in noncontradictory boxes; it often caused him to distort the Confucian classics by finding Christian doctrines in strange places! The literati could agree with most of what he taught, but:

What they regretted to see, however, was his wandering about amid strange doctrines searching for notions concerning the Creator, the immortality of the soul, heaven and hell, sin and the crucified Saviour.[25]

Finally, Ricci's effort at indigenization, although not rooted in present-day Catholic theory that sees Christ already working in a target culture by the Holy Spirit, recognized that the "natural theology" of the Chinese was a vehicle for God's truth.

Despite the efforts by Ricci and the Jesuits to accommodate their faith to the Chinese scene, they never compromised on what they thought was basic— idolatry; evil marriage practices such as concubinage or polygamy, or marriage contracts between children; superstitious practices related to the five elements (metal, wood, fire, water, and earth), and geomancy. They insisted on fully Christian burial services—in fact, the first sodality developed in China, termed the Sodality of the Blessed Virgin, had as its purpose "to supervise the funerals of the converts . . . and to make certain that their obsequies were conducted with strictly Christian ceremonies" [Ricci, *Journals*, 542].

The serious commitment the Jesuits had to their faith can be seen in the nature of the charges brought by opponents in the Chinese court against Adam von Ball Schall, leading Jesuit and director of the Bureau of Astronomy, in 1665. He was accused of:

1) Preaching Christ crucified, 2) baptizing annually two or three hundred converts, 3) claiming that the emperor had accepted Christianity, 4) preaching that Adam was created of God and was the father of the human race, 5) seducing the people by the preaching of repentance and by the administration of baptism and anointing, 6) preaching that Heaven *(T'ien)* is the seat of God and not God himself, 7) forbidding the worship of ancestors, 8) holding, four times a year, suspicious meetings with Christians and collecting money from them, and lastly 9) having suspicious relations with the Portuguese at Macao [Rowbotham, 313, n.11].

Clearly, then, the Jesuits were aware of the danger of syncretism and sought to avoid it. In this connection, they also made it clear that the final authority on questionable matters would reside with the pope—his authority was clearly a part of what they deemed to be the central core of the gospel.

Translation of European Classics

Translation of important books was also a part of the Jesuit strategy. This included not only the *Summa Theologiae* by Aquinas, the *Imitation of Christ* by Thomas a Kempis, Loyola's *Exercises* and other religious works, but a volume on mathematics, *The Elements*, by Euclid. Ricci had no hesitation in including Euclid in his gospel:

In the course of the centuries, God has shown more than one way of drawing men to Him. So it was not to be wondered at that the fishers of men employed their own particular ways of attracting souls into their nets. Whoever may think that ethics, physics and mathematics are not important in the work of the Church is unacquainted with the taste of the Chinese who are slow to take a salutary potion, unless it be seasoned with an intellectual flavoring [*Journals,* 325].

One writer confirmed the wisdom of this policy:

Nothing pleased the Chinese as much as Euclid. This perhaps was due to the fact that no people esteem mathematics as highly as the Chinese, despite their method of teaching, in which they proposed all kinds of propositions but without demonstration. The result of such a system is that anyone is free to exercise his wildest imagination relative to mathematics, without offering a definite proof of anything. In Euclid, on the contrary, they recognized something different, namely propositions presented in order and so definitely proven that even the most obstinate could not deny them [ibid., 476].

CHINESE CONVERTS

The response of the Chinese to the Jesuits and their gospel of religion-science was mixed. Scholars such as Wang Zhuanshan dismissed the new teaching out of hand, labeling it "falsehood and heresy." Many were attracted by the scientific knowledge of the missionaries but felt that the faith they proclaimed placed too little emphasis on traditional virtue and self-cultivation. Some of those who studied at the feet of Ricci and his colleagues became fervent converts.[26] These noted followers, often belonging to the highest scholarly ranks in China, were able to help in writing and translation, composed books on their own, commended the Jesuits to friends, paved the way for correct relationships with the government, often provided refuge in times of difficulty, and helped in innumerable ways. For all of them it was extremely important that the Jesuits had taken the specific strategy that they had: to show that the original teaching of Confucius, as contrasted with the debased neo-Confucianism current in the 16th and 17th centuries, was diametrically opposed to the superstitions practiced by the Buddhists and Daoists.

The support given by high-ranking converts is most clearly seen in a memorial written by Xu Guangqi to the Wan Li emperor of the Ming dynasty and preserved on a marble slab erected at the Jesuit church outside the southern gate of Shanghai. Written in 1617 at a time of incipient persecution, this appeal to the emperor argues that only these Christian missionaries are able to promote the "fidelity, filial piety, compassion and love" that the emperor desires to be universally exercised throughout the empire. Buddhists and

Daoists alike, he asserts, are "imperfect in their doctrines and incomplete in their laws of instruction." Christians, by contrast, are "able to serve Heaven" and "truly competent to repair and augment the royal Institutes, to strengthen and maintain the arts of the literati, and to restore and correct the laws of the Budha [*sic*]." He defends them against various accusations and pleads that they be granted a status equal to that of the Buddhists and Daoists.

In statements reminiscent of Ricci, who assumed the humble role of "barbarian," Xu (Hsü) explains the motivation of the Jesuits in coming to China:

> Now the reason of their coming thousands of miles eastward, is because hearing that the teachers, the sages and worthies of China, served Heaven by the cultivation of personal virtue, served the Lord of Heaven, and knowing that there was this correspondence in principles, they desired, notwithstanding the difficulties and dangers by land and by sea, to give their seal to the truth, in order that men might become good, and so realize high Heaven's love to man ["Apology," 118–26].

Xu and other converts obviously were impressed by much more than Ricci's knowledge of science:

> The knowledge of Matteo Ricci can be divided into three categories: the more important one is to serve Heaven and cultivate oneself; the less important one is to investigate things and their principles; the least important are the applied sciences such as mathematics and astronomy.[27]

On another occasion Xu commented:

> Matteo Ricci was very well known to every one in the country. All the scholars and gentry earnestly desired to meet him. Once they heard him speak, all felt satisfied and acknowledged that they never heard anyone like him before . . . for his learning is all-embracing and its most important element is conversion to the true God, and to serve him in true piety.[28]

Some have wondered if the devotion of the converts matched that of the Jesuit priests. Franke, for example, has claimed that for educated Chinese converts, "their traditional Confucian outlook remained predominant" [*China*, 54]. He refers specifically to a Christian official during the dynastic change of 1644 who, when imprisoned, wrote a series of poems that reflected only Confucian thought on matters of life and death. On the other hand, Paul Xu (Hsü) appears to have been a man of deep devotion, at least in the Catholic tradition. One historian tells us that he "meditated half an hour daily at the foot of a Crucifix in his oratory," an important observation in light of Ricci's reluctance to speak or write about the cross.

Mary Louise Martin, a critic of the quality of the spiritual experience of both the missionaries and their converts, has observed:

For Jesuits . . . spirituality is necessarily based on the Spiritual Exercises of St. Ignatius, basic to which is a notion of the Creator as a person God, not just a "Source of Morality," and deep faith in the Incarnation which carries with it a decision to follow Jesus as a person, not as an abstract concept. Fr. Hu maintained that this foundation must have been passed on to the early converts, who also would have been drawn to a personal God and the person of Jesus His Son [M. L. Martin, 155].

From what has been said thus far it must not be inferred that missionaries neglected the Chinese rank and file. Outside Beijing, the Christian faith reached the masses. Catechists, as well as elders or headmen in rural villages, assumed much of the responsibility for them. Sodalities were organized to meet special needs. One such sodality was a group of female catechists organized to teach children and to visit in the homes of Christians.

PROBLEMS FACING THE JESUITS

The Jesuits were not without their problems. Despite the lack of European political or military backing, they were suspected of having some type of relationship with the Portuguese through Macao. This was particularly true when they were just beginning in southern China in the province of Guangdong, which was often the scene of foreign depredation by marauders and pirates. This overall situation was not helped by an attempt of one of the early Jesuits, Ruggieri, to arrange for a papal delegation to be sent to China to seek official permission to preach the Christian faith.

Did this fear of outside support for the Jesuits create the problem that the "gospel of power" would be for later Protestant missionaries? Hardly! Moreover, the context of the early seventeenth and early nineteenth centuries was quite different. In the earlier period, Chinese civilization was thought to have something important to contribute to Europe, even possibly in science. The earlier missionaries were not at all inclined to be condescending or to tie Christianity and culture so tightly together in one package.

The major problem for the Jesuits was that missionaries from other orders, usually the Franciscans and Dominicans who came later, accused them of overaccommodating their faith in order to please their hearers. The complaints usually took two forms: what the Jesuits did, and what they did not do!

"Sins of Omission"

One accusation, certainly verified in some of Ricci's writing and preaching, was that the Jesuits did not preach the crucifixion of Christ. Ricci's reticence can be traced to an experience he had in 1600 while on his way to Beijing. He was detained by some eunuchs who, when they found a crucifix in his baggage, thought it was meant for casting a curse upon the Wan Li emperor. Although Ricci was finally able to clear himself of this serious charge, he felt that any public display of the cross, particularly with the figure of a dead man impaled upon it, would only be misinterpreted [Dunne, 75].

However, Giulio Aleni in his book *Tianzhu Jiangsheng chuxiang Jing jie* ["sacred explanation of the life of Christ illustrated with pictures"], published in 1635, twenty years after Ricci's death, includes a powerful description of the crucifixion as well as several pictures of the events surrounding the death of Jesus. I have noted above that one of the charges against Adam Schall was his preaching of the cross.

There were differences of opinion on the best way to present the crucifixion to the Chinese. Ricci on one occasion stated that an almost nude pictorial representation of Christ on the cross would be a mistake because a nude figure in art was forbidden by Chinese law. His earlier experience with the eunuchs was an indication that the crucifix could be considered a Daoist curse or charm. The Franciscans, not so restrained by cultural considerations, were much bolder in their public witness. "They considered it their sacred duty to preach in city streets, aided by an interpreter, garbed in their Franciscan habit, with a crucifix in hand."

The Jesuits were unwilling to discuss with the Chinese the eternal fate of their ancient worthies such as Confucius or the legendary heroes Yao and Shun. To a direct question, "Is Confucius in hell?," they were likely to answer ambiguously:

> All those who know God and love Him above all things, and who pass out of this life with such knowledge and love, are saved. If Confucius knew God and loved Him above all things, and passed out of this life with such knowledge and love, without doubt he is saved [Dunne, 274].

The Jesuits failed to enforce various external ecclesiastical laws: fasting, abstaining from work on Sundays and feast days, and other like matters. In adopting such a policy, basically as an accommodation to the economic realities of life in the Orient, they were continuing the precedent established by Aleosandri Valignano in Japan. Not to work on certain days would force the Chinese into even deeper poverty, and fasting was deemed impossible for them to observe. Francisco Furtado, writing in defense of this policy to Pope Urban VIII in 1639, noted:

> So far as fasting is concerned the Chinese live so close to the margin of subsistence, that in Europe itself Christians of long standing would be exempted from fasting if they lived in like circumstances. For most Chinese live simply on rice and herbs, to which they sometimes add a few vegetables . . . they are so poor and earn so little each day, that to forbid them to work would be the same as to forbid them to eat [Dunne, 272].

Another charge that a leading critic, Juan Bautista de Morales, made against the Jesuit missionaries was that "the Fathers in baptizing women fail to apply saliva to their ears, salt to their mouths, and oil to their breast and head" [ibid.]. This policy was dictated by the Chinese practice of forbidding any contact with the opposite sex except among members of the same family circle. Desiring to avoid any unfounded rumors and scandalous tales about their conduct, the Jesuits were unusually careful in their relationships with women believers. They made special arrangements, for example, to conduct confessions in a large room at one end of which stood a Chinese Christian of unquestioned integrity, who could see all that transpired but who was beyond the range of hearing the actual confession.

"Sins of Commission"

Over the years the Jesuits have been faulted more for what they did than for what they did not do. The terminology they developed to express their faith, the attitudes they espoused, and the practices they were prepared to accept as not contradicting the gospel have been the thorny issues for which their work in China has been most remembered.

The question of language, a common problem in all cultures and certainly faced also by the church in the first century, was sparked in China by the desire of the Jesuits to present older men as candidates for the priesthood. Older men would have finished taking the civil service examinations and would not feel any conflict between those prestigious studies and the ones required for the priesthood. Furthermore, they would have already reared their families, and celibacy would be less of a moral or cultural burden. A problem, however, was the difficulty these older men were having in learning Latin. The Jesuits were able to obtain permission to put the Catholic liturgy into Chinese. This led to the problem of terminology, a large part of what came to be known as the "rites controversy," a conflict that rocked the Catholic Church in China for over one hundred fifty years. My purpose here is not to discuss the intricacies of argument and counterargument, but to note only those matters that relate directly to the content of the gospel in Chinese.

The "Rites Controversy"

The most important question of terms had to do with the correct name for God in Chinese. In the Chinese classics were to be found the terms *tian* and *shangdi*, either of which could be interpreted impersonally as referring to the overall principle of the universe or personally as having theistic implications. Although recognizing that the terms were somewhat ambiguous in Ming China, most Jesuits appealed to the manner in which *tian* and *shangdi* were used by Confucius and in the ancient Chinese classics that predated him. Claiming that God had been revealed in ancient China as Jehovah through these two terms, they ignored all later accretions with their unacceptable connotations, and sought to reinterpret them in terms of Christian truth. This, they felt, was merely a return to their original meaning. Their conclusion was the same for several other terms: *tianshen* for angel and *linghun* for soul. They argued that they were supported in this stand not only by the Chinese classics, but also by the most prominent Chinese scholars, some of whom were Christians, such as Xu Guangqi, Yang Tingyun, and Li Zhizao.

A smaller number of Jesuits, principally Nicolo Longobardi, as well as later Dominicans and Franciscans, were not convinced. They remembered all too well Xavier's disastrous mistake in Japan when, after giving up on the Latin *Deus*, he chose the Japanese *Dainichi* to translate God. He learned only too late that "the term had a fixed significance in Japanese Buddhism . . . [and] that in summoning the Japanese to worship Dainichi he was sponsoring the cause of a Buddhist deity quite different from the Christian God" [Dunne, 283].

In the view of these more conservative missionaries, then, Ricci and his followers were hopelessly compromising themselves with idolatry. A safer path, in the conservative opinion, was to use the term *tianzhu* ("Heavenly Lord") to signify God. Although it had some roots in Daoism and Buddhism, it was, unlike the other two words, almost of zero value to most of the populace. After decades of controversy, this was the term ultimately authorized by the distant Vatican, and to this day the Catholic Church in China is known as the Church of the Heavenly Lord.

A second major issue in the rites controversy was the degree to which Christians could participate in ceremonies intended to honor departed ancestors. The ancestral cult, the focal point of filial piety, consisted of a complex of four activities: burial; ritual in the home before the ancestral tablets—wooden plaques that bore the names of the departed dead; annual sacrifices at the grave; annual services in the ancestral hall. The most important part of the funeral itself was the selection, by divination and geomancy, of the proper time and place of burial. When this had been completed, relatives prepared the wooden ancestral tablet, inscribed with the name and date of birth and death of the deceased and thought to be the abode of that person's spirit.

Following this, the survivors held a ritual in the home, and large sums of money were expended to provide the dead with symbolic paper miniatures of everything needed in the spirit world: house, clothing, bed, and perhaps slaves and concubines. Other major services followed at prescribed intervals, and eventually a routine daily ceremony was established, conducted morning and evening before a home altar either by the father or the oldest son and consisting of prostrations, the burning of incense, and offering of food.

Ricci's initial reaction to these ancestral ceremonies was that they were superstitious and that Christians ought not to observe them. But he later concluded:

> All this has nothing to do with idolatry, and perhaps it can also be said not to involve any superstition, although it will be better to change

this into giving alms to the poor where it is a question of Christians [Dunne, 291].

Ricci's opinion, never rigidly dogmatic, was probably based on several considerations. First, he undoubtedly felt, as many have since, that given the avowed agnostic attitude of Confucius toward the afterlife, the sage's concern in advocating filial piety toward the dead was not basically to provide for the dead, but to promote the virtue of filial piety among the living. Secondly, the materialism of contemporaneous neo-Confucian thought would indicate that, for most of the populace in late Ming China, the ceremony had little or no religious significance, but was meant to serve practical ends. Thirdly, Ricci was prepared to see many acceptable elements in this complex of ceremonies and to believe that they could be practiced by Christians, at least temporarily. He was convinced that over a period of time they would have a better understanding of Christian truth and practice, and would then be able to make proper and mature decisions on their own.

In contrast to their divided opinions on the matter of the name for God, the Jesuits were apparently united on the issue of the ancestral rites, and their policy became the practice among many rank and file Chinese Christians. An early Qing dynasty Christian ancestral tablet illustrates their emphasis. In the center of the tablet, with the same external features as those used by non-Christians, is the phrase, "Worship the true Lord, creator of heaven, earth, and all things, and show filial piety to ancestors and parents." The text to the right of this explains that the Heavenly Lord has created all and rules over all, punishing the evil and rewarding the good. In the column to the left is the explanation of the meaning of the rite:

It is through father and mother that one receives his greatest favors from God. After death, whether they receive punishment or reward, they will not return home. Therefore, the filial son or kind grandson sets up a tablet or a picture by no means that their spirits might dwell therein, but in order to serve as a reminder of his debt.[29]

In this matter, the Jesuits appealed to the example of the revered Augustine who tolerated certain drink and food offerings made on the tombs of the dead. Certain points they made very clear: no paper money could be burned before the tablet; participants must not affirm belief that the dead derived nourishment from the food used in the ceremony and they must not pray to the dead; ancestral tablets, as well as flowers, candles, and incense, could be used in the home, but this must not be considered any type of worship.

Almost of one piece with the issue of alleged ancestral worship were the rites offered to Confucius, at the granting of the *xiutsai* degree and twice a year in Confucian temples. Involving obeisance, the offering of incense, and animal sacrifices, these rites, largely the prerogative of the officials and gentry, again had the external appearance, if not the internal reality, of idolatrous worship. The Jesuits' position on this was consistent with their judgment on other matters: "the rites were originally mere civil ceremonies which had in the course of time become infected with erroneous preternatural or superstitious beliefs" [Dunne, 294].

One Catholic scholar observes that the Jesuit attitude was similar to a decision at the Council of Elvira in 303 when Christians were allowed to occupy an office associated with the imperial cult. Later scholars reasoned: "The line which separates Christian discipline from idolatry could change its position by reason of the laicization of idolatry" [Dunne, 297].

The Jesuits, even where disagreeing among themselves, as on the name of God, were able for the most part to maintain a spirit of love and unity, and not allow their disagreements to disaffect their converts. The Franciscans and Dominicans, however, were belligerent in their attitudes toward the Jesuits. Any degree of compromise to Chinese culture, even a painting of the Lord's table portraying Jesus' disciples with Chinese sandals on their feet, was outright idolatry! They were equally scandalized by a wooden plaque, on a table in one of the Jesuits' chapels, with the inscription, "Long live the Emperor!"

The theological issues had political overtones. Outerbridge suggests, correctly it seems, that differences between the Franciscans and the Jesuits were basically national. The Jesuits in China, chosen largely for their scholarship, came from areas in Europe not dominated by a strong nationalistic spirit (ten from Italy, three from Portugal, one each from Germany and France). The Franciscans were from Spain where there was a deep identification between nationalism and the Catholic Church.

And so the battle was joined! It waxed and waned over a period of one hundred fifty years. In general, most of the Jesuits were aligned with the Chinese emperor against the pope and others of the Catholic missionary orders. At various times during this long period one side or the other seemed to be ascendant. Eventually a hard line was adopted: the Vatican took an inflexible stand against the Jesuit position. Christians went through many periods of intense persecution, until the faith finally was prohibited in China (1724), many priests deported, the Jesuits disbanded (1774), and irreparable harm done to the cause of Christianity in China.

Not everyone agrees that the rites controversy caused such harm. Latourette, for example, although conceding its importance in leading to the retrenchment of Catholic presence in China, feels that it was only one item. He affirms that, even had the emperor's favor continued, the church could not ultimately avoid conflict with Chinese culture and persecution. Furthermore, Latourette believes that "had the Church made its peace with some of the more important religious practices of China, deterioration would almost certainly have followed" [*History*, 154]. Therefore, in his opinion, the decision by the central authority of the church to reject Jesuit accommodation to Chinese culture preserved the integrity, vitality, and uniqueness of the Christian message. Latourette's conclusion is echoed by Rowbotham:

It is probable that, had the Jesuit position been wholeheartedly accepted, the Catholic church in China might sooner or later have lost its identity and become merged in the relatively formless chaos of native philosophical thought. As has been shown earlier this was the fate that had overtaken Nestorianism in China—in which country the high mysticism of ancient Taoism had also degenerated into a system of magic and charlatanry [*Missionary,* 296].

By 1838, Catholics in China may have numbered as many as three hundred thousand, but they were bereft of leadership. Macao, Nanjing, and Beijing were without a bishop, and the leadership structure was in disarray. This was *meaning* hardly the success for which Ricci, a quarter of a century earlier, had hoped. Yet is it not naive to suggest that this state of affairs resulted, exclusively or chiefly, from the Jesuit efforts to present the gospel in Chinese? What other factors help explain this "failure" in China?

1. More important than the doctrinal issues that emerged in the rites controversy was the organizational clumsiness of the church, a disunity apparent to all its enemies, if not to the Christians themselves, and a struggle that was allowed to drag on interminably with solutions, countersolutions, and more counter-countersolutions! In a certain sense, the original issues were swallowed up by questions of power deriving from the ever accelerating European hubris that was to characterize nineteenth-century attitudes toward China. All this was much different from the earliest Jesuits who came to China as "barbarian" learners anxious to serve its felt needs in any way possible. Failure came with the abandonment of the unique spirit and attitude of the Jesuits. Ricci had "class" the others lacked.

2. Initially the Jesuits stressed the need to win officials and the gentry to Christ. This gave a high status to Christianity, often resulting in the conversion of entire rural villages, and also provided help, particularly during times of persecution, for missionaries in high places. Following Ricci's death in 1610, this policy was not consistently followed, and although the church might periodically find favor with a Kangxi or another emperor, support was lacking among high-ranking government officials, who tended increasingly to think of the church as on a par with popular Buddhist or Daoist sects.

3. The late Ming and early Qing dynasty periods were unsettled times with threats and near threats from many foreign enemies. This intensified the xenophobia of the Chinese to a high pitch, causing them more than ever to believe all foreigners were spies and in the direct service of foreign governments.

4. The antiforeign sentiment of Chinese officialdom fueled its tendency to suspect all new religious sects as centers of incipient revolt. Ricci tried to overcome this attitude by his overt identification with orthodox Confucianism. In doing this, however, he and his colleagues became a threat to the gentry and officials who feared a loss of their power. With Ricci this was less of a problem than with his successors who were far less willing to accommodate and thus posed more of a challenge.

5. Despite all efforts of the Jesuits to accommodate to Chinese culture, there were still tension points where even they would not budge—polygamy and overt idolatry, for example. However, these issues would not have posed as serious and as extensive a problem as the Confucian and ancestral rites. Contrary to some criticism, the Jesuits never advocated a "wholehearted" acceptance of those rites. They were selective in their accommodation and viewed what they were advocating as a "transition" strategy until the church would become well founded. Furthermore, their "failure," such as it was, did produce a church larger than that of the Nestorians and one that has continued until the present day. They were a bit unrealistic in their expectation, often expressed in letters to friends in Europe, that the Chinese emperors might be converted. As Franke has commented:

> As the Son of Heaven and as the representative of Heaven the Emperor possessed an exclusive position which was simply irreconcilable with subjection to a foreign ecclesiastical organization and its head. The conversion of the Chinese Emperor to a foreign religion would have seemed almost as monstrous as if the Pope had become a Mohammedan and still remained head of the Catholic Church [*China*, 55].[30]

Although the Jesuits may not have succeeded to the extent they desired, Ricci's principles in seeking to put the gospel into Chinese continue to be recognized as having abiding validity. He saw clearly that before he could expect the Chinese to be changed, he must change in his approach and methods. Despite having a message with carefully defined content, he perceived that it could be meaningful only within the Chinese frame of reference. He must go to the Chinese ideologically and not always expect them to come to him.

Possibly more important than anything else, Matteo Ricci made haste slowly! He was no devotee of short-cut methods. The conversion of China, in his view, would be a long process. A proper foundation must be laid. The resolution of controversial issues could be delayed until appropriate cultural bridges had been built that would make it possible for controversies to be resolved amicably and with understanding. Patience and perseverance were more important than compulsive urgency. He learned early that the Orient will not be hurried!

Only missionaries with sterling personal characteristics and adequate educational training could implement such a policy. Professor Yu-ming Shaw has compared these early pioneers with their latter-day successors:

> The intellectual prowess and moral integrity of the sixteenth and seventeenth century missioners was superior to that of many who followed them in later centuries. . . . standards were not so high in the nineteenth and twentieth centuries, when missioners to China were not chosen as carefully as business managers of the same period. The quality of their

work, therefore, could not match that of the earlier missioners [M.L. Martin].

By the time that the Vatican had dissolved the Society of Jesus, Protestant missionaries were about to knock on the doors of China. Many of these new arrivals would publicly denounce Jesuit attitudes and methods—even when they were privately adopting them as a model and ideal for their own work in proclaiming the gospel in Chinese.

CHAPTER 4

The Gospel of Power—
The Protestant Approach

MISSIONS AND POWER BEFORE THE PROTESTANT PERIOD

Since the early nineteenth century, the Christian message in China was inextricably linked with external political, military, and economic power. As one Chinese national stated it succinctly, "You brought to us both opium and the gospel, neither one of which we wanted!"

Both the Nestorians and the Catholics of the Yuan, Ming, and Qing dynasties sought a power base *within* China that was often to exert political, economic, and, on occasion, even military influence. The popes of Rome, at the time of the Jesuits and during the Franciscan-Dominican period, sought to bring moral pressure on Chinese rulers to accede to their wishes, but these demands were never accompanied by threats and warnings of political, military, or economic sanctions. During the Jesuit period, Chinese officials were never perfectly clear on the exact relationships between the missionaries and Macao. Memories of the early Portuguese debacle at Canton in 1517 made them apprehensive, but their fears were never justified, even when Portuguese emissaries were imprisoned or executed only a few miles away at Canton.

For nearly one hundred years before the first Protestant missionaries arrived, both foreign and Chinese Catholics suffered intense persecution. Martyred church members and Chinese priests were quickly replaced by others of equal devotion. Deported foreign priests found their way back into China, stealthily brought back to former positions of service by an "underground railroad" of safe Chinese homes extending from the coast far into the interior. Technically, of course, this widespread activity to promote the Christian faith was illegal. Separately and cumulatively, the laws of the Middle Kingdom allowed no legal status for Christianity. But Catholic missionaries, unprotected by any internal or external political and military means, had calculated the cost and were prepared to suffer the consequences of their unlawful course of action.

PROTESTANT ATTITUDES TO CATHOLIC MISSIONS

When Protestant missionaries reached China, beginning with Robert Morrison at Canton in 1807, they tended to be very critical of anything Catholic. "Jesuit" was a dirty epithet that expressed the Protestant revulsion for almost every aspect of Catholic missionary strategy, such as "sneaking into China" in Chinese garb, working with the officials and gentry rather than with the common people, insisting upon the authority of the pope, and using "nonspiritual" means such as "the calculation of eclipses, or the arrangement of the calendar." Apparently forgetting Morrison's role as a translator and interpreter with the East India Company, some could piously comment: "We must assume no other character than that of preachers of the Gospel, and be determined to know nothing except Christ and him crucified" [Philosinensis, "Christian Missions in China," *Chinese Repository*, vol. 3, no. 2 (April 1835) 5.61]. Had they indeed held resolutely to this ideal, the subsequent history of the Christian church in China would have been far different.

Many Protestant missionaries could not help admiring Catholics for their attitude of "weakness" and their zeal in penetrating the entire nation. Charles Gutzlaff, that doughty firebrand from the Netherlands, frequently exhorted his colleagues, "being clad with the armor of God," to exhibit equal devotion and perseverance, even to the "peril of their lives." He argued that missionaries must "not be surpassed by the wily Jesuits, who sent the flower of their body to conquer China for the Pope. We fight for a mightier prince and ought to be more zealous." Reminding his missionary friends that the apostles and reformers did not wait until "governments proved favorable to the Gospel," E.B. Squire of the Church Missionary Society asked for "no gentlemen-missionaries; but men who are at all times ready to lay down their lives for the Saviour, and can wander about forgotten, and despised; without any human assistance, but their God." This is a gospel of high risk!

Practical considerations, however, indicated that Protestants had little hope to live out or preach such a gospel. They had no church base in China, no Christian contacts along the coast, none in whose homes they could safely hide either to give local witness or to advance inland. They would have had to follow the procedure of the early Catholic emissaries who risked deportation, imprisonment, and even execution before gaining the foothold they desired.

And in the years immediately preceding the initial treaties of 1812-14, Catholics were again feeling the pressure of persecution. Martyrdom was again common. In 1836 Father Perboyre, a Lazarist, one of the few remaining foreign priests, was hanged in Fujian. The sees of Beijing, Nanjing, and Macao were vacant. The church was still there, but the superstructure of a foreign priesthood was crumbling. Catholics were having difficulty with a system that had worked well for over two hundred years.

A WALL OF LIGHT AROUND CHINA

Precluded from entering China proper in any extensive fashion, both because of their own timid "no-risk" Christianity and because of changed external circumstances, what course of action could the newly-arrived Protestant missionaries take? They patiently occupied various centers on the border or just inside the empire, such as Canton and Macao, for more direct ministries, and then used Singapore, Penang, Malacca, Bangkok, and Batavia as bases from which they could reach out to Chinese emigrants who, it was hoped, could influence the spiritual destiny of their homeland. By this strategy they felt they could build a "wall of light around her [China]. Then, as the old wall tumbles down, there will be a bright light shining through every breach, and truth will win her way in even before her heralds" [*Spirit of Missions,* vol. 2, no. 2 (Feb. 1837) 90].

Building a wall of light around China meant many things: learning the language for future use within the empire; acquainting churches in the West about needs and opportunities in China; encouraging the development of better and expanded commercial relationships between China and the West; telling Chinese intellectuals in the border cities about the strange "barbarian" world of the west; producing literature such as the Bible, grammars, dictionaries, booklets, and tracts for use in China and among the Chinese diaspora; planning for and implementing model strategies for the future in evangelism, education, and medicine; establishing bases for limited forays around Canton, along the coast to the maritime provinces of China, and even up some rivers. This was an era of preparation as missionaries waited for China to be "open to the gospel." They waited also for God, and, despite some covert and clandestine low-profile efforts, they dared not throw their weight around in a situation that was always precarious and filled with potential danger.

Canton was the most strategic center for these many activities. Missionaries, never more than six or seven in number, translated the New and Old Testaments, wrote grammars and dictionaries, and produced many tracts and booklets on basic Christian topics for distribution locally and for shipment to Singapore, Bangkok, and other population centers. They actively engaged in literature evangelism in shops, marketplaces, temples, in the fields, by the wayside, and in hospitals. These casual evangelistic trips often extended beyond the city for two or three miles.

Evangelism was combined with a ministry of compassion as Dr. Peter Parker opened the Ophthalmic Hospital in 1835. Even within the first year, he was treating hundreds of patients and training three Chinese assistants to help him with the heavy work load. Although schools were prohibited in Canton, each missionary had one or two young men whom he was teaching, not as formal students, but as domestic help in the home. From personal contacts with recipients of free literature, hospital patients, and domestic help, a few conversions resulted. By 1838 a total of fifteen persons had been baptized. The most prominent of them, a printer named Liang Afa, played a significant role in working with missionaries of several different groups in spreading the gospel.

Not content to minister only to the Chinese masses, many of these early missionaries made special efforts to attract the intellectual elite. Elijah Bridgman and David Abeel were the first American missionaries to come to Canton. Bridgman prepared a two-volume history of America with the aim of giving the Chinese an accurate picture of a Western nation. Bridgman, Parker, Samuel Wells Williams, and others established a Society for the Diffusion of Useful Knowledge, designed to teach the Chinese "natural theology" and to "enlighten the minds of the Chinese and communicate to them the arts and sciences of the west." The Morrison Educational Society, founded as a memorial to Robert Morrison, established schools to teach English to young Chinese and introduce them to the learning of the Occident.

Limited opportunities to evangelize the Chinese inclined the missionaries to give special attention to the non-Chinese community in Canton. The spiritual needs of foreign seamen had brought David Abeel to Canton in 1830. Sabbath services in English were attended by as many as eighty persons, and prayer and Bible studies throughout the week were particularly directed to the needs of the non-Chinese working in Canton. The *Chinese Repository,* designed to acquaint outsiders with all facets of Chinese life, commenced publication in May 1832 with Elijah Bridgman as its editor.

Despite being the only active base within the Chinese empire, Canton had more disadvantages than any other location in the "wall of light." Chinese taught foreigners their language at the risk of death. The usefulness of the local patois extended little beyond the limits of the city. Literature distribution was illegal in Canton. Missionaries consequently risked banishment, and the compradores or hong merchants responsible for them faced imprisonment or worse, if this activity was detected. Twice, once in 1834 when thousands of copies of scripture lessons had been distributed to candidates meeting for the literary exams, and again in 1837, shortly after a coastal excursion had angered the emperor, many books were confiscated, the missionaries' Chinese helpers were beaten and forced to flee, and all production of literature ceased.

Missionaries were not allowed to travel more than a very short distance from their homes, were forbidden to use sedan chairs, and experienced constant surveillance in all their activities. Such converts as they did have could see them only with difficulty. Open evangelistic meetings were obviously out of the question in such a controlled and stifling environment.

Macao, the peninsula less than a one-day journey away, served as a haven whenever conditions in Canton forced missionaries to leave. Although the foreign community in the core area of the city was under Portuguese rule, the more numerous Chinese—about 85 percent of the total population of thirty-five thousand—were governed by their own officials who kept constant pressure on the foreign authorities. Although educational and literature work enjoyed more freedom than in Canton, in times of stress schools were closed, the presses were stopped, home meetings were disrupted, and, in July 1839, Chinese pressure forced the Portuguese to evacuate all British residents. In general, however, Macao was the "staging base" for access to

Canton, though it had developed many missionary activities of its own.

Christian work in the Straits Settlements commenced at Penang, Malacca, and Singapore from 1818 to 1820. Presses, schools, and dispensaries were established in each city. Worship services and Bible studies were started for the Chinese, Malays, Indians, and other segments of the population. Singapore, although fifteen hundred miles from China, had many advantages over other centers: more freedom under British control, much lower cost-of-living expenses than in Canton, more unhindered contact with the Chinese, better opportunities for learning the language, easier tract distribution by way of ships returning to the coast of China, faster communication with home bases in America and Europe. By 1840 it was, in Latourette's opinion, "the most important Protestant mission station among the Chinese" [*Early Relations,* 105].

Malacca was best known in Christian circles as the home from 1818 until 1842 of the Anglo-Chinese College. Founded "for the interchangeable communication of the languages of England and China, with a view to the promotion of Christianity in the latter country," the college not only instructed Chinese youth in the learning of the West but led ultimately to the first church of Chinese Christians, in 1837.

Another major segment of the "wall of light" being built around China centered in Batavia. In the twenty-year period from 1817 to 1837 missionaries of the London Missionary Society, the American Board of Commissioners for Foreign Missions, and the Domestic and Foreign Missionary Society of the Protestant Episcopal Church in the United States came to Java, learned Chinese—and often Malay—printed and distributed tracts and portions of scripture, held Bible classes, and ran Chinese schools. They frequently had opportunity as well to minister to a congregation of British and American residents, numbering as many as forty or fifty. Life under a Dutch regime was less oppressive than under the Portuguese in Macao, but in 1838 the Dutch government adopted a more exclusive policy, requiring missionaries to restrict their residence and work to Borneo. A debilitating climate made Batavia one of the most difficult posts among the Chinese diaspora.

Missionaries viewed their activities in Canton-Macao, the Straits Settlements, and Batavia as "holding actions" until wider doors were opened to them. They did not wish to continue this way indefinitely. Not that there were no results. Medhurst, writing in *China: Its State and Prospects* in 1838, indicated that in all these work sites missionaries and their helpers had distributed two thousand complete Bibles, ten thousand New Testaments, thirty thousand copies of selected scripture readings, and half a million copies of tracts. Ten thousand children had received some training in missionary-run schools. One hundred converts had been baptized, and several native preachers had been prepared for Christian service [Medhurst, *China,* 292].

The missionaries realized, however, that much of the literature they had distributed was not read or understood. Very little made its way to China. Converts were relatively few and not very stable. Work at any site but Singapore was severely restricted. Day schools made little impact upon the "heathenism" of their students' lives, although boarding schools or live-in arrangements in missionary homes proved more satisfactory.

Pessimism about the present and uncertainty about the future turned many prospective missionaries away from American and European mission agencies. And yet all the missionaries felt to some degree that if they did not "reach these . . . one million Chinese outside the empire and its edicts . . . how can we expect [God] to give greater opportunities."

BOLDER EFFORTS TO PENETRATE CHINA

As missionaries pondered and prayed about bolder ways to penetrate China, they reflected often on the way early Buddhists had used literature to gain a foothold in the central kingdom. Perhaps if they distributed literature and medicine more widely—a better method than the scientific expertise used by the "conniving" Jesuits—and sought personal contact with more Chinese in the empire, it would help to pry the door open. This kind of thinking, combined with the desire by merchants of all nations for "free trade" along the coast of China, now that the monopolistic control by the British East India Company over commerce at Canton was scheduled to end in 1834, created the climate for a series of remarkable efforts by missionaries along the coasts and up the rivers of China. This was the beginning of the "gospel of power." Initially, at least, the "power" was not military but the condescending and arrogant attitudes toward officials and those in authority betokened a disdain not heretofore seen along the "wall of light."

Gutzlaff's Voyages

The first three of these missionary voyages were taken by Karl Gutzlaff of the Netherlands Missionary Society, beginning in 1831. A specifically missionary trip took place under the direction of Edwin Stevens and Walter Medhurst in the late summer of 1835. Two other probes were made earlier in 1835 up the Min River toward the Bohea Hills and also to the Ankoy Tea Hills above Canton.

Gutzlaff's first journey, on the *Sylph,* a private commercial venture not sponsored by any particular company, extended from June 18 to December 13, 1831. Reaching as far north as the country about Tianjin, the crew sought trade with Chinese merchants in exchange for its cargo of "sugar and tin, sapan wood and pepper, European calico goods, and opium."

His second trip, on the *Lord Amherst,* sponsored by the British East India Company to explore the possibility of trade in major ports of the China coast, took place from February 25 to September 3, 1832. Because this exploratory mission was to be secret, the captain, Hugh Hamilton Lindsay, and Gutzlaff changed the transliteration of their Chinese names to conceal their identities, and posed as officers of a merchant ship proceeding from Bengal for Japan, but blown off its course by adverse winds. Wherever they went they argued for free trade, sought equality of treatment for themselves, and examined sites of military importance.

The last voyage that Gutzlaff describes in his journal was again on the *Sylph* from October 12, 1832, to April 29, 1833. During the remainder of 1833 he made several other excursions of a shorter nature along the coast on several vessels, with most of his expenses covered by the London Missionary Society.

On each of these journeys Gutzlaff engaged in specifically Christian ministries: personal conversations on religious topics, distribution of Christian literature, limited preaching, and the practice of simple medicine for eye and skin diseases. He spoke the language well, dressed in Chinese garb, and mixed well with the people "assuming one of their clan names."

How was Gutzlaff perceived by the curious Chinese whom he met on these journeys? Certainly they saw him as an interpreter, for this was his official role on those voyages. He was also a trader, a role he gladly assumed because he believed commerce to be a legitimate way by which China could be opened to the gospel. Were the Chinese able to separate his religious activities, carried on at one side of the ship, from the opium trading in which his companions were engaged on the other side of the ship? They must have identified him as a medical practitioner, a teacher, and a religious enthusiast. Inasmuch as they themselves had all three of these, the impact he had in these roles is questionable. Nor did he always have his best foot forward. When there was occasion to send some books to the Daoguang emperor, he chose appropriate ones on scripture and "Heaven's Mirror," a simple systematic treatment of the Christian faith, but also one on gambling. Gutzlaff's listeners also saw him as a barbarian come to learn and be under the shield of the "Son of Heaven." To at least one merchant in Tianjin who wished to buy him for $2,700 in a publicity gambit, he was a "front-office foreigner."

Gutzlaff viewed his target audience as sincerely interested in learning about Christianity, believing that had they not been restricted by the haughty mandarins, their reception of books and literature would have been even more enthusiastic. He was distressed by the idolatry of the Chinese but conceded that they appeared to be happy. He also granted that this happiness was due in measure to the fact that the highly exclusive laws kept outsiders at a distance and protected them from the internal strife of India, which he termed "Hindoostan."

Yet he argued vehemently against all such exclusiveness. To refuse to foreigners the "natural right to claim fellowship" with the Chinese is a "transgression of the divine law of benevolence." Although recognizing that earlier laws of the empire allowing for more liberal intercourse had been revoked and carried to extreme exclusiveness because of petty, non-Christian provocation by some Europeans, he still claimed that there are innate rights "to walk upon our common earth . . . which no human prohibition can destroy." This "common law of nations" permitted Chinese to enter foreign ports, and such "free intercourse" must also be extended to European traders.

What could be done about these exclusive laws? Certainly, he affirmed, they cannot be altered. "Yet we do not consider them as binding upon us." This did not mean they should be resisted by "violent measures," although he noted that the fact that the *Lord Amherst* carried "well-mounted long guns inspired the mandarins with respect." "Firmness and resolution," he found, always caused Chinese officials to back down. And if Christian emissaries persisted long enough, accompanying their enthusiasm with the concerted and constant prayer of the church, divine providence would gradually open the door. Even with it only slightly ajar, he noted, millions of Chinese are exposed to the gospel truth. He noted in his journal:

> Justice and forbearance should be on our side; we should do our utmost to conciliate; by unequivocal acts of kindness we should prove ourselves Christian by honest dealings, and philanthropists by our religion; yet we should never allow any native to be unjustly punished on our account.[31]

If Gutzlaff, and other missionaries to follow him, believed military force to be unnecessary for profitable voyages along the coast, their views were not shared by Lindsay who virtuously proposed that it would be no problem to stir up a war with China that would assure a firm basis for free trade [I. Hsü, "Secret Mission," 251–52].

Accounts of Gutzlaff's epochal journey were first printed in the *Chinese Repository* and then reprinted in almost every missionary magazine in America and Europe. The message could be summed up in one concise sentence: "Blot it from your missionary publications that China is shut" [*Missionary Herald* (Aug. 1834) 308]. The excitement was electric! The Episcopalians hastened to send three couples to Batavia. The Church Missionary Society, whose interest had been cooled after earlier conversations with the London Missionary Society, activated plans for outreach to China. No one wanted to miss out on the new opportunities. A spirit of optimism spread in the minds of many still building the "wall of light" around China. Was this indeed the day that the Lord had made—the day of destiny for this benighted land?

Some were convinced it was, others were not so sure. David Abeel, for one, believed that "contrary to received opinion, they [the voyages] have shown that the natives are fond of intercourse with foreigners—that they have a high opinion of our medical skill and that they receive Christian books with the greatest avidity." Most mission executives at home were euphoric. The *Missionary Herald* reprinted with no comment an earlier piece from the *Chinese Repository* of September 1832 stating, "Who does not adore the wisdom and goodness of Providence that is making use of the interests of men to bring about so important a result? And who will not pray that it may be speedily attained?"

Walter Medhurst and others had many doubts. They knew that Gutzlaff was rather eccentric, a claim he himself would not deny:

I am fully aware that I shall be stigmatized a head-strong enthusiast, an unprincipled rambler, who rashly sallies forth, without waiting for an indication of divine providence, without first seeing the door opened by the hand of the Lord;—as one fond of novelty, anxious to have a name, fickle in his purposes, who leaves a promising field, and restless, hurries away to another—all of whose endeavors will not only prove useless, but will actually impede the progress of the Saviour's cause [*Missionary Herald* (July 1833) 252].

Was Gutzlaff exaggerating his claims? Even if he were not, the argument went, who else knew the language as well as he, or had the ability to conform so well to Chinese habits as to be mistaken for a native, or was able not to incur the displeasure of the police in his travels from province to province? "Almost any other man, pursuing the same course, might awaken jealously, and be expelled from the country—perhaps lose his life."

And so the curiosity to learn more was whetted. Could Chinese laws be broken with impunity? Why was the situation in the maritime provinces so different from that in Canton and Macao? Was China really open to outside penetration? Was it right to have opium runners distribute Christian tracts? All these questions had significant implications for those manning the "wall of light" and impatient for something to happen. This, of course, was Gutzlaff's point. He was not "waiting" for divine providence—he was obeying the "great commission" and *making something happen*. This he felt was to emulate the zeal of the Jesuits, who, although blindly fanatic and "nourished by attachment to popery, [had] found ways and means to penetrate into these regions. . . ."

The Missionary Voyage of 1834

The London Missionary Society, with Robert Morrison's recent death still fresh in its memory, and the British and Foreign Bible Society were particularly anxious to do a rerun of these trips and objectively evaluate Gutzlaff's conclusions. This led to a "missionary voyage" up the coast of China that was totally under Christian sponsorship. The principal missionary figures were Edwin Stevens, seamen's chaplain at Whampoa with the American Seaman's Friends Society, who had come to Canton in 1834, and Walter Medhurst, a missionary with the London Missionary Society, who had begun his work with the Chinese in 1816. The American brig *Huron,* a small vessel of 211 tons, carrying a total of eighteen men, and armed with "two guns and a few swivels," was, with the help of the Christian merchant, David Olyphant, chartered from an American firm for $1,200 a month for a period of three months. No opium or articles for general trade were carried, although a few bags of rice were taken along either for food or to be sold if need should arise. The principal cargo was books: twenty thousand volumes—"Scriptures, Medhurst's *Harmony of the Gospels,* Theology, a Commentary on the Ten Commandments, The Life of Christ," and a variety of other publications.

Medhurst gave three purposes for this venture: (1) to find out the true situation along the coast; (2) to enlighten the people by scripture distribution so that the government "be led to sanction what the mass of their subjects might be induced to adopt;" (3) to inspire confidence in the "breasts of missionaries who might advance, step by step, to more extensive and permanent efforts for the diffusion and establishment of the truth." The center of their missionary activities was to be the *Huron*, at once a "home, asylum, church, dispensary, book depository," and a staging base for many forays into nearby areas, where they could go only by boat or by foot.

The extensive itinerary of Stevens and Medhurst in the *Huron*, commencing August 1834, took them north and south of the Shandung promontory, to Fujian and the Shanghai area. Their activities were similar to those of Gutzlaff—distributing literature, dispensing medicine, personal conversation, and some public explanation of the Christian faith. Trading, interpreting for opium dealers, and anything antithetical to the Christian faith were avoided. Attitudes toward them, as described in their own journals, differed with the persons involved, whether officials, the literati, or the general public. Always there was curiosity—Where did they come from, what was their purpose, did they have opium to sell? Frequently this turned into investigation, a willingness to take the books and examine them, at least in a cursory fashion. This was particularly true along the China coast to the south. The rank and file Chinese were glad to receive tracts and medicine if they were not interfered with. The officials and literati were usually another story. "Chinese authorities generally treat strangers with contempt, in order to degrade them in the eyes of their own people; the immediate effect of this is to prejudice the business of the foreigner, and, if not met by a uniform and steady resistance, it generally ensures the failure of his object."

Occasionally there was disdain—"What can you give us that Confucius cannot?" Even the peasants were often fearful, apparently having been told that "the barbarians" would attack Chinese villages with the guns on their brig or would ravage women and children, who hid quickly whenever Stevens and Medhurst passed through their villages.

Local officials, responsible to higher leaders and to the emperor himself for enforcing the exclusion edicts, accused the outsiders of being rabble-rousers or lawbreakers. To this the missionaries responded in several ways. First, God's law is everywhere the same and God wills that human beings have relationships with one another. Secondly, the prohibitions are directed against unlawful commerce, and the missionaries were not involved in commerce. Thirdly, the edicts are directed against the lawless, not those engaged in doing good. They described themselves as:

> A number of pious persons in our own country, who feared God and who believed in Jesus, felt themselves exceedingly happy in their profession, and wished to extend the blessings of their religion to other parts of the

world. They therefore caused books to be printed, and sent out agents to distribute them, to all who might be willing and able to read them. We further informed them, that our object was to instruct all who came to us in the knowledge of God, and to administer relief to the sick and miserable.[32]

This explanation hardly dealt with the heart of the complaint that they were lawless because they were disseminating "corrupt doctrines," a matter of concern to Chinese intellectuals since the earlier period of the Jesuit missions in China.

Fourthly, the missionaries replied that Western nations were allowing privileges of social intercourse with Chinese. Fifthly, they appealed to the example of Paul at Philippi who felt no need to abide by local law. Their final reason, utilized extensively by early missionaries to China and seldom questioned, was that they were really only opposing the officials and gentry, not the people, The "people have no sympathy with their officers, and never assist them, unless compelled by force."

With these many reasons to support them, Medhurst and Stevens carried on their illegal activities in a number of ways. To be illegal was only to follow in the path of the Jesuits. The problem is not here, but with the attitudes accompanying their work. When officials approached them to talk, they finished whatever they were doing at that juncture before agreeing to talk, thus avoiding public mention of any prohibition. Frequently, they ignored a prohibition, affirming that if the government was "so absurd as to design to prevent good men from speaking to their fellow-men," they must "obey God rather than man."

When arguments to change the mind of a recalcitrant official failed, the missionaries sometimes withdrew to other places to try again. If they knew that officials were anywhere near, they sought to avoid them. If avoidance seemed impossible, they ignored them and appealed directly to nearby crowds for support. Only where a very firm show of force indicated that the missionaries could not continue their activities, they yielded and turned back.

It was not easy to get rid of the officials. They appeared early in the morning before Stevens and Medhurst left their ship, often followed them through the day, and seemed to appear precisely at the time when they wished to establish close rapport with the people. When the missionaries sailed up rivers or streams, or along the coast, they were often followed by the "imperial fleet"— a flotilla of armed junks with naval officers.

The arrogance and impudence of the mandarins was usually matched by the missionaries. Declaring that Christian humility or prudence were not in question, they stated that they did not wish to be treated, even slightly, in a disrespectful manner. When Chinese officials wished them to stand in their presence, they deliberately sat down. Insults were exchanged for insults, disrespect for disrespect. If books they had distributed were burned by officials, then they did the same with gifts given to them in the name of the emperor. This "eye for an eye, tooth for a tooth" policy was justified, they claimed, because they felt that to do otherwise would encourage officials in their arrogance, would increase the difficulty of the next negotiation, and would prove beyond doubt that the missionaries were indeed "barbarians"— too ignorant to understood reality and too weak to stand up to it!

Medhurst enthusiastically reported on his trip, exciting many missionaries and mission executives to believe that, with continued persistence, the ancient doors of China would swing open. He was well aware that Gutzlaff's previous trips had alarmed the emperor, distressed to learn that "an English vessel is sailing about in an irregular manner regardless of laws." The emperor had issued a spate of prohibitive edicts, but Medhurst reasoned that the imperial restrictions were "hardly like the laws of the Medes and Persians," and could be altered at any time. Following the voyage of the *Huron*, the emperor threatened to terminate foreign commerce in Canton. Of the many activities engaged in by Stevens and Medhurst, he most feared the "distribution of foreign books to seduce people with lies" and subsequently exerted pressure that, combined with various political factors, forced the closure of the literature work in Canton.

River Probes

In November 1834, G.J. Gordon from India and Karl Gutzlaff visited the Ankoy Tea Hills up the river from Canton, to gather information about tea cultivation and to disseminate the gospel message. The latter activity, not carried out in a widespread manner close to the larger villages, appeared to be well received by the people [*Missionary Herald* (Feb. 1836) 75–76].

The next spring, from March until May, Gordon and Gutzlaff, accompanied by Stevens, projected a trip of about two hundred miles up the Min River, near Fuzhou, to the Bohea or Wooe Hills. The literature that they took on this expedition included Gutzlaff's *Life of Christ*, a booklet on the Ten Commandments, and a special booklet acquainting the Chinese with the English nation, elaborating on "free intercourse on Gospel principles," and appealing to "the best and most philanthropic feelings of man as a reason for mutual good will to subsist between our two nations."

The party was able to go only a short distance beyond Fuzhow before being turned back by determined opposition from the military, attacking both from junks and well-protected forts along the river banks. Stevens commented, "on our part not a shot was fired from first to last, but we left them, as we desired, to bear alone any imputation of barbarism which might attach to the infliction of violence on the unresisting" [*Missionary Herald* (Feb. 1836) 78].

This attempt, along with the earlier one to the Ankoy Tea Hills, convinced Stevens that "the interior of China cannot be traversed with impunity by foreigners." Detection, even with a Chinese disguise, could not be avoided and continued attempts to probe inland would threaten personal safety. But a closed interior need not "retard the zeal of the missionary, before whom lies a well inhabited seacoast of many hundred miles, to much of which access may be had in the way of transient visits at least."

Stevens's negative conclusion about inland China did not mean that he or other missionaries were willing to accept a closed door as the final answer:

> As to the law against intercourse with foreigners I acknowledge no allegiance to such a law, *so far as the legitimate means of preaching the Gospel are concerned.* We have a more sure mandate to preach the Gospel *in all the world*, than the monarch of China can plead for a title to his throne. . . . Against such spiritual tyranny [of the Chinese government] over men's conscience, and rebellion against high heaven, I protest; and if we take upon ourselves the consequences of governmental vengeance, who will say that we do wrong to any man? It is not to the government of my own beloved country that I look for protection from danger, or redress of *such* wrongs; nor do I ask the bloody hand of war to prepare the way for the heralds of the Prince of Peace [*Missionary Herald* (Feb. 1836) 80].

Gutzlaff, never to be deterred, commented after a later visit to the Dongsan area on the coast of Fujian:

> I hope a missionary will soon be sent to this district. As long as he avoids the presence of the higher mandarins, and does not force himself into notoriety, there is some hope of his effecting a residence; but he must be versed in the art of the leech; a devoted man of God; and ready to suffer and die for the Savior. . . . A regular tour through these villages to exhort, and console, displaying a love for the souls of our auditors, would certainly be attended with the best results. The prospect of this establishing a mission in China is not utopian; but we have not, yet, men who are sufficiently conversant with the language, and who have become Chinese, in order to win Chinese to Christ [Medhurst, *China*, 420-21].

Was China Open?

What, then, was missionary feeling about the openness of China to the gospel? Gutzlaff's initial trips (1831-1832) had created an expectant mood on the part of most, which lasted until the exploratory probe up the Min River in the spring of 1835. For Stevens and Abeel, this burst the bubble, at least as regards the interior. The trip of the *Huron* brought renewed encouragement to Stevens and Medhurst. The critical lack, as they saw it, was of personnel who could maintain the required degree of persistence to wear down Chinese persistence along the coast. Gutzlaff, ever the optimist, was prepared either for coastal or inland forays. Sacrifice, however, even on the scale of the Catholic effort, would be required. The missionary communities in Canton or Macao were ready to be convinced, but they appeared to be waiting for more dramatic evidence of God's intervention to throw the doors wide open.

Missionaries at a greater distance, in Singapore, wondered if the voyage of the *Huron* had really accomplished anything. Most of the Chinese, it was affirmed, could not read; "as a mass, [they were] much below our common sailors and soldiers in their capability to be influenced by books." Furthermore there was the direct opposition of the government, "which is as much respected, perhaps as any monarchy in the world is, by the lower class of its subjects." Finally, they argued, proposals of such efforts had come at a time when "the opium trade has made foreigners odious to the lowest of the people as well as to the mandarins" [a letter from missionaries in Singapore, Nov. 16, 1839, printed in *Missionary Herald* (June 1840) 238].

Catholics, for the most part living in the distant interior at far greater sacrifice, derided the Protestant efforts. Jean-Henri Baldus, a French Lazarist, commented in the 1830s, "They [the Protestants] have made their appearance on the coast only, like commercial travellers armed with a prospectus; they have done no more than toss Bibles from shipside upon the beach" [Fay, 242].

THE OPIUM WAR AND ITS CONSEQUENCES

From 1836 to 1840 relationships between China and Great Britain were progressively worsening, incident upon incident paving the way to a head-on collision. In the increasingly agitated political atmosphere, missionaries had little opportunity to explore further any creative options to penetrate China. All were waiting, even though engaged in the routine of their normal daily activities, to see how God was going to use England, even through the introduction of opium—"worse, if possible, than the introduction, sale and use of ardent spirits"—to bring China into the family of nations and to bring about those "changes and revolutions" promoting the "free and rapid propagation" of the gospel.

There were ways to give the gospel to China—either up the rivers or along the coast. But sacrifice was required in the face of the determined Chinese opposition, and Protestant missionaries, not reared in a tradition that exalted martyrdom, were not prepared to pay the price paid by earlier or contemporaneous Catholic missionaries. The only choice left was to keep "building the wall of light" and wait for God to act.

As they waited for God to act, the situation was now much different from what it had been before their excursions inland and up the coast. First, those confrontations had forced them to search for reasons why it was justifiable to break the laws of China. Secondly, contact with the Chinese in a new context, though it had opened up many new opportunities and excited them with new prospects, had brought out the worst in their attitudes. But they did not perceive themselves as overbearing, arrogant, or excessively self-assured in relating to the Chinese. These new contacts and the newly developing attitudes prepared them to raise few moral questions when God did act, as they judged, through the Opium War and the consequent humiliating defeat for China.

The shame imposed upon China opened a door for the West. Several stipulations were written into the treaties drawn up from 1842 to 1844: the cession of Hong Kong; the opening of the five ports of Canton, Amoy, Fuzhou, Ningbo, and Shanghai to consuls, merchants, and missionaries; a most-favored-nation clause; extraterritoriality; fixed tariffs; the right of Western warships to protect commerce and trade. Until this time relationships between the West and China had been based upon the ancient Chinese tribute system. The new conditions imposed upon China, euphemistically called "agreements," introduced an era of "unequal treaties" and power.

These treaty agreements did little initially to alleviate the condition of "wandering and hunted" Catholic priests in China or of the Catholic communities with which they were associated in inland China. Ultimately, however, the result of the first French treaty with the Chinese in 1844 and the subsequent treaties of 1858 and 1860 created what has been called the "French Protectorate." By this arrangement, the French government, seeking a greater sphere of influence in China, took the responsibility for protecting and aiding Catholic missionaries and Christians in China. This included providing special passports for Catholic missionaries, seeking to exempt local Christians from taking part in pagan festivals, backing Catholic missionaries as they assisted Chinese Christians in lawsuits, supporting the missionaries in efforts to repossess confiscated property, and resolutely insisting, in accord with treaty privileges, that missionaries be allowed to rent or buy land in inland China.

Protestant missionaries, unprotected by any one specific political power, sought the help of their respective governments in obtaining the same types of privileges. They gained all possible advantage from the treaty provisions as they carried the gospel by every political contrivance into most areas of China.

On the surface, at least, missionaries were not as unashamedly expedient as the traders and diplomats. Without exception, the missionaries despised opium and all its evil consequences. From the beginning of Protestant missionary work on the China scene, religious workers, to their obvious disadvantage, were identified with opium and the opium trade. Nor was war viewed with any more favor. Abeel commented, "It is true the spirit of war does not consort with the gospel of peace, but God is evidently employing the one in this country to prepare the way for the other." Many like statements appeared in missionary literature of the period, for these emissaries of the gospel were painfully aware that many detractors on the home scene accused them of hoping for war. And yet, divine intervention in the form of warfare was an easy conclusion to reach if one was convinced, as many apparently were, that "this is an age of the world when the prophecies relative to the universal spread of the Gospel" were about to be fulfilled. Despite the hand-wringing over opium and the war, "no one . . . seems seriously to have challenged the right of the British to compel China to open her doors or the propriety of missionaries accepting the opportunities this obtained" [Latourette, *History*, 231].

The inequitable treaties that ended the Opium War declared opium illegal only in the five treaty ports, and even this minor exclusion was bypassed by full-scale trading in nearby anchorages. Thus, an obvious moral problem, the occasion if not the cause of the war, was not resolved. It was easy for Americans, at home and abroad, to accede to the argument of a John Quincy Adams who claimed that the moral problem was not opium but rather the question of the "kowtow," a symbol of Chinese immorality in refusing to allow other nations to trade with it [Fay, 337]. The five treaty ports—Canton, Amoy, Fuzhou, Ningbo, and Shanghai—as well as Hong Kong, ceded to the British, were open to English residence and commerce, but nothing specific was said about "opening" China to the gospel. Even before the treaty, missionaries had started to preach and distribute literature in Hong Kong, Dinghai, and Gulangsu. Now they entered the open ports. Whatever hopes they may have entertained at one time or another about other alternatives were quickly forgotten. God had opened the door.

Moreover, inasmuch as their governments had now entered into a forced "legal" arrangement with China, it would have been difficult, if not impossible, for them to be content with other methods—continuing to wait and pray for God to act, or seeking legal entrance. Could they have waited for a better opportunity, when some kind of tacit official approval might have been granted to Christianity, and they thus would not have been party to a forced arrangement? The diplomats and traders would hardly wait, and the missionaries felt they had an even more urgent task. Furthermore, they believed their presence would ameliorate the effect of those with carnal motives.

Some Catholic travel and missionary work continued in the interior of the country. Those missionaries, with a church constituency scattered through all the provinces, benefited less immediately from the outposts along the coast. The Protestants were only now seeing the chance for some substantial footholds.

Nothing appeared to matter but to get into China. Failure to realize what was happening may have doomed the modern missionary enterprise from the very beginning. No realistic alternatives may have existed for them. This is not the critical question. The key issue was a failure to see what this kind of forced entry did to them, the message they proclaimed, the huge non-Christian society, and the few brave converts. From then until 1949 the gospel in China was proclaimed in the context of power.

To ride the coattails of political power that provided an "open door" to the Middle Kingdom helped to create attitudes that, although usually directed at the official class, spilled over toward the general populace as well. Missionary activities were frequently characterized by a certain arrogance, an insistence on "rights," an assumption of European superiority, an easy acquiescence in any action as long as it seemed to promote the progress of the gospel, a disdain for the need to adjust to Chinese culture, a satisfaction with mediocrity in carrying out their tasks, and a resignation to the alliance of the gospel with worldly power. The early Catholic efforts, although usually illegal, were not accompanied by political clout. The Jesuits and others were prepared to suffer the consequences of their unlawful activities. Unsupported by their governments, they had to make their way by personal skill and adaptability to Chinese circumstances. Their work and their lives were in the hands of God. No personal sacrifice was too great for them to make. They worked against the odds, rather than wait for more favorable circumstances.

The attitudes fostered in missionaries by associating the cross with the flag stimulated adverse reactions from the target society—largely, to be sure, from the official class, but also from the rank and file as they were embroiled in disputes over land, residences, street chapels, travel into the interior, and religious conversions. Particularly was this so when these same attitudes rubbed off onto converts, some of whom were already only marginal members of the larger Chinese society.

With no practical alternative to the path they took, the missionaries could have espoused different attitudes to moderate their alliance with political power. Far more concerted efforts by both missionaries and their European sending agencies could have been made against the opium trade. Would not British opinion have yielded to this even as it had to pressure exerted in the 1830's against slavery? Not that nothing was done. There were numerous articles, a book or two, homes and facilities for the rehabilitation of addicts, and always preaching.

Missionaries could have refused to insist on their rights—their right of extraterritoriality, their right to appeal to consular protection, their right to rent whatever property met their fancy even if there might be neighborhood opposition. They could have scrupulously observed the minimal treaty rights on travel and the purchase of facilities. They could have campaigned for the elimination of obvious injustices in the treaty obligations. They could have avoided continued alignment with power by refusing to give time to the purely political duties—interpretation, service as government representatives, and the like—that they were overeager to perform for their governments. They could have humbly studied the efforts of the early Jesuits and selectively pursued approaches that would have given them better rapport with local officials and more sensitive accommodation to Chinese culture. In a word, they could have acted like truly Christian emissaries. A later missionary, not always ready to heed his own advice, stated it succinctly:

I cannot but think (without quarreling with Providence, and laying all the blame on the perverseness of men) that all this might have been effected in a much better way; for had Christian nations displayed, through their centuries of intercourse with this empire, the beneficence of the religion which they profess, they would long ago have dispelled fear, disarmed suspicion, opened the whole country to their commerce, and the hearts of its inhabitants to the Gospel [W.A.P. Martin, "Two Embassies," I, 119-20].

CHAPTER FIVE

East Meets West—
Chinese Natural Theology
and Western Common Sense

PROTESTANT BIBLE CONTROVERSY

The heart of the Protestant gospel in Chinese is derived from the Bible. The principle of *sola scriptura* of the Protestant reformation nearly three hundred years ealier was evident in the work of the first Protestant missionary, Robert Morrison, who reached Canton in 1807. Ironically, a Catholic handwritten copy of a portion of the New Testament gave him both the inspiration and much of the content for his amazing achievement of translating the New Testament within six years after his arrival in China.

This unlikely tale began in the large, southwestern Chinese province of Sichuan one hundred years before Morrison's arrival. A French Catholic missionary, thought to be Jean Basset, was working furiously on a translation of the New Testament to be used among the large number of Catholic converts who had been won there. The translator's effort was tragically cut short by death after he had completed the first chapter of Hebrews. Fortunately, a copy of his manuscript made its way to Canton where it was discovered in 1739 by John Hodgson, Jr., a supercargo for the British East India Company. Recognizing its potential value, he had it copied and carried the copy back to England where he gave it to Sir Hans Sloane, then president of the Royal Society, who, in turn, presented it as a gift to the British Museum [Spelman, 26, 45].

In 1789, some forty years after the manuscript had been deposited in the British Museum, it was discovered by William Moseley, a Congregational minister, who immediately petitioned various Christian leaders to consider using it in the evangelization of China. Little attention was given to his appeal at first, but after the formation of several mission agencies in the 1790s his proposal received more formal consideration.

In fact, the first annual report of the British and Foreign Bible Society, in 1805, noted the existence of this volume but declined to print it because it was incomplete, containing only a harmony of the Gospels, the Acts of the Apostles, and the Pauline Epistles, because it appeared to be a Jesuit translation made from the Vulgate, and because of a printing expense that would have exceeded six thousand pounds.

Robert Morrison was appointed a missionary with the London Missionary Society in 1806. He learned about this unusual manuscript in the British Museum. Accompanied by a Chinese friend introduced to him by Mr. Moseley, he went to the museum over a period of several months and laboriously copied the manuscript page by page, character by character. Taking it with him to Canton, Morrison used this partial translation of the New Testament as the foundation for his own work, the first extensively used translation of holy scripture into Chinese.[33] He was always prepared to confess the help that he had received from this Catholic manuscript.

> The gospels, the closing epistles, and the book of Revelation, are entirely my own translating. The middle part of the volume is founded on the work of some unknown individual, whose pious labors were deposited in the British Museum. I took the liberty of altering and supplying what appeared to me to be requisite; and I feel great pleasure in recording the benefit which I first derived from the labors of my unknown, predecessor ["Eleventh Report of the British and Foreign Bible Society," 1815, p. 332].

Morrison's translation of the New Testament and the subsequent revisions and new translations, both by individuals and committees, made over the next several decades, revived the "term question," this time in its Protestant form.[34] For the Nestorians, who transliterated the name of God as Alopa, or for the Franciscans and Dominicans in the Yuan dynasty, who apparently only translated into the Mongol language, there was no controversy over the correct term to be used for God or for other key Christian concepts in Chinese.

For the Protestants, however, as it was earlier for the Jesuits, the problem was rooted in the natural theology of the Chinese. How were potential terms for deity found in the Chinese classics to be interpreted? How were these same terms being used by Chinese in the nineteenth century when the linguistic battle was being waged? When Walter Medhurst, revered LMS missionary, summed up all his arguments in one volume, he entitled it simply *A Dissertation on the Theology of the Chinese*. The Protestants, as the Jesuits before them, were engaged in a profound theological debate that consumed vast amounts of time, energy, ink, and paper! It was not uncommon for protagonists on either side of the controversy to write letters of seventy and eighty pages back to their home directors. Frequently, they used onionskin-type paper to reduce postal weight, and, even more confusing, wrote vertically on the same side of the paper on which they had already written horizontally!

Much of the dispute on the home front was private, confined to the exchange of correspondence between missionaries and mission board officials. Only occasionally was any hint of the intricacy, venom, and heat of the dispute publicly displayed in any mission publication.[35]

As was the case with the Jesuits, the most crucial question was, how to translate the term "God" (Hebrew *Elohim* or Greek *theos*) into Chinese? For most Protestants there were only two options. The term in earliest use was *shen*, adopted by Morrison and the earlier translators, following the Catholic work deposited in the British Museum. The Catholic translator may have used *shen* to designate God "because he wished to avoid becoming entangled in the Jesuit-Dominican debate and thus used a totally different term"—neither *tianzhu* nor *shangdi*.[36]

The other possibility open to Protestant translators was to use *shangdi*, preferred largely by British and Continental missionaries. This term had been favored by the Jesuits, but it was ultimately rejected by the Vatican in favor of the term *tianzhu* (Heavenly Lord). This latter term became an option for some Protestants in the 1860s and 1870s, but it did not gain widespread favor, largely because of its use by Catholics.

The nub of this vexing problem was that the missionaries felt they were unable to bridge the gap between the way the term for deity was used in Greek and European languages and the way it could not be used in Chinese. The term "God" in English could designate the supreme object of worship, just as the term "god" pointed generically to an entire class of worshiped beings. The same was true of *theos* in Greek. One term covered two areas of meaning: the generic usage and the idea of eminence and supremacy. In Chinese, however, the two most available terms referred either to one or the other of these two referents.

The most prominent protagonists in this prolonged struggle agreed that they desired to find and use the most appropriate generic term that would clearly signify all those beings that the Chinese worshiped as gods. Those advocating *shangdi* believed that it had this quality, but that, more importantly, it also conveyed the concept of the supreme diety who had created all things. Proponents of *shen* argued that it was the only true generic expression and that the idea of supremacy could easily be taught to the Chinese.

What did the advocates of *shang di* believe that this term would convey to the Chinese?

1. The literal translation for the phrase was the "ruler (*di*) above (*shang*)." *Di* and *shangdi* seemed to be used interchangeably in the classics.

2. *Di* is believed to have created all things.

3. In *Shu Jing*, one of the classics, *di* is said to have "conferred a virtuous nature on mankind."

4. *Di* is viewed as providentially caring for all of nature.

5. *Di* is believed to be the same as Heaven and also the Lord of Heaven.

6. The highest worship is ascribed to *di*.

7. In the religious traditions of the Chinese, a variety of deities worshiped by the Chinese are referred to as *di*.[37]

William Boone, American Episcopalian bishop in China and possibly the leading proponent for *shen*, was not prepared to accept Medhurst's positive evaluation of the terms *di* or *shangdi*. He claimed that, far from being a term for the supreme God or for a class of beings referred to as "gods," it was, in fact, a "*distinctive* designation of a false God." It referred basically to human and nonhuman individuals who were worshiped.

Boone sought to substantiate this conclusion from the classics as well as from the account of a religious inquirer who, after receiving a tract at a gospel hall exhorting him to worship *shangdi*, went to the nearest temple and offered his praise to a particular idol that he found there ["Bishop Boone and the Shin Question," *Spirit of Missions* (Jan. 1851) 45–46]. Boone pointed to the undisputed fact that many Chinese, upon hearing the term *di*, tended to identify it with Yu-huang Da di (the Jade Emperor). He stated repeatedly that *shangdi* was for the Chinese what Zeus was for the Greeks or Jupiter for the Romans.

Another argument Boone used was that the term *di* could also be easily confused with the term used for the emperor of China, *huang di*. The first commandment of the decalogue, then, might lead them to believe that only the emperor should be worshiped. He also argued that because *di* in the classics often seemed to be used interchangeably with *tian* (heaven), this would lead to the worship of *tian* with all its undesirable connotations. He was afraid that the idea of God would be confused with the Chinese triad of "heaven, earth, and man" and thus undermine the unity of God.

Boone further argued that the term *di* would not fit in those many passages where scripture warns against the worship of "false gods." No one had ever been heard to warn against the worship of "false *dis*." Because the term cannot be used in this way, any forced exhortation of this nature would not prevent the Chinese from following and worshiping the many *shen*.

To all these arguments put forward both by Boone and others who sided with him, Medhurst had his own counterarguments, which, in turn, were rebutted by Boone. Probably more fruitful at this point is to note the positive assertions that were made for *shen* as the proper term for God.

1. *Shen* is the generic name of the Chinese gods and is thus the proper term to translate *Elohim* and *theos* into Chinese.

2. *Shen* is a comprehensive term, so all-embracing that even *shangdi* was considered a *shen* according to many passages in the Chinese classics.

3. The term *shen* can refer both to the true God and to false gods. This is not the case with the term *shangdi*.

4. The term *shen* could be broadened by usage to mean "creator" or "ruler" in the same way, according to Boone, that this had been done to the Greek word *theos*.

Undoubtedly the strongest argument that some missionaries used against *shen* was that it more properly should refer to "spirit" or "spirits." Medhurst affirmed that "*shen* is a popular term which refers to all sorts of beings which could be labeled 'spirits, elves, ghosts or hobgoblins' " [Medhurst, 552-53]. Even more seriously, *shen* was used to designate the human spirit or soul. How, Medhurst asked, was it possible to use the same term to refer both to the Supreme God and to the human soul?

Faced with this dilemma that divided nationality against nationality and denomination against denomination, a number of prominent missionaries[38] suggested that the best approach might be to use a "transferred term" that in effect would have a zero or neutral meaning to the Chinese. They pointed, for example, to the way in which Buddhist terms of zero lexical value were introduced into China and gradually gained the meaning that their adherents desired. The most notable of these were *pusa* for bodhisattva (savior) or *Amitofu* for Amitabha Buddha. They noted that "this corresponds with our own experience; for, when we first arrived, the name of Jesus was comparatively unknown, but now it is familiar to everyone who has once heard us preach, or read a single tract."[39]

These missionaries concluded:

As they have therefore no appellative for God, in the Scriptural usage of the term, we must introduce one; and the one we propose is Aloah, accompanied by the following translation, "wherever Aloah is used, it refers to the beings whom men sacrifice to and worship. They do not know, however, that the most honourable and without compare is only one Jehovah, besides whom no other ought to be worshipped. Jehovah is the proper name of Aloah" [ibid., 11].

These noted missionaries gave four reasons for their proposal to "transfer"—introduce a neologism given a precise definition:

1. No mistake can be made in following such a procedure.

2. Such an approach would free them from syncretism, combining Christian truth with Chinese superstition. To use *shen*, they affirmed, meant that the concept of God might be confused with evil spirits, the human soul, or the Chinese system of the yin and yang. To use *di*, they believed, was not quite sufficient, for it did not really refer to a "Being of infinite perfections like Jehovah."

3. No rules of the Chinese language would be violated by this solution. "No philological difficulties lie in our way, but those inseparably connected with a new term, which will be rapidly decreasing every day, from the first moment after we have employed it, until they have entirely disappeared" [ibid., 12].

4. "We are much more likely to succeed in creating for ourselves a *usus loquendi*, by adopting a new term and translating it, than we are by taking an old term diverting it from its proper sense, and applying it to a use utterly revolting to the philological tastes of the people" [ibid., 13].

This solution did not commend itself to missionaries in China any more than the use of either *shen* or *shangdi*. The controversy was not settled then; indeed, it has not been resolved to the present day. When the New Testament of the Delegates' Version was published in 1850, the British and Foreign Bible Society edition opted for *shangdi*, and the American Bible Society edition opted for *shen*. In every other respect the two editions were identical. The Union Bible of 1919, the "King James" of Chinese Christians, came out in two editions to satisfy those who preferred either *shen* or *shang di*. All recent revisions of the Chinese Bible since 1975 for the diaspora use *shang di*; the one prepared for distribution in China proper uses *shen*.

Hard data do not exist to prove without a doubt that the inability to choose a proper term for God was a major factor in the failure of the gospel in Chinese to make the comprehensive impact that missionaries desired. Common sense, however, would seem to indicate that the Chinese must have been confused by a religion unable to decide whether they ought to believe in *tianzhu, shen,* or *shangdi*.

The attention given to the "term question" undoubtedly detracted attention from weighty matters of style and readability. As a result it could be said—and correctly, in all likelihood—in the latter part of the nineteenth century that "the Bible as we know it has not yet been placed in the hands of the Chinese; and that, as a natural consequence, Christianity has never yet had a fair chance in China" [Giles, 158].

ORAL COMMUNICATION OF THE GOSPEL IN CHINESE

In addition to believing that the gospel in Chinese must be firmly rooted in God's revelation in scripture, early missionaries were also firmly convinced that this truth must be communicated orally. Francis Wayland of the American Baptist mission agency stressed that oral preaching was "the only allowable kind of missionary labor." His development of this theme was generally agreed upon, at least in theory, by all Protestant missionaries:

> It would seem, then, that preaching, that is, the oral communication of divine truth by man to man, is the means appointed by God for accomplishing the great and peculiar work of Christian benevolence. It matters not how this is done, whether in the family or by the wayside, in private conversation or in the public assembly; if it be the earnest, loving communication of the message of salvation, with reliance on the power of the Holy Spirit, it is the means by which God has promised that he will save the souls of those that believe. . . . We may therefore consider it as an established fact that the oral communication of divine truth, and this as distinguished from everything else, is the means appointed by God for the salvation of the world [Wayland, "Report," 220].

In Wayland's view, "oral preaching" was Christian benevolence. It was not to be confused with Christian philanthropy, in which "every Christian should be foremost" and which included relieving the oppressed, feeding the hungry, clothing the naked, teaching the ignorant, improving civil and domestic conditions, and, in general, alleviating human misery, whether physical, intellectual, or social ["Report," 219].

"Oral preaching," he believed—and he and the Baptist missionaries may have been unique in their emphasis—must always accompany the distribution of the Bible and gospel literature:

> When . . . the gospel is first presented to a people, the distribution of the Scriptures must proceed hand in hand with the preaching of the word. It cannot precede oral teaching, and only in rare instances will it be efficacious without it; men will not read the bible until some interest has been awakened in its teachings. A Mohammedan who should bring a carload of Korans into a crowded thoroughfare in any of our cities, might easily distribute them all if they were handsomely bound. He might do this for a year without arousing an inquirer. Let him however begin to preach Mohammedism, and be treated indignantly and persecuted for his preaching, and it would not be long before men would begin to inquire about his religion, and some of his Korans would come into demand. The same is true of the Word of God. Until men know what it is about, and their attention is aroused by an appeal to their consciences, a great result is not to be anticipated from its distribution. While, therefore, we advocate the unfolding of the Word of God to the whole people, we believe that it will be found efficacious mainly as it attends upon or follows the proclamation of the gospel from the lips of the preacher ["Report," 225].

Good theory, but nearly impossible to follow for the earliest missionaries! First, it was difficult for them to preach without having the terminology available in written portions of scripture. Secondly, open preaching of the gospel in some areas, particularly at Canton and Macao, would have sparked open conflict with authorities and risked aborting any long-range plans for the evangelization of China. Thirdly, Chinese was a difficult language to learn; preaching too soon would perhaps lead to garbled communication. Fourthly, those working in the more distant portions of the "wall of light" were concerned with making an impact more upon distant China than upon their immediate environment. Therefore, a more appropriate means than oral proclamation, at least initially, had to be found.

PROTESTANT MISSIONARY LITERATURE

Faced with these difficulties, missionaries concentrated their efforts on the printed word—the Bible itself, tracts, books, booklets, and periodicals or magazines. From 1810 to 1867 Protestant missionaries, committed in principle to "oral preaching," translated, wrote, and distributed a total of nearly eight hundred books and pamphlets, of which about 90 percent were

Figure 1

A CONFUCIAN TRACT (1846)

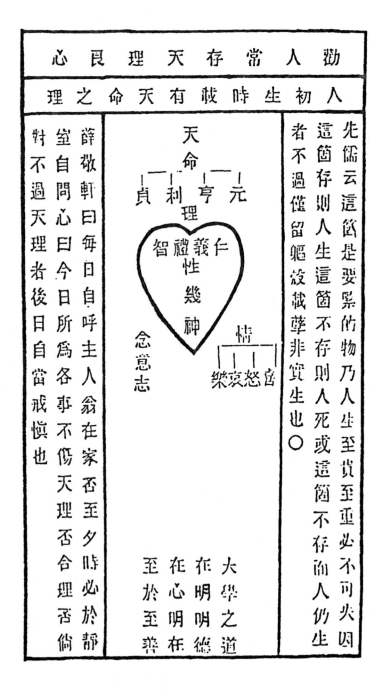

devoted exclusively to matters directly related to the Christian faith.

To use tracts and other Christian literature to exhort the population to believe in God, even as the Catholics had done earlier, was to adopt a tactic very familiar to the Chinese. Reproduced in Figure 1 is a nineteenth-century Confucian tract, a type often written by scholars to promote moral values in society. It illustrates something of the "competition" faced by the Protestant literature.

Printed on a large single sheet, this tract could either be posted on a wall or distributed to individuals. Its basic purpose, stated in the two horizontal lines at the top, was to exhort readers "constantly to preserve heavenly principles and a good heart." The rest of the material on the sheet falls into five sections. First is an initial summary-type statement in six vertical lines of print, three columns to the right and three to the left of the central section. Its theme is that the human being has been born with a heavenly principle; if due attention is not given to its care and preservation, only a bodily shell, not a living person, will result.

Section two, in the middle of the sheet, consists of key terms and phrases explaining the function of the heart. At the very top is the statement that "heaven (*tian ming*) gives benevolence, politeness, justice, wisdom." Below these terms is the pictogram of *li*, meaning "principle" or "nature." Directly beneath this key term is a representation of the heart; inside it are the terms "benevolence, justice, politeness, wisdom, nature almost divine." Outside the heart, but connected with it, are, to the right, the terms "affections: joy, anger, sorrow, happiness"; and, to the left, "thoughts, wishes, purposes." The entire page is summarized by several phrases at the very bottom. They define the aim of learning as restoration of the heart to its original nature or principle as given by God and outlined in the drawing above.

Section three, on another portion of the sheet (not shown in Figure 1), has two major divisions, the first showing how the heart, in six phases, grows progressively darker with the ascendency of evil desires until it is entirely black. The second division, also in six phases, represents the heart gradually becoming more white again as self and selfishness are put away and the "original heart is altogether restored."

In section four (not shown in Figure 1), the Chinese word for "heart" (*xin*) is presented in upright, inverted, transverse, and slanting positions with the comment that to have "a straight heart is better than to study the classics."

Section five gives a song that will help persons to "have a repentant heart and aroused reflections," which will lead naturally to restored virtue. This song, the tract relates, was used long ago by someone who urged others to repent and was cured of a long-standing ailment. How much more benefit can come if it is used to "correct our hearts and practice virtue!" The editor of the *Chinese Repository*, in which this tract was printed, comments: "These little fragments of ethical and moral writing are no unfair indices of the intellectual and moral character of the Chinese."[40] This "intellectual and moral character" even among the masses of the Chinese and their use of moralistic literature explain why first the Catholics and then the Protestants were to devote so much time to writing, printing, and distributing religious and moral tracts.

In fact, during the Jesuit period, particularly from 1570–1670, the moral climate among a few leading Chinese intellectuals reflected a remarkable improvement:

> [It] witnessed a deep awareness of the human proclivity to evil, an urgent need to counter this proclivity, a readiness for self-disclosure, and a deep anguish over one's own wrong doings, all to an extent and with an intensity never known before in Chinese history [Wu Pei-yi, 6].

Had this tendency toward self-examination and confession been more pervasive throughout the history of China, both Catholic and Protestant missionaries might well have utilized more of this specific type of moral literature.

What was the gospel in Chinese as determined from the content of these materials published in nine or ten Chinese languages or dialects?

About 6 or 7 percent of the total was either a translation of a portion of scripture or commentaries on scripture. This represented a far more direct approach to the Chinese mind than was to be found in the Jesuit literary efforts.

The largest portion of Protestant writing was devoted to theology or a rational explanation of the Christian faith. About 10 percent of this was negative in character—a confrontation with evils that the missionaries perceived in Chinese society, including idolatry in general, religious festivals, specific Buddhist doctrines such as transmigration, ancestor worship, and particular sins such as lying, gambling, opium addiction, and covetousness.

A major share of this category of theological literature dealt with foundational truths of the faith: the nature and character of God, important doctrines of the faith, the person and work of Christ, human nature, key sections of scripture such as the Ten Commandments and the Sermon on the Mount. Heaven and hell, the need for keeping the Sabbath, the doctrine of salvation, and "theological evidences"—indications from the natural order tending to substantiate the faith—were also given particular emphasis. Other books with specifically Christian content were catechisms, biblical biographies, hymnals, and prayer books.

Nearly every subject that was considered to be of relevance in communicating biblical truth to the Chinese public was included in this substantial array of literature.

The Confucian Frame of Reference

What exactly was the content of the more commonly used of these early missionary publications? In a large majority of them the writers specifically condemned Buddhism or any religious practices associated with Buddhism. The Protestant missionaries were one with the Jesuits in finding nothing of any help in the teaching of Buddhism. It was a foreign intrusion into the religious scene and was worthy only of condemnation.

One of many examples of this type of tract is Ferdinand Genähr's five-page work *Dialogues with a Temple Keeper*. The author, a missionary with the Rhenish Missionary Society, uses the popular dialogue format to explain Christian doctrine in the context of denouncing the follies of idolatry [Wylie, *Memorials*, 162, #4].

Much of this literature specifically related the biblical content to the Confucian frame of reference, such as to the five constant virtues and the five relationships. A notable example of this literary genre is *Questions about Christianity* written in 1855 by John Stronach, a missionary of the London Missionary Society. Written in a question-and-answer catechetical format in the fashion of a work by the famed Sung dynasty philospher, Zhuxi, this booklet of eighty-one leaves used 100 questions to sharpen the distinctions and point out the similarities between Confucius and the Christian faith.

The usual approach taken in Stronach's work was to quote a saying attributed to Confucius or Mencius, and then point out how the Bible treated the same subject. For example, the Golden Mean (*Zhong Yong*) stated that one should not "complain against heaven or bear a grudge against man" (*yuan tian yu ren*). The author indicated that the Bible tells us "Heaven" is God, and because all that happens is by divine decree, we should be satisfied. Furthermore, relationships among persons should never be on the basis of evil returned for evil.

Many of these early Protestant booklets quoted the alleged saying of Confucius that "before we know about life how can we know death?" This, for Stronach, gave the opportunity to talk about what God had revealed in the Bible about life to come, and, in the course of talking about the resurrection, to deny the reincarnation of the soul.

Not everything was negative. Christians, Stronach affirmed, can accept the Confucian emphasis on "self-cultivation, an upright heart, and a sincere spirit" (*xiu shen, zheng xin, cheng yi*), but they believe that this can be accomplished only through Jesus' salvation and by the help of the Holy Spirit. It is not wrong, he explained, for Christians to believe in filial piety, but this devotion must go beyond one's immediate kith and kin, and extend back to God as the source of all life.[41]

Karl Gutzlaff's short thirty-leaf tract entitled *The Perfect Man's Model* seems to have been directly fashioned on the Confucian ideal of the "superior person." He commences with a phrase calculated to interest the Chinese mind:

Man received his nature from Heaven and the morality of the five constants was complete; however, because man's ancestors fell into sin, evil has spread everywhere. . . . God (*shang di*) gave reason (*li*) to man enabling him to discern good and evil, but his heart [after the ancestor's sin] was now inclined to evil.[42]

The remainder of the booklet goes into God's solution for this state of affairs, using the Sermon on the Mount as the "perfect man's model," with special emphasis on Jesus himself, his teaching, the relationship of his teaching to God's requirements in the law, and the Lord's Prayer. He ends with a warning from Matthew 7 as to the consequences of neglecting this teaching of Jesus.

Even when missionaries denounced the Confucian faith, they held out much more hope for its adherents than they did for those of the other religions—Buddhism, Daoism, and Islam. The first Protestant missionary, Robert Morrison, for example, noted that Confucianism as practiced in his time—the early nineteenth century—was *incomplete*: it did not know God, only the material heaven; it espoused the five virtues, but had no knowledge of sin. He maintained, as did many others in subsequent years, that "the doctrine and knowledge given by God through Jesus was needed to complete the inadequacy of Confucianism."[43]

Transplanting a Foreign Gospel

In contrast with efforts to relate the Christian message directly to the Chinese context, there were other instances—numerous and inappropriate—when missionaries used materials developed largely for the British or American context.

One tract, revised and reprinted many times for the languages of all the centers of the "wall of light" and then in the five open ports, was entitled "Poor Joseph." It related the story of a poor working boy in London who, after first hearing and believing the gospel message in a chapel on a dingy side street, became seriously ill. The preacher from the chapel came and prayed for him, but to no avail. As he lay dying he asked the man of God to take the money that he had saved over many years and give it to Christians in need. The tract then went on to tell of another person who was quite rich but whose heart was hard and who died without repenting or believing in the Christian faith.[44]

Another popular tract translated by William Muirhead of the London Missionary Society and used widely to deal with the needs of Chinese inquirers was John Angell James's booklet entitled "The Anxious Inquirer." Useful as it probably was in England, this pietistic tract dealt with many subjects hardly fitting for China in 1856. Some of the chapter headings were: "Deep Concern for One's Salvation is Reasonable and Necessary"; The Importance of Retaining and Deepening Religious Impressions"; "Mistakes into Which the Anxious Enquirer May Fall"; "Discouragements."

The last topic was broken down into several aspects of discouragement: cold indifference; the low state of religion among those professing it; the prospects of opposition; a feeling that one is making no progress in attaining salvation. Despite one section that warned against looking too much to one's own heart rather than to Christ and microscopically analyzing all feelings and motives, this is the overriding emphasis of the booklet.[45]

Dialogue Tracts

One of the most popular of the dialogue-style tracts was *Dialogue Between Two Friends*. First prepared by William Milne of the London Missionary Society in 1819 at Malacca, this tract was used extensively at every place of Christian witness during the 1820–1860 period. Depending on the names used for the two who were dialoguing, it was entitled *The Dialogue Between the Two Friends Chang and Yuan* or *The Dialogue Between the Two Friends Chia and Yi* (*chia* means the first person; *yi*, the second person.

This tract was designed to cover the whole gamut of Christian truth, with particular attention given to matters that bothered the Chinese most. Care was taken, for example, to distinguish Jesus from a saint or a bodhisattva, a Buddhist savior. It was emphasized that Jesus had acted in history for human salvation, and that his power to save others was grounded not in fantasy, but in miraculous deeds. As in most Christian writing, not only in this period but throughout the history of Christian missions in China, sin was presented as a violation of God's law demanding punishment; Jesus came to substitute for humankind in paying the penalty for sin.

Eschatology had a place of considerable importance in this tract. Milne, and subsequent revisers, explained in detail the resurrection, the judgment to come, and the endless hell awaiting those who did not trust in Jesus. The resurrection was differentiated from reincarnation, and the author wrote specifically of the resurrection body and how it differed from ordinary bodies.[46]

The Literature of Natural Theology

Missionaries used the types of material considered above to reach the general population. However, if the same content were presented in the classical style and with references and allusions to the Chinese classics, it would also be useful for more intellectual readers. The most common way that some Christian workers used to reach the elite was by the approach of natural theology. The differences between the Jesuits and the Protestants were in their presuppositions; the former were committed to a Thomistic outlook in which nature leads to grace, whereas the Protestants brought with them a philosophical system of Scottish realism or "common sense."

Scottish realism was given its shape by Thomas Reid (1710–1796) who followed Adam Smith in the chair of moral philosophy at the University of Glasgow, and by two professors at the University of Edinburgh, Dugald Stewart (1753–1828) and Thomas Brown (1778–1820). This system of thought was popularized in America by John Witherspoon at Princeton Seminary and found its way into most American seminaries in courses of philosophy through which it influenced a generation of missionaries.

Although developed to meet philosophic problems in Europe, this type of apologetic appealed widely to American religious thinkers:

It supported orthodoxy in theology, raised no dangerous questions, invited no intellectual adventures. It was a restatement of Locke [who for Americans was a political idol] against David Hume and contradicted Hume's skepticism by a blanket assertion that idea and object correspond so faithfully that Americans, intent upon their business, need never give a second thought to be so unprofitable a worry [Miller, p. x].

The Scottish "common sense" philosophers and their many followers contended that objects existed independently of the mind and can be perceived directly as they are. Knowledge, they affirmed, is not gained through ideas or images of the real world, but from objects themselves. The truth of these assertions is self-evident through "common sense," in this system a synonym for reason. Belief in the objective reality of the external world and the doctrine of "cause and effect" led to an argument for God's existence. The basic premise was that "from certain signs or indications in the effect, we may infer that there must have been intelligence, wisdom, or other intellectual or moral qualities in the cause" [Grove, 147].

The Scottish philosophers and their disciples pointed out that human beings, in contrast with animals, have an intellectual faculty enabling them to perceive accurately, to organize their sensations, to remember, to imagine, and to make valid judgments. Therefore, idealistic assumptions concerning the unreliability of either the external world or of their minds must be rejected. Because the senses are reliable, science and philosophy are an invaluable means for Christians to erect an impressive structure of "Christian evidences"—"natural"—means by which Christians could explain or demonstrate the truth of their faith.

Christian doctrine elaborated in terms of this philosophy, brought to China by both American and British missionaries, fitted far better into Chinese patterns of thought than would many other formulations of Christian thought. As stated by one commentator on William Paley's *Natural Theology*, the most popular of all books on this topic for American students:

> Once then we know by natural theology that there is an intelligent mind behind the intricacies of the universe, then we may well leave to revelation the disclosure of many particulars which our research cannot reach respecting either the nature of this Being . . . or his character and design [Ferre, pp. xi–xv].

 The process, then, for many missionaries to state the gospel in Chinese was first to establish the reality of the spiritual world within the Chinese intellectual framework and then teach the truths of the Bible. James Legge stated it well:

> There is a broad standing ground in their own literature upon which the Christian missionary can take his position in communicating the truths

of revelation to the Chinese . . . the more it is sought for, the more will missionaries find among the Chinese that consciousness of God of which Tertulliam speaks, even in the simple, rude and uncultivated.[47]

Writing late in the nineteenth century Hampden C. Dubose elaborated in great detail on the need of the Chinese for "natural theology." He described how the five elements, human physiology, natural history, astronomy, and the "book of nature" in general should be used where there had not been an adequate preparation for the gospel—such as the preparation realized by the presence of Jews in the Roman empire. ["Preaching," 135, 137–39, 141–45, 154–89].

One of the best and earliest examples of this gospel in Chinese was W.A.P., Martin's *Tiandao Suyuan* ["evidences of Christianity"], written by him in 1854 within four years of his arrival in China, and printed in thirty or forty editions over the next sixty years. It was part of the language study program for new missionaries who came to China. *Tiandao Suyuan* was also used in theological schools for the instruction of Christian preachers. In 1907, prior to the China Centenary Conference, it was voted "the best single book" published in Chinese in a poll conducted by the Christian Literature Society.

Tiandao Suyuan was the only presentation of the gospel to which thousands of high Chinese officals and intellectuals, initially in Ningbo and later in northern China, were ever significantly exposed. When Martin served as an interpreter on American diplomatic missions to Tianjin and Beijing (1858–1860), and during his later years (1864–1894) teaching in and administering the government-sponsored Tung Wen Guan (Beijing University), he took advantage of his many contacts to distribute *Tiandao Suyuan* in the highest government circles. A classical Chinese version of the book was prepared in 1912 at the request of the North China Tract Society, which aimed to put a copy of it in the hands of every government official. Mandarin editions were also distributed among the general populace in northern China. Obviously, then, this book ranks of first importance for an understanding of the Christian message as it was articulated in nineteenth-century China.

The apologetic nature of this work was evident from the outset. Fan Yungtai, a friend of Martin's who wrote the preface for the first edition in 1854, observed that the Doctrine of the Mean and the Christian faith did not conflict; they were in perfect harmony. In his own introduction Martin picked up on this keynote, suggesting that the *dadao* (great doctrine) was not the property of either East or West; its origin was in heaven with a personal God who, he argued, might be referred to as *shen, tianzhu,* or *shangdi.* Martin stated that, contrary to what the Chinese thought, Westerners were not all merchants and destitute of knowledge of the *dao.* Some, he pointed out, were scholars from many countries who had labored hard to learn about Chinese life and culture in order to preach a faith that had its origins in the East.

The author divided the material in *Tiandao Suyuan* into three sections:

natural theology, evidences of Christianity, and revealed theology. The first section, on natural theology, contained seven chapters in which Martin appealed to heavenly bodies, the five elements, living things, the human body, the principle of life (soul), insects and animals, and all of creation to demonstrate the existence of God. The first appeal, then, was not to revealed truth but to an orderly world and the reliability of human perception and reasoning. This was almost exactly the plan used by Paley in his *Natural Theology*.

Martin's first appeal was to the heavenly bodies—the three lights—to illustrate the orderly nature of the universe and to emphasize that it consisted of matter activated by the principle of life. He explained scientifically how the sun, planets, and earth were thought to have orginated in the contradiction and spinning movements of the original stuff of the universe. Finally, he pointed to God as the hidden source of the gravitational principle that produced this creative activity.

The author next observed that ancient Chinese and Western theories to explain the nature of the universe did not reflect scientific reality, but that he would refer to a combination of physical elements—metal, wood, water, fire, and earth—to prove God's existence. He showed in detail how only the presence of a living creator could produce the marvelous interdependent functioning of these five elements in the universe. He often utilized simple scientific illustrations, unfamiliar to his listeners, but not difficult to comprehend. His very use of the concept, if not all the content, of the "five elements" appealed to the Chinese mind.

As Martin began to deal with the origin of life in his third chapter, the format of the text became more polemical, reflecting something of the give and take of the discussion in which the lectures originated. In each instance Martin's apologetic was directed toward a specific Chinese concept. A hearer argued, for example, that *li* (reason or principle) had given birth to all things and asked:

> What is the principle of anything if not its nature? What anything is by nature is Heaven's mandate; and Heaven is the Lord. Therefore, to say that principle gives birth to anything is no different from the theory that the Lord gives birth to it.

Martin replied that the nature or principle of anything adheres in matter and can hardly give birth to that thing. God the creator, he explained, has put a distinctive and unique principle in each part of creation, but God must be distinguished from it.

Martin noted the Chinese theory that the *taiji* (great ultimate) had given birth to the *yang* (male principle) and *yin* (female principle), which together produced all the rest of creation. Without condemning this view as superstitious or idolatrous, he observed only that it had no foundation in fact. Weather, environment, mutations, and survival of the fittest, he stated, were better explanations for the many different species of animal and plant life in the world than was the interaction of *yin* and *yang*.

When he presented the design of the human body as further evidence of God's creative ability, he drew a distinction between the popular Chinese proverb, *tian sheng ren* ("Heaven gives birth to man"), and the concept of creation, which implied careful planning. He described the human body, showing its complex detail and the interdependent functioning of each part. Martin may have been tempted to use Paley's famous example of the watch to reinforce his emphasis on design, but instead he pointed to what was obviously more familiar to his Chinese audience—a well-planned house or a metal tool. In the course of his argument, he used the illustration of Socrates, who called the attention of his disciples to a jade craftsman who, although he could carve a beautiful human figure, was not able to give it life. How different, Martin explained, from God, who could not only plan and execute but impart life.

The psychology of human nature was another significant aspect of Martin's natural theology. His starting point was that the human body had no life unless indwelt by a *linghun* (soul). He taught that each person has only one "soul," but the soul had five properties: consciousness, self-consciousness, memory, thought, and imagination. Thought, he stated, was particularly important because it separated human beings from even the highest level of animal, such as the orangutan. Martin used many simple illustrations to indicate the interdependence among the five properties. For example, he compared memory without thought to undigested food, and thought without memory to dysentery. The several stages in the process by which silk is produced were given as an example of the indispensable nature of each of the "spirit properties."

There were four "heart properties": desire, emotion, discrimination, and moral judgment. Each of these, as in the case of the "spirit properties," was further subdivided in great detail to show how God directed the working of the human heart and mind. Martin particularly emphasized that moral judgment was a result of the divine law written on the human heart.

This portion of *Tiandao Suyuan* closely reflected Dugald Stewart's *Outline of Moral Philosophy*, where, in part 1, Stewart described the intellectual powers of human beings, including, as did Martin, external perception, memory, imagination, judgment, and reasoning. Part 2 was entitled "The Active and Moral Powers of Man" and included an analysis of appetites, desires, affections, self-love, and moral faculty. Although undoubtedly indebted to Stewart in the development of this portion of his work, Martin did not bother his Chinese readers with any of the philosophic speculations of Western thinkers [Stewart, 28–143]. One difference between the work of the two men was that Martin made an occasional appeal to scripture to support his assertions, whereas Stewart completely separated natural and revealed theology.

Martin was indebted to both Paley and Stewart in analyzing the unique instincts of fish, birds, and beasts. He showed how the mating cycles of fish, for example, cannot be explained by learning, memory, or thought processes, but only by natural disposition. The Chinese term for this, *tianxing* ("heavenly" disposition), is not a Christian expression but lent itself, along with all its associated concepts, for use in Martin's argument. In effect, he linked his presentation to a ready-made doctrine of Chinese natural theology easily understood by even unsophisticated readers. The specific content that he presented was new, but not the concept with which he framed it.

Martin ended this chapter by emphasizing that, although the human and the animal worlds were different, they stood in a hierarchical relationship to each other. "Animals are subject to man and man is subject to heaven. Animals use their bodies to serve man, and man uses his heart to serve God." He perceived this unity among heaven, the human world, and the animal world, each in its own place and with its own responsibility, as a scriptural emphasis with deep roots in both ancient and contemporaneous Chinese thought.

Having used multiple arguments to establish the existence of God, Martin went beyond the usual province of an introduction to natural theology—certainly beyond Paley—to talk about God's nature. He argued from the worldwide unity of nature and humankind to the concept of one God over all—self-existent, with no beginning or end, and possessing the attributes of omnipresence, omnipotence, and omniscience. He quoted from many portions of scripture to buttress his statements, but only after he had fully appealed to the nature of the universe and human nature to deduce the nature of God. His method was to "investigate man in order to understand God." Could this God be approached by mortals? Martin answered yes, pointing out that Mencius had said that evil persons could prepare themselves, by fasting and ablutions, to sacrifice to *shangdi*.[48]

Martin had apparently read extensively about the work of the Society of Jesus in China under the Ming dynasty and liked to think of himself as a Protestant Matteo Ricci.[49] The natural theology section of *Tiandao Suyuan* was very similar in fact to Ricci's important work, *Tianzhu Shiyi*, in its apologetic approach and format. Although deeply indebted to Paley, Stewart, and other nineteenth-century apologists, Martin may also have been consciously patterning his book after that of the great Jesuit.

A similar attempt, on a much less elaborate scale, was made by Alexander Williamson who came to China in 1855 with the London Missionary Society. Writing over several months in the *Shanghai Serial*, a monthly periodical edited by Alexander Wylie during 1857 and 1858, he presented a cogent foundation in natural theology for the more detailed data coming from God's self-disclosure in holy scripture. Williamson commenced by using the order of the universe, the variety to be found in the animal world, and the complexity of the human body to argue for the necessity of a Supreme Being with the intelligence to bring this about.

Who is this Supreme Being or Force—the *dao, taiji,* or *li* (reason)? Utilizing a variety of quotations from Zhuxi, the Sung dynasty Confucian scholar, Williamson explained that the solution must refer to someone with life, activity, and wisdom. How else can we explain planets that move, water that flows, wind that blows, and the ocean tide that comes in and goes out? He points out that the *dao* is described as "extreme silence," *taiji* as a void or "nonplace," and the *li*, or rational principle in all matter, has no consciousness or knowledge. How then, he asks, can any of these be claimed as the source of all things?

Over the next several issues, Williamson went into detail about the attributes of God: God is one, all-knowing, without limits, self-existent and eternal, omnipresent, all-powerful, transcendent above creation, and spiritual in essence. Although appealing to "common sense" and a number of Chinese proverbs, Williamson here quotes scripture considerably more often than Martin did in his section on natural theology.

Under the broad topic of anthropology, Williamson deals with the human soul and human nature. From the human soul, the immaterial component of human nature, comes the ability to reason, to will, to feel, and to use the five senses. The soul, he affirms, never dies, and has only two destinies—heaven or hell. The ability of the soul to act as it does in one personality refutes, he argues, the doctrine of transmigration. Otherwise, he states, it would be possible for an insect to perform all of the functions normally associated with human life— talking, planning, reasoning, and so on.

In his discussion of human nature, the author quotes widely from the *I Jing* ["book of changes"], Confucius, Mencius, Xun Zi, and the Han Confucian scholar, Dung Zhungshu. In common with other Christian thinkers, he claims that God originally created humankind with a good nature, but that the presence of death in the world shows that humankind now has a sinful nature. Only in this way, he argues, can God be considered just, when a newborn baby, who obviously has not committed any specific acts of sin, is allowed to die.[50]

Defense of the Faith

Closely related to the way that the missionaries explained the foundation of the Christian message by natural theology was their use of "evidences" to prove that the faith was authentic. In the second section of *Tiandao Suyuan*, W.A.P. Martin explained the human need for revelation, mentioned the doubts that hinder understanding, and then analyzed five types of evidence: prophecy, miracles, the spread of the Christian faith, the transforming power of the biblical doctrines, and the wonderful nature of the *dao* (doctrine). Martin stressed that natural theology did not preclude the need for special revelation through the holy scriptures. He affirmed that although humankind was related to both heaven and earth, it was ignorant of God, its own nature, sin, and redemption. Nothing in the other world religions, he declared, could be compared to the Bible and the answers it gave to the deepest questions of humankind. He pointed out how the unity of the Bible, its consistency, and the applicability of its truth to all peoples attested to its divine origin. He stressed that, in contrast with other books, the Bible told both the good and the bad about the men and women it described. The God it portrayed was not a local deity, constantly changing and being superseded by new objects of worship, but was unchanging and controlled the entire earth. Although he was writing to Chinese readers, he left no doubt that the plight of humankind was universal.

Martin's phraseology, far from being a wooden translation of an American model, made frequent use of Chinese concepts. When Jesus was on earth, he was "filial" in his attitude to his family and to God—he "honored the King's law." In his incarnation he descended to the "dust" of the human level. Throughout, Martin placed stress on the fact that the Christian faith was a religion of morality and rectitude.

In discussing the major biblical evidences for the Christian faith, Martin first emphasized the importance of prophecy, showing how the New Testament fulfilled predictions uttered by the Old Testament saints in ways that defied human fabrication. He observed that these were unique to Christianity and constituted a formidable proof of its reliability.

Miracles were not performed, Martin asserted, in order to astound persons, but to provide evidence of God's unity in the Old Testament, and of Jesus' deity in the New Testament. He noted that Confucius did not even wish to talk of the miraculous, but he affirmed that what Jesus did often seemed strange only because it was new and beyond previous human experience.

In the second place, Martin devoted several pages to the resurrection of Christ as the supreme miraculous testimony to the reliability of the Christian faith. He presented the resurrected Christ himself as the continuing miracle. Jesus had worked only three years, but his influence had changed the world; although no one had served as Jesus' teacher, he had taught all the world; he never left Palestine, and yet the entire world had heard of him.

In common with other nineteenth-century apologists, Martin gave great evidential importance to the historic triumphs of Christianity as it was propagated throughout the world. The fact that the Christian faith had penetrated over two hundred countries was presented as a sure indication of God's protection and blessing. Other religions, he claimed, had not spread this extensively and were presently in a state of decline. Whatever measure of success they had attained in some areas of the world he attributed to accommodation—as when Buddhism entered China—or to dependence upon political and military power.

Martin contended dubiously that historically the Chrisitan faith had not relied upon anything but the spiritual zeal of its followers for its advancement. In his view the removal of religious restrictions in Japan and China was one further indication of this force at work. He marveled how God had providentially granted great material resources to Christian countries so that they could sponsor missionaries and build merchant fleets to bring them to their destinations. By contrast, he observed, non-Christian countries were getting progressively weaker and had very few ships. He predicted that under the impetus of this advance, the many *pusa* of China (Buddhist saviors) would be no more remembered in a few years than the old deities once worshiped in early European history.

According to Martin, the outward geographic expansion of Christianity was paralleled by the inward transformation of character that it brought everywhere. God had created human beings with a good nature and commanded them to walk in the true way. Although civilization was primitive, its moral state was good. As it improved its physical state, it soon deteriorated morally and wandered far from God. Many holy sages appeared to rectify this situation, but their strength and wisdom were insufficient. At this critical juncture, God sent Jesus into the world to enlighten humankind, to change its evil into good, and to save it. As human beings learned the truth of the Bible and believed in it, they were restored to God's will, their governments were reformed, and they developed an interest in science. When science had developed, their countries became strong and able to spread the Christian faith to other countries. The American thrust across the continent to the Pacific Ocean was cited as a prime example of the energy generated by the Christian faith.

Martin pointed out that the introduction of the gospel to the islands of the Pacific had initiated the same transformation all over again. Evil customs, such as cannibalism, human sacrifice, and idolatry, were put away as superstitious persons received the "efficacious pill" of the gospel. He noted that similar changes had occurred in India and Burma.

When Martin applied his convictions about the progress of Christianity to China, he was not as optimistic. He quickly dismissed Buddhism and Daoism because of their crude idolatry and their recourse to doctrines of hell and heaven to frighten and seduce their followers. Confucianism, although correct and beautiful in his view, was not complete, for it had neglected the divine dimension in its doctrines of the *wulun*, the five human relationships. Humankind, made in God's image, was first responsible to Heaven. The Christian faith embraced not five but six relationships. Martin argued that this firm foundation in God's will and grace was the prerequisite to a change in human morality.

In the final chapter of section 2, Martin answered a number of the more common objections that had been raised against Christianity. The first question dealt with conflicts between the age of the earth as presented in the Bible and in the Chinese classics. The former, based on deductions from genealogical records, had been thought to be about seven thousand years, whereas the latter seemed to imply forty or fifty thousand. Martin proposed no definite solution, but he claimed that the Chinese records with respect to *taiji*, the yin and yang, Pan Gu, "the first man, whom the Bible calls Adam," and the ancient kings, Yao, Wu, and Shun, were not clear enough for one to form any reliable comparative judgment.

Some of his Chinese audience had questioned the biblical assertion that the human race was a unity. Martin replied that differences in race, color, and language were not as important as the universality of human nature and the human body, and were probably related to climate and spatial separation. He pointed to the many languages of China to illustrate the world problem and noted that European and Indian languages both came from Sanskrit. He observed that the biblical Eden was in Asia and therefore very close to the first four centers of civilization—India, China, Babylon, and Egypt.

Martin dealt briefly with the theory of evolution. He acknowledged that scientists believed that human beings and animals came from a common stock.

He went on to state, however, that despite general consensus with respect to evolution—a gradual "creation" in contrast to a "sudden" one—several things could still be affirmed: the wonder of creation; the origin of human and animal life from the earth; and humankind's unique possession of a human soul. How could persons be human, he asked, if God had not given them a human soul? Martin had accepted some type of theistic evolution as he attempted to accommodate his faith to the impact of the evolutionary hypothesis that had dominated scientific articles since Darwin published his *Origin of Species* in 1858. Martin did not insist that the six days of creation be interpreted as literal, 24-hour days. To him, the order of creation was far more important than the passage of time it might have taken.

In reply to the query, "Why was Jesus born in a small country like Palestine?" he gave several answers: the monotheism of the Jews had uniquely prepared them to receive the Messiah; the land of Palestine, bordering as it did on three continents, was a suitable place from which the gospel would spread; Jesus' birth in Palestine symbolized the fact that he had not come to reveal his majesty and that the Christian church did not depend upon political might to make its way in the world.

A very important question that the Chinese people raised was, "If I follow this way, must I turn my back on Confucius?" Martin's basic principle was that "Confucianism and Christianity may be distinguished in terms of breadth and narrowness, but not in terms of truth and error." "How then," he asked, "can you talk about turning your back on it?" Without spelling out any details involved in this relationship, he went on to point out that Jesus was the God-Man—at once both teacher and Lord. He had come to redeem the human race by his sacrifice, not to wield political power or to change human customs. Jesus' first and last objective was to relate humankind to God.[51]

Secular Literature

If Scottish realism caused some missionaries to relate their theology and philosophy to the Chinese *dao* and all its implications, others put a high premium on science. The laws of the objectively real world, they contended, must relate to the heavenly way (*tian dao*) that was a part of the very stuff of the universe.

Of the nearly eight hundred Protestant writings during the first sixty years of their time in China, nearly 90 percent were religious in nature. The others dealt with secular subjects, including science. Until about 1850 most of the nonreligious writings dealt with history, geography, and commerce, and were intended to familiarize literate Chinese with the world in which they lived, and particularly those areas from which the missionaries had come.

Elijah Bridgman's noted *Brief Geographical History of the United States of America* (1838) was one of the most useful publications in this regard. In this book whenever he spoke about the school system, the books, or the educational system of America, he compared it with China, often introducing the religious element, even when writing about other topics. In chapter 19, entitled "Distinguishing Between the False and Correct Religion," he explained the Christian faith almost in the same fashion as would be found in a gospel tract. "The Five Relationships" was his theme in chapter 25, and he tried carefully to explain that there were more and bigger similarities than differences between China and America.[52]

After 1850, Protestant missionaries began to publish more works in the fields of mathematics, astronomy, medicine, and other sciences. Nearly all of them initially were translations of well-known Western writings such as Euclid's *Elements*, Newton's *Principia*, and John F.W. Herschel's *Outlines of Astronomy*. Unlike the Jesuits who used these kinds of books to establish rapport with the literati and government officials, the Protestants were more concerned with producing textbooks for the many schools they were starting. Except in rare instances, they were not specialists in the fields about which they were translating or writing, and the quality of their work did not reach the high standards attained by the Jesuits.[53]

How could missionaries justify using their time to publish this type of literature in China? First, it met the need for textbooks in schools. Secondly, if the Chinese were convinced that the missionaries were scholars, not barbarians, and able to speak intelligently on these matters, they would be more willing to listen to the gospel message. Thirdly, if the Chinese understood the rudiments of these several sciences, they would see the uselessness of continuing to hold to their many superstitious beliefs about the universe and daily life. They then would be more willing to become Christians. Fourthly, on a more positive note, truths of science were God's truth and thus a part of the gospel, although a secular one to be sure. William Martin noted that his book *Natural Philosophy* had one aim—to establish "that fundamental truth, the being and unity of God as the author and law-giver of Nature."[54]

Not all the missionaries were as anxious to equate science with the "gospel" in Chinese. Daniel MacGowan, an American Baptist Missionary in Ningbo, had his doubts:

> [He was careful not to] occasion an error, against which we often find it necessary to guard the native mind, namely that Christianity and science are the same, or so identified that in receiving the one they possess the other. As an illustration of this, I might mention that in exhibiting a drawing of a complicated machine to a very intelligent person, a short time since, he asked if it was not the invention of the Saviour! ["Lectures at Moon Lake College," *The Missionary Magazine*, vol. 21, no. 12 (Dec. 1851) 441].

Faced with this type of attitude, MacGowan determined that he would use his chapel only for preaching, and that his science lectures would be presented at a different site. In expressing this attitude, MacGowan may have remembered the example of the pioneer American Baptist missionary, Adoniram

Judson, who had little patience with missionaries who sought to prepare the Burmese mind to accept Christianity by using astronomical and geological concepts, with which they could not be familiar, to break down the cosmology of the Buddhist religion.

Nor were all Protestant missionaries as careful or as discerning in their use of science as those who saw its value but wished to separate it from the gospel essence. For many it was "bait" for the Christian message, a magnet of curiosity that would draw learners to hear the gospel proclaimed. Griffith John, an LMS missionary whose main base of operation was in central China, stated:

> Now the missionaries teach these things, not because they believe that history, geography and science can save human souls, but they know there is a great preparatory work to be done, a great amount of rubbish to be taken away. . . . Missionaries have taken an interest in the Chinese, not only in their moral and spiritual welfare, but also in their intellectual cultivation . . . but after all, my brethren, preaching is our great work in China [Wardlaw, 283].

Even as he said this, however, he could confess that the Chinese were arrogant and proud about not knowing geography, and, the "gospel necessary for that is a little geography." For other shortcomings in history and in understanding the natural forces, the "gospel is a little history . . . and a little science" [ibid., 282–83].

Hunter Corbett, an American Presbyterian missionary in Shandung after the 1860s, developed a museum located on a crowded street and placed all types of things in it to attract passers-by: stuffed animals and curios, mechanical toys, an electric engine, and other fascinating items. His biographer, James Craighead, entitled the chapter describing this approach, "The Gospel and the Tiger." Corbett reported that by this method—this gospel—he could attract nearly one hundred thousand persons a year to hear him preach [Craighead, 141–49].

An article in the early *Jiaohui Xinbao* ["church news"] presented various features of the Christian faith in the language of science. Jesus was called the sun. He was the source of light, pure and constant, even as was the sun for the physical universe. The rays of the sun were in three primary colors, even as Jesus is manifested in his ministry as prophet, redeemer, and king. Christian love was compared to gravity—a binding force in society; without it society would disintegrate [Bennett and Liu, 191].

Much of the material on science, particularly news items on recent inventions or short popular articles, appeared in the magazines, serials, journals, or almanacs published by missionaries at the several ports.[55] The *Chinese Serial* (Hsia-erh Guan-chen), was published monthly in Hong Kong from 1853 to 1856. Rather small, with only twelve to twenty-four leaves in each number, it was published by the Morrison Educational Society and edited successively over these few years by Walter Medhurst, C.B. Hillier, and finally by James Legge. The initial editorial commented on the vast resources of China and the greatness of its past. Now, during this time of initial Western contact, there were many problems, among them the forsaking of monotheism for idolatry. However, inasmuch as "all in the four seas are brothers," it was necessary for East and West to learn from each other, a task that could be partially accomplished through the *Chinese Serial*.

Although many of the items in the *Chinese Serial* were brief news items on contemporary events around the world, some space was given to applied science. In September 1853, for example, an article explained the basic principles of the steam engine. A few months later, in January 1854, there were "Notes on Geology." In September 1855 there was a treatise on heat and also a geographical article.[56] When it was necessary for the journal to cease publication in 1856, the editors lamented that nothing existed to "stir the Chinese mind from apathy and circulate among the people the lessons of 'universal history and the accumulation of Western knowledge.' "

A similar magazine was the *Chinese and Foreign Gazette (Zhongwai Xinbao)* published by Daniel MacGowan in Ningbo from 1854 to 1857. Local news of the five open ports and from around the world predominated, but several articles emphasized the application of scientific theory. The use of vaccination in England was highlighted in one issue. In 1855 the editor presented the Christian case against the binding of feet: the pain and inconvenience coming from this practice violated the basic Chinese virtue of *ren*.[57]

The *Shanghai Serial (Lu Ho Cong Tan)* continued for only a little more than a year. The number of its articles devoted to science or to natural theology was proportionately higher than in similar magazines. Almost every issue contained an article on physical geography or astronomy. The writers devoted considerable space to translations from Western literature, such as works by Homer and Thucydides.[58]

A work that continued over at least twenty years under slightly different names and with many different missionary editors and compilers was the *Anglo-Chinese Concord Almanac (Huafan hoho Tongshu)*, from 1844 to 1854. Articles on geography, accompanied with rather detailed, colored maps, on anatomy, natural history, telescopes, and steam engines were intermixed with gospel exhortations and detailed lunar and solar calendars. Only the most discerning Chinese reader would have been able to separate from this potpourri that which was gospel and that which was Western. By theory, implication, and application it was all one package.[59]

The emphasis that made natural theology and science, one of its principal components, a part of the gospel in Chinese continued into the post-1860 period when missionaries began to spread out over all of China. A leading spokesman for this view during this period of incipient reform in Chinese life was Young J. Allen, a Methodist missionary from the southern United States, who arrived in China in 1860. In common with other missionaries Allen was glad to confess that the Christian gospel was primarily concerned with a person's relationship to God as well as to one's fellow human beings. In his view, however, the relationship of humankind to nature could not be neglected:

[For him Christianity was composed of] ". . . religion to bind him [humankind] to God; morality to regulate his intercourse with his fellow man; [and] Science to teach him the properties and uses of things." Thus defined, Allen believed Christianity could be ". . . discriminated from all the known systems of the world, and hence proves its origin to wit: its comprehensiveness. It envelops the whole man; it develops the whole man; it illuminates and controls the whole man; yea, more, it comprehends (embraces and understands) his entire being and relations. In this, it is singular, extraordinary, alone—True." Such a system had made possible the "utmost development of our (The West's) intellectual and material resources. . . ." It was such a system that China was waiting for [Bennett, 75].

Allen believed that China could never be strong unless its leaders first understood the true principles of heaven, humankind, and nature—*tianli, renli,* and *wuli* [Bennett, 277]:

[Salvation] not only comprises spiritual regeneration, but restoration of man's long lost and forfeited relationships to God, to his fellow-man, and to all created things—his primordial relationship of sonship, brotherhood, and dominion [Allen, 192].

China, Allen affirmed, needed physical light from its coal mines, intellectual light to be gained from the "researchers, inventions, and discoveries of Western minds," and moral light that could come only from the gospel message.

Allen propagated his views on the holistic gospel in Chinese in two publications: *Church News (Jiaohui Xinbao),* from 1868 to 1874, and its successor, *The Globe Magazine (Wanguo Gongbao),* from 1874 to 1883. In addition to the religious articles and miscellaneous news items that comprised about 70 percent of the material in *Church News,* Allen used 17 percent of his space for scientific and technical interests—articles on railways, mathematics, chemistry, astronomy, zoology, coal mining, and other such subjects. When *Church News* was replaced by *The Globe Magazine* in 1874, the emphasis on science decreased dramatically, possibly because Allen felt that several other new Chinese publications were dealing adequately with this issue.

Another missionary committed to the holistic gospel in Chinese was William A.P. Martin. Feeling that modern science and liberal thought were the only way to "overthrow those ancient superstitions" that blocked both the central gospel message and social and material improvement in China, he and a group of his friends in Beijing organized the Society for Diffusion of Useful Knowledge.

Patterned on an earlier society by the same name in Canton, the society began publishing *Zhongxi wenjian lu*, known to the foreign community as *Peking Magazine*.

Up to this point all missionary-sponsored periodicals, whether published outside China or in Canton, Hong Kong, or Shanghai, had included some explicitly religious material and were not completely oriented toward reform. The *Peking Magazine* was the first exception. Described by Martin as "the first periodical besides the offical gazette ever published in Peking," it included articles on practical science, internal improvements, travel, adventure, moral fables, and world news, carefully selected to stimulate Chinese readers to reform according to what the editors deemed the superior achievements of the Western world.

No specifically religious articles or news items were included in *Peking Magazine*. God and Jesus did not appear more than once or twice and then only in a descriptive, not a dogmatic, manner. Martin and his colleagues apparently believed that this policy would gain greater sympathy for the West and its ways, and thus ultimately achieve a Christian objective.

Scientific articles in the *Peking Magazine* did not include highly technical data with detailed plans for the construction of machinery or for the use of a specific methodology. This more precise scientific function was later fulfilled by John Fryer's *Gozhi huibian*, which absorbed the *Zhongxi wenjian lu*, but Martin's purposes were broader and more popular. He intensely desired to convince the Chinese that science, like their classics of old, was "holy" and could be of great value to them. Even this kind of material could lend itself to a moral lesson. England, France, and Italy were reported, for example, to be submitting competing claims for a small volcanic island in the Mediterranean, only to find to their chagrin that it had disappeared. After an explanation of the reason for "salt seas" in various places, Martin commented that such data caused one to "reflect on the wonders of creation."

In other instances, however, direct aim was taken at superstitious beliefs. Martin noted, for example, that the comet of July 1874, and Venus passing by the sun in November of that same year, had been viewed by the Chinese as heavenly omens to explain respectively the Sino-Japanese conflict over Formosa and the emperor's death from smallpox. How, he asked, could these be omens for the Chinese alone and not for the rest of the world, some portions of which had enjoyed great prosperity and military success? Furthermore, he observed, when Venus passed by the sun about one hundred years earlier, Emperor Chien-lung had been at the height of his property and power. These laughable beliefs, he asserted, must be put away, and science must be used to "seek certainty and to pacify the minds of the people." The West, he added, had once believed similar things but had discarded them as without foundation.

Martin missed few opportunites to stress the orderly nature of the universe. He began an article on meteorological balloons with the observation that, because the human being was a creature who "wears heaven on his head and treads upon earth as his foot stool," he had the interest and the ability to investigate and control natural phenomena. As human beings made good use of their minds, "heaven and earth" would submit to them. Had not the wealth of England, he asked, come from the power of machines? He pointed out that when England was taken by the Romans in the Han period, its citizens were without culture, clothes, or wealth, and had extremely crude habits. Even their conquerors gave up on them. Now, however, having subdued nature, they were able to meet not only their own needs but those of an empire spreading around the world.

An obviously moral explanation was frequently slipped into the narrative. In the course of describing Naples, Martin digressed long enough to explain that the destruction of Pompei came from *tiandao* (heavenly way or doctrine), which blesses the good and destroys the licentious.

More often, the geographical articles aimed to stir the Chinese to emulate the development and progress that had taken place in a particular country. Chile, recently independent and without extensive outside help, had developed rail and ship transportation systems and greatly increased its trade. Hokkaido, the once desolate northern island of Japan, was using Western techniques to develop its agriculture and fishing, and the Japanese hoped to be able to sell some of its products to China.

The news items that Martin presented to his Chinese audience fell into a number of broad categories: internal improvements—industrial, commercial, financial, social, cultural, educational, political, diplomatic, moral, scholarly, military—and human interest. Western countries were the examples for desirable reform and progress, and non-Western countries, particularly Japan and India, were held up as Eastern models that had best emulated the West. Whenever possible Martin utilized Chinese news events to encourage his readers that China too was making progress.

A few rather short news articles passed moral judgments on a variety of social problems. From the first time he visited Macao in 1851, Martin had despised the Portuguese traffic in Chinese coolies. He reported how more than one hundred thousand Chinese, many of them young boys, had been either forced or lured to Cuba from 1848 to 1871. He recommended that Macao and China either enforce existing laws or create new ones to stop this traffic.

He commented gladly on progress in the fight against slave trading, with special commendation to those "benevolent princes" in Parliament, and to David Livingstone, the missionary who had fought to wipe it out in Africa. He reported its prohibition in Brazil and Cuba and noted that Egypt and England were seeking to stop slave trading at its origin in the Sudan.

Other things that Martin condemned, either directly or indirectly, were the opium trade, concubinage, wine, superstitious falsehood, and religious intolerance. He regretted that all British discussions of whether or not to prohibit opium planting in India considered only the economic aspects and never really raised the moral issue. But nothing was said in any of the thirty-six issues of the magazine to condemn the use of opium by the Chinese, or to indicate the various ways in which its social effects were being combatted.

Many articles and news stories that Martin reprinted in the *Peking Magazine* appealed to human interest. Some were of the Horatio Alger variety, and appealed to humanitarian and moral motives to think and do good. For example, he told the story of a young girl, on duty as a telegraph operator on a stormy night, who went out with a red light to warn an oncoming train of a tree fallen on the track. Although fatally injured when the train pushed the tree over her, she died with the satisfaction of having done her duty. A passenger on a late night train to Philadelphia saw a fire break out in a small village and jumped out to warn the residents of the impending disaster, breaking his leg in the process. Such response to human need, Martin observed, illustrated how someone might love another as oneself. His examples of altruistic heroism contrasted markedly with articles extolling the virture of celibate widows or loyal officials, then current in the *Peking Gazette*.

Both true stories and fables were used to illustrate the moral order of the universe. Martin believed that human beings everywhere possessed the same moral nature and were subject to the same principles of right and wrong. *Tiandao* was responsible for punishing evil, protecting from danger, and rewarding good.

Tiandao could not, however, be bent to respond to the whims of capricious individuals. Martin included a fable about a priest who was unable to pray simultaneously for the requests of his two sons-in-law—one a farmer needing rain for his crops and the other a pottery maker who required more rainless days in order that his pots might dry.[60]

In summary, what may we say about Martin's gospel in Chinese? The obvious aim of Martin's literary effort in the *Peking Magazine* was to challenge the sacral nature of the Chinese worldview. He appealed to *tiandao*, but he suggested that the Chinese could work with it to control a nature no longer perceived as mysterious, predetermined, and unmanageable. This attitude was epitomized in one of Martin's fables relating how several men were stranded on a beautiful island controlled, they learned, by the three fearful gods of water, wind, and fire. These gods were awe-inspiring, but gradually the men learned how to subdue them and harness their power for good. Martin appended a moral: "Whether these three things will harm or help men depends on whether the knowledgeable man will investigate their nature and use their power."

Martin's gospel in the *Peking Magazine* was a purely secular gospel. Although he believed strongly that the Christian God was the God of nature, personally involved in the physical world and in human affairs, he only presented an impersonal *tiandao*, no substitute for the Chinese "gods" he was replacing. His approach may indeed have suggested that the Chinese reformers were right in their stance toward the West when they said, "Chinese learning for the essence and Western learning for function." The *Peking Magazine* seemed to say that Western technology and science could be separated from the Western religious essence.

Why did Martin not brew a better mix of religion and science—one more appropriate for his own strong convictions? He may have had several reasons: many Chinese would not have read a religious periodical; the magazine was a "wedge" to create a desire for Western culture that Martin hoped would lead to an interest in the gospel; such an approach was necessary in Beijing where there was more than usual opposition to Christianity; Martin believed that the Christian message and European civilization, even when mediated through non-Christian countries such as India and and Japan, were but two aspects of the one message of salvation and progress. In some sense this was "the gospel."

Unfortunately, this gospel was essentially missionary. Its claim seemed to be that once ignorance, fear, and superstition were removed, all the economic, military, social, and educational problems of China would disappear. Martin often applied moral maxims and platitudes idealistically, in fact simplistically, to complex situations and gave almost no consideration to historical, economic, or sociological realities.

CATHOLIC LITERATURE

The Catholic use of literature in the nineteenth century was significantly different from that of the Protestants. The early Jesuits had written or translated many works on science and mathematics. They also had published various works on theology and ministerial functions, but they were to be used in training Chinese clerics, not to be distributed widely to the unconverted [D'Elia, 24].

The first contact that a non-Christian had with the Catholic faith was usually made by a Chinese convert, possibly a catechist. Once the commitment was made, either the foreign missionary or the catechist helped in the long process of preparing for baptism. This was fairly routine in all parts of China. Initially, the new convert learned the principal doctrines of the church and was instructed on how to make the sign of the cross.

The next step was to enroll converts as adorers, a process of confession, prayer, recitation of the Apostles' Creed and the Ten Commandments, and a celebration of the "five thanksgivings." If adorers fulfilled all their Christian obligations during the next year, they were regarded as catechumens. After another year of probation, probably accompanied by more serious instruction in the doctrine of the Christian faith, they were baptized and accepted as members of the church.

A great amount of literature was prepared by Catholics. It was far more circumscribed than that of Protestants, which tolerated wider-ranging frontiers of orthodoxy. The Catholic literature focused almost exclusively on the instruction of new converts. Few attempts were made, in contrast to the sixteenth and seventeenth centuries, to write apologetic material that would clothe the Christian faith in Chinese dress. Can we surmise that the Vatican suppression of the Jesuits with their innovative ideas and literature at the end of the eighteenth century contributed to this reluctance during the nineteenth century?

Kenneth Latourette, the noted historian, points out that the most significant kinds of adaptation were not verbal and literary but visual. The important festivals of the church, daily home worship, and images of Christ, Mary, and numerous saints were functional substitutes for Chinese customs and religious observances [*History*, 335].

THE GOSPEL ACCORDING TO CHINESE CONVERTS

This chapter on the gospel in Chinese would be incomplete without an examination, at least cursory, of records of what the missionaries' Chinese converts were saying about this gospel. Each missionary depended rather heavily on Chinese helpers—to learn the language, to prepare short sermons, to write and correct gospel tracts or longer booklets, and very frequently to go independently into nearby areas and preach the gospel truths learned from the missionary. These helpers often took the major responsibility for administering or teaching in the day schools run by the various mission boards. Eventually some of these men gained positions of responsibility, and, beginning in the 1850s, a number of them were ordained to the ministry.

What was the gospel in Chinese preached by these men? The most celebrated of the early Chinese evangelists was Liang Afa, a man led to the Christian faith by William Milne, an LMS colleague of the first Protestant missionary, Robert Morrison. Some authors, with very little direct evidence, have attributed to him the famous collection of tracts, *Quanshi liangyan* ["good works exhorting the age"], from which the Taiping leader Hong Xiuquan received his knowledge of the Christian faith. We do have one statement from Samuel Dyer, an LMS missionary who spent a period of time with Afa in Penang, that he "has written nine very good tracts."[61] Were these the "Good Words Exhorting the Age?" Very possibly, inasmuch as this collection was made up of nine short tracts. Whether Liang Afa actually wrote them or whether he had helped Milne and then Morrison in their preparation and revision, they reflect the gospel he was preaching.

Actually little more than a thematic compilation and organization of scripture passages, this influential work had nine sections, as described in Alexander Wiley's *Memorials of Protestant Missionaries*:

1. A true account of the salvation of mankind including passages from Genesis 3, Isaiah 1 (a statement against idolatry) and Matthew 5–7.
2. Following the true and rejecting the false. The principal passage here was John 3:1–21.
3. A miscellany on the true God, Christ's work of redemption, the state of man. This appears to be a compilation of several smaller tracts put together without any overall coherent theme.

4. Miscellaneous collections of Holy Scripture dealing with passages both in the Old and New Testaments, again with no sense of one particular topic.

5. Miscellaneous explanations of Holy Scripture. Apart from one portion from the Old Testament describing the destruction of Sodom and Gomorrah, this consists of sixteen passages from the New Testament with a very short explanation of each.

6. Perfect acquaintance with the true doctrine. To several Scripture portions is added the spiritual autobiography of William Milne, to whom, in some sense, this work is generally attributed.

7. On obtaining happiness whether in peace or peril. The ultimate good is received by believers in the future life, and those who reject the Gospel can only anticipate misery.

8. Excellent sayings from the true Scriptures. This section contains both short discourses as well as paraphrases on several sections of the Bible.

9. Selections from the ancient Scriptures. In addition to brief comments on several passages, there is a commentary on Colossians 4, a "refutation of various errors, and a Discourse on the day of Judgment."[62]

If, as has been speculated, much of Taiping Christianity came from this particular tract, received by Hong Xiuquan in Canton when he visited that city to take an examination in the classics, it is understandable why his understanding was so partial, so incomplete, so selective, and so eclectic! What indeed might have been the difference had he received a systematic exposition of the major doctrines of the Christian faith with the most significant scripture passages appended?

A common practice for early Protestant mission agencies was to ask their missionaries to send home translations from the experiences of their converts to be published in mission magazines. These reveal as well as anything else the emphases that were being made in the grass-roots preaching of the gospel. Unfortunately, however, anything really innovative and creative in its relationship to the Chinese context would probably have been excised by the missionary before he sent it home to his mission board!

If these types of documents are indeed representative, it is apparent that the gospel was always a confrontation with an unbelieving world. As these preachers exhorted others to seek the "true happiness of Jesus," they quickly mentioned that this meant "not to foolishly seek the false happiness of this world." Many inquirers wished to know the difference between Jesus and Pusa, Jesus and Confucius, and the Ten Commandments and Chinese moral truths. It was pioneer preaching, and truth was usually packaged as a positive affirmation and a negative denial.

Much emphasis appears in this preaching on the evil of idolatry and on the necessity to distinguish between Creator and creation, whether it be "heaven and earth" in general or whether it be, more specifically, particular trees, mountains, and streams. The ministry and work of Jesus was summed up as "at thirty years of age he preached the kingdom of heaven, and taught men to repent, until he died and made atonement for sin."

Frequently these humble preachers were asked if the Protestant faith ("religion of Jesus") and the Catholic teaching ("religion of the Lord of Heaven") were the same. In an answer that may have reflected faithful parroting of his missionary teacher's usual reply, one preacher replied:

> By no means, *this is silver, that is white copper*; this is genuine, that is counterfeit. Beware, gentlemen, that you are not deceived, and take the false for the true.

The usual way to handle a question that demanded some type of comparison between Jesus and Confucius was to say something like:

> Confucius was a great sage, who taught men how to enjoy happiness in this life; to practice benevolence, justice, propriety, truth, and other similar things; he was a scholar and a ruler, and the ruler who is unwilling to follow the instructions of Confucius, is a lover of evil, and injures the people; but I discourse of God, who gave His Son Jesus to teach the true doctrine to all nations, that they may be happy in this life and enjoy eternal happiness in heaven. God requires us to love other men as ourselves, and to refrain from sin.

In the course of preaching this gospel in Chinese, one of the most difficult questions to answer was social in nature. One preacher reported that he had been asked after a Sabbath service, "That man's teacher is a foreigner who sells opium; how can you talk of justice and harmony?" He replied, "He does not sell opium; but not fearing the sea, has come thousands of miles to teach men to worship the true God. . . . Opium smoking is the *heart's* sin; if you believe in Jesus, you can be cured; there is no other remedy."[63]

ANCESTRAL RITES AND THE GOSPEL

Whether preached orally or written in books or tracts, whether proclaimed by foreign missionary or native assistants, the gospel in Chinese sooner or later had to deal with the nagging problem of the ancestral rites. This had been a stumbling block earlier, for Catholic converts, and it was no less so for the Protestants two hundred years later. The handling of this particular matter would determine, in fact, if the gospel in Chinese was to be good news or bad news to the Chinese masses.

From the beginning of their labors in China, Protestant missionaries emphasized that the Bible, as well as the Chinese classics, commanded filial piety. In various writings the point was made that it was God's will that the Chinese be loyal to the emperor and that they show respect to their elders and all family members [McCartee, "Obedience"].

The rub came, of course, in seeking to determine what should be the attitude of Chinese Christians to those rites that seemed to imply worship of departed family members. In general, the missionaries tried first to take a positive line: the Bible, particularly in Ephesians and Colossians in the New Testament and many places in the Old Testament, exhorts an attitude of respect, honor, and obedience to parents. Only God is the source of life; the future life is under divine control, and those who follow God should not engage in the emptiness of rites designed to provide for departed loved ones.[64]

Some missionaries explicitly forbade their converts to participate in these rites; others strongly advised them not to. W.A.P. Martin confessed that one of his early failures was when he once insisted "on the surrender of ancestral tablets as a proof of sincerity on the part of an applicant for baptism" [*Lore of Cathay*, 277].

When speaking their gospel in Chinese, most missionaries did not take as radical or as unbending a line as when arguing among themselves over the issue. In *Evidences of Christianity*, for example, Martin posed the question, "Can the traditions passed down to us [Chinese] by our ancestors be observed along with the Christian rites [of baptism and communion]?" To this query, he replied, "You may observe those that do not contradict the Bible, but you must reject those that do." He supported this conclusion by quoting the Ten Commandments, noting specifically that there was no difference between idolatry and worship before the ancestral tablet, or between sacrificing to idols and presenting food to the spirit of deceased ancestors.

In very discreet and polite language, he empathized with Chinese views that saw failure to bow and to sacrifice as unfilial conduct producing dire consequences. He reminded his readers that Lu, one of Confucius's disciples, had said that "life and death, prosperity and all things" were under Heaven's control. If this were so, Martin argued, then one's first obligation was to God, the originator of all life and the one responsible for parents and care for their children.

Although Martin believed there was no need to offer food sacrifices to the ancestors, he stated that Chinese Christians should fix and clean the graves, put up pictures of departed loved ones, and take flowers to the burial sites. But above all, everyone should worship and praise God as the truest way of expressing gratitude for life. He closed his argument by affirming that when persons have understood the truth, they will be able to discern for themselves which of the ancestral rites to observe and which to abandon.[65]

In another of his books, Martin traced the details of the famed "rites controversy" and clearly took a stand with the Jesuits against the Franciscans and Dominicans. He claimed that if the ancetral rites had been permitted, even temporarily, Emperor Kangxi might have become a modern-day Constantine, bringing officials, gentry, and the general populace into the Christian fold. In his opinion, this would at least have bought time, if Chinese Christians had been granted liberty to practice customs that were such an integral part of Chinese life. He regretted the lack of Protestant unity on the "rites question"—

almost a replay of the earlier Catholic controversy—but believed the problem would have been settled much earlier if an "open policy," giving all groups liberty to follow the dictates of their own consciences, had been adopted.

When writing or speaking in English, Martin and a few other avantgarde thinkers of the Protestant missionary force seemed to be arguing for more radical positions. His first prominent opportunity to influence his colleagues was an invitation to deliver a major paper on the theme of the worship of ancestors at the General Missionary Conference in Shanghai in 1890. Far different from the well-prepared but inconclusive technical discussion of the subject presented by Matthew Yates at the first General Missionary Conference, in 1877, Martin's paper, presented for him by Gilbert Reid, sounded the only real controversial note of the conference, although Martin said nothing essentially different from what he had written ten years earlier in his book, *The Chinese, Their Education, Philosophy and Letters.*

At the outset of his lectures he stated that there were only two basic approaches to what was admittedly "the most serious impediment to the conversion of the Chinese." One was to remove the obstacle, and the other was to make a temporary accommodation while seeking a more permanent solution. He compared the first alternative to a man's attempt to remove a hill in front of his home rather than changing his habitation. The other option was to build a railroad track over the mountain while construction proceeds on a tunnel to go through it. Refusing to get bogged down in technical religious niceties, he concentrated on the historical and social role of the ancestral cult. He noted, for example, the historical function of the rite in announcing dynastic successions, reporting important imperial events, and in promoting morality and courage by appealing to the honor of the departed. He pointed out, moreover, that at the present time the system, although tainted by "a large intermixture of superstition and idolatry," still served a threefold social purpose: (1) to strengthen the bonds of family union, and stimulate to active charity; (2) to cherish self-respect, and impose moral restraint; (3) to keep alive a sort of faith in the reality of the spirit world.

Martin rejected outright both the possibility and the wisdom of abolishing a cult with such cohesive power in society; "Let us ask ourselves whether, if we had the power by a pen-stroke to sweep it all away, we should dare to incur the responsibility of doing so." Although he shared with his colleagues the conviction that the missionary must "avoid giving countenance to anything that can fairly be construed as idolatry," he affirmed that those features to which the church most objected were "its excrescences, not its essence." His approach unconsciously utilized techniques widely adopted by many agents of cultural change confronting adverse institutions. First, he rejected both the form and function of idolatrous elements—that is, invocations and offerings that implied that the deceased were tutelary deities. Secondly, he sought to modify both the form and function of certain "announcements" so that they would be regarded not as prayers but as mere expressions of "natural affection." Thirdly, he accepted both the form and function of kneeling and bowing, affirming that although these actions were idolatrous in certain contexts, they definitely were not in others. He put salutations and announcements to the dead in this same category. A fourth proposal, to develop functional substitutes, would have made his views more palatable to his colleagues, but was omitted from this presentation.

Martin claimed that much of the Protestant difficulty with the ancestral rites was related not to fear of idolatry but to repugnance for "any kind of connection with the dead," an aversion that he traced to an extreme reaction to the dogma of the Roman church. He urged restoring natural expressions of affection for the dead, if not among the tradition-bound churches in the West, then at least among congregations in China where "Protestant missions are still in the morning of their existence." He added that "the venerable usages of a civilized people should be judged by their own merits, and it is to be borne in mind that our aim is not to Europeanize the Chinese, but to make them Christians."

This approach, fraught with obvious dangers and demanding caution, "kept the way open for counteractive teaching" and avoided an "uncompromising conflict" that would "close the ears of the better class to all good influences." Martin argued that taking a rigid position on this issue would cause the "incipient conviction" of the rank and file Chinese to be stifled before it ripened "into practical conversion."

In the heated discussion following the presentation of this paper, Hudson Taylor, whom Martin once said had "erred in leading his followers to make war on ancestral worship, instead of seeking to reform it," asked "those who dissented from the conclusions of Dr. Martin's paper to rise." Nearly everyone did. Martin's views were defended largely by Timothy Richard, the noted English Baptist missionary, and Gilbert Reid. Martin stated later, however, that "many missionaries have assured me that they concur in the general sentiment of the paper."

When writing later about the ancestral cult Martin suggested that functional substitutes—bouquets of flowers, or planting flower seeds and shrubs—might be used in place of offerings of meat and drink. But because he had less difficulty with the original form and functions in the first place, he never pushed this option as hard as other liberal spirits did.[66]

Although conferences of Protestant missionaries in 1877 and 1890 went little beyond condemning most aspects of the ancestral rites as idolatrous, the third conference in 1907, sparked by the presence of many more Chinese delegates, seemed to be a bit more open to creative innovations. One commentator has noted:

It was agreed that while the "worship of ancestors was incompatible with an enlightened and spiritual conception of the Christian Faith," and that while the rites as customarily performed and understood could not be tolerated by the church, some observance expressive of filial piety by the church was desirable, and the hope was expressed that Chinese Christians themselves would find some generally acceptable and worthy way of meeting the need [Williamson, 294].

Chinese leaders are still seeking this "worthy way." The ancestral rites, even in the China of today, will not go away by themselves. The gospel in Chinese may spread widely throughout the land, but it will never truly take root until the church decides whether it preaches good news or bad news on these rites that continue to be the glue holding Chinese society together.

CHAPTER SIX

The *Dao* and The *Logos*

The buildings on the top of the small mountain in the Shatin Valley about ten miles from Kowloon City in the New Territories did not have the usual appearance of a church. Most prominent was an octagonal temple, with its roof curved in the familiar lines of Chinese architecture. Within this place for meditation and worship there was:

> [An] altar in beautiful Chinese style, with a red lacquer finish and adorned with golden symbols—the lily of purity, the cross of sacrifice, the sun of righteousness, the fire and water of the Spirit's cleansing, the swastika of cosmic unity and perfect peace, the fish of Eastern and Western sanctity, and the Greek monogram for Christ. Red candles, so often used in Chinese ceremonies, were used on the altar as was incense whose ascending smoke and fragrance were symbols of aspiration [Noren, 14].

Even more symbolic than the temple decor was the entrance into this complex of buildings—above the gate, a cross rising out of a lotus to show that the best of Buddhism was fulfilled in Christ. The title was also unique, Dao Feng Shan—"the mountain from which the Logos wind, the Christ-spirit, blows" [Reichelt, "Buddhism," 162]. The *Dao,* that ancient Chinese term signifying way, principle, reason, doctrine or speech, was identified with God's eternal *Logos,* manifest now in the incarnate Christ.

In formulating the gospel in Chinese, Protestant missionaries in one way or another had to speak in the context of a pervasive Buddhism that had been in China for eighteen hundred years. Karl Reichelt, with his innovative approach at Dao Feng Shan, was hardly typical of the missionary community. The initial Protestant reaction to Buddhism, in fact, was almost identical with that of the Jesuits—ignorance, misunderstanding, and almost total rejection.

DISPARAGEMENT OF BUDDHISM

Early Protestant missionaries spoke disparagingly to the Chinese, as well as to their church supporters at home, concerning the pagan idols and "silly ceremonies" that made up a large part of Chinese daily life. They perceived Buddhism as in a state of decline and saw no need to understand its function in Chinese society. Carstairs Douglas, an English Presbyterian missionary stationed at Amoy, stated it well for his colleagues:

Only one or two other missionaries had dived into the depths of Buddhism and Tauism as Dr. Edkins [LMS missionary in Beijing] had done. Missionaries ought to study Confucianism carefully, and thankfully use all that is good in it, pointing out its great deficiencies and wisely correcting [*sic*] its errors. But to spend much labour of that sort on Buddhism and Tauism would be unnecessary, for *as systems of thought* they are dead.[67]

A leading English sinologue, James Legge, did not give much attention to Buddhism, because it was a foreign import. Ernst J. Eitel, who came to China first with the Evangelical Missionary Society of Basel and later transferred to the London Missionary Society, was one of the first missionaries to make a serious study of Buddhism. Although more appreciative than many before him, he did not really enter into Buddhism as a religious system and could only commend its compassion toward all creation. For the most part he was harshly critical:

[Buddhism] arose from a feeling of spiritual bankruptcy and never recovered its mental equilibrium . . . a system of religion without hope and strictly speaking without God, a system of morality without a conscience, a system of philosophy which wears the mask of transcendental mysticism or of nihilistic cynicism . . . utterly incapable of comprehending or appreciating the claims of reality and the demands of the present [Eitel, 93ff.].

BUDDHISM AS A PREPARATION FOR CHRISTIANITY

A few other missionaries, though finding many deficiencies in Buddhism, believed that some of its features were preparing the way for the Christian faith. One of these was William A. P. Martin. During his first years in China, he had been strongly critical of the stoic negativism of Buddhism, its principle of self-annihilation, and its melancholy spirit. He once referred to the Buddhists as "religious atheists" whose highest motivation was to "escape from having their souls pounded in a spiritual mortar, or ground between spiritual millstones in Hades" [*Lore of Cathay,* 185, 188].

Most of the time he was more positive in his appraisal of the benefits of Buddhism. In his analysis of the Chinese religious system, Martin suggested that the three major religions, although different in their assumptions, beliefs, and practices, were supplementary in the Chinese experience. "In ordering their lives, they are regulated by Confucian forms, in sickness they call in

Daoist priests to exorcise evil spirits, and at funerals they have Buddhist priests to say masses for the repose of the soul." Furthermore, he argued, each religion represented a historical advance in religious thinking, and he was optimistic that Christianity would eventually become the "fourth stage" for the Chinese people.

Martin proposed that one way in which the Christian faith could be related to the Chinese religious system was as the "successor of Buddhism." He firmly believed that two basic elements in Buddhism—a belief in a divine being, and in the immortality of the soul—contributed "to make it [China] ready for the cultivation of our Christian epoch." The spiritual universe in which Buddhists believed, filled with Buddhas and Bodhisattvas—kind, just, and providential beings—was far different from that of the Chinese who worshiped "natural objects and . . . human heroes . . . not one of [whom took] any strong hold on their affections." The failure to restrict worship to one Buddha and the basic atheistic tendency of the religion did not deter him from stating that praise to the Buddhist divinities was "worthy to be laid as an offering at the feet of Jehovah." Few fellow missionaries took kindly to this suggestion. D. Z. Sheffield exclaimed:

> I have no sympathy with that sort of thing and think that Christian men, and above all missionaries, are in the poorest kind of business when they set out to coquet with heathen religions, magnifying their virtues and belittling their vices.[68]

Martin conceded that the Buddhist doctrine of the future life was "vitiated by mixture with the errors of metempsychosis."[69] This error was offset, he felt, by the strong emphasis on the immaterial essence of the soul and its future existence in a state that accorded with present conduct. These elements in Buddhist teaching constituted a better preparation for the Christian faith, he thought, than the materialism of Daoism or the agnosticism of Confucianism.

He also asserted that "faith, hope, and charity," cardinal Christian virtues, were taught by Buddhism. He showed how many Buddhist terms—heaven, hell, devil, soul, life to come, new birth, advent, sin, repentance, retribution—were taken by the earlier Catholic and later Protestant missionaries, "sprinkled . . . with holy water, and consecrated to a new use." He was persuaded that the hand of divine providence, preparing China to receive the gospel, as had been done for Europe in the Roman empire, could be seen in this provision of religious concepts and vocabulary useful for presenting Christianity. He believed that the mission of Buddhism was not completed, but that it served as the trunk of a tree to which the "vine of Christ" could now be grafted. Martin also viewed Buddhism as an example of a foreign creed winning its way and holding its ground in spite of opposition. Would not Buddhists themselves, taught by their own leaders to look for a fuller manifestation of their faith, see Christianity, also a non-Chinese religion, as the fulfillment of that hope?

Joseph Edkins, an LMS missionary who authored a major work, *Chinese Buddhism,* saw this preparatory work of Buddhism in a very practical way:

I do not in any way doubt that Buddhist doctrines have been, for the Christian teacher, most important preparation for Christianity; and that, through the spread of these doctrines, the Chinese people look upon Christianity with much less strangeness, and accept its doctrines with much less difficulty, than otherwise they would have been able to do [*Chinese Buddhism,* 370].

Edkins, even as Martin before him, saw this particularly in the many words and phrases of the Christian faith that had a foreshadowing in Buddhism. As Edkins pointed out, these terms gradually assume a Christian sense to Christian converts "in proportion as they are instructed in the Biblical message . . . but if not instructed, the views of the convert are Buddhistic." He noted, for example, that the Chinese term *mo,* used in the word for "demon," is largely associated with the idea of possession and that the Buddhist *mogui* is not nearly as "intensely wicked" as the concept of demon in Christian thought [ibid., 356]. In general, his conception of Buddhism as a *praeparatio evangelica* centers on its eschatology—it is the doctrine of heaven and hell that prepares Buddhists to consider the Christian message.

BUDDHISM AS THE GOSPEL IN CHINESE

The most radical of the nineteenth-century Protestant missionaries in his appreciation of Buddhism was Timothy Richard, an English Baptist who came to China in 1869. He found great affinity between the Christian faith and two Buddhist scripture portions: The *Lotus Scripture* of the Tien Tai school and *The Awakening of Faith* of the Pure Land school. Affirming that "it is incredible that [God] should leave all outside the Jews and Christians without any knowledge of the Way of Salvation," Richard held that the *Lotus Scripture* was God's revelation for Asia:

With regard to the doctrine of Immortality taught in the New Testament to Western nations—we can find that in the Far East, there is what might be called a Fifth Gospel, or "Lotus Gospel," which for fifteen centuries has shone throughout the Buddhist world in China, Korea, and Japan with such brilliancy, that countless millions trust to its light alone, for their hope of Immortal Life. It will be abundantly evident to Western students, that the wonderful truths taught therein have precisely the same ring as those taught in the Fourth Gospel, about the *Life,* the *Light,* and the *Love.* The bearing of the cross, by patient endurance of wrong and undeserved insults, is also inculcated over and over again, in the same gentle language as that of the Apostle of Love himself [*Buddhism,* 134].

Richard gives more detail to this Chinese form of the gospel when he comments on the role of Guanyin, the leading female bodhisattva or savior:

> For example, the story of Kwanyin, given in the 25th chapter of the Lotus Gospel, is an Eastern allegory, of the Infinite Love and Compassion of God. It matters little whether "Kwanyin" as an individual ever existed. The important point is that Infinite Love and Compassion is raised to an ideal, that inspires the life of all good men and women just as in the parable of the Prodigal Son in our Third Gospel we Christians have the ideal of Infinite Tenderness and Forgiveness presented to us as a model of what God the Father is [ibid., 135].

If the gospel was already present in these writings, why then did missionaries, in Richard's view, need to come to China? He claimed that these Christian truths found in the "New Testament of Higher Buddhism" (Mahayana) were so mixed in with the old doctrines of Hinayana Buddhism that only Christian missionaries, with their fuller knowledge of God's truth, could recognize them for what they are. The missionary then became the expert who discerned God's truth within the Chinese context and explained it to the Chinese. The gospel was already there in its Chinese form—it needed only to be discovered and expounded.

Richard was even more ecstatic in his praise for the sutras of the Pure Land sect, particularly the one titled *The Awakening of Faith (Qi Xin Lun)*. He first discovered a copy of this work in 1884 in Nanjing and eventually felt it to be of such importance that he published his own translation of it (1907)—still used today in its essential features.

What was it about this small Buddhist book that caused Richard to see it as an "Asiatic form of the Gospel of our Lord Jesus Christ in Buddhist nomenclature?" To him it best embodied the Mahayana Buddhism that had been brought into China and eventually into Korea and Japan. He found there the God who is both transcendent and immanent, salvation by faith rather than by works, a deep sense of compassion for the world, comparable to the Kingdom of God, and the reality of the Messiah who had come to bless all humankind.

The idea of "messiah" was the key to Richard's understanding of this book as well as his basic principle of translation. He knew of the sixth chapter of the Diamond Sutra *(Tin Gang Jing)* in which it was claimed that Gautama Buddha had declared:

> Five hundred years after my death there will arise a religious prophet who will lay the foundation of his teaching, not on one, two, three, four, or five Buddhas, nor even on ten thousand Buddhas, but on the Foundation of all the Buddhas; when that One comes, have faith in Him, and you will receive incalculable blessings [*Buddhism,* 47].

This expectation of a "coming one" in Buddhism and the appearance of this book written by a Buddhist saint, Ashvagosha, who lived in central and

northern India during the early part of the first century, influenced his translation of an important Chinese term, *Zhenru* or *Rulai*. Translated literally, this
would mean "true so" or "true like." In Sanskrit it is a term meaning "reality"
and has been variously translated as "suchness," "thusness," or the "cosmic
order." For some, all terms have been enigmatic, and they have used the
Sanskrit transliteration, Tathagata, which, of course, has almost no meaning
to anyone but the enlightened! Richard believed the term referred to God and
so translated it by a variety of expressions: True Form, True Model, True
Reality, and Archetype, some of which obviously could also refer to God
incarnate in Jesus Christ. He claimed precedence for this translation in an old
standard Buddhist work, *Wan Fa Kwie Sin Luh.* Although preferring to follow
another translation procedure, Alan Walton, a recent commentator on *The
Awakening of Faith,* concedes that the term refers to the One Mind, the
Cosmic Mind, the Divine Mind, whether of Buddhist, Neoplatonist, or Christian mysticism [*Awakening*, 21].

How would Ashvagosha have gained such insight into the true God?
Richard explained rather vaguely:

> It is getting clearer each year now that these common doctrines of New
> Buddhism and Christianity were not borrowed from one another, but
> that both came from a common source, Babylonia, where some of the
> Jewish prophets wrote their glorious visions of the kingdom of God that
> was to come. Babylon then had much intercourse with Western India and
> Persia, as well as with Judea, Egypt, and Greece. From this centre these
> great life-giving, inspiring truths were carried like seeds into both the East
> and West, where they were somewhat modified under different condi-
> tions.
>
> It is also getting clearer each year that different truths, wherever
> found, cannot be antagonistic. They do not neutralize, but complement
> each other; they do not destroy, but fulfill one another [*Buddhism*, 49].

In a much more explicit fashion, which other scholars have decried as pure
speculation and fantasy, Richard claimed that when the Apostle Thomas
traveled to India, he had direct personal contact with Ashvagosha and taught
him the truth of the gospel, such as was found in Philippians 2:12–13. This
intercourse with one of the early apostles of Christianity motivated Ashvagosha to write *The Awakening of Faith* and caused Buddhism to be transformed from its Hinayana form into the Mahayana form, which was then
brought to China [Richard, *Epistle*, 4].

Richard's understanding of Mahayana Buddhism, and particularly of
Ashvagosha's *The Awakening of Faith,* as the gospel in China for the Buddhist
context, was based, then, not only on general revelation but on some type of
historical contact, general or specific, between East and West. His views of the
specific contact between St. Thomas and Ashvagosha, his high estimate of
Ashvagosha's work, and his translation of the Chinese term *Zhenru* (itself a

parallel Buddhist translation of the Sanskrit *tathagata*) as the True Model beyond earthly appearances of the divine have not been widely accepted by other scholars—whether fellow missionaries or those with no particular desire to find an apologetic for Christianity.[70]

Critics point out that *Zhenru* was seldom presented as personal, and although seemingly self-existent, was hardly unique or the creator God. Richard undoubtedly was reading much of his own Christian concepts into the text, more eisegesis than a rigorous, historical exegesis. His principal biographer, W. E. Soothill, felt that, as wild as his ideas might have appeared to many other missionaries, they were not too far removed from what some of his Buddhist contemporaries were thinking [*Timothy Richard*, 317]. Richard was, in Soothill's title for him, a "seer" with a certain mystic spirit:

> His imaginative sense carried him into regions beyond the reach of other eyes, for vision leaps over chasms, leaving plodders to build bridges for feet to tread. To reveal a new point of view is the work of a prophet, and—to every man his gift! [ibid., 319]

FRIENDS OF THE *DAO*

Richard's vision was too radical to be implemented in any practical sense, but it, along with other factors, did help to motivate Karl Reichelt, a missionary with the Norwegian Missionary Society, to formulate a concrete plan to bring many Buddhists, whom he termed *dao you*, "friends of the *Dao*," to faith in Christ [Gluer, "Encounter," 50]. The "concrete plan" was to found the Christian Mission to Buddhists in Nanjing, on November 1, 1922. Desiring to build on the idea of a "lay brotherhood," much more familiar and congenial to seeking Buddhists than the very foreign Christian church, he established a "suitable apparatus" in the form of a monastery-type institution called Jing Feng Shan (Mountain of the Pure Wind). He stated its purpose:

> We will approach these religious people in sympathetic way, using the points of contact which exists in all the greatest systems of religion, at the same time faithfully laying stress on the uniqueness of Christianity, showing them that their highest aspirations may be fulfilled in Jesus Christ, the all-embracing Word of God, the Eternal Logos, which "shineth in the darkness" and "lighteth every man that cometh into the world." We firmly believe that all that is good and true in every religion and in every culture originates in Christ as the Eternal Logos, through whom all things are made and in whom they have their real life and light [Reichelt, "Buddhism," 161].

With a program that welcomed wandering monks and pilgrims to visit for religious conversation, trained those who made a commitment to Christ, and held retreats and conferences for seekers, the Christian Mission to Buddhists continued at Nanjing for five years. Faced with political turmoil in 1927, it transferred to a site at Dao Feng Shan near Hong Kong. There it continued its apologetic work until about 1950. Ten of thousands of believers—Buddhists, Daoists, and Confucianists—came to converse and to return to their tasks with a new understanding of the Christian faith. By 1949, two hundred twenty Buddhist or Daoist monks had become followers of Christ and been baptized.

Reichelt's greatest importance was probably as a practitioner who developed concrete strategies to bring the gospel to religious seekers. His theory was more ambivalent. On the one hand, he professed to adhere rigorously to the uniqueness of the historical Christ. On the other hand, he was often accused of equating general and special revelation to the extent that Buddhists, who were only influenced by the *logos spermatikos,* could experience the reality of salvation.[71]

One of the clearest expressions of Reichelt's views may be found in his essay "The Johannine Approach," prepared for the third ecumenical missionary conference at Madras in 1938. At the outset, although agreeing with Hendrik Kraemer's point that missionaries must be ready to say no to many features found in non-Christian religions, he affirmed that "grains of truth and beams of light" were present that constituted either "psychological stepping-stones" or even "real points of contact" for communicating Christ.

Reichelt's first appeal was to the prologue of John's Gospel, from which he concluded that Christ's activities in the world cannot be limited to the time when he was present physically. With Justin Martyr, Clement of Alexandria, Origen, and Augustine he wished to promote the *logos spermatikos*:

> This is to say that the Spirit of Christ, which like a grain of seed is lying behind the religious systems in the non-Christian cultures and religions, is sprouting forth, sometimes dimly and sometimes in real beauty and splendour, in poetry, rituals, holy scriptures and external arrangements (cf. Acts 17:23–28).[72]

Starting with this key idea, Reichelt then appealed to the experience of faith recorded in John 1:12–13, interpreting it to mean that those who received this "God-sent Logos-Life and Logos-Light," before the appearance of the incarnate *Logos,* whose arrival is described subsequently in John 1:14, were "born again, they became men of a new order, not only ordinary human beings born of the blood, or of the will of flesh or of the will of man, but born of God."

With the coming of Christ, "we have not only the Logos as a grain of seed or as small beams of light flashing out from the religious systems, but now we have God revealed in His fulness." Reichelt used later verses in John's Gospel, particularly 10:16, 11:52, and 18:37, to reinforce his interpretation. He also referred to Paul's experience at Athens, and to Melchizedek:

Who . . . did not belong to the elect people, and still he was wonderfully prepared and highly advanced as the High Priest of God. Further we may mention the Magi, the wise men from the East. . . . They were probably representatives of the Zoroastrian religion, deeply religious and prepared in a special way by the all-embracing spirit of Christ [ibid.].

Although Reichelt deeply believed that the ultimate aim of his efforts was to lead religious pilgrims to find Christ, he also rejoiced in the wide influence of the many whose lives had been changed short of conversion:

A considerably greater number have not joined the Christian Church but continue to feed upon the words of the New Testament and are bound to Christ our Lord in deep admiration, affection and love. These people have been acting as a vanguard for us in our work. They style themselves spontaneously "Tao-Yu," i.e., "Friends in the Tao" (Logos). Christ is for them the full realization and incarnation of the wonderfully rich Tao-idea, which holds the supreme sway in all the three religions in China (Buddhism included) [ibid.].

This "cosmic experience," he believed, was both an intellectual and religious awakening that brought enlightenment, peace, a sense of integrity, a wide variety of religious practices, moral transformation, and a new commitment to the world and its needs. Never, however, did he equate this with Christian conversion, which opened by faith the door into God's very life. Only the new birth would lead a person into full conformity with Christ [Noren, 28; Reichelt, *Meditation,* 13–16, 49].

With the conviction that it was Christ himself, the hidden *logos,* working within the religious systems of China, Reichelt probed far more deeply than most into the vocabulary that could best be used for presenting the gospel in Chinese to Buddhist devotees. He realized, of course, that many of the words and phrases used then, and even now, in Chinese congregations, in Chinese scripture translations, in hymns, tracts, and in Christian literature were originally borrowed from the Buddhist faith and had become an integral part of the Christian vocabulary. What Reichelt proposed was the use of many terms not previously considered appropriate.

He particularly wished to employ some of the rich expressions that spoke of conversion:

The first step is called *rudao* "to enter into the dao." The second step is called *dedao* "to receive the dao" or "come to a deeper understanding." The third step is to become perfect in the dao *chendao,* which points to a full and eternal salvation. But in order to arrive at this deeper understanding, the natural barrier of human thinking must be broken through. That the Buddhists of the Meditation School signify with the word *po ben can.*

He also suggested the words *kai lian hua,* "the opening of the lotus blossom." He noted as well that:

> The Buddhists have a very fine and useful expression which means . . .
> to return to the original ideals *fu yuan ben lai mian mu* . . . this means to
> return to one's original state, to find oneself again in one's original and
> ideal state, to restore the lost image of God in which men were created.[73]

Reichelt was committed to the principle of "points of contact." They were to be found:

> In the sanctuaries, cultures, literature and everyday life of the Far East
> [where] the wide-awake missionary will catch glimpses of "altars to the
> Unknown God," and he will not have read very far in the writings of
> Confucianism, original Taoism, and Buddhism before he discovers a
> profusion of sayings and concepts which point beyond themselves, and
> which, in an indirect and groping way, treat of the same great and
> fundamental problems of life upon which the New Testament has thrown
> full light [*Meditation,* 57].

Reichelt's sensitive, intuitive nature, combined with an aversion to use words with precision, caused fellow missionaries to believe that, far from merely advocating a point of contact with Buddhism, he was seeking some measure of integration. Hakan Eilert has observed:

> When he presented his views to fellow Christians they became a Buddhist
> Christianity. When they were presented to Chinese monks they became a
> Christian Buddhism [*Boundlessness,* 87].

Critics were known to refer to Dao Feng Shan as "that Buddhist monastery in Shatin."

Reichelt's ambiguity was not merely a personality trait—it was rooted to some degree in the very religious system that he was addressing. A key concept of Mahayana Buddhism was *sunyata,* best translated "emptiness." Intuition was the road to truth. "Language was empty, doctrines were of no use, holy scriptures were discarded." Only in this way could a person have direct contact with ultimate reality. This left little room for Western missionaries who could not divest themselves of Greek and Hebrew forms of thought. The synthesis of propositional revelation and an existential contact with reality he found in Jesus Christ:

> Christianity is not in the first place a fine system of dogmas and masterly
> definitions, although these are also helpful. Christianity is a person, a
> living working person, the unique revealer of God our Father and

Creator, who through this holy, unique life, his precious death and glorious resurrection has obtained eternal redemption for us all [Eilert, 136].

At this point he saw himself in the mystic tradition of Eckhart, Thomas a Kempis, and Bernard of Clairvaux [ibid., 132].

Whether or not this reality was personal constituted a critical question, continually raised in discussions that Reichelt had with Buddhist monks. Although not wishing to jettison any Christian truth, Reichelt carefully stated his position:

Even Christians know that it is not easy to use the word "personal" and "personality" with reference to God. God is *eo ipso* beyond all limitation. But knowing this difficulty, it is easier to remember that *we here use the words with a deeper meaning, thus every limited view is foreign to our thinking.* To some it has become helpful to add a "trans," i.e. *"transpersonal." The implication is then personal without the limitations of personality* [Eilert, 121].

A product of an age that ordered religions on an evolutionary scale from lowest to highest, Reichelt was convinced that the Buddhist reality of cosmic salvation would be caught up in the fullness of the kingdom of God when the aim of mission, world salvation, would be attained. At these times of exhilarating anticipation, distinctions between "cosmic consciousness" and "Christian conversion" were not so clearly marked [ibid., 158–68].

W. A. P. Martin, Timothy Richard, and Karl Reichelt had traveled a long distance in their concepts of and approach to Chinese Buddhism from the Protestant pioneers of mission. Their ideas were not always carefully honed, and, more frequently than not, their gospel in Chinese, the gospel of the *logos* and the *dao,* was not accepted. But in their earnest efforts to empathize with and understand this major religion, they blazed a trail that others may yet follow.

CHAPTER SEVEN

Buddhism in China—
The Contextualization
of a Foreign Faith

The indigenization of Indian Buddhism, a foreign religion in China, constitutes the best possible case study of cultural borrowing on a massive scale. Particularly is this so when the two cultures and the two ideologies that they represented were so totally opposite. No one could have predicted that this outside, "barbarian" religion would fit so well within a Chinese society having such a contradictory set of religious values. A Chinese scholar, Kenneth K. S. Ch'en, has commented:

> Buddhism as a religion in India aimed at individual salvation in Nirvana, a goal attainable by leaving the household life, to use the familiar phrase in Buddhist literature, and entering the houseless stage, which meant the life of celibacy and mendicancy. Upon assuming the monastic robe, the Buddhist monk terminated his ties with family and society, so that his wife became a widow; his children, orphans. When this religion was introduced into China, where filial piety and family life were the dominant features of society, the conflict was joined [*Transformation,* 15].

Chinese Christians have often expressed themselves as surprised by this phenomenon. Why, they ask, has it been possible for Buddhism to be transplanted to China, to gain acceptance by the masses, to spread throughout the country, to maintain itself over the centuries through alternating periods of ascendancy and persecution, and to gain for itself the status as one of the three religions of China, whereas Christianity has always been viewed as a stranger in the land, burdened with the epithet of "foreign"? Certainly, they go on to affirm, if Buddhism has been able to pull this off, it should be possible for the Christian church to do it as well. Seldom, however, have they really expended

133

the time and energy to investigate the matter in sufficient depth to come up with any definitive answers.

Scholars differ as to the nature of the process that enabled Buddhism to feel at home in China. Was it, as affirmed by the noted Chinese academician Hu Shi, an "Indianization of Chinese institutions, thought, art and life," or was it,

Diagram 2

FACTORS INFLUENCING TRANSCULTURAL ACCEPTANCE OR REJECTION OF NEW IDEAS

Factors	Hindering acceptance	Facilitating acceptance
1. Basic premises of source and receptor cultures	Very different	Very similar
2. Attitude of receptors toward their own culture	Very positive	Very negative
3. Attitude of receptors toward source culture	Despised	Respected
4. Openness to new ideas	Closed	Open
5. Pace of change at present	Slow	Rapid
6. Borrowing tradition	Nonexistent	Strong
7. Morale	Proud	Demoralized
8. Self-sufficiency	Strong	Weak
9. Security	Threatened	Stabilized
10. Flexibility	Resistant	Adaptive
11. Advocate	Nonprestigious	Prestigious
12. Perception of relationship of idea to felt need	Unrelated	Related
13. Fit of idea with present ideology	Incompatible	Compatible

Adapted from Charles H. Kraft, "Ideological Factors in Intercultural Communication," *Missiology,* vol. 2, no. 3 (July 1974) 300.

in the words of Kenneth Ch'en, the "Sinicization of Buddhism in China"? Despite its acceptance into the trilogy of Chinese religions, is there still much about Buddhism that would appear to be Indian? Or has it entered so deeply into Chinese life that Chinese values predominate? Interesting as it would be to explore, the various facets of this question are largely theoretical. What matters most is that Buddhism has been accepted in China by the masses and elite alike and that it functions as an indigenous faith.

In examining the reasons that enabled Buddhism to succeed in a venture in which Christianity has largely failed, we must beware of assigning too great an importance to ideological factors alone. Charles Kraft, utilizing some of the anthropological insights of Anthony Wallace, indicates that there are many psychological, social, and cultural factors that influence the adaptability of a given ideology in intercultural communication. He identifies thirteen such factors, which he grades along a continuum between the two poles of "hindering acceptance" or "facilitating acceptance" (see Diagram 2 above).

Even before examining specific historical reasons facilitating the acceptance of Buddhism, we may note that items 1, 9, and 13 are factors that would hinder the import of Buddhism. Apart from item 2, all the remaining items, largely of a nonideological nature, would encourage its adoption. The attitude of the Chinese toward their own culture at the time when the first Buddhist emissaries were coming to China (item 2) was probably neither highly positive nor extremely negative. Although looking for something new, the Chinese were confused and ambiguous about the lasting value of their own culture.

In analyzing the reasons for Buddhist success, I shall use the broad outline proposed by Hu Shi (Hu Shih). He divides this historical process into four periods: (1) mass borrowing; (2) resistance and persecution; (3) domestication; and (4) appropriation. He explains each of these terms:

By mass borrowing I mean not only the simple process of China's taking from India all those things which were either totally absent or weak in the indigenous civilization, but also that mass movement of religious enthusiasm which blindly embraced everything that accompanied the new faith. By resistance and persecution I mean to include those periods of history when the invading culture was openly opposed by Chinese thinkers and persecuted by governmental action. By domestication I mean to include all those tendencies consciously or unconsciously to make the Indian religion, art, thought, and institutions take up more and more Chinese colors, to make them more "at home" in China in order that the Chinese people might feel more at home in them. By appropriation I mean the culminating stage of successful borrowing when the essence, if not the bodily totality, of the borrowed culture was unconsciously "appropriated," recognized by the native population as their own ["Indianization," 223-24].

MASSIVE BORROWING

A long-persisting tradition, accepted by most of the early Protestant and Catholic missionaries, explained the introduction of Buddhism to China as a response of an embassy sent by the Han emperor, Mingdi, in 65 A.D. to Central Asia to enquire about rumors he had heard concerning this faith and to obtain Buddhist scriptures. Although no one takes this story seriously any longer, it was during the later Han dynasty, probably in the initial decades of the first century, that Buddhism entered China. How exactly this happened no one is quite sure. Lines of communication were open along the fabled silk route between India and China. Envoys traveled back and forth between the expanding Han empire and the Kushan empire in northwestern India. This type of contact, an informal context for the exchange of ideas, was undoubtedly heightened by the express attempts of Buddhist emissaries to introduce their faith into China. An early obscure reference, in fact, tells how a non-Chinese king, probably from the state of Yueh-zhi, later absorbed into the Kushan empire, explained the Buddhist sutras to a Chinese official at about the beginning of the Christian era.

Although the seed of Buddhism had been planted in the Middle Kingdom, it was not until about 150 A.D. that it began to root itself deeply and spread widely. This is not surprising in view of the fact that it was not until the later Han dynasty (25–200 A.D.) that China developed into a relatively stable and unified empire.

The coherence of the Han dynasty was promoted by its commitment to the Confucian ideology. The dynastic ruler viewed himself as the "Son of Heaven," using various rituals, astronomy, and the calendar to respond to those natural phenomena, both good and bad, that reflected Heaven's approval or disapproval of his reign. The emperor's mediative role extended from heaven to earth, consequently giving him responsibility for promoting agriculture and establishing programs for land use, advocating equitable taxation, and encouraging trade. He was committed to secure the livelihood of his subjects, and, beyond that, to educate all citizens in the virtue of heaven. His authority resided in the classical writings attributed to Confucius. If these written principles were to prevail, there must be state-supported centers in which they were taught and an official examination system that would screen successful applicants for official positions within this highly unified system.

This coherent worldview has been called "the intellectual response of the new gentry-elite to the problem of rationalizing the new imperial order and their place in it." Such a system helped both the elite and the emperor to resist the rise of feudalism, that disintegrating force that dissolved dynastic structures, and to promote stability. Supernatural sanction held power, position, and prestige in the right balance for all functionaries within society.

This age, then, was not a period in which the newly-imported faith could grow and prosper. As Arthur Wright has observed, "Buddhism could no more have established itself in the Empire of Han than Catholic Christianity could in the prosperous years of the Ch'ing dynasty" [*Buddhism,* 124].[74] In the latter half of the second century, new centers of power among feudal lords on their expanding landed estates, palace intrigues, a large peasant revolt in Sichuan in 184 A.D. to protest a critical agricultural crisis, and continuing strife between the government and warlords ended the Han dynasty, which, with all of its ups and downs, had brought stability to China for two hundred years.

All these troubles had taken a terrible toll of human lives, revealed very clearly in the decline of the population from about 50 million in 156 A.D. to only 7.6 million after 220 A.D. [Orr, 91].

In this period of political disunity, social disintegration, and culture chaos, nonofficial cults, always well-controlled in periods of stability, began to prosper. Daoism, a mystical school of thought, developed into an official religion that founded an independent religious state in northwestern China and gained immense popularity among the masses. Confucianism, the official religion, was greatly weakened; its waning power was insufficient to resist the inroads of heterodox thought into Chinese society.

Such a context of intense suffering was the environment in which Buddhism could begin to spread among the Chinese. It moved along the main routes of internal trade and communication from Dunhuang, Changan, Loyang, Shandung, and Anhui to the lower Yangtse Valley, about Wuchang, and then on to the coast at Jiaozhou. At the beginning of its major growth it does not appear to have influenced major social and intellectual movements within China. This initial period of expansion was among the masses, and the formation of what some have called "gentry Buddhism" came only in the late third and early fourth centuries [Zurcher, 71ff.].

Although Buddhism entered China without any imperial patronage, official government support came at critical junctures:

> In A.D. 65, a community of Buddhist monks was recorded as thriving in the northern part of present Kiangsu province under the patronage of the emperor's brother. A century later, in 166, Buddha was mentioned as a palace god along with the Yellow Emperor and the Taoist saint, Lao Tzu [Yang, *Religion,* 117].

As this quotation indicates, Buddhism was probably regarded initially as a sect of Daoism. Not surprisingly, then, it also depended heavily upon magic, particularly the magical power of its deities, to capture the mind of the Chinese. For the first two or three centuries after its arrival in China, Buddhism spread in its Hinayana form, which "emphasized attainment of magical power to ward off demonic influences which wrought misery in the human world" [ibid., 118].

Another factor in the early spread of the Buddhist faith among the masses of China was its concern to meet practical needs in the name of religion. Wright points out that the first time we really hear of Buddhist worship is when a local Han official, who built a temple in 191 A.D. in northern Jiangsu, an area ravaged by the Yellow Turban peasant revolt, instituted community welfare services designed to ameliorate some of the ills of an impoverished and demoralized peasantry [Wright, 34].

The progress of Buddhism in China was accelerated by a continuing flow of devoted and able foreign missionaries from a number of sending bases around China—India, Sogdiana, Khotan, and Ceylon. A prince from Parthia, named An Shigao in the Chinese transliteration, gave up his throne and came as a missionary to the Middle Kingdom. In the Buddhist center in which he worked at Loyang, he mobilized a number of scholars able to translate important sutras into Chinese. These early efforts were not the most successful. Goodrich comments:

> One group of these scholars included an Indian monk who knew no Chinese, a Parthian monk who could speak both Sanskrit and Chinese, and four or five Chinese scholars. The Indian recited the sutras and explained them orally; the Parthian translated them orally into Chinese as well as he could, and the native Chinese put his translation in writing. . . . many of the earliest translations had to be done two or three times [*Short History*, 61].

By the beginning of the fourth century the barbarian Huns (*Xiongnu*, in Chinese) conquered northern China, and over the next two and a half centuries a succession of non-Chinese peoples controlled that portion of the empire. These conquerors, as has always been the tendency, were sinicized by their Chinese captives except that they preferred Buddhism, at this point still viewed as a foreign religion, to the more traditional Confucian values. The peasants over whom the barbarians ruled, impressed by the power that they thought Buddhism gave to win battles, bring rain, and relieve sickness, converted en masse. In times of great chaos this faith provided more ultimate answers to the harsh realities of survival, suffering, and death.

In northern China the emperors were almost considered the incarnate Buddha with a relationship between state and religion comparable to caesaro-papism of the Roman empire. With this imperial patronage, many missionaries came to northern China during the fourth and fifth century, and, under the direction of the famed translator Kumarajiva they made new efforts at transla-tion that would disentangle the faith from its earlier mixture with Daoist terminology and concepts. So rapidly did Buddhism spread in this area that by early in the fifth century "nine out of ten families worshiped the Buddha" in Changan, the northern capital [Yang, *Religion*, 120].

The story in southern China, where most of the traditional elite had fled after the barbarian conquest, was considerably different. A greater degree of continuity here with the Chinese classical Confucian tradition made it impera-tive for Buddhism to adopt a more rational and intellectual flavor. Within the gentry circles there was much more interest in philosophical and metaphysical problems of how the new faith could relate to the teaching of Confucius and the Daode Jing. Cultured Chinese in the south began to wrestle with the knotty problems of karmic retribution, emptiness, the real nature of the *dao,* and the immortality of the soul.

As in the north, the Buddhist faith penetrated into the household of the emperors, although in this case the rulers were lay patrons of the faith and there was not the same kind of identification with the state. Once Buddhism penetrated the higher classes—officials and cultured gentry alike—it spread widely throughout society. Zurcher has commented:

> Monks come to take part in *ch'ing-t'an* discussions and to visit the imperial court and the estates of aristocratic families as preachers, chaplains, advisors and friends. Priests expound the meaning of Confucian Rites, write commentaries on *Lao-tzu* and *Chang-tzu,* answer questions about literary composition, politics and antiquities, and maintain a regular correspondence with influential laymen in which they express their opinion on doctrinal and other subjects. We find them compiling important biographical, bibliographical and geographical works in which they display the usual encyclopedic knowledge of Chinese literature and history [*Buddhist Conquest,* 75].

From this bustle of intellectual activity in the south was to come Huiyuan who founded the cult of Amitabha (*Amitofu,* in Chinese transliteration), the forerunner of the Pure Land school of Buddhism that was to be viewed so favorably by many Catholic and Protestant missionaries. Through him the Chinese "way" *(dao)* or "life principle" entered the Buddhist faith and helped transform it.

Several philosophical schools of Buddhism prospered in this environment. The foreign faith was no longer merely a "heterodox cult" favored by a few sinicized foreigners and an illiterate and semiliterate population. By late in the sixth century it could be considered the dominant religious tradition in southern China.

Ultimately, the more cultured Buddhism of the south would blend with the faith of the masses seen in the north and present a fully mature, sinicized Buddhism. I have explained the context in which this sinicization was occurring. Times were out of joint; the Chinese, rulers and masses alike, were seeking for a new rationale, a way to understand what was happening. A foreign faith appeared with new answers, many of them transcendental, in contrast with the Confucian ideology, and was able in a flexible manner, easily adaptable to differing conditions in north and south, to provide answers that all levels of Chinese society were able to appropriate for their own needs.

In this historical survey I have noted only one phase of Hu Shi's periodization: the mass movement of faith to Buddha. I now need to analyze in more detail the ideological and social factors that made for the success of Buddhism as they operated during his other three phases: resistance and persecution; domestication; appropriation.

THE WAY OF ACCOMMODATION

One factor that many authors have noted is the strong impact that this symbolic foreign faith must have had on the rather dull and drab life of the Chinese with their very "matter-of-fact" Confucian moral ethic:

Never before had China seen a religion so rich in imagery, so beautiful and captivating in ritualism, and so bold in cosmological and metaphysical speculations. Like a poor beggar suddenly halting before a magnificent storehouse of precious stones of dazzling brilliancy and splendor, China was overwhelmed, boggled, and overjoyed. She begged and borrowed freely from this munificent giver [Hu Shih, 225].

Specifically, it was the religious doctrine of salvation expressed and realized through this imagery that was the most attractive:

In contrast to the shadowy "immortals" of religious Taoism and its psychophysical regimens, Buddhism offered a rich iconography and mythology which would fire even the most tutelary divinities of an earlier time. Buddhism offered gods of great color and warmth, magnificent ceremonies replete with music and symbolism, and spiritual rewards undreamed of in the older religions [Wright, 82].

During the early period of mass borrowing as well as in the later era of domestication, one of the principal tasks facing Indian missionaries and their Chinese collaborators was to put the foreign faith into Chinese. The vocabulary of religious Daoism was a vehicle ready at hand to help them. The Chinese *dao,* for example, was used both for "doctrine" *(dharma)* and for "enlightenment" *(bodhi).* The Daoist term for "immortal" *(xian ren)* was the translation for enlightened one or saint *(arhat).* Nirvana, that slippery term with so many connotations, was translated by the Chinese term *wuwei,* literally meaning "nonactivity." The concept of morality was expressed by the Chinese term *xiaoxun,* "respectful and obedient."

In some translated material the Chinese ethical system demanded subtle changes from the Indian original text. Thus, the phrase "a wife comforts her husband" became "a wife reveres her husband"; "a husband supports his wife" was translated "a husband controls his wife" [Wright, 37].

The most significant way in which Buddhist views were related to the contemporary Chinese environment was by *go-i,* the "matching of concepts." In this method scholars placed groups of Buddhist ideas alongside a group of somewhat similar Chinese ideas—for example, the *wuchang* or five relationships with the five precepts of Buddhism, and the four elements of

Buddhism with the five Chinese elements. The Buddhist precepts, for example, are: do not kill, steal, commit adultery, lie, or drink intoxicating beverages. The Confucian virtues are: human-heartedness, righteousness, propriety, knowledge, and trust.[75]

However the task was done, it was not easy. A statement attributed to the famous translator Kumarajiva says it all: "Translating Sanskrit into Chinese is like feeding a man with rice chewed by another; it is not merely tasteless, it is nauseating as well" [Goodrich, 90]. This difficulty, combined with the growing desire to avoid the potential syncretism of using the vocabulary of the Daoists, not really their friends, caused later Buddhist scholars to replace translation with transliteration of Sanskrit sounds into Chinese. The Chinese word for "Buddha," for example, is *Futo*, which corresponds well in sound and meaning to the Sanskrit term.

For Buddhism to become at home, much more was necessary than to enter China at a time of crisis with an ornate symbolism and a vocabulary so adapted to Daoism that it could be considered a sect of that faith. The process of accommodation and appropriation had to deal with matters of ethics, politics, economics, education, and literature, all of which closely intersected with religion. This kind of total accommodation set the stage, as it were, for domestication and appropriation on the religious, moral, and philosophical levels.

RESISTANCE AND ADAPTATION

Ethical Issues

In many of the spheres in which it was relating to Chinese life, the foreign religion was confronting resistance and persecution. One of the most serious ethical accusations leveled against it was that it violated the precepts of filial piety. Buddhist monks were criticized for having no offspring and also for cutting their hair, making it impossible in Confucian fashion to return their bodies to their ancestors unharmed, intact. They usually defended themselves by appealing to the classics, which spoke of heroes who had mutilated their bodies for humanitarian purposes and even Confucius had praised some who had no children.[76]

Most frequently, Buddhist leaders went on the attack to present a positive image of their support for filial piety. They emphasized the sutra that told the tale of Shanzi, a Buddhist savior (bodhisattva), who, seeing a blind couple needing help, was born as their son and served them faithfully. By the time of the Sung dynasty Shanzi was proclaimed one of the twenty-four models of piety. Another famous story tells of Mulien, who, following his enlightenment, was concerned for his mother who had been reborn as a hungry ghost. With the help of the Buddha, he prepared sumptuous offerings on the fifteenth day of the seventh month of the lunar calendar for monks "of the ten quarters" (that is, everywhere) in behalf of present and deceased parents for seven generations back. Called Yulanpen, this feast was intended specifically to save or rescue parents and ancestors.

During the Tang dynasty, Zeng Mi, a leader in the Chan sect, wrote a commentary called the *Yulanpen Jing*. With little regard for history, he claimed that Gautama had left home because he wished to repay the love and affection of his parents. Zeng Mi affirmed that Buddhism, like Confucianism, regarded filial piety as the most important virtue. Other writers went further, stating that in fact the Buddhist concept of filial piety was better than the Confucianist because its ultimate purpose was to convert parents to Buddhism so that they might enjoy the benefits of a future life. This "great filial piety," *daxiao,* as they called it, could bring salvation to all living creatures and significantly influence the whole world.

Over the centuries, Buddhist leaders adopted the same attitude to the ancestral cult. The monks were careful to actively promote special memorial services in the monastaries in behalf of the deceased imperial ancestors. And they participated openly in memorial services for their own ancestors. They developed annual and triennial feasts that corresponded to the Confucian observance of *xiaoxiang* and *daxiang* (the small and big incense or sacrifice). They inaugurated the "seven-seven feast" (seventh day of the seventh month), designed to intercede for souls in the immediate state; because of their bad karma, they might be consigned to be reborn in hell.

Political Barriers

The political adjustment of Buddhism to every level of the Chinese state was at once the most difficult arena in which to indigenize and also the key enabling it to escape the opprobrium of a "foreign" faith. Differences between India and China were profound. In India the Buddhist *sangha* (order) was a community not responsible to the authority of the state. Members of the order had withdrawn from society and were, in effect, a law unto themselves. No outside law really applied to them. They need not revere the ruler or even render homage to him. More usually, it was the ruler who deferred to the monks. Often the highest ideal for a ruler in the Indian subcontinent, then and now, was to abandon imperial power and prestige for the ascetic and self-denying life of a monk.

China could hardly have been more different. It had an emperor whose power and authority extended to all persons and every part of the empire. The concept of *li* demanded that order, stability, and harmony within the empire could come only as each person and institution fulfilled their specific function within society. No group was exempt from submitting to or rendering homage to imperial rule.

This cultural difference between India and China precipitated an intense struggle between the *sangha* and Chinese officialdom that lasted several hundred years and ended only with the submission of the *sangha* to regulations imposed by the government. Without its coming to terms with Chinese law and giving up the types of freedom it had known in India, Buddhism would never have been indigenized in China.

What precisely were the tension points between the *sangha* and Chinese officials? First, the monks often refused to participate in rites of reverence for the emperor. Over a period of time they resisted less at this level. The state insisted that monks must register with it, that it was in its power to approve or disapprove of the ordination of new monks, and that it was its prerogative to defrock monks who committed certain offenses. Prominent items in this Tang code of "sins" were items such as healing, divination, use of weird books, incantations, riding on horses, marriage, quarreling while intoxicated, forming questionable cliques, going from door to door teaching, and presenting religious goods to government officials.

During this period when Buddhism was accommodating itself to Chinese life, the government was progressively asserting its bureaucratic control over the *sangha*. A specific government organ was established to deal with *sangha* affairs and continued over the centuries, although with a change in its name and the precise nature of its organization. In China there has really never been the principle of separation of church and state. Not surprisingly then, the "Buddhist monastic community became a Chinese religious organization, subject to the jurisdiction of the imperial bureaucracy" [Ch'en, 124].

Economic Integration

Although frequently criticized for their withdrawal from society, Buddhist monks and monasteries became an integral part of the Chinese economy. Very soon after their arrival in China, they began to accumulate large landholdings, whether by purchase, private donation, or as a gift from the state. Free from taxation, these temple lands, cultivated by temple slaves, tenant farmers, novices, and probationers, were important sources of income for the new religion. Unlike large, private landowners whose land was divided when the head of the household died, the monasteries were able to increase substantially the size of their holdings. Freedom from taxation was often an incentive for rich landowners to create "merit cloisters," an eighth-century version of a "dummy organization," enabling them to donate large plots of land to monasteries on which they need not pay taxes, but from which they still profited tremendously.

Monasteries often became involved in certain kinds of industrial enterprises such as running water-powered grinding mills. Millers working for the monasteries as tenant farmers rented the mills from them, and whatever excess of flour there might be beyond the quotas set by the monks they sold for profit on the open market. Monasteries also ran oil presses for cooking and lighting oil. They established what was called an "inexhaustible treasury," kept full by freewill contributions, which served as a bank of surplus items—seedlings, silk, and so forth. These were lent out at interest, which was then reinvested to produce more interest. No wonder that Buddhist monasteries were often viewed in the same way as were the nobility and the rich and powerful families of the empire.

Educational Efforts

During the Tang dynasty, when Buddhism reached the height of its impact on Chinese life, it was the dominant faith at all levels of society. Its educational process was obviously very effective to have reached so many diversified groups of persons. Some of this influence came informally, through the life and work of well-known literary figures such as Bo Juyi (772–846). The monasteries were favorite places of recluse for poets, and they made extensive use of Buddhist technical terms, doctrines, practices, and allusions to Buddhist scriptures to create a favorable impression.

In a more intentional fashion, the *sangha* had developed varied means of popularizing the sutras so as to make their teachings accessible to all levels of society. A principal figure in this process was the *jingshi,* master lecturer, who chanted the sutras from a high platform. If there were many unlettered listeners, a *dujiang,* assistant lecturer, after the master had completed his recitation, explained in the vernacular what the lecture meant. At the end of the lecture it was customary for the assistant to question the master on various points that he had made.

During the Sui and Tang dynasties, the most popular of the scripture expositors was a class known as the *changdaoshi,* whose lectures on the law were cast in the form of stories and parables. With an emphasis that could be both profound and simple, these teachers spoke to the specific needs of the audience. One type of lecturer, referred to as *sujiangseng,* exegeted Buddhist texts in much more detail than others, who tended to preach topically.

An unusually popular type of lecture was known as *bianwen* (reformed or changed literary form) or *bianxiang* (changed image), which involved the use of stories, parables, anecdotes, miraculous tales, and other means to present abstract truth as word pictures. Used by expert practitioners, these popular lecture formats attracted great multitudes into the temples for religious instruction.

As a part of their educational work, Buddhist functionaries organized religious festivals and drew the Chinese together with a sense of having one common religious faith. Once a measure of peace was restored between the *sangha* and the state, Buddhist monks entered deeply into the imperial cult, celebrating in the monasteries the imperial birthdays and memorial services for deceased emperors. They aggressively promoted the festivals that over the years had become uniquely Buddhistic: the lantern festival in the middle of the first lunar month, the birthday of the Buddha, and all-souls' feast on the fifteenth day of the seventh month. In conjunction with these festive days, certain monks, skilled in magic, mesmerized the masses with their art.

Buddhist leaders were active in forming many types of societies, some more specifically religious, but many to perform charitable activities. The Buddhist doctrine of compassion was based on the Mahayana concept that all living things have the Buddha-nature within and must be protected. As a result they established hospitals, dug wells, built bridges, helped the aged, infirm, and poor, and provided for weary travelers by maintaining hostels along well-used roads.

DOMESTICATION AND APPROPRIATION OF BUDDHISM

It must be emphasized that throughout the period of its domestication in China, Chinese Buddhism was never merely an extension of Indian ideas. Reinterpretation and elaboration of the original forms and meanings took place continually to help the new faith fit uniquely within a new context. Avalokitesvara, an Indian male savior (bodhisattva), became Guanyin, the goddess of mercy, in China. Maitreya, the coming Buddha, but now living in Tushita heaven, became the center of a mystic cult in China and eventually by the thirteenth century was portrayed as the fat, laughing Buddha to be found in most Buddhist temples. The Indian stupa evolved into the Chinese pagoda.

The art forms accompanying and facilitating the spread of Buddhism in China were also indigenized. Hu Shi comments:

> Music, painting, architecture, and the other fine arts which came from India together with the Buddhist religion were also subject to processes of domestication. The reciting and sing-songing of Sanskrit text have become entirely Sinicized; and Indian melodies have been made vehicles of Chinese songs in which their Indian origins are often forgotten. In painting, as in sculpture, the domestication went so far that later Buddhist paintings are essentially Chinese and differ radically from the early Buddhist art and also from the later artistic development in India herself ["Indianization," 232–33].

Pure Land Buddhism, emphasizing faith in Amitabha, and Chan, which advocated sudden enlightenment, were not Indian sects transplanted intact into China; rather they developed as a response to the Chinese context with its concern for simplicity, directness, and practicality. Schools of thought in India such as Vihnanavada, which were highly introspective and endlessly split hairs over obtuse doctrines, were discarded rather than digested by the Chinese.

The crosscultural impact was not unilateral. Not only were Indian concepts changed—they also gave new meaning to Chinese ideas. Zurcher has noted:

> Buddhism not only changed the morally indifferent Way of Nature [the Chinese idea of the *"dao"*] into an instrument of supra-mundane impersonal Justice . . . resulting from and consequently dependent on man's individual course of action and thought . . . but also brought this concept to its logical conclusion by introducing the dogma of rebirth, or as

the Chinese generally interpreted it, the "immortality of the soul" [*Buddhist Conquest,* 73].

The *sangha* retained much of its Indian form in China, but its meaning changed drastically. No longer a religious community of prestige that could assert its independence from all outside control as in India, it was never able in China to escape state control. Its role in society was far more similar to that of powerful landlords and aristocratic families than to that of an Indian mystical order of faith and meditation.

From its arrival in China until the time of its greatest success in the Tang dynasty, Buddhism had accommodated itself to a context of philosophic and religious Daoism that was basically naturalistic and nihilistic, as well as to a Confucianism that professed no interest in and no need for the supernatural. It moved into a vacuum, relating to whatever terms and concepts could carry, if only partially, its new ideas. It brought a transcendent hope to a struggling, suffering society, furnishing for it a point of revitalization or reintegration.

During the Sung dynasty (960–1279), Chinese philosophers began to reinterpret the Confucian classics in such a way as to find many hidden metaphysical concepts that they correlated with Buddhist teachings to produce neo-Confucianism. The emphasis on meditation and enlightenment unique to Chan Buddhism, for example, was appropriated by competing schools of Sung philosophers to produce either a gradual or immediate neo-Confucian enlightenment. The depth of the interpenetration of the two systems of thought is seen by the old question raised by many scholars: Is this ultimately the absorption of Indian ideas into a Chinese mold, or is it a reassertion of Indian ideas that refused to die? Depending on what choice of data is made, the evidence can go in either direction. Creel notes, for example:

We find them echoing the Buddhist idea that the universe is ceaselessly destroyed and recreated. This is interpreted in Chinese terms, however, as a function of the operation of the *yin* and *yang,* the five forces, mystic numerology, and the diagrams which are the basis of the *Book of Changes* [*Chinese Thought,* 167].

Hu Shi, however, comments:

It is in the peculiar exaltation of Divine Reason and supression of human desire that we see the best evidence of the deepening of the influence of the Indian religion through its secularization ["Indianization," 244].

From his viewpoint the secularization of Buddhism through neo-Confucianism helped to extend its appeal to the more intellectual elite who might not have been attracted to the popular faith of the masses [ibid., 242–43].

Again, this question does not need to be answered definitively. Either way, the outside faith has penetrated deeply into the warp and woof of Chinese society, not losing its identity entirely but mutually reinforcing and challenging the culture. Indigenization is not to identify totally, for this would be absorption, not accommodation. The Indian thought is there and will never totally disappear. But because it has so related itself to every facet of Chinese life and has spoken so tellingly to the deepest needs and inspirations of the Chinese, it is not called a "foreign faith."

SUCCESS WHERE OTHERS FAILED

In summary, then, what are the factors that enabled a "foreign faith" to become one of the three religions of China?

1. A relatively easy access route by land into China and zealous missionaries able to relate well to Chinese life within the overarching Asian milieu. Asians were evangelizing Asians.

2. A Han China desperately needing revitalization and open to new ideas.

3. An available and acceptable role to be a "sect of Daoism," asserting no exclusive claims.

4. A "people movement to Buddha" of such mass proportion that the faith gained hold with minimal social dislocation.

5. A faith perceived by the Chinese as adequate to deal with incredible human misery and suffering. Part of this, of course, meant catering to Chinese religious views in what even non-Christians would label syncretism.

6. No external power base to pose as a threat to the Chinese state.

7. A flexible methodology adequate to exploit differing opportunities in northern and southern China.

8. Penetration of Chinese life at all levels—linguistically, economically, religiously, socially, politically, artistically, and educationally—to overcome resistance and persecution and gain popular favor. Submitting to the state politically was of crucial importance.

None of these several advantages were available to the same degree to the emissaries of the Christian faith. Apart from the Nestorians in the seventh century, they came by the sea route—distances were great, communication with the home base was poor, they were not Asians, it was the "ocean faith" *(yang jiao)* or foreign faith. Nineteenth-century China was crumbling from outside pressures, but internally there was an ideological cohesiveness that resisted new ideas. Christianity was an exclusive faith. In its largely successful attempts to be orthodox, it was overrigid and could mount no aggressive ideological assault on the bulwarks of disbelief.

For the most part, with all its attempts to indigenize linguistically, the Christian faith was never perceived by most of the Chinese as doing anything for them that their own three religions could not do. The spoken and written gospel in Chinese did not theologically address issues of human misery and suffering, although Protestants and Catholics did many compassionate works of mercy. With a Damoclean sword overshadowing their every move, nineteenth-century missionaries operated from a power base and with an

Protestants

arrogant assertion of their universal rights that threatened the very existence of the Chinese state. Methodologically, with some exceptions, nineteenth-century missionaries showed little "give and take." They were largely inflexible. Only in the religious and educational arenas did they really penetrate Chinese life.

Apart from a few missionaries who speculated on its possibilities, "mass conversion" was out of the question. Missionaries promoted a highly individualistic, narrowly pietistic brand of Christianity. To move too fast, they thought, would only be to produce multitudes of "rice Christians," not grounded in the faith.

Possibly, at least for Protestant missionaries, their time of contact with China was not long enough. Now that the church in China has lost its external power base and source of supplies; now that it is Asians preaching to Asians; now that it is modeling as well as proclaiming a unique message of God's power for its society; now that the masses as well as many elite may be losing their faith in the Marxist ideology; now that it is coming to terms with the state; now that its very beleaguered presence requires it to be a Chinese church not turned in on itself but relating to all levels of life—there is for the first time a real hope that the gospel may be both indigenized and contextualized in China. With apparently millions believing in Jesus Christ in a people movement, the church may be entering a period of "mass conversion." This will undoubtedly bring even more resistance and persecution. But this is the path to domestication and appropriation.

Christianity was not the only religion that failed to be sinicized; Islam, Judaism, and Manicheism met the same fate. Several reasons are generally cited for the failure of Islam. First, the Muslims tended to make their way among the minority Hui peoples, who were discriminated against by the majority Han. Secondly, apart from their traders, they entered China by invasion and violence. This did not commend them as religious emissaries to the peace-loving Chinese. Thirdly, in common with Christianity, they refused to blend their faith with the Chinese religions. They preserved their purity and missed the chance to evangelize. The present government of China, however, views Islam as more indigenous than Christianity because it took root before the Chinese subdued the local tribes and asserted control over the frontier. The Islamic "foreign connection" has been far less imperialistic in recent centuries than that of the supporters of Christianity, a fact not forgotten by leaders of the People's Republic of China.

Buddhism related well to all levels of the Chinese population—Islam largely to the Hui, a peripheral group. The Christian movement also appealed to a marginal group people, a periphery. The initial Protestant thrust was along the coast to the five treaty ports, the littoral, where it attracted many "reformer" types whose influence never spread much farther. The core of Chinese culture, the heart of its legitimation, was in the hinterland, and the leaders there were not significantly touched, at least religiously, by the Christian faith.[77] Christians, then, much like Muslims, worked with a minority segment of Chinese life and could not penetrate the whole of society as did Buddhism.

Manicheism, introduced into China in the seventh century by Persians, did not adjust well to the Chinese environment. Manichean communities, largely limited during the twelfth century to several small centers in southeastern China, were extremely clannish. Followers of this religion differed significantly from the general Chinese populace in several ways: distinctive dress, teetotalism, clandestine meetings, a Persian-type worldview with brightness and darkness viewed as opposites, and refusal to worship either Buddha or their own ancestors. Their appeal was very limited and made no lasting impact on any segment of Chinese society [Li, 372].

Although the oral tradition passed down by the Kaifeng Jewish community indicates that its ancestors arrived in China as early as the Zhou dynasty, the earliest written records date from the eighth and ninth centuries. For a period of nearly seven or eight hundred years, the small Jewish colony, centered about Kaifeng, coexisted within the vast sea of its Chinese environment. Not an aggressive religion seeking to evangelize its neighbors, its members were gradually absorbed into Chinese life and, by the end of the fifteenth century, had lost any sense of strong Jewish identity and cohesiveness. Chinese Jews continued to live in Kaifeng, and until World War II were visited both by Christian missionaries as well as by interested Jewish friends.

Over the centuries most of the Jewish residents in Kaifeng resisted assimilation to Chinese life, developing a cohesive community experience that sought to preserve their ancient heritage. The loss by marriage of Jewish girls to Chinese life was balanced by the absorption into the community of Chinese brides for Jewish young men. The Jewish determination to preserve its own way of life was made easier by the tolerant Chinese who neither tried to "grind them down or . . . forcibly segregate them" [Pollak, 343].

Over the years, however, as this determination waned, as intermarriage increased, and as Jewish intellectuals were confucianized by attaining academic degrees and civil office, the die was cast and the community commenced its long decline to dissolution. Unlike Christianity, Islam, or Buddhism, which sought to increase their memberships, Judaism had no local reservoir from which to draw and maintain its identity. Intentionally separate from Chinese life over many centuries, it finally took the course of least resistance and succumbed to its friendly environment.

CHAPTER EIGHT

New Deities and Demons—
Taiping Christianity

It was a simple worship service held outdoors on a flat piece of land. Most of those present were dressed in military attire, summoned to the gathering by a trumpet blast. The captain was in charge, and he commanded one of the men to read from a scripture passage in Leviticus. This done, the group joined in a hymn of praise that was not exceptional in its content:

Praise God, the Holy Father of Heaven—the only true Spirit.
Praise the Holy Son, the Saviour of the world—the only true Spirit.
Praise the Three Persons, united in one—the only true Spirit.
The truth is proclaimed to us, the way is everywhere open.
The Heavenly Father's flood-like grace, immense and illimitable,
Spared not the Imperial Son, but sent Him down to mortal regions;
When men know this glory, the Heavenly road is open.
When men repent, their spirit shall ascend to Heaven.

Following the singing of this ode, the captain read a prayer addressed not only to God, the Heavenly Sir, but also to the Holy Mother—not Mary but God's wife! When the captain had finished reading the prayer, the paper on which it was written was burned. The concluding portion of the prayer asked the Father to forgive sins, and then, almost in the same breath, exclaimed, "We obey the Heavenly decree to slaughter the fiends." With this note of revenge all the worshipers sprang to their feet, waved their swords, and shouted loudly, "Kill the fiends!"[78]

For Taiping Christianity there were myriads upon myriads of fiends and demons in the land. Fortunately, however, there were new divine resources sufficient to assure victory. Among these were God's wife, the elder brother of Jesus, the Holy Spirit incarnate in one of their leaders, and God the Father repeatedly coming to earth to take direct charge of events. Our imaginary space visitor (chap. 1, above), confused by his several visits to earth to assess the

Christian scene, would have been puzzled by Taiping Christianity. It too, however, was in the line of Christian continuity—the first really indigenous effort to proclaim the gospel in Chinese.

TAIPING ORIGINS

This brand of Chinese Christianity developed in its own unique historical context. Southern China in the late 1840s was in a state of economic, social, and political turmoil. The drainage of silver to pay for the import of opium, and new lines of trade and commerce developing after the treaties of 1842 to 1844, which opened up new ports along the coast to the north of Canton, badly upset the local economy and put many peasants out of work. A severe famine brought on by natural disasters, combined with the oppression of the local populace by landlords and tax collectors, added to the financial burden of the people, causing many to join local marauding gangs of bandits. When local authorities sought to restore order, at the behest of the Manchu government, the unrest took a nasty antidynastic turn. As in the declining years of the later Han dynasty, the times were ripe for a new religion, an ideology that would give unity to the many disparate elements of society, and enable them to accomplish their political, economic, and social goals.

The man who was to head up the Taiping movement, the ideology that would move into this vacuum, was Hong Xiuquan, a Hakka born in southern China in 1814. In common with many aspiring young men of his generation, he sought to be qualified for government position by passing the civil service examinations. Three times he went to Canton to face this ordeal, and three times he failed, much to his own chagrin and to the disappointment of family and friends from his small village.

It was probably during the first of these visits to Canton that he happened to acquire a selection of nine Christian tracts written by Liang Afa. As recounted above (chap. 5), Liang was a Chinese evangelist who had been converted under the ministry of William Milne, a Protestant missionary serving with the London Missionary Society.[79] Usually referred to as the first Chinese convert from China proper, Liang worked as a printer and itinerant, free-lance preacher/evangelist available to help various mission works in Malacca, Canton, Macao, and Hong Kong.

As a result of severe pressure and fatigue from preparing for and failing his first examination, Hong Xiuquan suffered a nervous breakdown. While in bed for a period of forty days, he had a vision in which he was carried to heaven where he was confronted by an old man who identified himself as the creator. The command that this old man gave to him was to exterminate evil demons, for which purpose he was presented with a large sword. In his vision he saw Confucius and heard him being severely rebuked for his failure to keep human beings from worshiping demons. He also saw another prominent person, referred to as Elder Brother, who exhorted him to be zealous in killing demons.

Following this period of illness, which occurred in 1837, Hong recovered and spent the next six years teaching school either near or in his native village. In 1843, his cousin Li borrowed the tracts, and, in returning them, remarked on their unusual contents, motivating Hong to study them intensively for the first time in the six years they had been in his possession. As he pondered the meaning of this material, he was amazed! The interpretation of the visions he had experienced was now clear—the old man was God, the elder brother was Jesus, and the demons referred to were the multitude of idols that the Chinese people worshiped. Furthermore, it seemed apparent that God had directly given Hong a life mission—exterminate idols in all the land and lead the Chinese masses to believe in Jesus.

Hong believed this vision, and he and his cousin professed their faith by baptizing each other. As he began to proclaim this new message, several others were converted, among whom were two distant cousins, Hong Rengan and Feng Yunshan. They became iconoclastic religious zealots, destroying idols, throwing out ancestral tablets, and abandoning their long-professed Buddhist religious rites. Feng moved to a nearby area, commenced preaching to all who would listen, and won several thousand converts, largely among the Hakka people. He soon organized them into what was called the "God-worshipers" society (*Bai Shangdi Hui*).

About this time Hong heard that there was a foreigner in Canton preaching the doctrine he had espoused. He went with Rengan to learn more. Here he found an eccentric Baptist missionary, Issachar J. Roberts, with whom he spent about two months expanding his knowledge of the Christian faith. Very possibly, Hong, whose primary language was Hakka, and Roberts, who spoke only Cantonese, could not communicate directly with each other ["Letter from J.L. Holmes, Shanghai, June 29, 1860," *The Commission*, 5 (Nov. 1860) 142].

Hong's learning was probably mediated through some of Roberts' helpers, who quickly became jealous of his unusual experience. When Hong asked for baptism, one of these assistants suggested that he request Roberts to give him some financial help, knowing full well that this would cause Roberts to doubt his motivation and deny him baptism [Hamberg, 31–32].

Following this disappointing experience with Roberts in Canton, Hong Xiuquan returned home. He soon left on another tour to Guangxi to continue the task of preaching, to Chinese and to Miao tribes. He was a man of high standards, strict in regard to his own conduct and demanding of others. To urge others to believe in Jesus and to help them destroy their false idols became an obsession with him. He often used to say:

Those who believe not in the true doctrine of God and Jesus, though they be old acquaintances, are still no friends of mine, but they are demons. On the other hand, all who believe in the doctrine of God and Jesus, are true brethren of Heaven and true friends. If they do not believe my words, every one must go his own way; I cannot bring them into heaven, and they shall not draw me to hell. If my own parents, my wife and children, do not believe, I cannot feel united with them, how much less with other friends! Only the heavenly friendship is true, all other is false. A short happiness is not a real one; only eternal happiness can be called real. What others gain, they cannot impart to me; and what I gain, I cannot share with them. I only desire that very many may enter into heaven, and grieve that they should go to hell. Therefore I cannot withhold preaching to them the true doctrine [Hamberg, 42].

To apprehensive authorities, the society led by Feng and Hong appeared purely religious, not political, but its violent inconoclasm disturbed them. Within a relatively short period of time, however, the movement took on an antidynastic stance in order to deal with the many and varied problems faced by the people. With this broadening of the purpose of the "God-worshippers," the organizational structure was expanded to include others besides Hong's friends or relatives, or even those who worshiped God. Efforts were made to form and equip an army. A military code was drawn up with strict religious and moral observances. The leaders required participants to sell their property to help buy and make arms. Two beliefs motivated the soldiers: first, all who died fighting for the cause would go to heaven; secondly, there would be repeated "descents" or further revelations from heaven, directly from God or Jesus, when things went bad militarily and special help was required.

These expanded activities and the coming of more devotees, many from questionable backgrounds in secret societies, to learn the faith and to be trained for fighting led to conflict with the Manchu forces, the imperialists. The first major battle and Taiping victory came in January 1851, after which Hong officially took the title of *Tian Wang* (Heavenly King) and referred to his movement as *Taiping tianguo* (Heavenly Kingdom of Great Peace). Any who joined, such as members of the Triad Society, had to pledge loyalty to the Heavenly King and follow the instructions and rules of his kingdom.

The growing movement, now a powerful magnet for anyone with religious, economic, or political complaints, moved out from its original base in Guangxi province and took Nanjing, from which it moved both north and east to conquer huge sections of central China.

Nanjing became the rebel capital, and to it came four official visits (two English, one French, one American) by foreign governments contemplating official recognition. Most visitors were impressed by the moral vigor, high ideals, and Christian beliefs of the Taipings, but they were repulsed by their demands for total subservience—so similar to what they had experienced from the Qing dynasty before the Opium War. An unsuccessful attempt was made to take Beijing, but the rebels were able to consolidate their position up and down the Yangtze River. From 1856 until 1863 the Taipings, increasingly plagued by internal dissension, outside suspicions about the purity of their Christian profession, disregard for life and property, and poor relationships with foreign powers whose support they desperately needed (they tended to disrupt trade wherever they went because they would not deal with opium), were on the defensive militarily. Eventually, in 1864, they were defeated by a combination of Chinese and Western forces under Li Hongzhang, Zeng Guofan, and Charles Gordon (an English officer nicknamed "Chinese" Gordon).

The demise of the Taiping movement can be traced to its failure to obtain a working alliance with the numerous anti-Manchu societies, whose members were disappointed because it vigorously opposed idol worship and was determined to create a new kingdom rather than restore the Ming dynasty. Even more critical was the fact that the Taipings were not able to obtain support from Western powers. Western governments, particularly that of England and America, adopted a neutral stance at first, realizing that their treaty privileges were contingent upon the continued existence of the Manchu dynasty. This neutrality changed to opposition when it became apparent that the Taipings would not be successful in their efforts to establish a new dynasty.

THE TAIPING CONSTITUTION

The nature of the Christian faith espoused by the Taipings can be gleaned in part from the main features of the constitution that they adopted:

1. A type of primitive communism was introduced to replace the private ownership of land and other property. The Taipings believed that land should be distributed equitably, that it did not really belong to the recipient, and that any surplus produce should be contributed to a public storehouse. Unsettled conditions wherever the rebels went made it difficult for them to implement this policy uniformly.

2. The military and civil administration was unified according to ancient prescriptions in the Rites of Zhou. A group consisting of 13,156 families was ruled over by a commander who was responsible for five divisions, each of which had five brigades. Under each brigade commander were five captains, each of them having four master sergeants. Each master sergeant was in charge of five corporals who were responsible for four soldiers each. Military leaders were also civil rulers:

> Every twenty-five families formed a basic social unit, each with a public storehouse and a church under the charge of the master sergeant. He administered the civil, educational, religious, financial, and judicial matters of his twenty-five families and took charge of their litigations, marriages, and funerals [I. Hsü, *Modern China,* 285].

Church attendance was required every day for the children of the twenty-five families. The master sergeant was in charge of these services, as well as of the worship service on Sunday.

3. The Taipings had strict moral requirements. "Opium smoking, the use of tobacco and wine, prostitution, foot-binding, the sale of slaves, gambling and polygamy were all forbidden" [ibid., 284]. Special catechetical instruction was provided to accomplish this ambitious goal. Instructors prepared a "Three-Character Classic," comprised of 478 sentences of three characters each,

embodying Hong's central teaching. This work, along with "Odes for Youth," was prepared in a type of colloquial language that was a prototype of the later literature to come from the literary revolution of the 1920s. The Taipings also proposed an alternative civil service examination system, again written in a vernacular style—thus easier and open to many more applicants—based not on the Chinese classics, but on the Bible, Christian tracts, and the teaching of the Taiping rebels.

4. The Heavenly Kingdom of Peace wrought a social revolution. Most notable was that men and women were considered equal. Women were military officers and had responsible positions in the civil administration as well. Special efforts were made to care for the "disabled, the sick, the widowed, and the orphaned."[80]

In their pietistic morality, use of the Bible, church attendance, and compassion toward the needy within society, the Taipings were undoubtedly seeking to establish a type of theocracy. All these topics are worthy of extensive investigation, but the primary concern of this book is to see more precisely the nature of their gospel in Chinese.

SOURCES OF TAIPING IDEOLOGY

Of prime importance among the sources of the Taiping ideology was the material Hong received in Canton, *Quanshi liangyan* ["good words for exhorting the age"], given to him by Edwin Stevens, an American missionary working with the American Board of Commissioners for Foreign Missions. Selected from many portions of both the Old and New Testament, this material was a running commentary on diverse passages and did not give a sustained treatment of any one biblical topic. The omissions in his theology for which Hong has often been criticized may have derived from lacunae in this literature, his introduction to Christianity. He probably attached an almost magical quality to it.

Equally significant to the Heavenly Kingdom was the Christian Bible translated by Gutzlaff. Many critics have been so intrigued with the Taiping use of indigenous Chinese materials that they have overlooked the authority that the Taipings attached to the scriptures. Thomas Meadows analyzed Hong's treatment of Confucian texts when compared with the Bible:

> Wherever Hong detects a clash between the Four Books and the Five Classics on one hand, and the Old and New Testament on the other, he either by a re-interpretation makes the former conform to the latter, or declares them in so far wrong. The Bible is his highest standard [*The Chinese,* 420]

During the time he was in Canton being instructed by Roberts, Hong attended Bible class two hours daily, probably memorizing the more important sections being taught. He was most impressed with passages dealing with idolatry, as well as with Robert's firm attitude on this subject. "Hong even forbade his followers to write *pai*, 'to worship,' as translated by Roberts, on their visiting cards, because 'I was taught at Canton that it was wrong' " [Yuan, "Rev. I.J. Roberts," 420].

Some have speculated that Hong was also influenced, particularly in the harshness of his morality, by the Constitution of Roberts's church, the Uettung Baptist Church of Canton. It included the following provisions:

6. He who smokes opium shall be turned out of the church.

7. He who tells falsehoods should be excluded from the church.

8. He who gambles should be excluded from the church.

10. The disciples of Jesus should daily read the Scriptures and pray to God.

11. He who trades or works on the Lord's day should be excluded from the church [ibid.]

Hong was undoubtedly selective in what he took from Roberts. The church Constitution, if indeed it did influence him, contained many statements about the nature of the Godhead. These truths apparently were considered of less importance to Hong than the alleged direct revelation he received from God on his first visit to heaven.

Hong's understanding of the Christian faith was augmented by continuing contact with Protestant missionaries who were deeply concerned about the purity of the movement. Missionaries, as already noted, were prolific in their writing, and by this time had produced nearly three hundred tracts or booklets that had been distributed widely in many of the Chinese languages. By 1850 they had available to them the revised translation of the Bible prepared by Karl Gutzlaff and Walter Medhurst. During the early 1860s several missionaries, including Roberts, personally visited the Heavenly King or his fellow leaders, but by this time any effort to influence their Christian beliefs was to little avail.

Chinese missionaries affiliated with Gutzlaff's Chinese Christian Union, an ill-fated attempt to evangelize inland China by "native" evangelists, probably had contact with rank and file members of the Taiping movement. Upon the disbanding of the union, they may have become lower-level leaders with some opportunity of contributing to the Taiping understanding of Christianity.

Another Christian source for the Taiping movement was Hong Rengan, the Taiping king's cousin, although his influence, coming in the late 1850s, did not have the sustained impact that had been anticipated. Rengan had had much more extensive contact with many Protestant missionaries (Legge, Medhurst, Joseph Edkins, William Muirhead, Griffith John, E.C. Bridgman, Hamburg, Roberts, Piercy, and others) than had his cousin, and his beliefs represented "nearly faultless Protestant orthodoxy."[81]

When he made his way to Nanjing in April 1859, Rengan carried with him the hopes of the entire missionary community that he might become the "Martin Luther of Taiping Christianity." Although he initiated a number of ecclesiastical and ritual reforms, he had much less success in modifying Hong

Xiuquan's heretical views, particularly those regarding the Trinity. He wrote a number of pamphlets that were lucid expositions of doctrine and ethics in the Chinese context. Jen Yu-wen comments:

> There was, for example, his elaborate theory about the purification of the "human mind" or *hsin* (from concern for superficial external actions to concern for inner spiritual growth through self-discipline) which brilliantly incorporated the teachings of Confucius, Mencius, the great Sung and Ming philosophers, and even Wang Yang-ming, the exponent of intuitional philosophy or "philosophy of mind" (*hsin-hsüeh*). This and his many other religious formulations give Hung Jen-kan a right to an important place among those Chinese theologians who have for so long pursued the elusive goal of an indigenous Chinese Christianity [*Taiping Movement,* 365]

Had Rengan been able to make this type of contribution a few years earlier, the nature and quality of Taiping Christianity might have been much different. Hong had been too long under the influence of the other Taiping leaders whose political ambitions far overshadowed any type of religious commitment.

The ideology of the Taiping movement was rooted in the Christian Bible, but its doctrine was both reinforced and informed by the Confucian tradition. The *Gongyang zhuan*, an interpretation of the *Chunqiu* ["the spring and autumn annals"], one of the five Chinese classics, was a popular commentary taught widely in the Guangdong area by advocates of the Confucian reform movement during Hong's school days. The term *taiping,* used by Hong in the name of his proposed new dynasty, was used in this commentary to describe a utopian age to come when the people of China would return once again to the period of its ancient wisdom, which, for Hong and his followers, meant the time when they worshiped the only God, *shangdi.* In this *datong* or "great equality" to come, the land was to be distributed equally, men and women were to have equal footing, and all oppression and inequality were to be banished. The fact that the name for this revolutionary movement, *Taiping tianguo,* was composed of one word taken from the Bible—*tianguo,* "heavenly kingdom" or "kingdom of heaven"—and one word taken from a Confucian reform document—*Taiping,* "of Great Peace"—testifies to the breadth of ideological influences bearing upon Hong's intellectual process [Levenson, "Heaven," 450].

In addition to drawing upon the Confucian tradition in which they were immersed, Hong and other Taiping leaders were undoubtedly influenced also by a complex of animistic religious practices such as magic, trances, and divination [R.H.J. Lin, *Taiping Revolution,* 59].

THE TAIPING GOSPEL IN CHINESE

Although the easiest way to analyze the Taiping gospel in Chinese is to utilize its major documents and organize the material into some of the major doctrines of the Christian faith, we must not ignore the obvious fact that their doctrines did not develop all at the same time and that there were changes through the years.[82] Thomas Meadows points out that Taiping teaching developed in at least two stages: the early period when Hong received his initial revelation of God's truth and his mission in the world, and the subsequent period when God and Christ made new descents into the world and allegedly revealed themselves in new ways through and in the name of the Eastern and Western princes, Yang Xiuqing and Xiao Chaoguei. These later revelations were much more political and often seemed radically different from Hong's earlier teaching.

The Taiping documents furnishing much of the material in the following sections are: *Taiping Zhaoshu* ["imperial declaration"], *Taiping Tianri* ["Taiping heavenly chronicle"], *Tiantiaoshu* ["book of heavenly commandments"], *Taiping Jiushigo* ["Taiping songs on world salvation"], and *Tianli Yaolun* ["important observations on heavenly doctrines"].

God

The Taipings put a singular emphasis on monotheism, the doctrine of the one true God. For them there was but one God, Lord of all humankind. Merciful, forgiving, and all-powerful, God intervened in behalf of the Taipings, coming to earth on seven occasions over the four-year period from 1848–1852. Their "god of battles" aided them in defeating the enemy. There was only one God, and God's name, following the terminology of Liang Afa's tracts, was *Shangdi*, a term going back to the ancient Shang and Zhou periods, and taken over by Confucius along with *tian*. Later, probably under the influence of Gutzlaff's translation, Hong used the title *Huang shangdi*, which linked Taiping Christianity even closer to the old Chinese classics.

Taiping literature also designated God as *Tianfu* (Heavenly Father) and *Shenye* (God-father). The latter term grew out of Hong's misunderstanding of a term *Shenyehuohua* (God-Jehovah) found in Morrison's translation of the Bible. Unfamiliar with biblical names, Hong analyzed this name to mean *Shenye* (God-father) whose given name is *Huohua*. Because of this mistaken interpretation, the name of Jehovah was not used in Taiping Christianity [Jen, *Taiping Movement*, 157].

One of the major Taiping publications, *Tianli Yaolun*, is virtually a duplication of a tract written by W.H. Medhurst shortly after his arrival in Batavia.[83] Its several sections on the existence, unity, spirituality, eternality, unchangeableness, omnipresence, and omnipotence of God are no different from what would be found in any perfectly orthodox presentation. In common with much contemporaneous Protestant missionary writing, Medhurst made extensive use of the logical "natural theology" to draw out God's essential attributes.

Despite using Medhurst's work, the Taiping editors deleted long sections in which the author presented God as immaterial and invisible. These passages obviously did not fit with their anthropomorphic view of God nor with Hong's claims to have personally seen God.

Several years later, in 1860, when Joseph Edkins, LMS missionary, visited Nanjing, he presented the Heavenly King with an essay entitled, "That God has a Body is Allegorical; That God Is without a Body is True." Commenting on this essay, Hong countered:

> God is angered most over the idols and images;
> The likeness of the Father may not be looked upon by earthly men.
> Christ and myself were begotten by the Father,
> And because I was in the Father's bosom, I have seen God.
> The Father created Satan after the original model. . . .
> If you recognize this truly you may still be pardoned.
> The Elder Brother and I have personally seen the Father's sage face;
> The Father, the Son, and the Elder and Younger Brothers are not uncertain.
> The Father and the Elder Brother have brought me to sit in the Heavenly Court;
> The good guests shall enjoy happiness in ten thousand forms
>
> [Michael, III, 1204–5].

At an earlier period, possibly when Hong was teaching school in the Guangdong village of Huaxian in 1845, he penned a poem in praise to God that then and now would fit well into the worship service of any Christian church:

Ode Of Praise

1

The ways of our Lord, being abstruse and profound, are indeed wondrous;
The worldly and the ignorant, how are they to understand?
Three are united in one body, of which there is no origin;
Combined in nature but separated in duty, it shall never be changed.
The Father, the Son and the Holy Ghost, fixed are their names;
To create, to save, and to convert, each has his individual function.
Concentrate your mind, seek wisdom, and eventually you will know;
Ignorant of Heaven's nature, you will remain foolish forever.

2

God the omnipresent knows all;
How can the clever devices of mankind ever succeed?
Plots and conspiracies, before exposure, are fully recognized.
As a desire arises in the mind, it is observed in completeness.
Not just for a day has the whole world practiced evil.
Mankind has long been wicked.

If one fails to seek salvation through Jesus Christ,
How can one's sins be redeemed?

3

The Heavenly Lord, the Supreme God, is most sublime and just;
He rewards and punishes without prejudice and rules over heaven.
The good and the virtuous may encounter physical suffering;
The wicked and the treacherous may chance to prosper for a time;
It is so because in the present life they are hard to distinguish,
But the coming of the next life will certainly make things clear.
Disaster and happiness are men's own choice,
But the soul will receive justice according to one's deeds.

4

God is omnipotent and eternally active;
All the things of the world were created at one word.
The stars, the constellations, the sun, and the moon, he created them all;
The rivers, seas, mountains, and the streams, he determined their length.
Men and things even yet are shaped and nourished by him.
As years and time fall into antiquity, there never has been change.
Heaven is manifest and the divine power is marvelous;
Let men throughout the universe praise the name of our Lord
                                                    [ibid., II, 22–23].

Much of the Taiping teaching on God came from the Pentateuch, which, along with the book of Joshua, is apparently all that they published of the Old Testament. In most instances they followed the biblical account faithfully, and their sense of history, although extending only from creation to the giving of the law, was substantially accurate. Hong's literal, anthropomorphic concept of God led him beyond the biblical record in creating an entire family for God. The Heavenly Father had a wife referred to as the Heavenly Mother, and the Heavenly Elder Brother, Jesus, had a wife whom Hong identified as his own Heavenly Sister-in-Law (these terms are found in *Taiping Tianri*). Is it possible that Hong's humanistic and familial extension of the God-head was his way of bringing into balance the human personality of God to offset the usual emphasis by the educated elite on a nonpersonal ultimate principle of the universe?

The imagery of Hong's heavenly vision was distinctly indigenous with relations among the heavenly family members patterned on typical Chinese families. The Heavenly Mother lovingly cared for Hong when he arrived in heaven and arranged for his own mother to wash him in the river to cleanse him from the dirt of the "dusty world." The Heavenly Mother interceded tenderly on his behalf when the Heavenly Brother, Christ, became enraged at his slowness in learning how to read and sing the Psalms. The Sovereign Lord, Hong, demonstrated marital faithfulness, for when he arrived at the gateway to heaven, carried in a sedan chair supported by angels, and "beautiful maidens beyond number approached to receive him, . . . the Sovereign cast no sidelong glances at them."

Heavenly family life took place in the celestial imperial palace, where all the niceties of the Beijing royal court were observed. Hong needed to bathe before he could enter the presence of the Heavenly Father. After he knelt before the august presence in a posture of greeting, he stood properly to one side. The Great God taught him:

> When seated one's clothing must be neat and orderly, the head must be raised and held high, one's body must be erect, with the two hands on one's knees and the feet with the heels together and pointed outward.[84]

God's wrath against the demons, who have at every turn sought to thwart the divine purposes, was strongly emphasized. This was most evident in superstitious practices, idolatry, and the magic of Daoism. The Heavenly King's commission was to act on God's behalf "to exterminate the demons, awaken the world, and soothe the myriad states that they might equally enjoy true felicity" [Michael, II, 240].

The Chinese were well known for their immersion in idolatry. Although the Taipings did not speak about God's having had a covenant with the Chinese comparable to that with Israel, they did affirm that from of old their ancestors had known God. The writer of the "Trimetrical Classic" comments:

> Throughout the whole world,
> There is only one God,
> The great Lord and Ruler,
> Without a second.
>
> The Chinese in early ages
> Were looked after by God;
> Together with foreign states
> They walked in one way.
>
> From the time of P'an Ku
> Down to the Three Dynasties,
> They honored God,
> As history records. . . .

This state of affairs continued until:

> Coming to Cheng of Ch'in—
> He was infatuated with the genii;
> All were deluded by the devil,
> Those two thousand years.

Tracing the worship of God back to the very beginning of history not only was an effective antidote to idolatry; it also helped to refute the common accusation, to which the Taipings were extremely sensitive, that "to worship the Great God is to follow barbarians' ways." They replied:

[Those who accused them of this] do not know that in the ancient world monarchs and subjects alike all worshipped the Great God. As for the great Way of worshipping the Great God, from the very beginning, when the Great God created in six days heaven and earth, mountains and seas, man and things, both China and the barbarian countries of the West have continuously walked in the great Way. China also walked in the great Way, but within the most recent one or two thousand years, China has erroneously followed the devil's path, thus being captured by the demon of hell [*Tiantiaoshu*; Michael, II, 113–14].

Sin

God gave the Taipings the Ten Commandments as an ethical standard for the life they were expected to live. The Taipings made extensive use of these, adding flourishing clauses from Chinese proverbs and elaborating where they deemed necessary. The First Commandment, for example, was not only given a positive turn, "Thou shalt honor and worship the Great God," but appeal was made to the "common saying, 'Produced by Heaven, nourished by Heaven, and protected by Heaven.'"

The prohibition against adultery in the Seventh Commandment was expanded to include "intermixing of the sexes . . . the casting of amorous glances, the harboring of lustful imaginings about others, the smoking of opium, and the singing of libidinous songs." Included in the Tenth Commandment, "Thou shalt not conceive a covetous desire," is a phrase forbidding the type of gambling that "buys lottery tickets and bets of names," probably a reference to the gambling clubs in Guangdong organized to bet on those candidates who would succeed in the state examinations [*Tiantiaoshu*; Michael, II, 119–23].

How did Taiping Christians view sin? Above all, it was an abandonment of God's original purposes for the created world. They affirmed that, "the great origin of virtue (*Dao*) is Heaven." In the beginning:

Heaven and man were of one mind, there were no two principles . . . from the time of P'an Ku down to the Three Dynasties, both princes and peoples as one body honored August Heaven. During that time when the sovereigns honored God, nobles, scholars, and commoners all did the same . . . whether west or north, whether south or east. Every fibre and thread depends on God; Every sip and morsel comes from the Heavenly Majesty [*Taiping Zhaoshu*; Michael, II, 25–26].

Humankind fell from this high pinnacle of worship and praise because of the serpent's deluding Eve in the garden:

> After [Eve] died the deceiving serpent also had a second generation; they [serpents] can still be born, and in all generations women have greatly believed the talk of devils, to the point where they have destroyed lives [Hong Xiuquan, *Annotations*; Michael, II, 225].

Despite being deluded by demons throughout history, humankind is culpable. *Tiantiaoshu* commences with the question, "Who in this mortal world has not offended against the Heavenly Commandments?" The most culpable among the Chinese was their great sage, Confucius.[85] He, in fact, according to a proclamation issued by the Supreme Lord and Great God, in Hong's hearing during his forty-day vision, must bear "all the ultimate guilt for inciting the demons to do wrong . . . [because his] books of teachings are very much in error."

During this confrontation between God and Confucius in heaven, the Father:

> Charged Confucius, saying, "Why did you teach people to carry on their affairs in such a muddled, confused manner, to the point where the people of the world do not even know me, but your reputation on the contrary is greater than mine?" At first Confucius argued stubbornly, but in the end he though silently and had nothing to say.

As a result:

> The Heavenly Father, the Supreme Lord and Great God, thereupon dispatched the Sovereign [Hong in heaven during his vision] to go with the angels to pursue Confucius [seeking to return to earth with the demons] and to bring him, bound and tied, before the Heavenly Father, the Supreme Lord and Great God. The Heavenly Father, the Supreme Lord and Great God, in great anger, ordered the angels to whip him. Confucius knelt before the Heavenly Elder Brother, Christ, and repeatedly begged to be spared. He was given many lashes, and Confucius' sad pleas were unceasing. The Heavenly Father, the Supreme Lord and Great God, then considering that his meritorious achievements compensated for his deficiencies, granted that he be permitted to partake of the good fortune of heaven, but that he never be permitted to go down to the world.

Taiping Zhaoshu, one of the earliest of the Taiping documents, spelled out in detail the types of sin that human beings must conquer if their "natural conscience is to be restored to its original state."[86] Listed first, and labeled as "chief," was licentiousness: "when man becomes demon, Heaven is most enraged."

Second in importance in the Taiping category of wrong was disobedience to parents:

> The man of true filial virtue loves his parents all his life;
> He discerns their formless wishes and hears them, unexpressed.
> To be filial to one's parents is to be filial to God;
> The cultivating and nourishing of one's own origin alone will cause the
> self to flourish.
> To be disobedient to your parents is to be disobedient to God.
> The cutting and maiming of one's own origin alone will cause the self to
> fall.

The third sin, murder, by which apparently the Taipings did not mean what they were continually doing in their attempted conquest of China, was labeled specifically as the "worst of crimes." "Wanton killing," it was affirmed, did not exist in "former days." Killing is wrong because:

> Under heaven all are brothers;
> The souls of all come from heaven.
> God looks upon all men as his children.
> For men to destroy one another is extremely lamentable. . . .
> To practice forgiveness through your life is your duty.
> Make faith and charity your masters,
> Modesty must be known.

Many historical references were used to illustrate robbery and thievery as the fourth kind of wrong.

The fifth type of sin listed in this important document was witchcraft. To engage in such practices was condemned because "death and life, calamity and sickness, all are determined by Heaven," not by useless charms. Witchcraft is also wrong because it is service of demons. "The devils' agents, having served the devils, are eventually possessed by the devils."

The sixth specific sin that the Taipings condemned was gambling. Gambling, particularly if done with "deceit and fraud," was regarded as wrong not merely because it produced "unrighteous gain," but, more importantly, because "the acquisition [of wealth] lies in fate":

> If fate provides for you, why need you gamble?
> If fate does not, although you gamble, you will not obtain your wish.
> In the end, poverty and riches are arranged by Heaven.
> Follow your proper avocations, and you shall be at ease.
> Confucius and Yen-tzu were happy on water and thin gruel;

Knowing their fate they were content in poverty, and their spirits soared.
Man's life in this world is like a dream at the third watch.
Why ponder? Why worry? Why hope?
Small wealth comes from diligence and great wealth from fate.

Salvation

What, in Taiping teaching, was the antidote for sin? At times the solution seemed largely Confucian, despite Hong's aversion for Confucius and his doctrine:

The great origin of virtue is Heaven;
Let us reverently take Heaven's way to arouse the multitudes of the
    virtuous.
The way of Heaven is to punish the licentious and bless the good;
Repent while it is early; be the first.
The root and source of the true Way lies only in rectitude
[Michael, II, 123]

But Heaven to the Taipings was more than an impersonal principle, and thus they urged that, "without distinction between noble or lowly, all must reverently worship him." Salvation had an Old Testament flavor and was to be obtained by forsaking the false and learning how to worship the true God:

Give full evidence of a true heart,
And then you can ascend to heaven.
In sincerity worship God;
Believe not in the monster's falsehoods;
Abandon all worldly views,
And then you will ascend to heaven [ibid., 25].

Heaven was worthy of worship: from the beginning Heaven had sought to rescue humankind from its plight. Heaven had called the Israelites, and given them the Ten Commandments. When humankind "was caught by the devil's schemes . . . [and] fell into misery," Heaven sent:

[The] first-born son, the Heavenly Elder Brother, Jesus, down into the world to save mankind and to suffer extreme misery and grief in order to redeem mankind's sins. Amongst meritorious deeds of the greatest kind nothing can be found to exceed this. If men did but know the basis of their redemption, consisting in the sacrifice of life for the salvation of the world, they would be able to estimate how worthy of all honor our Heavenly Elder Brother is; still more would they feel that our Heavenly Father ought constantly to be regarded with pious reverence [*Taiping Jiushiguo*; Michael, II, 239–40].

God not only commissioned Israel and his Son, he sent Hong, the Heavenly King and the Heavenly Father's second son, into the world, as the third phase of the divine redeeming activity:

> From whose coming the true doctrine began to be clearly manifest.
> Wisdom and intelligence endowed by Heaven far exceed the common order;
> His disposition is benevolent and kind, truly beyond calculation.
> In beheading the evil and preserving the correct, he upholds Heaven's command;
> With rewards and punishments clearly distinguished, Heaven's law is manifest [ibid., 243].[87]

This "manifestation of Heaven's law" took concrete form in the initial Taiping uprising, in routing the demons, in establishing the "heavenly capital" at Nanjing, and in the various other exploits that fulfilled God's purposes. Hong was assisted in this saving activity by five other kings, of whom the most important were the Eastern and Western kings, Yang Xiuqing and Xiao Chaoguei.

Although the Taipings followed the Chinese classics in promoting rectitude (*zheng*) and propriety or morality (*li*), their concept of sin was basically superficial. Consequently its solution, although using some of the right phrases, was also superficial. Vincent Shih has commented:

> The idea of original mind and the original goodness of human nature is probably the reason the Taipings did not and could not understand sin in the same way as Christians understand it. For the latter, it is sin which is original and not the goodness of human nature. This opposite conception of human nature explains why the Taipings failed to grasp the deeper meaning of repentance. For them, as indeed for all Chinese whose pattern of thought has been conditioned by traditionalism, the idea of original sin and repentance appears very strange. Repentance for them does not exist. [V. Shih, 183].

Religious Ceremonies

The Taipings observed a number of ceremonies, of which baptism was probably the most important: it was used by Hong and his followers to indicate freedom from sin. Candidates came to a table on which were placed two lamps and three cups of tea. A previously written confession of sins was burned to indicate acceptance with God. Applicants then had to agree orally not to worship corrupt spirits or to commit acts of evil. They pledged to follow the laws of heaven. When they had responded correctly, water was poured over their head, and they said, "My sin is washed away. I have put aside the old man and am now made new." They then arose, washed their chest with water, drank a cup of tea, and went to the river to immerse themselves, calling on the Lord for forgiveness.

The Sabbath was carefully observed. On Fridays a large flag was displayed, signaling the approach of the Sabbath. Its observance began at sunset on Friday. The principal worship service, celebrated with cakes and fruit, was held at midnight. "When constructing a hearth, building a house, piling up stones, or opening up the ground," it was customary to "offer up sacrifices of animals, delicacies, tea and rice." These sacrifices were offered in the Old Testament tradition, invoking the blessing of God and beseeching God "to grant peace to every member of my household, both great and small, to ward off every kind of fear, to cause all demons to flee and hide, and to make everything accord with my desire, accompanied by great bliss and great prosperity." Apparently this was not intended to gain merit, for it was followed by a phrase acknowledging that this prayer was through "the merits of our Saviour and Heavenly Elder Brother, Jesus, who redeemed us from sin."

Prayers and Eschatology

In the Taiping "Book of Heavenly Commandments" several forms were given to direct believers in their prayers on various occasions. First in importance were the prayers to be used when repenting of sins and declaring one's commitment to God. Other prayers were suggested for use at morning or evening, when giving thanks to God at mealtime, and when "suffering from calamity and sickness." In keeping with their strong emphasis on the family and filial piety, the Taipings developed (or adopted) prayers appropriate for birthdays, marriages, and other special family events. These occasions were also times for the offering of the same sacrifices as at the erection of a building. A special funeral service for those who had "ascended to heaven" was substituted for Buddhist ceremonies. At one point in the service:

> When the coffin is closed down, the mourning clothes put on, the coffin carried out to the place of interment and lowered down into the grave, all should cry out in a loud voice, saying "Having received the commands of the Supreme Lord and Great God, the commands of the Saviour, Jesus, and the commands of the T'ien Wang, Monarch of the Great Principle (*Hung Hsiu ch'üan*), may every kind of fear be driven away, may demons be compelled to flee and hide, may everything accord with my desire, accompanied by great bliss and prosperity" [*Tiantiaoshu*; Michael, II, 114–19].

In discussing eschatology, the Taipings made more use of the New Testament than of the Old. "Kingdom of Heaven" apparently was often taken to refer to China, and the Taipings were an embodiment of this. Heaven itself was to be a place of endless bliss, and hell a place of punishment and never-ending misery. In common with other Christians in China, they used Buddhist terms for heaven and hell in their literature.

WEAKNESSES OF TAIPING CHRISTIANITY

The most obvious place where the Taiping gospel differed from historical Christianity was in its view that Jesus Christ was not deity and not to be equated with God. Hong asserted repeatedly that Jesus was the Son of God, and because this was true, he could hardly be considered equal to the Father. Note some of his comments—annotations on various verses in the New Testament:

> *Mark 12:28–34.* The Elder Brother clearly proclaims that there is only one Supreme Lord. Why did later disciples through some error feel that Christ was God? If that were really true, this would be so: there would be two Gods. Respect this.
>
> *Luke 4:12.* The Elder Brother says not to tempt God; he does not say that he himself is God. This is essential. Respect this.
>
> *Acts 7:55–60.* Stephen clearly proves that Christ stands at the right hand of God; therefore God is the divine father, Christ is the divine son. They are one and two. And all the more, since the Elder Brother has himself also proved this, how can we now mistakenly understand that Christ is God? Respect this.
>
> *Romans 8:6.* Paul clearly proves that God is God and Christ is Christ. Respect this.

Shocking as these views were to outside observers, they were compounded by the numerous other quasi-divine personages on the Taiping stage. Foremost, of course, was Hong Xiuquan, the Heavenly King himself. From the time of his vision in 1837, he viewed himself as the second son of God and the brother of Jesus Christ. He took his name, Xiuquan, meaning "accomplished and perfect," after the vision as a replacement for earlier names, believing that it had been given to him directly by God when God commissioned him for his work.

Given this view of himself, Hong, obviously at the instigation of others who wanted his leadership fortified, progressively found other biblical evidence to support his position and even extend it. He saw himself, for example, as Melchizedek of the Old Testament:

> This Melchizedek was none other than myself. Formerly when I was in heaven I descended into the world and made manifest these real events, as proof of my descent into the world at this time to become the sovereign. As for the things Heaven does, there must be a previous allusion to them [Hong Xiuquan, *Annotations* (comment on Genesis 14:17–24); Michael, II, 225].

And again, in commenting on Hebrews 7:1–20, he observed:

> This Melchizedek is none other than myself. Formerly in heaven our Old Mother bore the Elder Brother and also all those of my generation. At that time I knew the Father was going to have my Elder Brother born of Abraham's descendants. Therefore I comforted the officers and troops, and congratulated and blessed Abraham, for Abraham was a good man [ibid., 233].

With such a divine ancestry, Hong exercised absolute power over his followers and was not ready to brook any interference by outsiders, even missionaries, in his megalomania. Troubles developed, however, when he traveled away from his base of operations. Others were waiting to receive heavenly revelations and to share power with him, or even to seize it as their own.

Foremost among them was Yang Xiuqing, who claimed that God had descended to the world in 1848, possessed his body, and given him the right to speak for God and to act as "Redeemer of Sickness to transfer the sickness of fellow Society members to his own body."[88] Jen Yu-wen observes that Yang's claims cleverly brought together two strands of thought: the work of Christ who redeems humankind from sin, and the work of spiritual mediums well known to the adherents of the popular religious cults. Jen Yu-wen notes:

> Belief in the ability of spiritual beings to possess the body of a human and to speak through the human so possessed was widespread in China at the time and especially in Kwangtung and Kwangsi, where professional mediums were flourishing on small fees received for communicating in this way with the people's ancestors and other beloved dead [*Taiping Movement*, 50].

Xiao Chaoguei's story was very similar. He too claimed that God had descended to earth and was speaking through him. Following his announcement, what had once been thought of as a unique experience became increasingly a common occurrence, resulting in a diminution of the authority of Hong and an increased fragmentation of the movement.

Yang, the Dong Wang (Eastern King), and Xiao, the Xi Wang (Western King), along with other kings, were given designations corresponding to the natural elements. One document, not circulated as extensively as others, includes this hymn of praise:

> Praised be God, the Holy and Heavenly Father, who is the one true Deity.
> Praised be the Heavenly Elder Brother, the teacher of the world, who
>   gave up his life for mankind.
> Praised be the Tung Wang, the Wind of the Holy Ghost, the Redeemer
>   from Sickness.

Praised be the Hsi Wang, Master of the Rain, the noble one of high
heaven.
Praised be the Nan Wang [Southern King], Master of the Clouds, the
upright one of high heaven.
Praised be the Pei Wang [Northern King], Master of the Thunder, the
benevolent one of high heaven.
Praised be the I Wang [Assistant King], Master of the Lightning,
the righteous one of high heaven.

[*Tiantiaoshu*; Michael, II, 119, 20].

Eventually a power struggle ensued, which led to the assassination of Yang
Xiuqing and a leadership vacuum in Nanjing. Hong himself had never been a
capable administrator, and the entire movement might have collapsed even
earlier had not Hong Rengan, Hong's cousin and one of his earliest followers,
appeared on the scene. As noted earlier when considering the origin of Taiping
religious beliefs, Rengan, for several years a catechist of the London Missionary Society, espoused relatively orthodox beliefs. He held to the deity of Christ,
derived most of his doctrine from scripture, emphasized the individual and his
personal salvation, talked more about the compassion than the wrath of God,
and sought to clarify Hong's rather muddled ideas about the Trinity.

Although Xiuquan had granted to Rengan the chief administrative position
with the title of Gan Wang (Shield King), this power base was not sufficiently
ideological to compete effectively with the teaching of the many others who
gained their power through supernatural claims. Rengan was far more the
teacher than the prophet, and his attempts at reform, whether religious or
administrative, were too late to effect any change in the direction of the Taiping
movement.

Possibly because of his relatively long association with Protestant missionaries, Rengan believed in the "gospel of progress." In his opinion, the Taiping
movement needed something more than religious principles. China needed to
be modernized, and among the useful things required were "steamships,
trains, clocks, modern guns, and other practical Western inventions" [Mi-
chael, I, 135–68].

EVALUATION OF THE TAIPING GOSPEL IN CHINESE

How can we evaluate Taiping Christianity? Was it the gospel in Chinese or
was it no gospel at all? We do not need to take seriously the accusation by some
historians in the People's Republic of China that the religious views of the
Taipings were a smoke screen for their revolutionary political program, the
typical Marxist dismissal of religious motivation. But if they were indeed
serious in their religious profession, how can we evaluate their deviant doctrines?

In answering the question about whether the Taiping movement was really
Christian, we might wish to respond as Thomas Meadows, the interpreter for

Sir George Bonham, British plenipotentiary in China from 1848 to 1854: "What kind of Christians do you mean?" he asked. "Do you mean Romanist Christians, or Lutheran Christians, or Nestorian Christians, or Calvinist Christians, or Armenian Christians, or Abysinnian Christians, or Coptic Christians, or Greek Christians?" [Meadows, 412]. We are back to our imaginary space visitor (chap. 1) and his efforts to make some sense of differing Christian views and practices.

Scant Knowledge of Christian Truth

One approach to the alleged deficiency of Taiping Christianity takes note that Hong Xiuquan, within in his own frame of reference, was an Old Testament Christian. Many portions of the tracts written by Liang Afa that he used so extensively were from the Old Testament. As he read the Old Testament, particularly the Pentateuch, which was about the only portion available to him, he saw the variety of ways in which God spoke to Israel. He found no indication anywhere that these revelations were to cease. The use of sacrifices of many types on important occasions was integral to Old Testament life and fit well with his Chinese environment.

Closely related to this explanation is the indubitable fact that Hong and his followers, with the exception of Rengan whose influence came too late to make a marked difference, knew little about distinctively Christian truth. Liang Afa's tracts were rather randomly organized and were essentially homiletical in style. Certain areas of the Christian faith were totally neglected: a systematic presentation of basic facts in the life of Christ; the Trinity; the sacraments; the teaching of the parables; the value of love. Early missionary tracts were weighted more toward denouncing superstition and idolatry than toward a positive statement of doctrine. Liang Afa used the first edition of Morrison's Bible translation for his material. It was not a good translation, and, undoubtedly, Hong found much that was simply not understandable. Its very incomprehensible nature, in fact, could have added to its mysterious quality and convinced Hong that it was of supernatural origin.

At only one place did Liang's tracts refer to Christ as the "only" Son of God. Usually, the phrase was merely "Son of God." In adding other divine sons to the heavenly family he was really doing nothing to contradict Liang's christology. The term for Holy Spirit in Morrison's Bible was *Shengshenfeng* (Holy God's Wind), a phrase so ambiguous that Hong could apply it to the Eastern king, Yang Xiuqing.

The very fact that the Taipings did have Christian literature—various bibles, tracts, and booklets—and yet innocently twisted some portions to their own advantage, caused a number of mission theorists in England during the nineteenth century to question the wisdom of indiscriminate scripture dissemination. They favored a serious effort to annotate the text or give explanations of geography, history, and customs. They argued that biblical Christianity always implied the presence of a teacher, at least an informal kind of magisterium, that would help to guarantee continuity with the historical understanding of the faith. Thomas Meadows comments:

> While un-annotated copies of the Bible may answer well enough among illiterate Polynesians or Africans, who *must* read it under the guidance of a teacher; such copies, spreading among millions of reading Chinese, who may never see a foreigner, cannot fail to give rise to much greater diversities of opinion than exist in Western Christendom [*The Chinese*, 412].

Why Was Jesus Not Considered Equal with the Father?

It is well to point out that Hong's diminution of Jesus Christ was not done to promote a hidden agenda. He did not deny deity to Christ because he deemed it impossible for a man to be God or because he thought it unnecessary or because he did not believe the Bible. He was, in fact, trying to protect Christian truth: he wished to claim unreservedly that there was only one God, and to press this claim on the evils of the polytheism so rampant in Chinese society.

Hong's denial of Christ's equality with God did not lead him to reject Christ's divinity (Hong could say that Christ was divine, but not that he was God). Nor did Hong doubt that Christ was indeed the savior of the world, whose death was essential for the forgiveness of sin. Hong's capacity to think abstractly on this matter was limited. The expression "son of God," in all its bleak concreteness, could only mean to him that Christ was less than God.

Was Hong Demented or Led Astray by Colleagues?

Some commentators have believed that Hong Xiuquan himself was devoted to God and to seeking God's truth, but that he was led astray by other leaders, such as Yang and Xiao, who played on his vanity and claimed new revelations and authority for both him and themselves. Without doubt, the earliest formulation of the Taiping teaching was much more in conformity with traditional Christianity than that which later developed. However, it must be noted that Xiuquan's visions came at the earliest stage of the movement and that they were always viewed as foundational, even by Rengan in his much more orthodox formulations.

Other critics of Taiping Christianity have speculated that Hong was demented, noting that his earliest vision came at a time when he had been critically ill with a persistent fever. Franz Michael observes that, following his illness when he had talked irrationally, often in fits of rage, his "personality as well as his appearance had changed."[89]

"Only a Political Movement"

Joseph Levenson, although not following a Marxist interpretation, identifies the Taiping movement as basically a "political rebellion," claiming that

"Taiping Christianity" is really a misnomer, inasmuch as it had no separate existence apart from the political movement that produced it. Unlike Buddhism or Daoism, or even non-Taiping Christianity, this brand of Christianity did not exist as such preceding the rebellion or following it. "Christianity of the Taiping stamp," Levenson claims, "was purely rebellion-bred, rebellion-nourished, with no social existence in China, except as an ideological concomitant of violence" ["Heaven," 439].

Most irksome to Levenson is that the Taipings were Chinese and sought so successfully to pour their Christian concepts into Confucian forms, thus twisting these forms and their meaning into something non-Confucian. Specifically, he refers to the concepts of heaven, the mandate of heaven, the classics, the civil service examinations, universalism (*tianxia*), and barbarians (*fanguo*). In each instance, he complains, the Taipings were misusing Chinese concepts and coloring them with Christian dyes.

He believes this "ideological concomitant of violence" was politically motivated, because it did not accept the usual Confucian interpretation and because it had no precedent or continuity in Chinese Christianity. In short, he finds it to be neither Confucian nor Christian. Is this the only possible conclusion? Can it not be viewed as a legitimate effort by the Taipings to put the gospel into Chinese—an effort both to use and to combat Confucianism? Violence was indeed an integral part of the movement, but the Taiping ideology was far more than a rationalization for violence.

THE CHINESE CONTENT OF THE TAIPING GOSPEL

Whatever the reasons for the Taiping failure to adhere to the more usual formulations of the Christian faith, no one doubted that it had included heavy dosages of the Chinese context in its content. Kenneth Latourette concludes that "the Taiping movement was a Chinese sect, displaying some interesting results of contact with Christianity, but drawing most of its beliefs and characteristics from its Chinese environment and the erratic genius of its leaders" [*History*, 298].

Thomas Meadows would not go so far. Comparing Hong with Swedenborg and his vision of angels and sense of being transported out of the body, Meadows comments:

Swedenborgianism is Protestant Christianity modified by an extensive knowledge of physical science; Tae-pingism is Protestant Christianity modified by Confucian philosophy [*The Chinese*, 439].

Jen Yu-wen notes:

Hung's [Hong's] interpretation of Christian doctrine was molded by his own social and cultural milieu, the special needs of the Taiping Revolutionary Movement, and a reverence for the ancient truths of Confucianism [*Taiping Movement*, 156].

Jen Yu-wen, along with Eugene Boardman, has been more concerned with what the Taipings omitted in their teaching rather than with the ways in which they twisted Christian truth. He claims:

> The charge of heresy made by some missionaries was irrelevant since Hung . . . did not grasp his divergence from orthodoxy. Arguments as to the heterodoxy or orthodoxy of Taiping Christianity are therefore academic and perhaps becloud the true significance of this great religious phenomenon [ibid., 155].

These critics have noted that, specific theological issues aside, the Taipings did not understand the concept of love and forgiveness among men, the teaching of the Golden Rule, the welfare of one's neighbor, the *spiritual* nature of the kingdom of Heaven, and Christian humility. This causes Jen to conclude:

> It became a case of "reverting the guest to the host," to use a Chinese set-phrase, for the Taiping religion in its ethical content turned out to be more a Christianized Confucianism than a Confucianized Christianity [ibid., 156].

Boardman, even more blunt, baldly states, "Taiping religion was not Christianity" [*Christian Influence*, 114].

Although reserving final judgment as to how "Christian the new faith may have been," Franz Michael makes the pertinent observation:

> The belief that united the members of the new society differed *fundamentally* from the vague Buddhist, Taoist, and Confucian concepts used by the traditional societies. The members of the God Worshippers Society accepted a new religious faith, a faith quite contrary to *all* tradition of Chinese imperial society, a faith in a personal God and his guidance for one's personal salvation as well as in all matters of daily life and in the larger problem of economic, social, and political affairs [I, 29; italics added].

Surely a faith that differs "fundamentally" from Chinese religions, is "contrary to all Chinese tradition," and puts different meaning into the forms of Chinese culture and ideology is to be labeled something more than "a Chinese sect." Is not the Christian component more dominant than the Confucian element?

MISSIONARY EVALUATION OF THE TAIPINGS

How did Protestant missionary contemporaries of the Taipings evaluate the Christian element in the revolutionary movement? John Littell, although emphasizing the political more than the specifically religious, notes that missionary "feelings about the rebels may be divided into four groups: (1) enthusiasm; (2) moderate sympathy; (3) opposition; leading to (4) pleas for intervention."[90] Not that missionary views were constant. Although some missionaries and groups tended to be consistently either positive or negative, the thermometer of missionary impression rose and fell as news on almost anything filtered out from Taiping headquarters.

Enthusiasts rooted their excitement in the belief that God was about to fulfill the prophecy in Isaiah 49:12 that there would be those coming to the Lord "from the region of Sinim," believed almost without exception to refer to China. From this, it was easy to claim that the Taipings were the "instrument of a superhuman power" whose desire was to bring about the conversion of the Middle Kingdom.

One of those most enthusiastic about Taiping prospects was W.A.P. Martin who often expressed himself on the subject. He defended the Taiping brand of Christianity against charges that it was heretical:

When has Christianity in its incipient stages not presented the appearance of being spurious? The process both with nations and individuals is purgative . . . was not the religion of the Middle Ages exceedingly crude and imperfect? And yet light was made to shine out of darkness [Covell, *Martin*, 85].

He suggested that the New Testament itself revealed ignorance and irregularities that could easily be labeled false by a critical outside observer.

From this perspective, he wondered if Hong's visions and trances differed in kind from Constantine's vision of the "cross-emblazoned banner"? Hong's pretension to be the "son of God" was not, he believed, a claim of natural identity with God but only a title of dignity to maintain status before his followers.

Missionaries of the London Missionary Society were generally positive in their evaluation of the Taipings, wavering between enthusiasm and moderate sympathy. Granting that their religious beliefs tended toward "wild and blasphemous fanaticism," James Legge concluded that they had three convictions going for them: an earnest abjuration of idolatry and a desire to serve the living and true God; a belief in the future life; and a belief in the value of the sacred scriptures.[91]

Others expressed similar opinions:

In opposition to the pantheistic notions of the philosophers of the Sung dynasty, they hold the doctrine of the personality of the Deity; in opposition to the popular polytheistic notions, they have the clearest conception of the unity of God; and in opposition to the fatalism of philosophical Buddhism, they believe in and teach the doctrine of an all-superintending Providence ["Visit of Messrs. Edkins . . . and Hall to the Chinese Insurgents," *Missionary Magazine* (Oct. 1860) 753].

Many of these missionaries were as disturbed as their colleagues about the gospel the Taipings proclaimed, but they were convinced that even this would prepare the soil for a widespread turning to Christ in truth. William Muirhead tested this hope in the one month he spent preaching at Nanjing in the spring of 1861. He found the people ready to give assent to and receive the truth of God once they had heard it repeatedly. He excitedly exclaimed:

How different is all this from our experience in Shanghai and elsewhere. There we have a hard and strong ground to work where ignorance and *opposition* prevail in abundant measure. Here on the part both of military and civilians, there *is* knowledge, and there *is* appreciation of the truth to a certain extent, which renders the spiritual enforcement of it a more easy and pleasant duty [Lin-Le, II, 471–72].

Because they were convinced that the soil was being prepared for widespread preaching of the gospel throughout China, particularly in the area controlled by the rebels, missionaries were anxious to make arrangements to go to Nanjing and get started. In this they were helped by Hong Rengan, the Shield King, who belatedly realized the need for foreign support and invited missionary leaders to visit Taiping headquarters at Nanjing and Soochow. Several groups of British and American missionaries accepted this invitation in 1860 and 1861. They were generally impressed with the Taiping leaders' Christian faith, their friendliness and desire for trade, and the fact that the cruelty and destruction, so widely reported in the foreign press, were nowhere evident [Teng, 178–79].

In a journey to Hankow late in 1860, Griffith John of the London Missionary Society obtained from rebel leaders an Edict of Religious Toleration granting missionaries the right to live and preach the gospel in the insurgents' territory [Thompson, 147]. John also transmitted to his colleagues the following memo from Zhong Wang the Loyal King, at Nanjing:

You have had the Gospel for upward of 1800 years, we only as it were eight days. Your knowledge of it ought to be correct and extensive. Ours must necessarily be limited and imperfect. You must, therefore, bear with us for the present, and we will gradually improve. As for the Gospel, it is one, and must be propagated throughout the land. Let the foreign brethren all know that we are determined to uproot idolatry and plant Christianity in its place [Thompson, 148].

Attractive as this possibility was, an apparent change of heart by Hong Rengan and other leaders seemed to indicate that, rather than depend on missionaries, they preferred to use "native means" to evangelize China.

These direct contacts with Taiping leaders gave missionaries the opportunity to change things right at the source. Joseph Edkins explained, for example, how he and Griffith John prepared a theological statement of several important subjects. They presented it to the Zhong Wang that he might forward it to the sovereign for his views. They had high hopes that every doctrine "commonly received" among them would be clarified:

> We first spoke on the Trinity, especially on the Divinity of Christ, and His perfect equality with the Father, and also the Personality of the Spirit. The second subject was the Atonement, showing that sacrifices are unnecessary under the Christian dispensation. A third article described the connection of the Old and New Testament, their comparative value and authority, and the differences in the institutions existing under the Mosaic and Christian economies, for example, in reference to marriage. A fourth article spoke of the future state. The insurgents have a notion among them, that the dignitaries enjoyed by them under the dynasty in this life will be continued hereafter. We therefore stated the Scriptural doctrine of rewards and punishments. Lastly we spoke of inspiration, and the ordinary influences of the Holy Spirit ["Visit . . . to the . . . Insurgents," *Missionary Magazine* (Oct. 1860) 755].

A Southern Baptist missionary, J.L. Holmes, spent eight days in Nanjing in the summer of 1860, but he had no direct contact with the most influential leaders. Probably slighted by the kind of attention or lack of attention he received, he was critical:

> I went to Nanking predisposed to receive a favorable impression; indeed, the favorable impressions of a previous visit to Soochow led me to undertake this journey. I came away with my views entirely changed. . . . I found to my sorrow nothing of Christianity but its names, falsely applied [*North China Herald*, Sept. 1, 1860].

Issachar Roberts, the missionary who had first met Hong in Canton, came to Nanjing on October 13, 1860, and remained there until January 20, 1862. Taiping leaders treated Roberts graciously: he was given a rank similar to that of a British marquis; he was offered and refused three wives; and he was offered the post of director of foreign affairs, which he declined. Nevertheless, he helped Hong Rengan in diplomatic matters and performed other tasks, dressed usually in the robes worn by all the kings and other leaders. In terms of status and privilege he should have been able to have made a significant impact upon Taiping Christianity.

But how, William Martin once asked, do you give advice to those who receive direct revelations from God? Even more of a problem was Roberts's personality. A rigid fundamentalist who could brook no variant interpretation of scripture and who held to the usual inflexible Western attitude toward any type of deference to human leaders, Roberts could only butt his head unsuccessfully against all aspects of Taiping life and belief. Although most concerned over blasphemous claims Hong made about his relationship with

Christ, Roberts could be upset by the Taiping failure to have "regular immersion," by their worshiping so much on the Sabbath (both the night before and
in the morning) that they could not really rest, by genuflections made to Hong
at the beginning and end of worship services, by their refusal to distinguish
between church and state, and by their lack of properly ordained ministers.

Things went from bad to worse, until, dismayed by Hong Rengan's precipi-
tant murder of his servant before his very eyes, Roberts left Nanjing never to
return. His final comment:

> I have hitherto been a friend to his [Hong's] revolutionary move-
> ment. . . . But after having been among them fifteen months, and
> closely observing their proceedings—political, commercial, and
> religious— I have turned over entirely a new leaf and I am now as much
> opposed to them. . . . Hung Hong . . . has been exceedingly kind to
> me. But I believe him to be a crazy man, entirely unfit to rule.
> . . . He is violent in his temper. . . . He is opposed to commerce . . .
> and has promptly repelled every foreign effort to establish lawful com-
> merce. . . . His religious toleration, and multiplicity of chapels, turn out
> to be a farce—of no avail in the spread of Christianity—worse than
> useless. It only amounts . . . to the spread of his own political religion,
> making himself equal with Jesus Christ, who with God, the Father,
> himself, and his own son constitute one Lord over All![92]

Walter Medhurst once expressed his regrets that the Taipings "had not
enjoyed the teachings of intelligent missionaries" ["Critical Review"]. All the
missionaries had some interest in the Taiping movement because it interfaced
with so many vital topics: the evangelization of China, the question of the
proper name to use for God, the nature of baptism, the issue of the Sabbath,
and the shape of an indigenous Chinese Christianity. Only a relatively few,
however, were bold enough to brave the dangers as well as the wrath of their
home governments, which sought almost to the very end to preserve a facade
of neutrality. Unfortunately, with some exceptions, although they were relatively open in attitude, they were inflexible intellectually and unable to really
understand and build upon the dynamics of what they were experiencing.

Not all missionaries, as already pointed out, were as exuberant as others
about the propects of the Taiping movement. They often expressed fears
similar to that of Samuel Martin that "should the Revolution finally be
defeated, it will almost inevitably [harm] the cause of missions and especially
native Christians" [Presbyterian archives, Ningpo, 1845-53, no. 249; in Littell,
"Missionaries"]. Dr. Happer, physician with the American Board of Foreign
Commissioners in Canton, was one of the few missionaries most consistently
opposed to the Taipings, advocating ultimately, in exact opposition to William
A.P. Martin, that foreign governments ought to interfere in the revolution on
the side of the Manchu dynasty.

It is easy enough to find fault with a Roberts or a Holmes who, with more understanding and patience, might have used their unique positions to influence the Taiping leaders. Robert Lin widens this accusation to include most of the Christian missionaries when he quotes M. Searle Bates's observation:

By far the greater part of the American missionaries had only a general, biblical knowledge of the Christian religion, with experience of Christian homes, churches, and instructions, rather than theological competence. They were workers and teachers rather than theological scholars or thinkers [*Taiping Revolution*, 94–95, quoting M. Searle Bates, "The Theology of American Missionaries in China 1900–1950," in Fairbank, *Missionary Enterprise*, 137].

Diagram 3

PROTESTANT CRITERIA FOR ASSESSING THE AUTHENTICITY OF TAIPING CHRISTIANITY

Unacceptable starting points	*Dubious starting points*	*Acceptable approaches*	*Ideals*[*]
Confucian classics as authoritative		Scripture and visions	*Sola Scriptura*
Worship of many deities	Divine descents	Allegiance to the one God	Christ equal to God
A merely human savior	Leaders as quasi-divine	Belief in Jesus, divine son of God	
Animal sacrifices to redeem from sin			Salvation by grace
		Belief in the salvific death of Jesus	
Salvation by works			Worship of the Trinity
		Belief in the total efficacy of the work of Jesus, plus pursuit of a sincere moral code	

[*] If these ideals are understood as an indivisible *set* defining the Christian, then the Taipings were not Christians.

To say that the educational background of most missionaries at this point in the missionary movement in China was certainly deficient begs the question. Some of the American missionaries who were highly critical of the Taipings had had four years of college and three years of seminary training. They could not have done much better for that period. Their failure to relate to the Taipings was due more to specific theological views than to a lack of theological training. Furthermore, insights of modern missiology that would help them understand the dynamics of this type of religious movement were totally unavailable to them.

Catholic missionaries were never comfortable with Taiping Christianity. With mistaken iconoclastic zeal the rebels often attacked Catholic churches in the interior of China. Frightened Catholic refugees fled to Shanghai, as well as to other treaty ports. To them and to their religious leaders this brand of Christianity was a Protestant offshoot and could only mean trouble for them.

"NOT ONCE IN A THOUSAND YEARS"

The Taiping rebellion failed for many reasons—internal dissension among its leaders, inability to win foreign support, its puritanical attitude on trade matters, its failure to take a base in the north, the opposition of foreign or foreign-trained armies, its loss of support among otherwise antidynastic sympathizers, and its threatened attack on Shanghai, center for foreign trade, which tended to crystalize foreign opposition. The rebels' Christian profession, though the major component in their ideology, did not contribute measurably to their success when successful or to their failure when they ultimately failed. It both gained and lost friends for them, but it did not significantly affect the dynamics of success or failure.

The Taiping period represents the first and possibly last example of a real "people movement" to Christ that sought to embody the gospel in Chinese. Many, if not most, of their teachings were substandard. But, in terms of people movements to Christ worldwide, they were not uniquely aberrant. Their beliefs in God, the Bible, Christ, the atonement, and Christian life were at least acceptable "starting points." Charles Kraft and Paul Hiebert argue that there can be an acceptable range of variation in both behavior and belief so long as persons have a faith commitment that is heading them toward an attempt to do God's will[93] (see Diagram 3 p. 179).

Within the Taiping movement, the Christian faith does not seem to have developed beyond a very rudimentary stage. The rebels had the Bible, wished to implement God's will, believed the divine Christ died for their sins, and expressed their loyalty to God and God's will. Were they as far along as those converted in the mass movements in Europe? In Europe there had been godly missionaries and the resources of the monasteries to help conserve and deepen the commitments that were made. Possibly all that the Taipings needed were missionaries to make longer commitments to the movement, swallow their pride, and really seek to understand the movement from the longer perspective of history. A better evaluation of the incipient Christian faith could conceivably have influenced some diplomatic decisions and brought a different end to the struggle. However we speculate on the pluses and minuses of the movement, we can probably agree with W.A.P. Martin who concluded that "an opportunity was lost such as does not occur once in a thousand years" [*Cycle of Cathay*, 142].

CHAPTER NINE

The Gospels of Pietism and Revolution— The Daoist and Confucian Contexts

THE CONTEXT FOR CHANGE, 1860–1949

From the demise of the Taiping movement in the mid–1860s until the liberation of China from the decaying Manchu dynasty in 1911, the nation sought in vain to meet the intensifying challenge of the West. The real turning point was not the Taipings but the "unequal treaties" of 1842–44, which helped to trigger the kinds of internal problems that could occasion a Hong Xiuquan and his fanatical followers.

Of this period John Fairbank has observed:

> Until that time [1842] relations with the West had been based upon the ancient Chinese tribute system; after that time they were based upon the "unequal" foreign treaties. Under the tribute system foreign trade had been restricted to the picturesque "factories" of old Canton. But 1842 began a new era—the opening of China to Western commercial exploitation [*Trade and Diplomacy,* 48].

With the renewal of these treaties at Nanjing, in 1860, the interior of China was opened to all phases of Western penetration: missionary evangelism in many remote areas; the development of railways, mining, and manufacturing; the sale of imports into China at prices low enough to undercut local products. Foreigners were put in charge of the Chinese Maritime Customs, and foreign shipping along the coast and to distant ports was extensively developed.

The initial response to this challenge was for China to shore up its coastal defenses, promote "self-strengthening" through Western studies, develop arsenals for the production of arms needed for self-defense, promote industrializa-

182

tion in the form of cotton mills and coal mines, and build a few telegraph lines. These efforts, the awakening of a long-slumbering giant to a modern world, were helpful but fell far short of the demands of the time or of what missionary reformers such as Timothy Richard or William Martin were recommending. Staid Chinese conservatism needed something more drastic to prompt radical change from its traditional ways.

Impetus toward more radical reform came from a rapid succession of external events from 1870 to 1900: British aspirations in Yunnan in 1875; Russian aggression at Ili in Sinkiang, 1871–81; the French conquest of the tributary state of Annam and the war of 1884–85; Japanese militarism in Korea; the tragic Sino-Japanese conflict of 1894–95; and the subsequent efforts by France, Germany, Russia, and Great Britain to carve up China.

China was prevented from responding to these external pressures because of internal disunity, the tug-of-war between disparate groups favoring different answers for its ills:

> [It was a] power struggle between the emperor and the dowager, the conflict between the conservative and the progressive, the strife between the moderate reformers and the radicals, and the racial antipathy between the Manchus and the Chinese [I. Hsü, *Modern China*, 423–24].

New leaders rose up to direct the destiny of China at this juncture. Zhang Zidong, governor-general of Hunan-Hubei from 1889 to 1907, made moderate proposals for reform. In his well-known work, "Exhortation to Learning," he proposed a program to save China by education—converting colleges to primary schools in provinces, prefectures, and districts—and by industrial development. He clung to Feng Guifen's slogan, "Chinese learning for the fundamental principles, Western learning for practical application," and he also advocated the revival of Confucianism to save the Manchu dynasty.

Kang Yuwei was a radical reformer. Although never in a high official position, he used his brilliant literary gifts to influence his contemporaries. He drew upon the Confucian classics to promote reform. He argued that Confucius had devised the idea of a past utopia to convince rulers of his day to reform society even as the earlier rulers Yao and Shun had done. The socialistic utopia that he envisioned included a single world government with popular elections at both the central and regional levels, freedom, equality and independence for all, government care for children, and state ownership of property.

Kang did not wish for dynastic change. He wanted to find in the old classics both the "essence" of China and the "functional" attitude necessary to incorporate Western values. He chose Japanese modernization through constitutionalism for his model. With the help of Liang Qichao, who later took a more liberal path to republicanism, and Tan Sitong, Kang founded the "Society for the Study of National Strengthening" and promoted the reform movement in many areas.

In the early formation and later development of his reform ideals, Kang gave much credit to missionary influence. The Guang Xuehui (Society for the Diffusion of Christian and General Knowledge among the Chinese, or SDK), formed in Shanghai in 1887, claimed such distinguished missionary figures as Young J. Allen, Timothy Richard, and Gilbert Reid as members. They promoted modernization and reform through translations of Western works on science, history, and literature, and through lectures, editorials, and discussions [Covell, *Martin*, 219–20].

The widespread and radical political, economic, educational, and social reforms proposed by Kang Yuwei and others in 1898 came to a grinding halt when the dowager empress put herself firmly on the side of the conservatives. Unfortunately, this meant support for the Boxers, a secret society that laid all the economic, social, and political ills of China at the door of foreigners, particularly Christian missionaries, their converts, and their churches.

Encouraged by this official support, not only in Beijing, but in their base in Shandong as well, the Boxers provoked an uprising that spread over Shandong, Zili, Shanxi, and southern Manchuria. Burning churches, killing a number of foreign missionaries and hundreds of their converts, and destroying all signs of "foreign" modernization, they promoted widespread chaos, which ended only with their defeat in Beijing by an allied force representing eight nations. The Boxer Rebellion was the climax of an antiforeign animus that had been ignored by Christian missions and churches for forty years.

Within a short time after the treaties of 1858 to 1860 were signed, antimissionary riots began to occur with regularity wherever the gospel was preached. Poor communications, a certain unwillingness to face facts, and a typically defensive attitude caused missionaries to pay attention only to the major incidents between them and local or national officials—about twenty such incidents between 1860 and 1890. Studies by Professor Lu Siqianq of the department of history at the Academia Sinica, Taipei, indicate that from 1860 to 1874 alone there were over four hundred separate conflicts between missionaries and local officials involving destruction of property and serious misunderstanding [Lu, *Zhongguo*, 202–60].

In the aftermath of the Boxer tragedy, the extreme conservative faction within the Chinese government was broken up, and the dowager empress, yielding to the force of events, allowed a number of moderate reforms to be made. Prominent among them were abolition of the civil service examinations, the development of new educational institutions, an investigation into constitutionalism, the building of a modern army, and important changes in the areas of law, industry, communication, banking and finance, and journalism.[94]

Even as these various reform programs were being implemented, Sun Yatsen was advocating a more radical solution: not constitutional monarchy, which the Manchus had manipulated to reinforce their domination over the Chinese, but republicanism with nationalism as its banner. In 1905 he organized the Zhongguo tongmeng hui (Chinese United League), allying various Chinese revolutionary groups in a concerted effort that led to the Wuchang revolution of October 10, 1911, and ushered in the fall of the Manchu dynasty.

Sun Yat-sen was made the provisional president of the new republic, but yielded to Yuan Shikai, who was inaugurated to succeed him on March 10, 1912.

Yuan continued as the leader of China until his death in 1916. China then entered into a period of prolonged internal political strife that at various times pitted warlord against warlord, Sun and his followers in southern China against Beijing, and eventually the Guomindang (Nationalist Party) against the communists, officially organized into a political party in 1921. This era of instability, disorder, and disunity was ultimately resolved only with the ascendancy in 1949 of the People's Republic of China to rule the Middle Kingdom with a firm hand.

From the founding of the republic until the mid-1920s, China had gone through extreme ideological ferment. It established much of the political, social, economic, and cultural agenda for the remainder of the twentieth century. Of great importance for the propagation of the Christian faith in China, particularly for the translation of the scriptures into Chinese, was the literary revolution of 1916–17 against the traditional classical style of writing. It substituted a written popular vernacular (*baihua*) as the literary medium. Led by Hu Shi, a literary figure who claimed John Dewey as his disciple, this communication revolution facilitated the spread of new ideas throughout China.

During this period China was looking for national models. The liberal Western model, with its pragmatic and utilitarian views well advocated by John Dewey who lectured extensively in China over a two-year period, was championed by Hu Shi and Cai Yongpei, chancellor of the National Beijing University. For many students and the more radical leaders it lost much of its authenticity when the Versailles treaty failed to rectify the great injustice China had suffered in Western acquiescence to the twenty-one demands of Japan for control over German holdings in Shandong province.

The widespread discontent sparked by this injustice erupted in the May 4th movement, which ushered in a new era of cultural upheaval marked by nationalism and anti-imperialism. Lu Xun's novelette *AQ* became the symbol of a new China seeking to escape from its chrysallis of control by feudalism, imperialism, and bureaucratic capitalism. In this moment of high resentment against past tradition and encroaching imperialism by the capitalist West, many Chinese leaders turned toward Marxist thought. Russia was an attractive new model, particularly inasmuch as its government, newly in power following the 1917 revolution, revoked the treaties that had been disadvantageous to China. Attraction to Russia and its new revolutionary thought led to the formation of the Chinese Communist Party in 1921.

Both Marxist thought and liberal Western ideologies produced a New Culture movement, as well as an anti-Christian reaction in the early and middle 1920s. The chief sin of Christianity was that it was an ally of both imperialism and capitalism, and thus, in essence, an enemy of the Chinese people. To Chinese students, enamored of Dewey and other anti-Christian Western philosophers, the Christian faith lacked the scientific attitude capable of carrying China into a new age of progress.

By this stage in the history of China, the size of the Christian movement made it sufficiently visible to be a ready target for the new renaissance-type thought. Latourette has noted:

> While between 1902 and 1912 the number of Roman Catholics increased from 720,540 to 1,431, 258 . . . , or a growth of not quite one hundred per cent in eleven years, from 1900 to 1906, the number of Protestant communicants increased from 85,000 to 178,251, or a little over one hundred per cent in six years, and to 235, 303 in 1914 [*History*, 567].

By the mid-1920s, when the anti-Christian movement was in full force:

> A fairly large Christian community arose. In 1927 it probably numbered between two and a half and three million baptized persons, of whom somewhat more than four-fifths were Roman Catholics and a little less than one-fifth Protestants. If made to include those under Christian instruction, the total was not far from three and a half million [ibid., 831].

Even more significant, Christians exerted more influence than their numbers would indicate. They occupied posts of prominence in education, medicine, rural reform, commerce, and even politics. Their influence extended far beyond their less than 1 percent of the total population of China.

Furthermore, the Chinese Protestant churches had reached the point where indigenous leadership was coming to the fore. In 1920, for the first time, Chinese ordained ministers outnumbered ordained missionaries, 1,305 to 1,268. At the second national missionary conference (1890) there had been only two Chinese present in a gathering of 445. By 1907 there were seven Chinese out of a total of 1,170. When the China Continuation Committee was organized in 1913 as a follow-up on the world mission conference at Edinburgh in 1910, one-third of the delegates were Chinese. By 1919 half of those participating in the work of this committee were Chinese. When the National Christian Conference met in 1922 the majority of the 1,200 present were Chinese.

The Catholic Church did not proceed as rapidly in its efforts to develop an indigenous hierarchy. From 1918 to 1926 the number of Chinese priests rose from 834 to 1,184, an increase from 35 to 41 percent of the total clerical body. By late 1926 the further step was taken of raising six Chinese to the episcopate. Despite this progress, the most significant positions in the church were held by missionaries, and 90 percent of the bishops were foreigners.

How were Chinese churches and their leaders going to respond to the new context characterized by (1) national political independence from foreign domination; (2) an ideological ferment producing radical new ideas to deal with the ever-worsening ills of China; (3) a frontal anti-Christian attack depicting them as forces opposed to China?

Protestant leaders chose one of two approaches: (1) a movement to local church independence accompanied by a pietistic withdrawal from the world to nurture a quiet, spiritual life; (2) a stress on writing and a radical involvement in social concern, social action, and finally social and political revolution. These were, respectively, the gospels of Daoistic pietism and Confucian activism. Each had articulate proponents.

THE GOSPEL OF CONFUCIAN ACTIVISM

Cheng Jingyi

One of the first noted Chinese leaders to wrestle with the concept of an indigenous Chinese church was Cheng Jingyi, secretary of the China Continuation Committee and a man well respected by his colleagues, both foreign and Chinese. Cheng proposed a two-step approach to develop a church truly at home in its Chinese environment (see Diagram 4).

Diagram 4

Step 1: Western Christ   -   Western Culture   =   the Essential Christ

Step 2: Essential Christ   +   Chinese Culture   =   Chinese Christianity

Cheng felt that for this model to be realized church-mission relationships must be shifted from the traditional "mission-centric" to the "church-centric" principle. Furthermore, church thinking must advance from an anti-Chinese cultural position to one that would appreciate and embrace the very best in the Chinese cultural tradition. Only a Chinese Christianity, deeply rooted both in continuity with the historical church and in its own cultural reality, would be able to enter fully into Chinese life and effect the widespread social regeneration that was needed. He expressed hopes that the Essential Christ, identified intimately with Chinese culture and society, would be able to produce a christianized Chinese culture and society.[95]

Zhao Zichen (T.C. Chao)

Another significant leader was Zhao Zichen, professor of religious philosophy and later dean of the School of Religion at Yenjing University. For over thirty years, beginning about 1918, he was one of the leading spokesmen for Christianity on college campuses and among the better educated or the intellectual class. A man with broad interests, Zhao's most important concern was for the "indigenization of Christianity." Christianity had always been viewed as a foreign faith in China, particularly during the anti-Christian agitation of the 1920s.

In Zhao's thought the indigenization of the church must be considered under two headings.[96] The Chinese church must first engage in purification, both institutional and doctrinal. Under institutional purification he dealt primarily with denominationalism and forms of worship. The church must also become more independent from the West, but not to such extremes that it would become highly nationalistic. He felt that churches ought not be "separated either by nation or by race." He considered not cooperating with those missionaries who placed themselves under and depended upon the "toleration clauses" of the inequitable treaty arrangements of 1842 and 1858–60, provisions that were not abrogated until 1943.

Zhao, at least in the middle phase of his pilgrimage, was liberal in his theology, and doctrinal purification meant that everything seemingly contradictory to science (and science was very highly revered in the China of the 1920s) and reason must be excised with vigor. Included here were cardinal points of the historical faith, such as the virgin birth, the resurrection of the body, and miracles in general. To a China steeped in the mysteries of the Buddhist religion, none of these should pose any problem. But Zhao viewed modern Chinese thought as composed of an updated Confucian philosophy plus a new scientific spirit, and indigenization meant that the faith must conform to this newly developing culture. And from his perspective what he wanted to give up was not all that central. He believed that the person of Jesus was the central doctrine of Christianity and that it must be held to and propagated in China.

Beginning in 1932 Zhao's messages centered more upon the cross, not so much in its atoning significance, but as a means by which sacrificial love triumphed over the evils of the world. The cross meant that the church needed to identify with those suffering and participate in a loving way in programs of national recovery and social reconstruction that would refuse to compromise with corruption—any form of evil.

In the late 1930s and early 1940s, influenced both by neoorthodox thought and the disappointment of his earlier efforts to produce change, Zhao became a little more traditional in his theology. He believed Jesus to be unique, the Bible to be more trustworthy, and sin to be considerably more than intellectual failure. Salvation, grace, and revelation came to have the more usual orthodox meanings to him, although human effort was still a pivotal point in his thinking.

Before the communist regime came to power in 1949, Zhao saw no way for communism and the Christian faith to coexist. Once communism was established, however, he seemed to throw aside his theological fears and enter fully into promoting the "three-self" principle, as well as many activities of nation building. Gradually he lost some of his euphoria and initial idealization as to what the church could accomplish in a Marxist environment. "Finally Christianity no longer held any relevance for him in view of the achievements of the New China" [Gluer, "Legacy," 168].

The second prong of indigenization in Zhao's thought consisted in properly relating Christianity to Confucianism. He believed that Jesus was the complete revelation of God, but God had also been revealed *to a lesser degree*—Zhao did not see the difference as one of *kind*—to Confucius, Mencius, Moti, and others. The doctrines expounded by these religious thinkers were of such a nature as to make them "akin to some of the Old Testament prophets." And just as Jesus was seen as the fulfillment of the aspirations of the Old Testament prophets, persons of other nations and cultures would see Christ as the fulfillment of their aspirations. This "universality of God" to all cultural expressions meant that there were many points of contact between Christianity and Confucianism.

Zhao was very broad in his development of this concept:

> [When] Christians know that their faith is broad enough to take in all the truths of all philosophies and religions, then, and only then, can Christianity be attractive to those not yet of the faith [Ng's translation of *The Appeal of Christ to the Chinese Mind*, in his "Evaluation"].

Zhao believed a purely humanistic interpretaion of Confucius' teaching was erroneous. "Heaven" in Confucius' thought, Zhao believed, really represented the essence of all things and was religious in nature. As the Chinese attempted to become one with nature, they were revealing a religious spirit. He regretted that Confucian philosophy was rather passive—promoting resignation, or withdrawal from life—and tended to swallow up the individual. The function of Christianity, Zhao affirmed, was to be an antidote for such tendencies.

Zhao well states the way in which the Christian faith will do in China what is impossible for Confucianism:

> We must not forget, however, that Christianity is the social gospel for mankind. Christ did come to preach the gospel to the poor, to liberate the oppressed, to give light to the ignorant and to proclaim the joy of heaven to the whole earth. As such a social gospel, as a gospel of salvation for the down-trodden, the publicans and sinners, the outcasts of society, Christianity must make its appeal to the Chinese people. As such a social gospel it will make its specific contribution and prove its superiority to Confucianism. The teachings of Confucius do not, indeed, prevent Confucians from giving of their best to the poor and oppressed, through active loving service and self-sacrifice. But history has not shown that Confucianism has within itself that religious fervour and enthusiasm which would carry its life in full abandonment to the needy souls, to the ignorant and oppressed people of the country ["Christianity," 596–97].

Zhao also emphasized many points of contact with the ethical system of Confucianism. He wished to see the central idea of "benevolence" or *ren* in all social relationships—on both the local and international levels. He equated this concept with the "kingdom of God," a phrase he understood as a kind of "brotherhood of man." Zhao saw the Christian faith as the energy necessary to achieve many of the idealistic goals of Confucianism. Furthermore, he was well aware that traditional concepts of Chinese life, such as filial piety, although not wrong in concept, could easily cause subservience, blind obedience, and feudalistic oppression. The Christian faith gave dignity to the individual and kept the individual from being swallowed up in a system. Finally, he believed that the Christian faith could be the foundation of a new society. Lee-Ming Ng comments:

> Christianity could, and already did in some instances, help to break down some of the social customs and structures of China, and this was the "destructive work of emancipation." Then Christianity could introduce a new basis of society, consisting of the idea of freedom, equality, and democracy [Lee-Ming Ng, "Evaluation," 35].

Zhao, in terms understandable to us today, did not stop with indigenization—he wished to see the Christian faith contextualized within Chinese society. Salvation was not merely for indivduals but was to embrace all of society. The problems of China, in Zhao's analysis, centered in a malaise in its people:

> The rise and fall of a country rest with her ideals, From now on, if China can revive her spirit, she will survive; if she fails to revive her spirit, she will perish [ibid., 14–15].

The need, then, was for a "spiritual reconstruction." The Chinese like other peoples, were sinners—they had strayed from the path of love. Confucianism did not have the dynamism to do anything about this. The primary function of the church, however, was directed at reviving the spirit—to bring about spiritual transformation, to seek the good of others, and to work for the benefit of an entire society:

> Christianity has not given any plan of organizing a political party. It has not provided us with any education method, economic systems, or social philosophy, although the content of Christianity is not without relevance to these areas. What Christianity has given us is not Eastern culture or Western culture, nor is it its arts or literature. Its contribution is Christ, and the religious experience of Christ [ibid., 18].

In retrospect, writing in 1950 at the celebration of the fortieth anniversary of Nanjing Theological Seminary, Zhao deprecated the efforts he and other Chinese theologians had made over the years:

For the last forty years there is nothing in the Chinese Christian theology which is worthy of being recalled. In cultural exchange, education, medicine, social and welfare exercises, the Church has contributed significantly and deserves careful attention. But in the theological areas of exegetical and Christian theology, let alone apologetics, there is hardly a single case which deserves our attention. The so-called Chinese theology is nothing more than Western-imported theology, spelled out by Western missionaries and completely digested by Chinese Christians. There has been no contribution by the Chinese on their own ["Possibility," 14–21].

This may be a harsh judgment. Such a failure, Zhao perceived, came because of dominance by Western missionaries and because of a certain antidoctrinal stance of the Chinese church. Other Chinese who made contributions during these years were more positive in their evaluation.

Despite his pessimism about the past, Zhao expressed some hope. Looking into the crystal ball for the future, how did he project the shape of a gospel in Chinese for the 1980s? First, he affirmed that the theology of the future must be done by the Chinese themselves. Secondly, in the course of doing this, Chinese theologians must have available to them "selective translations" of the classical works of the past, such as the writings of Augustine and others. Thirdly he advocated cooperation between philosophers and theologians that would deal adequately with "the relationship between knowledge and revelation, or the question of religious epistemology."

In Zhao's view any gospel in Chinese must be integrally related to the traditional Chinese faiths:

The task of Chinese theological labor lies in the study of Confucian Chinese (Ru Jia) thinking, as well as of the Dao, and Buddhist thinking. Then we need to make a comparative study of the former three with Christianity. We ought to make discoveries of the areas of similarities and dis-similarities; the areas needing dialogue, and other areas which need not be harmonized. Confucian teaching on human ethics (Daode Lun) ought to be used to stimulate Christian theology. Also, Christian theology can point out the unstable characteristics of Ru Jia and Dao Jia's teachings on human nature. The Dao and De in the teaching of Daoism can reveal some truth of the incarnation, while the incarnation can criticize Lao-Tzu's teaching on Guan Fu (to watch, returning to Dao), as well as Zhuang Zi's Xiaoyao (free wheeling or feeling at ease), for not meeting needs of the human quest. Meanwhile, Christian teaching on God's absolute revelation in space/time truth can be a basis for criticizing Buddhism's teaching on "all emptiness in human nature and its opposing forces." Christianity is a religion of faith and life. Whenever it encounters a civilization, it ought to utilize the philosophy of its culture to explain itself. In the second century, the early Christian fathers often used Greek philosophy to explain Christianity. Leaders like Origen, Tertullian,

Augustine (4th century) used Platonic and Aristotelian terms to explain Christianity to their environment and time. But many times they went too far with the result that the essence of Christianity disappeared [ibid.].

With remarkable foresight he projected that, although the theologians of the future may not need to be seminary graduates, they should be the "product of theory and practice." Admitting that the church in China, together with its leaders, has not often gone through trial and suffering and been "put on the scale of 'heavenly justice,' " he claimed that:

The Chinese Augustines, Tertullians, and Origens must come out of churches which go through hard and long suffering. There will be theological students and seminaries. Life, faith, and experience can give interpretation to faith and life [ibid.].

A major task of the Chinese theologians of the future, Zhao affirmed, will be "the interpretation of the fundamentals of our [Christian] faith, which is also Christian theology." He predicted:

Forty years from today, the Chinese Church will be narrowed in scope (and limits); with its abundant experience and its yeast-like effect, it will certainly draw many to the cross of Jesus Christ. I am sure that it will provide the standard of truth for which people will want to search: the moral (ethical) foundations, security of values, selfhood, meaning of life and sense of belonging to which we are drawn. . . . The Lord sees 1000 years as but one day, and the next forty years is nothing but to demonstrate the wonders, power, and authority of God [ibid.].

Wu Yaozong (Y.T. Wu)

Wu Yaozong, converted to the Christian faith at an evangelistic rally conducted by Sherwood Eddy in 1918, found spheres of Christian service in the YMCA, the Student Christian Movement, and, after the advent of the Peoples' Democratic Republic of China, as a leader in the Three-Self Movement. He was far less interested in structural indigenization seen, for example, in the formation of the Church of Christ in China, or in the cultural indigenization that occupied a fair share of Zhao's thought and writing. However, he did believe that only an indigenized church could reach broader goals and be committed to the broader idea of "social reconstruction," which also, as we have seen, was part of Zhao's concern.

Wu saw love at the center of the Christian faith, but he understood it chiefly in terms of action. He believed that to act by God's love and not by selfish desire was to be saved. He reacted to the motto of the Five-Year movement (1929), "Revive the church, Lord, but first revive me," by proposing that a more adequate objective might be the "Kingdom of God . . . an ideal society in this world wherein men would be freed and liberated from material wants and political and social injustices and oppressions" ["A Study of Y.T.Wu," *Ching Feng,* vol. 15, no. 1 (1972)].

The needs of China, in his view, were both internal and external. He viewed its internal problems as not unlike those of the entire globe:

> [Chinese society] is based on the principles of private property, laissez-faire and competition no less than the capitalistic society. And the exploitation, oppression and inequalities it has produced are no less than those produced in capitalistic societies [ibid.].

Externally, China must resist all foreign aggression, whether military—as had come from Japan—cultural, economic, or political.

Social services previously performed by the church through schools and hospitals were essentially an application of the "Band-Aid" philosophy and did not deal with the "roots of evil" or with society as a whole. The church, in his view, must regain a prophetic perspective and also be revolutionary in spirit. "To be revolutionary in spirit" meant dissemination of revolutionary ideas, concentrating more on urban problems related to industrialization, and organizing the people into a revolutionary force. Wu felt that Marxism shared some common goals with Christianity, although he could not espouse the violent tactics of Marxism or its promotion of class hatred. Reconciliation by the cross, he felt, must always be the Christian stance. Despite this "ideal" position, he did believe that in certain situations violence might be justified as a lesser evil than continued oppression.

Eventually, Wu espoused Marxism and, after 1949, entered fully into its program of reeducation and liberation of the people from years of bondage under external imperialism and the internal feudalism produced by Confucianism. An unreconstructed church could never accomplish this: it was too closely allied with the capitalistic influences of the West. This task, for Wu, became "Christianity." "To do what was necessary for the benefit of society was Christianity" [ibid., 52].

In his pilgrimage Wu had moved from spiritual reform to social reform and then to social revolution. For him the gospel in Chinese had taken on a Marxist tinge. The West had orchestrated a worldwide example of the bankruptcy of capitalism, seen particularly at the time of the 1929 depression, and the church in China, tragically in his view, was linked with this evil of capitalism. Increasingly he felt that the only path for the church in its ideological stance was the route of communism. Revolution was really the only solution for the ills of China [ibid.].

Theoretically, Wu believed that the church should act as a prophetic voice within society, a conscience that would proclaim the righteousness of God's kingdom. In reality, a weak view of the corruptive influence of sin in all social structures, not least of all the state, left him with no standard to really speak as a prophet. Furthermore, prophets were and are without honor in a Marxist society. The capacity for thoroughgoing criticism, although praised as a virtue, is scarcely tolerated when directed at the state.

Wu Leizhuan

A fourth important Chinese leader during this critical period of the history of China was Wu Leizhuan, the first Chinese president of Yenjing University.[97] As with others in this era, as a Christian he was under attack for being unscientific and for being "half foreign." He responded to the first criticism by seeking to rid Christianity of some of its "irrational dogma." To escape the label of "foreign," the Christian faith, he believed, must relate itself far more deeply than ever before to Chinese culture.

In his book *Jidu Jiao Yu Zhongguo Wenhua* ["Christianity and Chinese Culture"] (1936) he tried both to reinterpret the Christian faith and to relate it more integrally to his own culture. He viewed sin as evil, crimes, or selfishness, all created by society rather than being something innate in human nature. With the locus of sin in society rather than in individuals, the task confronting the church was to change society. This effort to achieve God's righteousness— right relationships among members of the same society—was the best way to demonstrate God's love.

Jesus' role in this process, according to Wu, was to provide that selfless, persevering example of devotion to God's will even in the midst of opposition. Jesus, he believed, had been as confused in his day as to the right way to do God's will within society. His early attempts at wielding political power had failed because of Jewish opposition, causing him then to turn to reforming the spirit of the people, an effort that also ended in failure when even the people misunderstood him.

Wu's reading of the gospel record led him to believe that Jesus taught a kind of socialism—no need for private property; equal distribution of wealth. To attain this goal—a new society equated with the kingdom of God—required revolutionary action in China, although he himself did not wish to use violence. This option, however, was a much lesser evil when compared with the Western-imported capitalism that he saw in China.

Wu's recommendations for the sinification of Chrisitianity were not unique. Along with others, he was impressed with similarities between Christianity and Confucianism: a comparable ethics; the concept of truth or a cosmic principle behind the universe; and the possible equation between the idea of *ren* (benevolence) in the classics and the Holy Spirit. He felt that both faiths were humanistic in emphasizing that, by their own power and moral strength, people could achieve the status of superior persons. Jesus had achieved the divine goal by prayer and struggle, and, because he was essentially not different from others in nature, his victory could also be theirs.

These varied attempts by leading Confucian-like Christian activists to contextualize the gospel to their Chinese milieu were thwarted by several "rocks of stumbling." First, in what might be viewed as the narrower task of indigenization, efforts made to stress points of commonality between Christianity and Confucianism probably worked to the disadvantage of both. Would outsiders have been led to believe that both protagonists were giving up their uniqueness—that which identified what they really were? And was it not futile to seek accommodation to the Confucian ideology at the very time when Chinese intellectuals were discarding it as impotent to face the problems of a modern, technological world?

More serious was the reality that the gospel by its very nature must always operate from a position of what the world calls "weakness":

> Yenching voices [e.g., Wu Leizhuan] would speak of comprehensive solutions, but they were unconnected to any program for creating power to implement them and thus remained largely voices of protest. The social gospel promised social justice, but the *means of delivery* were never clearly spelled out. The Christian formulas for national salvation did produce new social patterns, a new vision of society, new tasks to perform, like teaching, and the training of skills for carrying out those tasks. But these tasks involved only a small segment of society and had little effect on the reshaping of a new political order. . . . Yenching followers, furthermore, were unable to tap the one resource which Chinese patriots increasingly identified as the means to national salvation, namely the mobilization of the masses in the countryside [West, P., 245].

Actually, their failure was rooted in the lack not merely of a power base, but of a detailed program that could be labeled "uniquely Christian." None of the four men who sought to put the gospel into Chinese during this period started with a specifically Christian position. Rather they opted for this or that social philosophy and then sought to christianize it. This would not have been fatal if they had claimed less. But to say that "Jesus had the answer," without being able to deliver, left them vulnerable and destroyed their credibility. If the Christian faith had no unique social validity, could not the same be said of its religious claims?[98]

THE GOSPEL OF DAOIST MYSTICISM

Was there another gospel in Chinese in the turbulent twenties? The route advocated by several prominent and popular preachers was that of a Daoist-like mysticism. These evangelical pietists did not overtly adjust themselves to the Daoist spirit, but, in essence, they advocated this path—the gospel of subjectivism, intuition, and individual, personal quietism. If enough persons are in harmony with the Dao (God and God's purposes), they seemed to say, all will go well in the universe. Trust God and do nothing socially (*wu wei*).

Who were these pietists—who probably have had more effect at the grass roots than all the Christian activists? They also were products of the independent spirit of this age.

Ni Duosheng (Watchman Nee)

From 1901 until 1931, but particularly after the fall of the Manchu dynasty in 1911, over six hundred independent Chinese churches were orgainzed. This happened most often with the emergence of a strong Chinese leader who had a vision of starting a church in a particular city, probably with branches reaching out into the surrounding area. One such leader was the well-known and widely followed Ni Duosheng. He was born in Swatow in southern China in 1903 and died in northern China in 1972. He is known as the founder of the Assembly Hall churches, sometimes referred to as the "little flock," after a hymnal issued by these churches.

Ni published many books in Chinese as well as some thirty-four works in English, some of which have sold hundreds of thousands of copies. The church group that he founded in 1922 grew to have seven hundred local congregations with a membership of seventy thousand by 1949. When the communist government came to power, Witness Li continued the movement in Taiwan, and by 1970 it could count a membership there of thirty-five thousand.

In general, the "little flock" fared little better in China than did the mainline denominations that were much more visible. More indigenous at least in structure, Ni's group was still accused of being tainted by imperialism, and, more than some others, had difficulty in relating to the Three-Self Movement, the touchstone of survival tactics in liberated China.

Structurally, this church group was considerably more "indigenized" than most of the mainline denominations. The Chinese non-Christian did not immediately dismiss it as "foreign." The local church was the basic expression of the Body of Christ. All leaders were Chinese. The Assembly Hall pattern was usually that of a central congregation with several district halls clustered about it. Radiating out from these district halls were many "home churches."

Although "gifts of the Spirit" were emphasized, there was also a strong leadership pattern centered in Watchman Ni and Witness Li, the only ones with the rank of "apostles." Local assemblies could choose their own elders and deacons, but they had to be ordained by the apostles. Ni was influenced strongly by the Brethren movement in London and North America, and even as they were rebels from Anglicanism and its highly structured church life, so he found denominational patterns in China intolerable. The only way to go, in his view, was to seek primitive worship patterns, albeit modified by authoritative leadership patterns found in the Orient. Significantly, the rank and file of the Assembly Hall movement were far different from the elite, "compradore-like" Chinese leaders who were the usual product of the foreign missionary movement and who found it difficult to move far beyond a kind of a weening dependence on outside funds and direction.

In general, the Assembly Hall churches were antiforeign, antidenominational, and antimission. They were pietistic and otherworldly, which is what might be expected from a movement influenced by the English Brethren and the annual English "keswick" conference for the deepening of spiritual life. They stressed a tent-making ministry, "man in community," with many small group meetings, widespread use of literature, stewardship, and extensive evangelism. They were a nationalistic type of church that wanted to do things the Chinese way, a view that was reinforced by Ni's concept of the church.

Ni believed in the idea of a universal church, but the local church was far more important to him. According to this view, locality is the only scriptural basis for the division of the church into churches. It was possible to have fellowship with other groups, but it was not right to accept denominational prejudices or to give denominational representatives responsibility in church services. These persons, Ni felt, were Christians, but they had lost the correct basis of what constitutes a true local church.

In terms of "theological indigeneity," doctrinal concepts overtly related to their Chinese context, these churches might just as well have been non-Chinese. They used the Chinese Bible that incorporated much Buddhist terminology, as noted earlier. They sang Psalms, prayed together out loud, separated men and women in their seating arrangements, and followed other Chinese customs in their gatherings; this, however, is generally true of all Chinese churches of whatever persuasion and polity.

To what extent, though, were their beliefs shaped explicitly by their Chinese environment? Very little, it would seem. In fact, Ni's doctrine, far from being purely biblical, is modeled on many strands, including heretical, of Western theology. At an early age he went to mission schools in Fuzhou, and his initial alma mater was Trinity College in Fuzhou, an institution operated by the (British) Anglican Church Mission Society.

One of the early influences on Ni's life was Margaret Barber, a CMS missionary who had gone to China in 1899 but later became independent and developed strong relationships with British independency, particularly the Plymouth Brethren Movement. From her library he read widely on the lives and writings of Martin Luther, John Knox, Jonathan Edwards, George Whitfield, David Brainerd, and others. Probably nothing was more influential on his thinking than the works of Jeanne de la Motte Guyon, the famous French mystic imprisoned by Louis XIV in the Bastille for her fervent and very mystical faith. Other authors who made an impact on his life during those formative years were Andrew Murray, F.B. Meyer, Jesse Penn-Lewis, Charles Finney, and Evan Roberts.

In 1932 and 1938 Ni made visits to England, developing informal ties of fellowship with the London Brethren, who were so exclusive that they deeply resented the fact that he also visited the Christian Fellowship Centre, whose leader, J. Austin-Sparks, was a friend of Miss Barber's. Although the rigid exclusivism of many of these groups precluded the development of any ongoing organizational ties with them, he imbibed deeply of their philosophy: a reaction against the worldliness, sterility, and bureaucracy of the major church groups; a rigidly separatist lifestyle in view of the imminent second advent of Jesus Christ; the rejection of all creedal formulations; emphasis on individual conversion; and a resistance to futile social reform activities as opposed to the essential calling of the church to pluck men and women out of a rapidly deteriorating world.

All Ni's writings reflect this pietistic, otherworldly viewpoint that Richard Niebuhr would classify in his classic *Christ and Culture* as basically anti(Chinese) cultural. His works are a warmed-over version, with a slightly Oriental flavor, of Brethren doctrine. This ability to communicate the gospel in an indigenous fashion within the Chinese environment led to noninvolvement with the broader political, economic, and societal issues of the Chinese context.

The Spiritual Man, written in 1928 when he was nearing his twenty-fifth birthday, is a representative sample of his theology. The "spiritual" person was one who was able to be victorious in the Christian life. To Ni this meant that the "spirit" must overcome all the constraints of soul and body. For him the body was the means of world-consciousness; the soul the means of self-consciousness, including the will, mind, and emotions; and the spirit was the vehicle for God-consciousness, being composed of conscience, intuition, and communion.

Ni claimed that the ideal held forth by God is for the human spirit to rule over the soul and body. In the fall of humankind, the soul gained ascendancy over the spirit that had died and lost its sensitivity to God. When a person is regenerated, the spirit is revived, but this new birth "has no relation to soul or body." For the Christian, to live under the control of the spirit is to be spiritual, whereas to live according to the body is to be carnal, and to live under the control of the soul is to be "soulish."

In practical terms, the soulish Christian places too much stress on will, mind, and emotion, whereas to live spiritually means:

> To walk according to intuition . . . to have all one's life, service and action in the spirit, ever being governed and empowered by it.[99]

The spiritual Christian, then, is guided more by the "inner voice of intuition" than by logical thought processes. Prayer is more important than planning and may in fact replace it. In *Sit, Walk, Stand,* for example, Ni states, "we have sought to make it clear that Christian experience does not begin with walking, but with sitting" [p. 22]. Ten pages later he asserts, " . . . nothing is so hurtful to the life of a Christian as acting." How indeed like the Daoist mystic:

> Let things go on their own way, not interfering, not imposing one's will on nature, letting things happen of their own accord, not trying to reform the world, not trying to "improve" the world, but simply accepting things as they are [Raymond M. Smullyan, *The Tao Is Silent* (published privately by the author, 1977) 147].

I am not, of course, suggesting that Ni and his followers were Daoists. They firmly believed in a transcendent, personal God who created and controls the universe. They had a high standard of Christian ethics. But the essence of the Christian life was to relate to God directly through "intuition," not far really from the soulish "emotion," rather than to be governed by anything external or artificial, such as mental processes, planning, common sense, organization, education, or even the more conventional methods of interpreting the Bible. God was experienced directly within the soul, the personal perception of the will could not be challenged by others (except the Apostles!), and an individualistic, quiet type of faith was more authentic than any attempts made outwardly to reform the world. The world was, in fact, so under Satan's control that any attempts to employ the Christian ethic were both useless and unbiblical [Ni, *Love Not,* 42–43].

If our imaginary space visitor (chap. 1) were to examine this, he might well wonder if it were any more anomalous than the Nestorian faith or indeed than some of the beliefs of Hong Xiuquan. What continuity is there here with the "orthodox" Christian faith? If one, however, is guided by "intuition" in faith and action, then the question of continuity and normativeness is not all that significant.

Is it possible that Ni Duosheng, with extreme inward mysticism inherited from Madame Guyon and Jesse Penn-Lewis, inadvertently did better in creating a gospel in Chinese than we might at first surmise? Does this help explain his popularity and the widespread success of his movement? It is no secret that many of the Christian groups that have mushroomed in the China of today are in a line of descent from Watchman Ni and other like-minded Chinese preachers. Evangelicals would say the Christian house meetings are more scriptural. But is it conceivable that their antipathy to organization, their suspicion of anything that would limit their freedom, their emphasis on the "inner life," their disinterest in reforming society, and their inability to develop any kind of church-state doctrine may derive more from the traditional Chinese context than from a commitment to biblical Christianity?

Just as believers should not seek to reform the world, according to Ni, neither should they truck with the state. The church stands above the state, whose primary function is that of an instrument wielded by God to create conditions in which the church can carry out God's will, a rather restricted task in Ni's view. Ni urged his followers not to pray either for a Chinese or a Japanese victory in World War II, but for the outcome that would most benefit God's people [Kinnear, 117].

Ni's premillennial, apocalyptic eschatology made him pessimistic about both the world and the state. The ever increasing problems that China faced demanded escape rather than a solution.

Although much of Ni's teaching was continuous with the classic creeds of Christendom, serious questions have been raised about some of his doctrines. His atomistic analysis of human nature has not been the usual Christian view. He made a rigid distinction between justification and sanctification, distinguishing between the blood of Christ, which brings forgiveness, and the cross, which deals with original sin and gives deliverance [Ehrling, "Story," 150]. Some have noted a tendency toward Sabellianism in his view of the Trinity. God is not simultaneously Father and Son, but rather there is a transformation (*hua shen*) of one member into another—God *revealing* the divine nature through different persons [Carl Henry, "Footnotes," *Christianity Today* (May 9, 1975) 799–800]. Nearly everyone has noted the extreme subjectivity in Ni's hermeneutics—the "hermeneutic-of-spiritual-man principle" that sees the Bible as an inexhaustible mine of hidden allegorical and typological meanings.[100]

Ni's gospel in Chinese demanded that Chinese nationals be its prime evangelists. His strong nationalism, necessary for the period in which he lived and ministered, did not preclude the need for missionaries. He advocated, however, that they ought not to be associated with a mission society, and that in the complex culture of China it might be well for them "to wear for the first ten years of their service something like the L-plates attached to the car of English learner-driver's" [Kinnear, 112].

In consulting with leaders of the China Inland Mission shortly before their withdrawal from China in 1950, Ni, when asked how missionaries could serve best in the future in the Middle Kingdom, replied:

> First of all, provide us with Bible commentaries. You have so many and we have so few. Translate Bishop Lightfoot's commentaries, for example, and other similar works. And then, when you can come back again, come *not as evangelists*, but as teaching elders in our local churches. You will receive a very warm welcome [Lyall, 90; italics added].

Ni has had a profound influence on Chinese Christianity. He may not have been the most accurate interpreter of the Christian faith for believers everywhere, and he may not have done as well as he could have in translating his commitment into the Chinese context. None will doubt his evangelistic zeal, his commitment, and his perseverance during later years of suffering and imprisonment. And in ways beyond his own planning, a concept he decried, the style and ethos of his brand of Christianity were uniquely Chinese.

Wang Mingdao

Nearly equal with Ni Duosheng in his impact upon Chinese Christians was Wang Mingdao, best known for his steadfast and costly refusal to submit to the demands of the Three-Self Patriotic Movement. This organization, named after the "three-self" concept (self-governing, self-propagating, and self-supporting) long espoused by foreign missionaries as the epitome of an indigenous church, was the link between the Christian community and the new government. Pastor of the Christian Tabernacle in Beijing, Wang's influence spread not only through proclamation from this important platform in the

Chinese capital but through the many readers reached by the Chinese quarterly *Ling Shi* ["spiritual food"].

Converted at the age of fourteen, Wang had considerable contact with foreign missions through the London Missionary Society and the Presbyterian Church. He undoubtedly was also influenced by Ni and the doctrines of his pietistic Christianity. Any "dynamic equivalence" of biblical truth into the Chinese idiom was difficult because of his belief that the scriptures, in their entirety, were dictated by God. Form and content, for him, were of equal importance and must be doggedly preserved.

Early in his life Wang intended to be a politician to save China from its political and economic ills. Once he was converted and received a vision of "eternal life," however, he believed that it was futile to try to improve the world. The world, in fact, had really almost gone beyond the point of redemption, and it was God's will that it be destroyed. All human efforts to build an ideal society were doomed to failure, because they lacked moral vigor and could not lead to God's perfect kingdom.

What has been the nature of Wang Mingdao's gospel in Chinese? In general, he has held to the principal tenets of classic orthodoxy. Within these parameters, one of his main emphases has been on the way in which God delivers the Christian from death. In Wang's view, conversion resulted in a new person, replacing the "old man," almost in an organic sense, which would then never die. Behavior was always the product of faith leading to a strong emphasis on works, although never as a means of salvation. Faith, in Wang's theology, was more a matter of the will than of the intellect, an emphasis that made him popular with the common people.

Despite his insistence that the Christian should be separate from the world and that faith and politics are not to be mixed, Wang frequently insisted that Christians should set a high standard of moral conduct in the world. China in these turbulent times was undergoing a moral crisis. Jiang Jieshi was promoting the New Life movement, calling especially the young to return to traditional Confucian virtues. Wang's preaching well fit the need of this context:

> The Chinese term for "ethics" is *Dao-de*. *Dao* means doctrine, while *de* means virtuous conduct. He takes this as an illustration of how the Word of doctrine is the basis for virtue. Without it, one has no way of knowing what virtuous conduct is. It would be like trying to build a road, but having no origin [Jonathan Chao and Christopher Morris, "Wang Mingdao Today," *China and the Church Today*, 2:2–3 (March–June 1980) 4].

Wang's ethical emphasis, however, reached little beyond the individual, the pietistic devotional life of the individual. He gave little thought to ways in which sin was enmeshed in the very structures of society and demanded as a solution anything more than a very individual approach.[101]

Wang's perseverance in holding to unpopular convictions both frustrated his enemies and attracted many followers. During the time of the Japanese occupation of Northern China in early 1940, he refused to join a Japanese-sponsored Northern China United Christian Promotion Association. In the early 1950s, appalled by the efforts made by the Three-Self Patriotic Movement to organize Chinese Christians under what he deemed to be the traitorous Christian Manifesto confessing past church complicity in imperialism, he refused to cooperate. Disregarding repeated warnings, he persistently headed down a path of confrontation. In June 1955, he published an article, "We Because of Faith," in which he attacks an essay written by Wu Yaozong delineating the differences between fundamentalists and modernists. Affirming the inerrancy of scripture, the virgin birth of Christ, salvation, the resurrection, and the second coming of Christ, he denied that there was any basis for unity in China among Christians of widely diverse opinions.

Wang Mingdao saw his differences with the Three-Self Movement as *theological*—it was a modernist organization and he was defending the faith. Later, in a forced statement, the truth of which is open to question, he confessed that his position was *political*—he had ridiculed socialist society and had undermined his hearers' readiness as Chinese citizens to work toward national reconstruction.

The issues between him and the Three-Self Patriotic Movement were probably both political and theological. They were theological in the way he understood them as a defense of orthodox Christian beliefs, but theological-political in the sense of defining the relationship between religion and society, the Christian's role in the world. To him the issues were clear-cut with no room for compromise: the new government was communist; it had stimulated the leaders of the newly-formed Three-Self Movement to issue the manifesto; some of these leaders had espoused liberal theology; the faith must be defended at all cost. He, even as the Son of man twenty centuries earlier, was being betrayed into the hands of sinners.

It was a simple gospel, ignoring all of the immense complexities of history, the contemporaneous interplay of social, theological, and political issues, and the many strands of New Testament teaching instructing Christians in their relationship to the state. But, even as in the case of Watchman Ni, his central thrust had an irresistible appeal:

> His exposition of the basis of a spiritual life as lying in a close relationship of doctrine, virtue, and practical life is a refinement of the general pietist ethic, set largely in traditional Chinese ethical terms. It is consonant both with traditional Confucian values and with the practical, common-sense Chinese outlook [Lam Wing-hung (M. 101), p. 4].

CATHOLIC RESPONSES

Whereas some of the more articulate spokesmen for Protestant Christianity adopted views that deviated from the classic Christian creeds, the few significant Chinese Catholic leaders held firmly to traditional theological positions as they expressed their gospel in Chinese. These were not the days of post–Vatican II when many would dare to challenge long-accepted views.

Nor could leaders or institutions within Catholic hierarchical structures operate or speak in independence of control by the Congregation for the Propagation of the Faith. There was no freedom comparable to that of the Protestant churches.

Catholic thinkers, however, were ready, at least within narrow limits, to dress their message in Chinese garb—always careful to balance their theological bent toward accommodation while avoiding the pitfalls of compromise that had plagued their missionary efforts during the late Ming and early Qing periods. Bishop Paul Yu-pin, vicar apostolic of Nanjing and apostolic administrator, traces the authority for such accommodation to an instruction given by the Propaganda in 1659:

> Do not in any way attempt, and do not on any pretext persuade these people to change their rites, their customs and their manners, unless they be openly opposed to religion and morality [*Eyes East*, 114].

Bishop Yu-pin devotes a chapter of *Eyes East* to the Chinese Catholic Culture Movement. He argues the classic Thomistic position on culture (what Richard Niebuhr identifies as the synthesist "Christ above Culture" view) when he states:

> Actually there is no conflict between religion and culture properly conceived, because they are in different spheres. Culture is the ennoblement of man by human ingenuity; Christianity is the divinization of man by divine generosity. Where culture finishes Christianity takes up. By Christianity I mean Catholicism, which alone is integral Christianity. Where culture leaves imperfect, Christianity fulfills. For Christianity is a supernatural religion; it builds on the natural; it destroys and conflicts only with the unnatural [ibid., 112].

Yu-pin urges that, in the pattern of Matteo Ricci, Catholics need "to form an intellectual elite and to work specifically to satisfy the needs of China's elite."

In giving this challenge he then refers to the instruction of December 8, 1939, with respect to Confucian rites:

> Since the Chinese government has several times openly declared that all are free to profess whatever religion they choose, and that it is far from their minds to issue laws or orders about religious matters; and that consequently the ceremonies in honor of Confucius which are either performed or ordered by the public authorities, are done not with a view to offering religious worship, but solely in order to encourage and manifest traditions;—it is permitted to Catholics to be present at ceremo-

nies of honor which are performed before an image or tablet of Confucius in Confucian temples or in schools [ibid., 142].

NO INTEGRAL, INTEGRATED GOSPEL FOR THE TIMES

What may we say in conclusion about the gospel in Chinese preached by the Chinese themselves in the period of the Chinese republic (1911–49)? One dominant Protestant strand was clearly pietistic, almost Daoistic, as I have suggested. It had characteristics similar to the Mukyokai (nonchurch) in Japan, whose doctrine appealed strongly to the traditional Japanese sense of "spirituality." Carlo Caldarola, in his brilliant work *Christianity the Japanese Way*, has commented:

> Obviously, as Christians, the Mukyokai people accept the dualistic conception of reality [objective external reality—e.g., God and human reality], but the exclusion of institutional requirements and the emphasis on interior experience, immediacy, spontaneity, and the identification of religion and ethic are so genuinely Japanese in flavor that the final synthesis can in a sense be defined (as some respondents called it) a "Zenlike Christianity" [pp. 89–90].

This brand of Christianity, although pointing many seekers to the eternal Christ, did little to change the issues that kept Christianity from being an option for the Chinese masses. Its leaders opted for the status quo, a very specific political stance, with the result that:

> Christian missions and the churches they have fostered have throughout presupposed and disseminated the capitalist culture of the West and have been allied with such forces in China as were sympathetic to or could be the tools of the captialist and imperialist West; and therefore, objectively speaking, the mission and the Church were fundamentally reactionary forces, opposed to the true interest of the people [Paton, 37].

The activist, Confucianlike social reformers—Cheng, Zhao, Wu Leizhuan, and Wu Yaozong—saw the social issue much more clearly and tried to place the church and its message on the side of forces seeking to change China. In the process, they accommodated themselves so thoroughly to contemporary human philosophies that there was little unique Christian gospel left. Their Christianity had no more solution for the total ills of China than did that of Ni Duosheng or Wang Mingdao. Although many Protestant Chinese preachers sought a balanced position between these polarized extremes, there were no preeminent advocates for a gospel in Chinese that addressed itself to the totality of the needs, both spiritual and social, of China.

Catholic leaders probably struck a better balance in this troubled period of Chinese life. Holding fast to their theological mooring, they promoted Catholic involvement in many deeds of mercy, and sought as well to lead in indigenizing their faith to Chinese culture. Did they, however, do any better than the Protestants in proclaiming an integrated gospel that could provide possible solutions to the gnawing social, economic, and political problems of Chinese society?

CHAPTER TEN

The Gospel about China

The late nineteenth and early twentieth centuries marked a crisis of national identity for China. The pat phrase, "Chinese learning as the essence; Western learning for practical ends," was convenient. Unfortunately, no one was perfectly sure what the "essence" included! Was it the Confucian faith, either in its classical form or in some kind of modern reformulation? Could it be an up-to-date Buddhism or the *dao* in a more generalized sense? Or was it all or part of this plus new universals such as science, democracy, and pragmatism?

For the Christian churches and their leaders, both Chinese and foreign, the issue was hardly theoretical. Any indigenous theology must be sure of its context, and this was a question of the Chinese "essence"—its identity as a people and a nation. This period, then, was one when many thinkers were devising ways and means to put the gospel in Chinese. These were not necessarily the practitioners actually preaching the gospel in Chinese; more often it was outsiders proposing suggestions for how the task should be done.

CHINESE PICTOGRAMS

A classic approach, familiar to many missionaries, made use of Chinese pictograms, and was first published in written form in *Genesis and Chinese* by C. H. Kang in 1950, and in *The Discovery of Genesis and Chinese* by C. H. Kang and Esther Nelson in 1979. Based on the assumption, not without some evidence, that the earliest Chinese culture was monotheistic and only later degenerated into polytheism, this method analyzes Chinese pictograms to discover evidences of God's primitive revelation to Moses.

These analysts have pointed out, for example, that the Chinese pictogram for *chuan* (船), meaning "boat," is made up of three elements: 舟 also meaning "boat"; 儿 meaning "eight"; and 口 meaning "the mouth of a person." The entire pictogram, eight persons in a boat, derives, it is claimed, from the biblical account of Noah escaping with his family from the flood.

In similar fashion the character 魔 , meaning "devil," is broken apart as follows:

$$ 厶 + 儿 + 田 + \text{'} = 鬼 + 林 + 广 = 魔 $$

secret + man + garden + alive = devil + trees + cover = tempter

Admittedly there are interesting resemblances, but the authors' detailed analysis requires some imagination. They explain that in picturing the fall of humankind several pictographs were combined in early Chinese:

A garden, field or landed property 田 represents the Garden of Eden; a man, son 儿 shows the humanoid aspect of the devil, who spoke as a man to Eve, even though through the medium of a serpent; and the word secret, private 厶 conveys his clandestine approach to Eve. These three symbols, together with the "pien" ヽ indicating 'alive,' are combined in the devil 鬼 .

But to be more specific, the devil 鬼 radical is then placed under the cover 广 of protecting trees 林 . The devil 鬼 waited for Eve in the forbidden tree, which was located in the middle of the garden next to the tree of life—hence the two trees 林 . Furthermore he was under cover 广 , being hidden in the tree and also camouflaged as a serpent. By uniting these primitive pictographs into an ideographic character, the word tempter 魔 appears to have been designed [Kang and Nelson, 3–4].

In a similar fashion, either soberly or more imaginatively, the words for "create," "walk," "spirit," "ancestor," "blessing," "want," "naked," "hide," and so forth, are analyzed to find indications of this primal revelation. The authors speculate that the Chinese themselves may have participated in the rebellion at Babel. By this method, the Chinese language itself becomes the launching pad, as it were, to present the gospel in Chinese, revealing to the Chinese God's concern for them as a people from antiquity.

Peter Lee of the Chinese Research Centre at Dao Feng Shan in Shatin, Hong Kong, suggests that in a milder, more restrained form, this use of the Chinese language is an appropriate way to present theological truths:

The Chinese language is adept at using concrete imageries, suggestive rather than discursive, and conducive to the communication of intuitive knowledge. When Chinese Christians write their own theology, they should take full advantage of the special qualities of their native tongue, and their works would then contain genuine indigenous elements [Peter Lee, "Indigenous theology," [Ching Feng, vol. 17, no. 1, 1974].

He specifically points to the Chinese character for belief 信 , which may be divided into 亻 "man" and 言 "word," with the implication that faith is a person leaning on God's word. Another common illustration is the Chinese character for righteousness, 義 which seems to be a picture of a "lamb" 羊 positioned above "me" 我 , teaching that God's righteousness in Christ is associated with the covering for sin provided by the Lamb of God.

Most modern writers who appeal for a Chinese contextualized theology, although not ignoring the rich cultural tradition of China, wish to be much more specific about current realities, whether on the mainland or in the diaspora. Lee, for example, seeks a theology that speaks to the current Chinese struggle for modernization. He notes that in Hong Kong there is much freedom but little sense of justice; the opposite condition prevails in China. What, he asks, should this mean theologically for the Hong Kong Christian? He further wonders what perspective the Christian ought to bring to the problems of Chinese history.

MODERN NEO-CONFUCIANISM

It is to these kinds of issues—science, democracy, economics, education, politics—that a new, modern neo-Confucianism seeks to speak. "New Confucianism" has had several proponents. Zhang Junmai (Carson Chang), first on the mainland and later in Taiwan, was most responsible for a 1958 Manifesto to the World on Behalf of Chinese Culture. Denying that the Confucian faith was interested only in ethics and morals, and was devoid of any truly vertical, religious dimension, this declaration affirms that the Chinese concept of the Unity of Heaven and Man (*tian ren he yi*) is no less "religious" than the faith of Christians.

A key idea in this apologetic is the Chinese expression *xinxing* (心性), translated by most Westerners as "human nature" but in the manifesto as "transcendental mind":

Man's nature is essentially good, not bad, as in the Christian doctrine of original sin. Since man's nature partakes of the universal (heavenly) nature, it is best translated as "Transcendental Mind." When man develops or exerts his "Transcendental Mind" to its fullest, he approaches the celestial virtue, Heavenly Reason and the Cosmic Mind, so achieving a unity or harmony with Heaven.

The manifesto declares that, to the Chinese, human activities are ultimately always directed toward attaining this identity with Heaven, whether interpreted as God or as ultimate reality. The Chinese have not been so interested as Westerners about "seeking knowledge for the sake of knowledge," a Greek legacy, but about knowing and developing the moral principles inherent in the idea of the unity of heaven and earth. The time has come, the manifesto asserts, not only to develop theoretical science alongside this ethico-religious system but also to promote the concept of democracy, present in seed in the teaching of Confucius.[102]

Another form of neo-Confucianism founded by Chen Jianfu in Taiwan in the mid-1950s has a more distinct Christian component—in fact, its founder calls it "the Chinese form of Christianity." Seeking to find some kind of middle ground between total surrender to westernization and a stubborn clinging to classical traditionalism, Chen confesses his debt both to Christianity and Confucianism. The gospel of neo-Confucianism has little resemblance to classic Christian formulations. God is not clearly transcendent, but has existence primarily in human nature. No clear line separates the creator from the creation. Jesus is not unique, but as he realizes fully the potential of the *dao* within him, he serves as a model for all humankind.

Not rigidly bound by historical Christian dogmas, this form of Christianity is better able to promote the kind of scholarly thinking needed to reach Chinese intellectuals, those most responsible for welding society together in a matrix of books, poetry, rites, and morality. This intellectual bent, free from all absolutes, means also that it will better be able to develop a scientific attitude committed to research and debate. Human nature is autonomous, with no need really to depend on God. In its self-sufficiency and independence, it is the measure of all things. Dogmatic religion need no longer shackle and inhibit human beings from conquering nature and its secrets.

This movement, popularized in Taiwan, Hong Kong, and other Chinese centers by its magazine *Xin Ru Jia* ["the new Confucian"], has not attracted a large number of adherents. Its very existence, however, testifies to the frustration of Chinese intellectuals, many of them Christians, who seek to relate the Chinese "essence" to whatever function the West may provide.[103]

THE POTENTIAL FOR HYPHENATED CHRISTIANITY

Speaking from a more traditional Christian standpoint, Julia Ching argues for the need among Chinese of what she calls "hyphenated Christianity"—a Christianity open to the values of Eastern religions, but not giving up its own essence:

I consider belief in Christ as the revelation of God . . . as *the* essential characteristic of Christianity. There can be no hyphenated Christian in cases of persons who do not fulfill this condition. And there can only be hyphenated Christianity where the *other* religion—Zen Buddhism, Confucianism, etc. allows for this central belief without offering any ground for fundamental conflict. In other words, in the life of the Zen Christian or Confucian Christian, the Buddha and Confucius can remain as models for behaviour and as sources of inspiration, but only as secondary to Jesus Christ, whose life and teachings are normative for all forms of Christianity. . . . The Christian message is not Jesus' teachings *plus*. It can only be *his* teachings. . . . Jesus Christ is *more* decisive for Christianity than Confucius is for Confucianism ["Hyphenated Christianity," 34].

Today

What is her view of the status today in Asia of Confucianism, which she calls neither a religion nor a philosophy but a "teaching *(jiao)* that has both religious and philosophical dimensions"? The Confucian values, she affirms, continue to persist, but Confucianism no longer has a privileged position as a "state religion" in any area—it is but one ideology in the midst of pluralistic societies. No longer established or supported by any type of political power and having no social relevance even as a cult, it finds its strength diffused throughout many cultural and social traditions.

Even less, of course, does Confucianism have any role in the life of the People's Republic of China. Confucian thought was labeled "feudalistic" and criticized rigorously in the first few years following the establishment of the new regime. From 1957 to 1963 the evaluation was a bit more positive, to the extent that in 1962 the Historical Institute of Shandong could invite over one hundred sixty participants to attend a weeklong conference to discuss Confucian philosophy. Liu Shaoqi, one of the supporters of this conference, could go so far as to suggest the need to " 'supplement' Communist ideology with Confucian ideas of ethics and personal cultivation."[104]

Following the traumatic Cultural Revolution, Confucius was attacked in an increasingly violent manner. In analyzing why Chinese leaders should continue to fear Confucius twenty-five years after their ascendancy to power, Ching concludes:

> One should not rule out the deep-seated influence which Confucianism may still exert in people's minds today. As the Chinese newspapers point out, Confucian sentiments and values are preventing the youth from fully accepting Maoist ones, and from participating whole-heartedly in the reconstruction of the country. . . . It seems that many young people still regard a higher, professional education as an important priority, together with urban life and the rise on the social ladder, just as many members of the government administration remain supporters of an educational system which gives more importance to formal content than to political ideology. The campaign against Confucius appears designed to help uproot such "old" tendencies and give room to Marxist-Maoist values. In this sense, the entire campaign aims literally at "brainwashing" in order to assure that the great Communist revolution will have worthy successors, those with "pure minds" [*Confucianism,* 63–64].

Ching affirms that among Chinese of the diaspora, Confucianism continues to be a part of the context addressed by the gospel. It has died only to rise again in a new synthesis. It continues to be very relevant as:

A dynamic discovery of the worth of the human person, of his possibilities of moral greatness and even sagehood, of his fundamental relationship to others in a human society based on ethical values, of a metaphysics of the self open to the transcendent [ibid.].

And mainland China is no exception to this tendency. Confucian values persist even as the government frantically seeks to eradicate their roots. Immanuel Hsü comments on the historical continuity that he finds in the China of today:

> Historical continuity manifests itself in many ways. The once sacrosanct imperial ruler is replaced by a deified party leader, and the old bureaucracy by party elite and cadre. Political indoctrination to ensure conformity of thought can be construed as a modern variation of the ideological orthodoxy of Confucianism. The "Mandate of Heaven" . . . is now reflected in the "will" of the people as expressed by their vanguard, the party. . . . The tradition of large-scale public works—the Great Wall and the Grand Canal—is manifested by the numerous gigantic material accomplishments of the Peking regime. The Middle Kingdom concept is furthered by Communist China's intense drive toward big-power status, ideological leadership of the socialist camp, and atomic parity with the United States and the Soviet Union [*Modern China*, 797].

CHINESE THEOLOGIES

Feng Shangli

Some Chinese thinkers have presented a specific agenda for the content of a gospel in Chinese. Feng Shangli has sketched the contours of a Chinese theology. Starting with what he calls a "Chinese-oriented theology," he makes statements about thirteen doctrines, many of which are usually found in creedal formulations. Note how each concept has both indigenous and biblical roots:

> Just as [God's] unmistakable revelation was vouchsafed to Israel, so has the seed of his *Tao* been operative among the Chinese people.
> [Jesus] the Light of the world and the Saviour and Lord of all . . . came, not to destroy, but to fulfill China's many-faceted culture.
> The Holy Spirit . . . awakens man's mind and his four hidden *shan-tuan* [*jen, yi, li* and *chih* or humanity, rectitude, propriety, and wisdom—concepts found in Zhuxi], so that he may know God and Jesus Christ and repent.
> The Bible contains the Word of God and is our norm of truth. . . . We do not feel ourselves tied to Hebraic expressions or enslaved by thought-forms of by-gone ages, nor are we free to change God's truth.

We accept the Apostles' Creed, but at the same time we uphold China's lofty ethics as embodied in the entire teaching of Confucius and Mencius. . . .

All men are sinners . . . and cannot of themselves attain to the perfection of our heavenly Father. . . . Man's goodness is not totally destroyed, for latent in every man is "the possibility of becoming a Yao or a Shun," . . . the righteous will obtain eternal life while the evil will receive eternal punishment.

God's Word . . . should be elucidated by the use of the philosophy of our sages and of concepts, expressions and forms with which our countrymen are familiar. . . . We should adhere to the Confucian principle of "equal regard for words and actions."

[In worship] the Chinese Church should be free to choose its own usages. . . .

The Confucian ideal of the "nobleman" and the Christian ideal of the "saint" should be applied throughout life. The virtues of the nobleman—sincerity, resolution, truthfulness—should blend with those of the Christian profession and constitute the all-embracing principle of daily life ["Contours," 13–16].

These basic doctrinal concepts, he affirms, must then be expressed in programs of evangelization, social service, religious education, and theological training that will produce a "confluence of the Chinese Church and Chinese culture, both marching forward with clasped hands [that] will lead to the formulation of a truly Chinese theology both in content and form."

Jung Young Lee

A less precise format has been contributed by Jung Young Lee who wishes to use the Chinese concept of yin-yang to develop a methodology for "ecumenical theology." Lee is attracted to this model because, in his view, it overcomes the Aristotelian "either/or" pattern of thinking that has "created some of the serious problems that Christianity has to deal with in our generation."[105]

Lee believes that this rational system of thought has overintellectualized Christian doctrine, made it difficult for the Christian faith to relate meaningfully to other religions in the world as well as to nonrational aspects of life, and has created a dichotomy between humankind and nature, thus destroying the sense of the unity in life. He contends that these weaknesses make it much less fit to be a framework for presenting the gospel to the Oriental mind.

He concludes that a framework for Oriental thought must be more inclusive, allowing for "both/and" rather than "either/or." The model for this is the yin-yang found in the Chinese Book of Changes (*I Jing*). This provides for paradoxical thinking:

The characteristic nature of this symbol is not the conflict, but the complementarity of opposites. It is the category of wholeness rather than of partiality. It is the category of becoming rather than of being. It is the transcendental category of expression, because it transcends the logical and analytical categories of our rational thinking. It is therefore possible to express the divine nature which transcends every dichotomy and conflict of opposites [see M. 105].

Lee proposes that the yin-yang method of thinking will better help Chinese theologians to formulate the gospel in Chinese. Such a gospel will teach the transcendence *and* immanence of God, the divine personality *and* impersonality, the divinity *and* humanity of Jesus, and the unity of the human person (body *and* spirit). This approach not only fits better with Chinese ways of thinking, he argues, but also conforms better to the categories of biblical thought.

THE THEOLOGICAL MEANING OF "NEW CHINA"

Both Chinese and Western theologians have given some of their most creative thought since the mid-1950s to the conundrum of China—trying to make sense out of what was happening on the mainland. Every external indication was that something unique and new was occurring—progress in society on such a scale that it could be attributed only to God. The euphoric reports were reminiscent of what Marco Polo had reported to a disbelieving Europe in the thirteenth century and the letters sent to Europe by Jesuits during the seventeenth and eighteenth centuries. China could do no wrong! God was at work there in the task of "ultimate contextualization." God was directly implementing the divine agenda in meeting the needs of China. The task of the church was to cooperate with God, faithfully doing God's will. This might not produce an institutional church, but it would bring salvation to the Chinese masses.

What was it in the thinking of many theologians that caused them to feel this positive about the China from which missionaries had been driven and in which the institutional church was finding it difficult to survive? Most important was that many foreign visitors were nearly unanimous in reporting a wide variety of "astonishing achievements." Even as sober an observer as J. Lawrence Burkholder, president of Goshen College (Goshen, Indiana), was deeply impressed by what he saw. In his list of achievements he included:

A productive, noninflationary economy, almost self-sufficient. . . . Socialized medicine . . . resulting in excellent health . . . Universal education on the primary level, dramatic improvement in literacy. . . . A strong sense of national destiny. . . . A general social ethos of peace and tranquility. . . . Unparalleled personal and national morality. . . . A strenuous work ethic with emphasis upon manual labor, simple, unostentatious living and sharing. An egalitarian social system which precludes private wealth and abject poverty. An ethic of selfless service to society within which personal pride, aggrandizement and "elitism" are discouraged. An authoritarian social system resulting in unparalleled "law and order" ["Notes," 1-5].

How were these accomplishments of a "new China," affirmed by many observers, to be evaluated? Were they illusory? Were they phantoms created by Chinese officials who deluded visitors by showing them only what they wanted them to see? Critiques given by Chinese themselves, particularly at the time of the cultural revolution, and later government revelations about the post-Mao period would indeed indicate that there was very much more than met the eye. China was definitely *not* all-perfect. But tremendous progress in nearly every area except "human freedom" had been accomplished.

Such achievements were hardly surprising, given Mao's belief that a people could be educated to discard the burdens of imperialism and feudalism, and could be motivated toward an inner-directed change, which ultimately would produce a totally new society.

Some critics were prepared to grant that China had made revolutionary gains, but only at tremendous cost. Others asserted that Mao's new society was a good start and to be applauded, but that the jury was still out as to whether such moral and social exertion, with no real spirit of religious transcendence, could really continue and produce permanent changes. Not that a spiritual dimension was totally lacking. Maoism was a type of secular religion—a sacred book not totally unlike the old classics, songs of praise for Mao, the savior from the East, and fervent testimonies to Mao's power, of a nature to help skilled Chinese players win international ping pong matches!

In the opinion of many observers, the changes in China demanded serious reflection and explanation. Raymond Whitehead reports on a humanist and a Catholic priest who had visited the new China:

So a Christian and a Humanist visit China. Both are baffled—the Christian because he finds the Chinese living good lives without what he calls religion, the Humanist because he finds that to do so the Chinese seem to need what he calls religion! ["Christ," 9].

Explanations for the new China were many. For the humanist it was a vast exertion of human energy, a tapping of the potential always there within the human spirit. Why was it necessary to appeal to God? For Christian thinkers, God's presence had been indispensable. A common approach has been to see God's providence at work in a general way:

Should we consider China under Mao as Persia under Cyrus in the Old Testament? In the prophecy of Isaiah, Cyrus, a pagan king, is referred to as "his anointed." "I girded thee, though thou hast not known me" (45:5). Could it be possible that God may have "anointed" Mao to serve His purposes? Would it be appropriate for us to look at Mao in the providence of God as one called to "save" some 800 million from chaos and destruction. Could God be using Mao as a leader to call the church, and indirectly the Western nations, to justice, order, peace, simplicity and morality? Could it be that God has given up the West to moral and economic disintegration and He looks paradoxically to China as the fulfillment of His purposes? [Burkholder, 4].

For these commentators God had an agenda beyond that which the church was either willing or able to accomplish, but this could not be construed as a substitute for an ongoing agenda that envisioned more specific, transcendent salvation. In this vein Don MacInnes has concluded:

Finally, even as we praise God for all signs of his continuing work of creation and salvation in the secular world, we reaffirm our conviction that beyond the needs of the body and mind—food, shelter, employment, schooling, health care, justice—is the human dilemma, man's cry for liberation from the existential dichotomy between personal ideals and dreams, and man's finitude and sinfulness. . . . The elimination of social and economic inequities will still leave man searching for self-understanding and ultimate meaning. . . . Salvation for each person, and for all mankind, has been given and will be *fully* known only in God's work of grace and love in Jesus Christ ["Implications," 443–44].

Catholic Approaches

Domenico Grasso concludes that one can speak of God's "saving" activity in China in the sense that God has been dealing with those "great problems of humanity's origin and destiny." What, then, has God been telling us in China? First, God wishes to show us what humanity is capable of achieving even without explictly knowing or recognizing God and God's grace. The depravity of human nature has not utterly destroyed its capacity for significant moral and social progress. Secondly, all the achievements of the new China reveal clearly what human effort *cannot* accomplish—namely, eternal salvation. Grasso then asserts that China needs to be evangelized and that it is not true that "God has become so disgusted with the 'believers' that he has decided to turn the moral future of mankind over to nonbelievers" [*New China*].

In a less positive spirit one of the workshop reports from an ecumenical colloquium on China held in Louvain, Belgium, in the fall of 1974 recognized that "fulfillment [of salvation] is both within and beyond history" and that even in a secular sense "the revolution will prove to need the gospel . . . to keep it radical, honest and human."[106]

Paul Rule, professor of Chinese studies at La Trobe University in Australia, recognizes that Maoism is a type of religious faith, or at least looks like one. He concludes that it is in a sense preparing the Chinese people to receive the Christian message ["Maoism," 40].

In this same vein the Vatican Congregation for the Propagation of the Faith has affirmed:

> Through accepting Marxism, China has also opened itself, for the first time in its existence, to certain ideas . . . such important values as a spirit of poverty, of sacrifice and renunciation. . . . Mao's directives are the "most authentic expression of the social doctrine of the church" [Chu, 16–17].

Robert Faricy, who teaches at the Gregorian University in Rome, sees a clear distinction between Mao's thought and Christian belief. Both have something to say to the other. Inasmuch as Mao's "ideology"—Faricy does not give it the status of religion—has influenced "hundreds of millions of Chinese," it behooves Christian thinkers to formulate their theology in Marxist terms. Only by finding something "naturally Christian" in Chinese culture may dialogue occur. Faricy points preeminently to Mao's idea of universal struggle, including as well the idea of permanent revolution. He suggests that only the resurrected Christ, conqueror of individual and corporate mortality, is able to give ultimate meaning to the communist emphasis on continuous struggle to bring about progress and development. Faricy also sees the death of Jesus as a significant doctrine vis-à-vis Maoist thought:

> In his public life and in his passion and death, Jesus is in an *antagonistic contradiction* with the powers of darkness, with the forces of sin and death and of all that oppresses people ["Mao's Thought," 41; italics added].

Other Catholic writers have sought to relate the suffering of the Chinese—both in their conscious struggle to develop their nation and in their passive submission to all types of injustice—to the suffering of Christ. Gerald O'Collins characterizes this as *"passio Christi apud Sinenses* (the passion of Christ among the Chinese)" [Chu, 132].

Jean Charbonnier and Leon Triviere ask the question, "Do not freely accepted sacrifices for the good of the people reveal the cross of Christ in the life of the Chinese people?" ["New China," 101].

An important statement from Vatican II describes the church as "the universal sacrament of salvation." In the light of this affirmation how does the Catholic Church specifically relate itself to either the "religious" or the "secular salvation" of the Chinese people? Francis A. Sullivan suggests that the former may be ascribed to "the intercessory role of the praying and suffering church" among the Chinese diaspora and in the worldwide community of faith.

How though has the church, relatively nonexistent in the People's Republic of China, effected the deliverance of the Chinese from feudalism, oppression, injustice, and poverty? This, he declares, can only be the work of the Holy Spirit, whose very presence is inseparable from the church. Sullivan's argument then has two implicit dimensions: implicit faith for "religious" salvation and the implicit workings of the Holy Spirit for "secular" salvation ["Implications," 155–62].

If the Church is indeed the agent of this salvation, it also has the responsibility to reveal it to a skeptical world. "Christians have to proclaim the good news of this salvation as it is unveiled in the very depths of Chinese history and not as a foreign element brought by strangers" [Charbonnier and Triviere, 101].

Many Catholic scholars have sought to relate God's work in China to the church as a "sacrament of salvation" for the world, but usually with the affirmation that the institution, per se, must not be concerned about its own survival. Rather, following the example of its Lord, it must as a grain of wheat fall into the ground and die—rising then to new life appropriate to the circumstances and the priorities of God. Even if the existence of the church in China is precarious, can anyone question the increased pervasiveness of Christian values? [Pro Mundi Vita, 5–40].

Protestant Approaches

A very optimistic approach, best represented by Raymond Whitehead, affirms that Christ is working anonymously and incognito in China and that, eschewing all distinctions between secular and sacred, the product is biblical salvation. He claims that "insofar as justice is done, the oppressed liberated, the broken healed, there is salvation." What is the meaning of faith in a secular society? Whitehead suggests that a sense of trust, "of being part of a historical movement toward justice, peace, and human fulfillment" may be found in Maoism and is similar to the kind of faith found in the Synoptic Gospels where various persons "believed" who "had little chance of knowing and believing the teachings of Jesus." Whitehead does not believe that salvation is complete in Maosim, but he sees little role for Christians or the church in attempting to deal with the problems that he feels still remain: "contradictions, class struggle, corruption, crime, selfishness, laziness, and pride." Indeed Whitehead wonders if "the Christian who approaches China today has any exclusive, ultimate, absolute truths to proclaim to the Chinese people?" ["Christ," 1–17].

To Charles West's abrupt dismissal of his approach with the statement, "it is idolatry, not theology. In other words it is a worship of human objects in the name of God" ["Reflections," 39], Whitehead makes a further affirmation:

On these grounds the biblical writers are idolatrous. The liberation of the people of Israel from bondage in Egypt, a violent event in which Pharaoh's army was drowned, is interpreted by the biblical writers and remembered by the people, as God's saving act ["Christ," 4–5].

A more serious rejoinder to Whitehead and others like him comes from Bishop Ding Guanqxun:

> From our situation we have to say that socio-political liberation is not a good enough description of our theology. The message we have received from God and have to transmit centers on reconciliation in Jesus Christ between God and man ["Evangelism," 310–11].

C.S. Song, much more the theologian than Whitehead from whose position he differs only in degree, gets right to the heart of the problem for many who try to equate Mao's Long March (the "Chinese exodus") with the scriptural account of the deliverance of Israel from Egypt:

> The crucial question is obviously this: Is the salvation history intensely exhibited or demonstrated in both the Old and the New Testament to be looked upon as the absolute norm by which events in secular world history get chosen arbitrarily to be incorporated into God's salvation in Christ, or, is it to be regarded as a pattern or a type of God's salvation manifested in a massively concentrated way in ancient Israel and in the history of the church and therefore to be discovered in varied degrees of intensity and concentration in other nations and peoples also? Presumably Cullmann and most Western theologians will take the position of the former. But we want to argue in the following pages . . . that it is in the latter position that we will find a new theological framework for our quest of the meaning of nations and peoples, in this case New China, in the salvation of God for the world ["New China," 57].

For most evangelical Christians, scripture is the "absolute norm," and the meaning that God gives to specific events, God's interpretation—revelation in act and word—makes these events to be included in "salvation history." For Song, Whitehead, and many others, no particular distinction exists between special and general revelation, between sacred and secular history, and the events recorded and interpreted in biblical history, such as the exodus, are not unique to Israel. They are patterns to be repeated frequently in a salvific sense in the history of many nations.

Song's position, which he presents as distinct from "Western" theologies, is hardly Chinese except in its benefits! He does not appeal to any biblical content but to several "Western" theologians. Of greatest importance is Wolfhart Pannenberg, who has equated revelation with history. This insight, called by Carl Braaten a "new departure in modern theology," allows us to recognize God as "the Lord of the nations, not a local, tribal deity of Israel." God's activity is no longer confined to the narrow spectrum of the history of Israel, but to the totality of world history, through which God is revealed in every generation.

But the agenda of history is immense; how may God's acts be identified?

Which among many events are God's acts? Song depends here on the insights of Schubert Ogden:

> Wherever or insofar as an event in history manifests God's characteristic action as Creator and Redeemer actually *is* his act in a sense in which other historical events are not [*Reality*, 183].

Reacting strongly against the view that "Christian mission is viewed as the extension of Western Christendom," Song argues for God's direct intervention in the history of China as creator and redeemer:

> It is in the light of Jesus Christ, and not on the basis of the Western version of historical Christianity, that we can begin to see the profound meaning of God's acts in New China. The order that now prevails in New China seems to reflect partially the order which God brought into being out of chaos and disorder. The land which used to be torn and laid waste by natural disasters and by man's inhumanity and brutality has begun to function again for the welfare of the Chinese population. And the society in which fear and darkness dominated seems to assume its constructive role again for its members. The *tohu wabohu* of the war of resistance against Japan and the civil war is now a thing of the past. New China seems now destined to represent the possibility of a future classless society in which the dictatorship of the proletariat will prevail completely ["New China," 611].

More so than Whitehead, Song recognizes that "power exercised in an absolutist political state alienates a man from God and from his fellow man." Consequently, he predicts that, with "salvation" only attained in the struggle with poverty, starvation, and exploitation, "the drama of salvation history [not restricted to Israel and events recorded in the Bible] in China in the days ahead will therefore be the drama of the human spirit fighting for the freedom to be human" [ibid., 67].

From the perspective of a decade later, Song apparently is not so sure that this higher salvation has been attained. In a "parable of people's political theology," he quotes from a Beijing "underground poem" whose author yearns for a time when "people will no longer be a powerless hand forced to raise in unconditional acceptance of the dictator's order" [*Lady Meng*, 58].

Apart from his attempt to interpret the gospel about China, has Song constructed a gospel in Chinese, the message to be preached to the Chinese people? Although his language is framed with Oriental illustrations and symbols, Song would deny that his gospel is a Chinese gospel; he undoubtedly would prefer to think of it as a universal theology.

What are the characteristic elements of this theology? First, it is a gospel of God's creative power, implying God's deep involvement in and judgment upon cultures, society, history, and politics. The opposite of what Song calls "mission-compound Christianity . . . where mission . . . consist[s] in counting the sleeping heads of converts," this gospel and its followers "thrust themselves more and more into the vortex of actions in which the power of the Creator-God and the powers that be intersect and interact" [*Christian Mission,* 48].

This emphasis results in a political gospel. Unlike secular politics, dependent on power and arrogance, this gospel is characterized by tears shed by those weeping in their misery and weakness. Paradoxically, however, this tearful weakness, because it has truth—reality as perceived by the common people—on its side, is able to overcome in the ongoing strife with evil, although the victory will be marked with suffering and death. As in the biblical record, however, death is followed by resurrection and the ultimate vindication of God's will. Song portrays this gospel of political theology for audiences under a totalitarian regime in the delightful framework of a well-known Chinese parable, "The Tears of Lady Meng."

A second major strand in Song's gospel is the incarnation. This term, for him, expresses the aim of mission better than does indigenization, an idea that he feels is theologically wrong. He denies that the gospel can be made indigenous; this is possible only for a religion such as Buddhism. The ultimate criterion for Christianity is not whether or not it has a "native" flavor, but:

> Whether it is a humble and obedient instrument which serves to manifest the pain and love of God incarnate in Christ our Redeemer. . . . Our discipleship should be turned to the discovery of what the incarnating love of God in Christ is saying to this or that the particular form of culture, philosophy, or religion, and not to how much or how little we can make use of them in our communication of the Gospel ["Analysis," 21–22].

The incarnation leads naturally to an emphasis on the Christian gospel as a message of God's pain-love (*tengai*), a truth rooted deeply both in scripture and in the Asian spirituality influenced most by Buddhist teaching. The world, according to Song, is not to be understood and explained essentially in intellectualistic formulations and theological propositions; rather it is to be understood and interpreted as a world of pain and suffering. A crucial dimension lacking in Eastern spirituality, which Song feels must come from Christianity, is the "resurrection that turns the tragedy of a life of pain into a life of hope and celebration." This dimension of God's love is seen most intensely in Christ, but it also appears, though to a lesser degree, in other religious traditions of the Orient [*Third-Eye Theology,* chap. 2–3].

How Song perceives the relationship of his gospel to the gospel of the Buddha needs to be explored in greater detail. In talking about the leading symbols of the two faiths—the cross and the lotus—he notes:

> The expression of Buddha's compassion for the masses in his vow and the way he toiled unselfishly for their emancipation from pain and suffering

are not without redemptive significance. Can we not say that Buddha's way is also a part of the drama of salvation which God has acted out fully in the person and work of Jesus Christ? . . . There are redemptive elements in all nations that condemn human corruption and encourage what is noble and holy. Our evaluation of the history of a nation is not complete until such redemptive elements are properly recognized. . . . The Bodhisattvas themselves are not redemptive from the viewpoint of Christian faith, but they are evidence of God's redemptive power and of humanity's hope in the future [ibid., chap. 5].

Song's gospel seeks bridges between the new and the traditional, particularly in its emphasis on suffering and pain, and the continuous plight of Third World peoples. Song refers repeatedly to Kazoh Kitamori's *The Pain of God*, and to Endo Shusaku's *Silence*, both of which sought to interpret the universal reality of pain and suffering to Japan at two periods of crisis in its national life.

The aim of this gospel of the Creator-God, who has become incarnate in human society to reveal the divine love-pain, is that humankind be liberated from all forms of oppression, exploitation, and injustice. Such a gospel does not merely pronounce moral judgment upon humanity for its immoralities but seeks to deliver it from social bondage. Conversion will result in the "emergence of a new social order" [*Christian Mission*, 122]. This gospel justifies Christian support of liberation movements "so as to humanize the power held in the hands of revolutionaries and liberators" that they might recognize clearly that they are under the sovereign power of God [ibid., 154].

Although eschewing dogmatic formulations in his gospel, Song does not wish to promote syncretism. He does not like the idea of "anonymous Christianity," for it smacks of imperialism and arrogance, implying that persons do indeed believe what they have rejected. Nor does he like the concept that traditional religions are a kind of *praeparatio evangelica* for the Christian faith, for this seems to put the various faiths on an evolutionary scale. The gospel, he affirms, must be the person of Jesus Christ, presented as personal truth in such a way that he may directly penetrate the facade that religions erect to keep him out [ibid., 200].

As this gospel roots itself in the lives of ordinary persons, a "selective fulfillment" will take place bringing certain elements of the past into fruition in Christ. Song quotes with approval a statement of A.D. Bouquet:

It might not be improper for believers to exist who called themselves Christian Buddhists or Christian Confucians, and even perhaps Christian Vedantists or Christian Moslems, without in the least abating their adherence to the Catholic faith, and while paying a respectful tribute to the religious insights of their forefathers, and to their enlightenment by the One Logos. There are already some who dare to call themselves Christian Communists [*Christian Faith*, 424].

Interpreting the Church in Maoist China

Although many evangelicals have had their say in a variety of magazines, journals, and denominational organs, the gospel that sought to interpret Maoist China during this period was best articulated by Jonathan Zhao (Jonathan Chao).

Zhao affirms his belief that "God, as the Lord of history, is at work among all nations, and uses the acts of man to accomplish his will." But, in common with other evangelicals, Zhao does not see God's activity in China exhausted by what God was doing through secular means ["Record," 184]. In fact, God's primary deeds of power have been among the community of faith, though not necessarily within historical ecclesiastical structures.

In the pre-1949 period, the Chinese church, according to Zhao, had a gospel characterized by "Western traditionalism, divisive dogmas, hardened structures, and fragmented denominationalism." It emphasized an institutional form, was highly individualistic, and did not relate well to the Chinese family, particularly in the way it viewed the ideas of ancestor veneration and filial piety.

Little wonder, then, with this perspective, that Zhao has welcomed the change molded by the new context in which the church has been living out its life:

> Chinese Christianity, originally a missionary product modelled on Western institutional Protestantism, has been stripped of its buildings, professional clergy, denominational organizations, budgets, foreign funding, hospitals, schools, orphanages, social programs, heavy overheads, and that "Christian" subculture so typical of American evangelicism [sic]. Believers have been scattered throughout the secular social structures of communes, production battalions, and brigades. As a result, the believers have had to radically diffuse or mold their Christian fellowship forms into the existing social institutions, such as the family or production brigades, and to internalize a vital faith into every aspect of their daily lives [Guidelines, 17].

As Zhao views the state of the Christian faith in China from the outside, he notes those ways in which Christians are already accommodating to their environment. He emphasizes the significant fact that the gospel is being diffused into the warp and woof of Chinese life rather than adopting a high institutional profile. He and others argue that this model best accords with the traditional ways in which religion has permeated Chinese life and that it works better under antagonistic political regimes than does the use of "open churches" for public worship.

The gospel that will work in China today, in his view, is a gospel of the "mean." He claims that Christians are learning "to sustain a dual worldview simultaneously: an inner Christian worldview and value system in which they truly believe, and an outer Communist worldview in which they have to live" ["Gospel," 32]. This, states Zhao, is a retreat from the more confrontational attitude of the 1950s, although it is being revived under the more relaxed rules of the early 1980s. It represents the bending of the grass under a vicious, antagonistic wind, or, in biblical terms, being "wise as serpents, but gentle as doves."

The kind of gospel in Chinese that Zhao advocates—and which, he claims, is working with unparalleled results—is a gospel of high morality. Chinese Christians "testify to Christ by high ethical standards, industry, gentleness, forgiveness, and tact, especially during moments of common despair." Chinese Christians are incarnating themselves in Chinese society and, through their homes and the fellowship shown there, are demonstrating a community that appeals in practical terms to a society characterized by contradiction and alienation. This concrete, pragmatic kind of contextualization—learned from praxis—is more of a "subjective theological-faith experience than it is a set of objective analyses by outsiders" ["Gospel," 33–34].

Zhao does not believe that there is hope for any creative kind of dialogue with the state. First, the government and its various organs have "politicized the entire Chinese social and cultural sphere" with their own ideology and see anything else, as in ages past, as heterodoxy. Secondly:

> The Maoist criterion of truth is not based on philosophical validity, but on practice, practice in the productive struggle, the class struggle, and scientific experimentation [ibid., 33].

A Closed Door

China was the largest field of religious work for Western missionary agencies and its fall to an atheistic regime in 1949 was viewed by them as a highly traumatic event. Many hands were wrung in despair in New York and London as mission thinkers struggled to analyze what had happened. More often than not, the blame was placed on faulty methods and attitudes. Seldom did the many Monday-morning quarterbacks point a finger at the message. And where the gospel message itself was analyzed, no uniformity of opinion emerged as to what God was indeed doing in China and what God's people on the outside ought to do.

This brings us, then, to consider the community of faith in the new China—how was it contextualizing its message in the new environment? What was the gospel in Chinese for the Marxist context?[107]

CHAPTER ELEVEN

Jesus and Mao in the New China— The Chinese Gospel in a Marxist Setting

On October 1, 1949, the Chinese people stood up! This event, in culmination of a revolution that started in 1911 with Sun Yat-sen, brought more changes to China than any previous dynastic turnover in its long history. Politically, economically, educationally, socially, and intellectually the Middle Kingdom underwent a drastic metamorphosis. Although there is historical continuity with the past, usually with some type of functional equivalency to the traditional Confucian framework, instances of discontinuity abound. Immanuel Hsü has chronicled a number of the latter:

Dialectical materialism, class struggle, democratic centralism, and democratic dictatorship.

Mass organizations, psychological remolding, control of the communication media . . . mass campaigns and mass demonstrations.

The idea of progress has superseded the cyclical concept of history, and political and social activism has become the new creed of the country.

. . . industrialization, rapid agricultural collectivization, and communication. . . .

The vicious denunciation of old thought, old customs, old habits, and old culture. . . .

Family honor, individual heroes, filial piety, and "face" are all discarded as feudal vestiges; in their place have arisen the new concepts of the labor hero, public confession, criticism and self-criticism, and the denunciation of parents by children.

. . . the new alliance between workers, peasants and the petty and national bourgeoisie has replaced the old stratification of scholar-official, farmer, artisan, and merchant [*Modern China*, 797–98].

The advent of this drastic national change also forced the Chinese churches to stand up. Long committed theoretically to the concept of being indigenous—self-governing, self-supporting, and self-propagating—God's people was now faced with the sober reality. No longer would there be leaders, money, and expertise from abroad. The church would no longer operate from a base of power, but from a position of weakness. It was now faced with the necessity, certainly for the first time in the modern period, of "putting its house in order" (a euphemism used by Zhou Enlai [Chou En-lai] in early meetings with Protestant church leaders in Beijing).

THE CHURCHES IN CHINA, 1949–1985

Initial Adjustments, 1949–1956

To understand the gospel in Chinese during this period, we must first overview the phases through which the Christian churches passed from 1949 to 1985. What follows here is not a detailed history of the churches during these years—only a framework for sketching the basic substance of the gospel that was preached.

From 1949 to 1956 the Protestant churches were directed to gradually align with government policy. The constitution of the new government provided for "freedom of religion," which, broadly interpreted, meant toleration of church activities for such a period as believers continued to sense a need for religion. The implicit assumption, often articulated explicitly, from the beginning was that the context of the new, improved China would gradually make religion unnecessary.

In the year or two following "liberation," Chinese government leaders worked with a nucleus of church leaders to form what was initially called the Three-Self Reform Committee. Under the aegis of the Religious Affairs Bureau and the United Front Work Department, the committee coordinated government policy and procedures with church bodies. Even before the formal organization of this committee, church and government leaders issued a Christian Manifesto, eventually to be signed by over four hundred thousand Protestant Christians. It upheld the responsibility of the churches to support the common platform of the government, to recognize and eradicate all elements of American imperialism in churches, to accept no funds or personnel from abroad, and to cease all except Sunday services during the upcoming period of land reform.

During the next few years the Three-Self Patriotic Movement (the name was changed in 1953) exerted pressure on the churches to hold accusation meetings against some of their own leaders as well as missionaries, to engage in intensive political indoctrination sessions, and to support current political goals, such as the "Resist America, Help Korea" campaign in 1951 and 1952.

Leaders of traditionally conservative church groups—Wang Mingdao, Jing Tianying, Watchman Ni, Isaac Wei—firmly resisted the efforts of the Religious Affairs Bureau and the Three-Self Patriotic Movement to control their churches. Claiming that there was no place for politics in the church, that the charge of imperialism against the missionaries was grossly exaggerated, and that the Three-Self leaders were liberal and procommunist, these men refused to knuckle under to the tremendous pressures put upon them. As a result, they were accused unmercifully in public meetings, defamed for alleged moral and political crimes, and sentenced to long prison terms. Wang Mingdao, one noted example of this pattern, was released from prison in 1980 and lives with his wife in Shanghai, where his home, wisely or unwisely, is a mecca for both Chinese and Western visitors to China.

Period of Forced Unity, 1956–1966

During the period from 1956 to 1966 the Religious Affairs Bureau put pressure on churches to merge and unite, a measure that made some sense in view of the fact that attendance at public worship services had decreased dramatically, and not as many buildings or pastors were needed to care for the diminishing flocks. Special ground rules were needed for these unions that brought together groups with widely divergent theological positions and with no tradition of this kind of ecumenical fellowship. The "articles of union" formulated for the churches of Taiyuan, capital of Shanxi province, included the following kind of provisions:

> Each church shall surrender its own individual ritual and use an edited and united hymnal.
>
> [In] books used in the interpretation of the Bible . . . only [those] favoring union and socialism shall be used.
>
> There shall be no more preaching about the Last Day, or about the vanity of this world. This is negative and pessimistic teaching. Instead we shall emphasize the need for the union of faith and practice, the dignity of labor, the control of nature, and the dividing line between ourselves and our enemies, between right and wrong.
>
> Belief and unbelief shall not be made an issue in determining the marriage question.

Included were a few regulations that related to special practices of the Little Flock, the Salvation Army, and the Seventh-Day Adventists [Patterson, 126–27].

These union churches were faced with a variety of demands, many of which were at least quasi-political in nature and seemingly were geared specifically for religious institutions. Among the "five don'ts" listed in the late 1950s from a list of "Patriotic Resolutions" issued by a Shanghai district were items such as "don't preach reactionary doctrine, use healing promises to get converts, invite free-lance evangelists, and attend or preach in home services." The "five musts" included the need to "expose free-lance evangelists and home services" and "to take part in every socialist campaign." Members were exhorted to:

The five loves (love country, party, socialism, the Three-Self Movement and labor), and the five excellencies (to improve the openness of one's thinking through the criticism of others and self-criticism, to go further in self-reform by destroying capitalism, to increase mutual respect among believers and between believers and nonbelievers). . . .

Pastors were exhorted to learn "six patriotic songs before May 1, to guarantee participation of 85 percent of church members in every social campaign, and to have a criticism meeting once a quarter to check progress on all these points." Christians were urged to "support government efforts in public hygiene, and to heed the call of the government for birth control, in one's own family and by commending it to others."[108]

During the period when Mao allowed "One Hundred Flowers" to bloom, in the late 1950s, a noted evangelical leader, Marcus Cheng addressed the People's Political Consultative Conference in Beijing. In the course of his address, he gave a kind of apologetic for the gospel and explained the nature of the gospel he preached.[109] Obviously bothered by the closing of some churches, unrestrained abuse against Christians, and other forms of discrimination, he pointed out:

The contradiction between belief and unbelief, between theism and atheism, is a contradiction among the people, and not against an external element. We are all citizens of China, and this is not a contradiction between friends and enemies of the people, but an attempt at discrimination, at finding the truth. It is a contradiction of the "hundred schools" [category] [Document 65 in MacInnis, *Religious Policy,* 201-7].

Cheng appealed for religious policy to be rigorously implemented in such a way as to give dignity and respect to all persons:

The attempt in this controversy to discover the truth should be carried out calmly, without abuse or name-calling. You speak out your atheism and I will preach my theism, and in this controversy you must not take to abusing my mother, defiling my ancestral graves or reviling my ancestors. In the eyes of us Christians, God is the supreme Being, and the churches are His temples, the place where Christians worship Him. In the argument over theism and atheism you must not revile God, or blaspheme His name: you must not take our churches by force [ibid.].

Referring repeatedly to epochs from the revolutionary history of China itself, Cheng masterfully quoted from communist sources, including Friedrich Engels, to the effect that Christianity had "always been a people's movement opposing the ruling class." He referred to Mary's magnificat, that Jesus would:

scatter the proud in the imagination of their hearts, he would put down the mighty from their thrones, exalt those of low degree. He would fill the hungry with good things, but the rich he would send empty away [ibid.].

He went on to explain that:

> We stress the fact that Jesus was a carpenter; the Son of God was incarnate on earth and lived here thirty-three years, of which more than twenty years was spent in common labor, both in a manual trade and in farming, so that he thereby raised the position of labor, and we who are followers of Jesus should follow Him in loving labor and the produce of labor [ibid.].

Affirming that "we still proclaim that his precious blood is the way of salvation," Cheng noted that some communist tenets of "political economics" had given help in pointing to doctrines of the faith often neglected. He called attention particularly to the importance of productive labor and to the coordination of these efforts as principles taught repeatedly both in the Old and New Testaments.

In the years prior to the Cultural Revolution, if documents on various religious activities are indeed to be taken at face value, the gospel in Chinese for many included faith healing, the exorcism of demons, and the observance of various religious customs, such as the Lord's day, which authorities found harmful to agricultural production quotas. More and more believers were meeting in homes, some because they feared the connection with imperialism in tainted public worship services, and others because they were resisting the creeping control over local church activities by the Three-Self Patriotic Movement.

Possibly under the pressure of the Three-Self Movement, some Christian leaders rued the fact that their gospel in the past had been for the elite. Theoretically, it was a message for the masses, but many Chinese preachers, because of the nature of their education and background, were "intellectuals of the propertied class" and served the interests of this clientele—the landlords in rural areas and business interests in the cities [Document 86, "To What Social Class Does A Preacher Belong?," in MacInnis, *Religious Policy,* 274–82].

The Cultural Revolution, 1966–1976

The third phase through which the Chinese church passed in the post-1949 period was that of the Cultural Revolution when a leftist clique within the government, encouraged by Mao himself, sought to create a new Chinese society by destroying all vestiges of imperialism, feudalism, and bourgeois ideology. Rather than wait for religion to wilt away, these elements sought to destroy it as a hotbed of superstition. Christianity, along with the traditional Chinese religions, came under vicious attack. The Christian faith ceased to exist in its overt institutional form, but Christians were dispersed throughout society as worshiping house communities, a structure much more appropriate and enduring for a time of harsh persecution.

While the Cultural Revolution was in full force, almost no word came from China on the fate of the churches. Gradually the silence was broken, and bits and fragments of news came out, particularly from southeast China where the Christian faith had traditionally been vibrant, indicating that the churches in China were alive and well, although not without their problems. Beginning with President Nixon's visit to China in 1972, numerous contacts developed between China and the Western world culminating with President Carter's official recognition of the People's Republic, January 1, 1980.

The experience of Catholics under the new regime was similar to that of Protestants. Under the guidance of the Religious Affairs Bureau, Catholics loyal to the new state founded the Patriotic Association of Chinese Catholics in 1957. A large segment of the Catholic Church in China, however, could not identify itself with this association, because it repudiated any kind of even tenuous relationship with the Vatican.

Since the Death of Mao, 1976–1985

Following the death of Mao, in 1976, China began to reveal a willingness to rejoin the family of world nations and started on the "long march" of the Four Modernizations (of agriculture, industry, science-technology, and defense) under the moderate leadership of Deng Xiaoping. A climate was created that enabled Christian churches to experience new life. In order to encourage religious groups in China to join forces with all Chinese citizens in promoting the progress of the country, Deng reestablished the "united front" policy, which restored to institutional religious groups the religious toleration wrenched so violently from them during the Cultural Revolution.

In 1979 the government restored the Religious Affairs Bureau, dismantled during the cultural revolution, and very shortly Protestant Christian leaders were encouraged to revive the Three-Self Patriotic structure and Catholics the Patriotic Association of Chinese Catholics. Daoists, Buddhists, and Muslims reestablished comparable organizations.

With this type of official encouragement, members of all the major religions of China, as well as those committed to myriad superstitions, came out of the woodwork. They were the vanguard of a tremendous religious revival that swept over the country, surprising the many observers who had concluded that communism had inaugurated a postreligious era. In this general resurgence of the Chinese religious spirit, the Christian faith in both its Protestant and Catholic forms expanded rapidly. With government encouragement and help, nearly five thousand Protestant churches were reopened and now four to five million worshipers crowd Sunday services. Many times beyond this number—even conservative estimates range as high as 30 to 40 million—are meeting informally in homes scattered throughout China, either because ideological reasons keep them from associating with "open" worship services, vulnerable if the government religious policy does another zigzag, or because there are no formally established services where they live.

With religious revival has come the restoration of many institutional forms of the church. In addition to the Three-Self Patriotic Association, which oversees relations between Protestant churches and government organs, the Protestants have organized the China Christian Council responsible for matters of ministry, leadership training, and church life. Church leaders have taken the lead in publishing hymnals, devotional materials, limited editions of the Bible, and the monthly magazine *Tian Feng* ["heavenly wind"]. The YMCA and YWCA have been reestablished in a number of Chinese cities.

In February 1981, church leaders reopened the Nanjing Theological Seminary. In November 1982, the Northeastern Theological Seminary was opened in Shenyang. Lower-level training schools have been established in ten centers. A total of over seven hundred students are in training in these institutions and many others in extension branches scattered throughout the country, some in church facilities.

Initially, only skeletal activities were conducted in the newly-opened church facilities, but now a full range of services is offered in addition to public worship: Bible classes, prayer meetings, baptisms, weddings, funerals, memorial and thanksgiving services, choir practice, observance of the sacraments, and regular visitation of the sick and elderly. Most of the leaders, both clerical and lay, are elderly and have only recently been restored—from church-related inactivity in factories, labor camps, and prison cells—to posts of pastoral duty.

The same types of ministries have been restored within the Catholic fold. The work of the Patriotic Association of Chinese Catholics has been supplemented by the services of the Catholic National Administrative Commission, which supervises pastoral concerns such as church marriages, baptisms, funerals, confessions, pilgrimages, the various sacraments, and Bible study. Seven Catholic seminaries for leadership training have been opened. The Catholic journal *Zhongguo Tianzhu Jiaohui* ["the Chinese Catholic Church"] has resumed publication.

Merely to recite the activities of the Chinese Catholic Church overlooks the intense conflict going on within Catholicism in China—a struggle directly related to the nature of the gospel in Chinese.

Traditionally, the Catholic Church has affirmed its faith in the "one, holy, catholic, and apostolic church," a confession that demands submission to the pope as the universal head of the church. Yet the Patriotic Association of Chinese Catholics (PACC) has repudiated the Roman connection and is running its affairs in total independence of the Vatican. This independent spirit has gone so far that in recently opened Catholic churches "mention of the name of the Pope appears to have been deleted from the Latin Canon of the Mass" [Lazzarotto, 75].

To multitudes of believers who continue to think of themselves as loyal *Roman* Catholics, such an attitude is a denial of the very essence of the church and of its faith. Protestants are not united around one spiritual ruler, and for them to reject any external ecclesiastical authority or patronage ruptures only an international fellowship, not the universal church itself.

The refusal of the Vatican to acknowledge the apostolic legitimacy of the fifty bishops elected and consecrated since 1958, its sometime condescending attitude to the PACC, and its insistence on maintaining diplomatic relations with Taiwan do not augur an early solution to this theological and political problem. In theory, however, the emphasis of Vatican II on the particularity of local churches may provide the key for recognizing the legitimacy of a *Chinese* church that seeks to establish its own identity apart from Rome.

THE GOSPEL IN CHINESE UNDER COMMUNISM

With a basic understanding of these several phases through which the churches in China have passed, I can now address the question that is my primary concern. Throughout this period, from 1949 onward, how have church leaders related the gospel they preach to their new environment? Is it "business as usual" in terms of gospel content or has the gospel in Chinese assumed a different shape to meet new needs? Does the innocuous term "self-propagation" go beyond reliance on one's own efforts in evangelism to the creation of a theology that will fit the values of a new society?

The Apologetic of the Gospel

Judging from Marcus Cheng's speech delivered to the People's Political Consultative Conference and reported in a Beijing newspaper, the "contradiction" between theism and atheism was a hot issue at that time, but not so by the late 1950s in any locality where any real dialogue had taken place. T. C. Zhao, writing in 1950, could pose the question of whether Chinese theology could have productive dialogue with Marxism—a hope not to be realized.

A remarkable example of one attempt, in June 1957, to speak to issues raised by Marxism is Bishop Ding Guangxun's message to graduating seniors at Nanjing Theological Seminary. Entitled "Christian Theism: A Theology of Society," Ding's address dealt with problems current among intellectuals. In typical Oriental fashion, he denies some of the antithetical categories that nonbelievers or even believers like to use either to defend or attack the faith. Christianity, he avers, cannot be classified neatly either as materialistic or idealistic. This would imply that it is principally an ideology, which could then be compared as such with communism, an undertaking that Ding says is impossible:

We must ever remember that what we preach is the Gospel, is Christ, something in nature entirely different from an ideology, something which moves in a different orbit from any system of thought, and then we will have a clear understanding from which to perceive that all talk of comparison of Christianity with Communism, or likenesses or differences, is beside the point and superfluous.[110]

Ding expertly deals with an indubitably common question, "Is Christianity an opiate of the people in socialist China?" He grants that members of any society use any number of means to numb themselves to social responsibility, and that religion, or even nonreligion, may be among these means. This psychological state, even if bad, hardly speaks to the issue of the objective reality of the Christian faith or of whatever ideology has a numbing effect:

> To analyze the effect which religious belief has had upon some individual is one thing. But the question whether God exists or not is an entirely different thing. Let us grant for argument's sake that you have discovered that the religion of certain individuals has had a narcotic effect upon them. But this discovery does not at all prove that the universe is without a Creator [ibid.].

Exhibiting a realism that enables him to affirm his faith without denying the social improvements that have occurred under a Marxist regime, Ding notes that "Christians need not go around looking for flaws, trying to make someone lose face, as if the only way to satisfy us were to discover that someone else was wrong." He applauds the fact that the "level of moral action" has been raised, even as he affirms anew:

> The change of social system can only limit the effectiveness of sin, it cannot solve the problem of sin. Sin can only be healed by forgiveness, salvation, and grace. It is not a matter of social progress. These two matters should not be confused [ibid.].

Ding concludes his pungent essay with a short analysis of why, over the ages, some persons have refused to believe in God. Granting, as he had earlier done, that religion may be an opiate, he contends that an equal danger is that persons "may drug themselves by a denial of God's existence, so that they can continue to sin, avoid responsibility and stifle the reproaches of their conscience." Boldly he declares:

> They are morally reprobate, but refuse to repent, and the result is that having departed from God they gradually come to deny his existence. The only way they can recover their faith is first to repent of their sin [ibid.].

He points his finger at the community of faith and contends that many have refused to believe because the church has failed to manifest God. The God whom they see through the church is one "whom their own sense of morality and justice does not allow them to believe in."

In this message Ding effectively separates the fact of God's existence from communist propaganda, declares the impact of the Christian faith on society, analyzes reasons for unbelief, denies the power of any human solution for sin, and points to Christ as the answer for the human dilemma. How different and yet how much more effective for this environment than a bombastic, direct confrontation that serves only to alienate rather than to challenge.

Possibly the only book published under the new regime that dealt at any length with these kinds of questions was written by Wu Yungzhuan, the editorial secretary of the China Inter-Varsity. Entitled simply *Xinyang wenti* ["questions concerning the faith"], it dealt with certain vital questions:

> "What is the origin of matter? Which comes first: plan or order, the architect or the builder's blue-print? What is the difference between spirit and matter? Does matter influence spirit or spirit influence matter?" He went on to discuss the difference between the eternal existence of God and the so-called eternal existence of matter. Communism teaches that there is a built-in sense of direction within matter, and it is that which is responsible for the evolutionary development of the human race. But this leads to the question of whether materialism is another form of pantheism. The communist says that man's effort creates the world. Mr. Wu insisted that it is the Word of God which provides the creative power. Other relevant questions, such as "Is there such a thing as absolute truth?" were also dealt with in this little book. All the discussion led up to a final chapter on Christ the center of the Christian faith [Adeney, *Students,* 78].

A Political Gospel

In general, the gospel as practiced and proclaimed by the institutional church in China, whether early in the "liberation" or much later in the post-Mao period, has had a political content. This has made it contextual in its environment, where, as we have seen, every aspect of life has been politicized. This stance of the church vis-à-vis the state, and the attitude and expectations of the state toward the church, is of a piece with past church-state relationships:

> As long as a religion did not threaten state security, it was usually tolerated by a watchful government. This was true even though many of China's institutional religions—Buddhism, Islam, Judaism, and Christianity—were imported, from the second century A.D. on. From time to time, however, when these faiths offered notions of virtuous government and distributive justice that inspired their devotees to seek

the overthrow of a dynasty, the court moved quickly to suppress them [Bohr, "Religion"].

At the beginning, and even now, the burden of proof was on the churches to demonstrate that they were not centers of dissidence and revolt. Past connections with Western imperialistic efforts and with the inequitable treaties imposed on China—not merely an "accident of history" as one author superficially states it—the unwise activities of some missionaries, the rather obvious anticommunist stance of nearly all missionaries, and their direct support of Jiang Jieshi's discredited government, as well as support for America in the Korean conflict, were all strong indicators that the fears of the new regime had some basis in fact. Dramatic steps were needed to prove otherwise, and the Three-Self reform movement led the way in asserting that, without embracing Marxist ideology, it was going to be supportive of the new regime, cut off all compromising relationships with churches in the capitalist West, and join with all their fellow Chinese in building a new society. The fact that "house churches" could begin in the early 1950s and continue, with ever increasing strength, to the present must be attributed to the fact that there was an institutional Christian church prepared, at great cost and with much difficulty, to cooperate with the government. Were it not for this "buffer," the community of faith in China would have found it difficult to survive, particularly had the government determined to exterminate it.

This politicizing of the gospel, though possibly begun on pragmatic grounds, has been given a more sophisticated theological articulation. Ding Guangxun notes, for example, that the pre-Mao gospel was hardly apolitical in its support of the Guomindang and its deep antagonism toward communism:

> We found that all the strong doses on original sin, on the fallen state of the world, on the meaninglessness and absurdity of history, on the complete separation and antithesis of grace and nature, on the so-called pride in human works and on justification by faith could very easily be turned into a sort of anti-nomianism which, in the name of faith, gave blessing to any sort of political stance required by the Kuomintang and U.S. policy ["Religious Policy," 121–24].

He also argues forcefully that God is a "living, immanent, ever-working God" who can use human instruments (institutions) to accomplish the divine will in human societies, and to destroy the exploitive systems of colonialism and feudalism that have oppressed whole peoples:

> And we seem to feel that there is a pre-given engracement of all people through the incarnation of the Son of God. He united himself to every man and woman in some fashion and, there, you will find Chinese Christians not only talking about the Redeemer Christ, but more now about the Cosmic Christ, the Incarnational Christ, Christ as the crown

and fulfillment of the whole creative process, the clue to the meaning of creation, the One whom we find very much talked about in the New Testament, especially in the Fourth Gospel, in Colossians and in Ephesians. And in this way we think that many contemporary thoughts and movements are not in contrast with the divine revelation or destructive of divine revelation, but rather means of illuminating that revelation [ibid.].

Bishop Ding is careful, however, not to *identify* the gospel with the liberating acts of God in history—what God may indeed accomplish through political means. Denying that the products of "liberated" China are the new men and women of whom Paul speaks in his Epistles, he affirms:

We in China needed liberation. We do not want to return to our preliberation days. Yet we do not think that political liberation is a solution to that much more ultimate problem—the problem between human beings and the ultimate ground on which the whole universe is structured. The question of life in Jesus Christ—[is something that] we feel that liberation theologians have not dealt with adequately [ibid.].

Nor does Ding believe, in the same vein, that he and other Chinese theologians are prepared to absolutize the poor as God's ideal:

In post-liberation China we still have poor people. . . . [Yet] the very suffering that we experienced during the days of the Cultural Revolution was exactly due to the doctrine of perpetual revolution of the poor against the wealthy, and that is why we would hesitate to idealize the poor.[111]

Prophetically, to be political in calling human governments and society to stand under God's righteous judgment demands that the churches of China be ready to witness courageously to the Chinese government. Obviously, this has to be done with care and tact. Only through this kind of witness were Christian leaders able to persuade political leaders and officials to remove from the Constitution the offensive clause enabling nonbelievers not only to have freedom of unbelief but "to propagate atheism." Will Three-Self leaders be ready to speak out on issues that will confront the Christian faith in the days ahead? Time will tell!

Some evangelical leaders outside China can find little good to say about the Three-Self Patriotic Movement in its politicizing of the gospel. They doubt whether it can be called Christian and feel that its leaders, willingly or unwillingly, have been almost totally duped by Marxist manipulations. You cannot cooperate, they argue, with a communist government addicted to lies.

Some leaders associated more directly with conciliar ecumenism are prepared to defend the Three-Self Patriotic Movement in all its decisions. Francis Jones suggests that this extreme polarization is not needed:

There is a mediating position possible between these two extremes. We have come to see that it is possible to condemn a specific act as unchristian without thereby denying the essential Christian character of the perpetrator—otherwise who could be called Christian? [*Church,* 113].

Again, it is noteworthy that the gospel in Chinese for groups meeting in homes is not purely "spiritual" just because Christians refrain from talking about politics. Their very silence shouts out their reactionary position. Claiming that they are loyal to their country, they hesitate to affirm their support for the government in the way that the government seeks it. Why should the government consider them patriotic and not prohibit meetings outside the structures of public worship? What indeed have they specifically done that would cause the "powers that be" not to see them as centers of revolt? They do not overtly proclaim their support of the government, they often refuse to worship in public gatherings, they change their meeting places in order to escape government detection, they listen to broadcasts coming from outside the country, and they receive bibles smuggled in from organizations and persons known to be anticommunist. The whole style of their lives, although morally exemplary, militates against their claim that their gospel is only the spiritual principles of the Bible.

An experienced China-observer writes that these Christians "do not associate the supply of bibles with imperialistic activities" and that those providing the bibles have "no wish to interfere with the church in China." This is really beside the point! In any kind of communication the message transmitted is the one perceived by the target, not merely the one intended by the source. Both sides in this unwise exchange are signaling a clear political message, regardless of their own intent, which may indeed be very honorable.[112]

The fact that many Christians are asking for help in the form of bibles is also beside the point! In the midst of an antagonistic society, they do not see the total situation. Neither do they and those helping them seem to realize that a bible for every Christian, or even for every few Christians, is a luxury that history has denied to many, and is necessary neither for orthodoxy nor for Christian growth. The rather slow procedure of the China Christian Council in providing bibles is not likely to produce sudden results, but it will prove better for Chinese Christians in the long run.

The churches of the China Christian Council, on the other hand, although not adhering to the atheistic tenets espoused by the government, wish to live within the constraints of their religious policy, which countenances a wide range of church activities. In local religious conflicts between government officials and Christians who meet in homes, they have only two options—to side with the officials or with local Christians. If they stand up for their Christian brothers and sisters, as many expect them to do, they also are suspected of counterrevolutionary activities and lose the limited freedom their position has brought not only to them but to these independent Christians as well. Such a policy, if pursued on a nationwide scale, could totally change the government attitude and inaugurate an era of persecution that would exceed that of the Cultural Revolution. The other option—to side with government officials—seems to betray fellow Christians, thus leaving themselves open to charges of callousness.

If Christians meeting in homes do indeed wish to be apolitical—almost an impossibility—then it behooves them to refuse outside help and eschew any activity that would compromise their alleged neutrality. More positively, they need to find appropriate means to alleviate legitimate fears by government officials that they are potential centers of revolt and not loyal Chinese citizens. They need to find ways to symbolize their submission to the government, as did the Buddhists in the fourth and fifth centuries when they sought to acclimate themselves to Chinese life.

An Incarnate Gospel

Another prominent element in the current gospel in Chinese, according to Bishop Ding, is that the church has identified with the Chinese people—it shares a common ground with and speaks a common language to the people. The Chinese have all alike "been sinned against" in that they have suffered from the three mountains of "imperialism, bureaucratic capitalism, and feudalism," which have created exploitive situations leading to hunger, disease, homelessness, and many other things not in the will of God. It has always been easy, confesses Ding, for the church and its leaders to take a Confucian attitude that would exalt them as an elite over the masses. Furthermore, Chinese Christians participated in the benefits of the "unequal treaties," and the Chinese masses could scarcely detect their Christianity, covered over, as it was, by a thick layer of foreignness.

With this kind of heritage, the Three-Self leaders and their churches felt the need to become:

> Conscious of respecting the faith and beliefs of others, thereby promoting unity among the people and avoiding conflicts between believers and non-believers, and among the different faiths. Was this not limiting the scope of the gospel? No, for the wonder of God exceeded all our hopes and expectations. With the change in style of our preaching, the work of the Holy Spirit was no longer limited or obstructed by numerous conditions, and even more people were willing to come and hear the gospel message.[113]

Ding Guangxun uses this need for Christians to identify with the Chinese masses to develop a positive attitude to the "human collective":

> More and more Christians are realizing that the transcendent is encountered not so much "out there" as within the interpersonal relationships of finite beings. We really open ourselves to the holy and to the sacred and to

meeting God himself as we plunge ourselves into the depths of human relations, no matter how secular they seem. God being love, it is only in love that we come into touch with the uttermost reality of the universe and get ourselves attuned to the character of God.[114]

Ding admits that a new sense of Christian reconciliation with the masses of the Chinese people has meant an abandoning of "certain conceptual frameworks in which we have felt secure for many years." Grace and nature, for example, have been brought together in what Chen Zeming has called a "monistic synthesis."[115] Preliberation theology, he affirms, overemphasized the "axis of belief and unbelief . . . to bring about enmity between Christians and the revolutionaries who are mostly non-believers." This gospel in Chinese helps Chinese Christians to:

> Discover the immanence of the transcendent God in history, in nature, in the people's movements and in the collectivities in which we find ourselves. After all, the God who is worthy of our worship and praise is not so small as to be concerned only with a few million Chinese who profess to believe in him. God's love and care is for the whole of humanity and the whole of the Chinese people. He does not mind terribly much if many, for good reasons, do not recognize his existence . . . but I think liberation in China, with all the material and cultural elevation it has brought to our people, does make it more possible for our people to ponder on such a God. We hope we are able gradually to be an instrument of introducing this God to our people [Ding, "Religious Policy," 124].

In a word, whether or not outsiders may like the way in which God has done it, the Chinese churches are no longer painted with the brush of "foreign." They are Chinese through and through, and the common people know it. This desire to be "Chinese"—self-governing, self-supporting, and self-propagating—means, in Ding's words, that the church has erected a spiritual "protective tariff" against outside help or interference whether from Brother Andrew (evangelical head of Open Doors) or from an ill-conceived project promoted by the United Board for Christian Higher Education in Asia.[116] This self-reliant spirit, smacking at times even of arrogant nationalism, is not unlike that of the government in its relationship with the nations of the world. This ideological stance may thwart well-meaning plans of all those outside who wish to help China, but if it helps to maintain the "Chineseness" of the churches and to protect them from further limitation by the government, we must respect it. To do otherwise is seen as perpetuating the pattern of foreign paternalism and dependency of the past.   *church universal implications*

Dealing with Contradictions

How do Chinese church leaders within the China Christian Council relate their gospel to features seemingly antithetical to it in a Marxist society? How, for example, can they justify support for communist values, such as hating and denouncing class enemies, when the gospel clearly demands that Christians are to love even their enemies? They have used several approaches to deal with these kinds of matters. First, they point to times when Jesus condemned the scribes and Pharisees, even to the extent of cleansing the temple. Secondly, they cite the ways in which the Old Testament prophets denounce injustice and oppression. And, finally, they seem to have accepted the Marxist idea that injustice and exploitation derive from class interests. Bishop Ding, in his well-reported message at Riverside Church in New York City in 1979, suggested that a Chinese beggar's plight might be the result of "his own passivity." The church:

> Must help the beggar see it is not the will of God for him to be so degraded and for his lot to be begging while a few at the top of society are running everything, enjoying all the good things of life and out of their wealth giving alms to beggars [see n. 114].

New Approaches

One of the clearest expressions of how a few church leaders see the gospel in Chinese came from the Montreal Conference held in October 1981. Citing once again earlier indications of the freedom of the churches to be Chinese and to identify with the masses, Ding describes a new unity among believers and in the gospel they proclaim:

> The fundamentalists and evangelicals are definitely there, but they are much less obsessed by the belief-unbelief syndrome which has been the axis around which everything else revolved. They are presenting an eschatology much less harsh, and an understanding of history more humanitarian, more loving, more people-oriented, more democratic. All of this we welcome. Christian liberals, denominational traditionalists and neo-orthodox intellectuals are giving up their pacifist sentiments and the reformism of their social services, and are feeling for the immanence of the Transcendent God in history, affirming in a new way the Trinity and the unity of God's total work of creation, redemption and sanctification towards the emergence of the commonwealth of truly free, loving men and women, in the image of God, who is a community himself.[117]

Ding is fearful that the rapid growth of the church in China and an overemphasis on "church growth" is producing an impure church. He called for priority on "up-leveling the church in China, making the church in China more purely the church."

Chen Zeming, vice-principal of the Nanjing Union Theological College, is more forthright than Ding in seeing "God's salvific purpose in the historical event of the liberation of the Chinese people, under the 'mask' of God as it were." Inasmuch as God sides with the "oppressed, the poor, and the sinned against, . . . so all who choose to side with the people are actually on God's side." This does, indeed, blur the distinction between unbelief and belief, between law and gospel, between secular and salvation history, between nature and grace, and between progress and the kingdom of God.

Chen wishes to replace traditional Christian categories—he would probably call them Western—with something more appropriate for Chinese communal-type thinking. Consequently, he proposes that, even as "man's being is realized only in community," so we should understand the idea of the Trinity, not ontologically, but as God's activity within the human community, the only arena in which God can be recognized. He suggests that sin is not so much a rebellion against a sovereign God as it is a violation of God's will in human relationships, especially failure to attain the *summum bonum* of social justice within the community.

Eschatology, as traditionally understood, he views as much too harsh in its indictment of humanity. He reports:

> One senior teacher in our Seminary shifted his chiliastic view from premillenarianism to postmillenarianism because he saw new China as too good for him to wish it to be destroyed, and he would like to see it develop and grow and progress for at least another thousand years before the final judgment [ibid.].

Chen affirms, in essence, that it is still too early to articulate specifically the shape that the gospel is going to take in a Marxist China. There must be a longer period—time for a "hundred flowers" of divergent views to emerge. In general, however, he affirms that "it is a theology rediscovering God's greatness, goodness, and gracefulness to our people and to humanity as a whole, a theology full of hope, a theology full of struggle to live a communal life more bountifully and harmoniously . . ."

Despite the Marxist context and many innovative views by a new generation of Christian leaders, the gospel in Chinese continues to deal with universal questions. One observer at the Montreal Conference stated that "the renewal of religious practices in China today seems to be rather anachronistic," as if he were expecting something totally new, perhaps on the order of a Louvain or Bastad consultation [Woo, 186].

Jiang Peifan, president of the Jiangsu Christian Council, gives examples of the kinds of questions that Christians at the grass roots are asking:

> Why did God allow a few ultra-leftists to create such suffering during the Cultural Revolution?
> Under what conditions should we turn the other cheek?
> God is just, but will those good people who do not believe in him someday go to hell?
> Why does the Bible say that there is not even one righteous person?
> How should Christians express their social concerns?

What special contribution can Christians make to humankind?
In addition to urging people to be good, what else can Christianity do for
the human heart? [ibid.].

Throughout all the papers delivered at Montreal is the note of Thanksgiving
that the gospel and the churches are now free from foreign control. The
Christian church and its message are no longer in a privileged position that
gives them prestige or power:

We have thereby gained the respect of the Chinese people because the
Christian church is now entirely a Chinese enterprise with full sover-
eignty in its work of evangelism. For the first time, we are no longer
dubbed as a "foreign" religion. . . . Christianity in China has been too
long a "foreign" religion and this foreignness has brought about a
process of alienation from our own people. We thank God that through
the instrumentality of the Chinese Communists and through the historical event of Liberation, we Chinese Christians are now given an opportunity to make a new beginning to reconcile with our own people and to
bring Christ's witness to them [ibid.].

Outside observers of Chinese Christianity have been grieved that it seems to
have such a nationalistic spirit and that it is seemingly unwilling to enter into
bonds of fellowship with other churches around the world. The fear has been
expressed that it is isolating itself from the universal expression of the faith. To
this type of criticism Bishop Ding replies:

This Christianity [Chinese] does not take European and American Christianity as the norm, but we understand that Chinese Christianity cannot
talk of making contributions to world Christianity unless it rids itself of
its colonial nature, ceases to be a replica of foreign Christianity, does not
antagonize or dissociate or alienate itself from the cause of the Chinese
people, but joins them in that cause, plants its roots in Chinese culture,
forms a Chinese self, and becomes a Chinese entity ["Retrospect," 30].

The way in which sophisticated, international Chinese church leaders articulate the gospel in Chinese must not be confused with the typical preaching done
by pastors in the open churches. The gospel message heard Sunday in and
Sunday out is almost identical, it would seem, to the missionary message
proclaimed in preliberation days. These pastors stress the truths that will make
for real differences in the lives of their parishioners: God's love, the cross of
Christ, the forgiveness of sin through faith in Christ, the value of prayer, and
the way in which the Christian life is to be lived out in the midst of daily
problems. Outsiders who have been present at these services throughout China
unanimously agree that what they have heard is the traditional gospel message.

The Gospel in Home Meetings

Over four thousand public meeting places are now open for Protestant worship in China. Most of them are facilities that were closed during the Cultural Revolution and have now been renovated. Some are new buildings erected by church funds in areas where previously there was no Christian witness. Connected with these open churches are about twenty thousand "meeting points" as well as a number of what are called "home meetings." These are used by Christians who do not live close to the open churches and for whom it is more convenient to meet in smaller groups.

In addition, there are reported to be a large number of "free meeting places." These are places of worship for those Christians who are not related in any way to the Three-Self Patriotic Movement. Their reasons for this choice may be varied: they recall the past attitude of Three-Self leaders toward dissidents such as Wang Mingdao and Ni Duosheng; they may fear "going public"; or they may live in areas where there are no open churches or small groups affiliated with them.

The Gospel of Spiritual Power

The gospel in Chinese as proclaimed in some of the "free meeting places" is very similar to that heard in the various kinds of Three-Self gatherings, but there are unique features. Without doubt, the gospel in these meeting places, particularly in rural China, is the gospel of spiritual power. Great emphasis is placed upon acts of exorcism, healings, and miracles to meet daily needs. Some who have been put in prison for alleged illegal activities report many ways in which God has miraculously acted on their behalf.

In preaching, expecting, and praying for miracles Chinese Christians are not far removed from the New Testament scene, from the "signs of the kingdom" that Jesus promised to his early followers. Unfortunately, neither are they far removed from having government officials step in and forbid certain types of activities. Although granting "religious freedom," the government has tried to extirpate:

> Feudal superstitions . . . including sorcerers, magic potions and drugs, divination and fortune-telling, getting rid of calamities and praying for rain, praying for sons and daughters, controlling demons, healing sickness, practicing physiognomy and palm reading, practicing geomancy. . . .[118]

Overzealous cadres can easily confuse some Christian practices with outlawed superstitions, and have recourse to prohibitions or even persecution. Such practices may be also proscribed by local Three-Self committees, fearful of what the government may do. Undoubtedly, acts of healing and the exorcism of evil spirits have helped spread the Christian faith in China. Nothing else has so convinced men and women of the direct power of God. God's miraculous intervention in the lives of ordinary persons forms the content of most of the testimonies given in house meetings and is the backdrop for the sermons given.

"Signs and wonders," on this scale, although not unknown, were not characteristic of past revivals in China. In fact, one missionary who made an in-depth study of demon possession in China was surprised at how little attention missionaries gave to this phenomenon:

> No Protestant missionary, so far as I know, has ever given native converts instructions as to casting out spirits; and few, if any, have dreamed that their converts would have the disposition, the ability, or the opportunity to do so [Nevius, 14].

Indeed, in his opinion, missionaries did not give much credence to the subject. Possibly, they did not think demonism was prevalent: they were not in close contact with grass-roots village life; they explained it away on rational grounds; or they did not hear about it because others were ashamed to mention it to their missionary friends.

If we are to talk meaningfully about the contextualization of the gospel in the China of today, nothing could be more relevant than the subject of sickness and demon possession. Even in contemporary China, where medical help has been decentralized right to the village level, vast physical needs abound. And with the greater religious freedom that has allowed a resurgence of the institutional religions, rank and file Chinese have returned to a myriad of superstitious practices. A gospel of action that promises healing and freedom from evil spirits speaks much more directly to the Chinese rural context than does an intellectualized verbal message emphasizing propositions beyond the grasp of peasants, who, if able to read at all, are minimally literate.

In an extremely insightful article, "C.S. Lewis's Contribution to a 'Missionary Theology': an Asian Perspective," Paul Clasper, longtime missionary resident in Asia, and now professor of theology at Chung Chi College, Hong Kong, comments on the prominence of Satan and his minions in much of Lewis's writings. This emphasis, he affirms, when not presented as an unbiblical dualism, is very relevant to many Asian Christians who are "animists-at-heart." Clasper observes:

> Many voices are now being raised to question whether the scientific world-view, just behind us though still popularly influential in the West, may really *not* be a graduation from "childish things"; perhaps it is a peculiar desensitization to essential conflict which the dark powers have inflicted upon a non-discerning world.[119]

A Family-Centered Gospel

The message proclaimed in the free meeting places is a family-centered gospel. Much of the zealous evangelistic witness carried on by these simple peasants is directed toward intimate friends, family members, and relatives who, when converted, become the nucleus of a group of believers. Their natural communal life and fellowship, strengthened and deepened by their new bonds in Christ, are the basis of a dynamic home meeting. In a society where alienation and anomie are predominant features, this type of fellowship is what unbelievers are seeking. This is the current context in China.

Lay-Centered Activities

For the most part, the activities of the free meeting places are lay-centered. In larger gatherings of several hundred closer to urban centers, there may be one or several leaders who have had some type of formal Bible training and who might be classified as "clergy." Some of these might have been released from prison during the period of relaxation since 1979 and have been allowed, along with some other occupation in society, to take up part-time duties working with a home meeting or even an open church.

Because of the many untrained lay leaders and the general lack of bibles, free meeting places are very simple in nature: times of prayer, testimonies of what God is doing in the lives of unbelievers, singing, possibly some Bible reading, and a short message. Those who serve as leaders are ordinary men and women who seek to exercise gifts of the Holy Spirit in appropriate ways. With their own indigenous hymns and with varying "forms of service," these gatherings are structurally more indigenous than the Western-style worship services of the open churches.

Sermons also are very simple and apply directly to the lives of the participants. A favorite doctrine, also occasionally preached in the open churches, is the second coming of Christ. Some local groups have been so obsessed with this teaching that they have left jobs, home, and relatives to go to secluded places to await, even for several months, the return of the Lord.[120] One message on the birth of Jesus stressed how Satan could enter into the heart of a leader such as Herod and turn him against God to the extent that he would seek to kill someone as innocent as Jesus.

Prayer

Another common topic, emphasizing the power of God to meet human needs, is prayer. The policy of religious freedom is implemented unevenly throughout China, and believers often feel that they are discriminated against as "second-class citizens." They face trials and opposition daily. Prayer, for them, is the primary resource for spiritual power. Without it, they claim, their lives would be hopeless. They are disillusioned with human solutions; they depend only on God. This sense of hope in a society increasingly filled with hopelessness has also proved to be a powerful magnet, bringing many young persons to faith in Christ.

Community

Undoubtedly, one of the greatest gospel attractions seen in these simple meetings is the sense of mutual care, love, and compassion. Even with hardly enough to meet their own needs, many of these Christian families have extended themselves in caring for the families of Christian brothers and sisters who have been arrested and put in prison for long periods of time. Christians have shown loving concern even for those who have mistreated them and sought to disrupt their activities. This kind of love, excelling even the "serve-the-people" attitude engendered in China today, has been a unique witness for the gospel. It has spoken directly to a context often filled with mutual distrust and suspicion.

Funerals have been one of the principal occasions when Christians have been able to reveal their sense of community, their devotion, and their mutual love. They accompany the coffin to the burial plot, sing, eulogize, read the Bible, give testimonies and, when appropriate, preach short sermons. Open witness to Christ, generally forbidden, is engaged in boldly at these times.

The Gospel of Suffering

The gospel in Chinese in recent years, both for those inside and outside the open churches, has been a gospel of suffering. Before, during, and to some extent even after the traumatic Cultural Revolution, some Chinese Christians not associated with the Three-Self Patriotic Movement have suffered difficulties and persecution because of their decision to meet on their own and not to affiliate with the more official brand of Christianity. They are often very bitter because they believe that the Three-Self leaders, directly or indirectly, have been responsible for their difficulties, including long years of imprisonment. To them the choice has been simple: "it is better to obey God than to obey man." In their view, the decision has been a spiritual one and not at all political.

But the suffering has not been on just one side. During the Cultural Revolution, in fact, it was the Three-Self officers and pastors who suffered the most. They were the most visible to the Red Guards and other followers of the leftist clique that was bent on destroying all vestige of religion. Their fellow believers who met in homes were equally as committed, but, gathering in secret and in frequently-changed meeting sites, were more elusive and less obvious targets for radical fanaticism. Many of those associated with the official church were cursed, beaten, imprisoned, separated from their families, and sent to difficult and distant places for cruel, manual labor.

Undoubtedly, some Christians in China have developed an overworked martyr spirit, coming almost to the place of Catholic saints of past ages who went out of their way to court martyrdom and, in fact, to glorify it as the highest expression of the Christian life. They have espoused the idea that it is impossible to be a true Christian without some very obvious suffering. Thus, now that former harsh government restrictions have been relatively relaxed, they constantly test the limits of toleration rather than being satisifed with the measure of freedom that they have.

Some Christians seek to preach publicly, making this the litmus test of real religious freedom. They seem to forget the fact that, in the providence of God, the great growth that has come to the church in the last several years has come by a much more quiet, and probably much more effective, witness to Christ. Why, at this point, does it become the mark of spirituality to press for yet more? And where, because of the tolerance of local officials, there now are opportunities for witness in one area, some preachers have tried to move into other areas where regulations are more rigidly enforced. The inevitable clash, usually involving officials of the Religious Affairs Bureau and, on occasion, local Three-Self leaders, is then made a cause celèbre to Christians outside China as another example of religious persecution in that land.

Jonathan Zhao and others have pointed out that some leaders of house groups have become more militant than in the past, confronting government officials at every possible turn. Such action may be praised as "spiritual courage," but it also may be direct disobedience to Jesus' admonition to be "wise as serpents and harmless as doves." The interpretation is by no means as clear as many superficial observers would have it.

Nontraditional Features of Home Meetings

If the free meeting places are not nearly as conventional or "westernized" as those of the open churches, their gospel may also take on some nontraditional features. Some house groups have been extremely separatistic, refusing to meet with others whose members may have a denominational background. Disputes that missionaries naively thought had been laid to rest in the new China have resurfaced again as "indigenous" problems—speaking in tongues, the form of baptism, the role of women in the church, and authorization for ministry.

It has been reported that in one area a leader arose who claimed to be Jesus. Some Christians are known as "shouting Christians," and the noisy nature of their assemblies has caused authorities to limit their activities. With some groups the loudness of the "amen" at the end of prayers has been the mark of spirituality. Some have practiced the rite of baptism by having the practitioner touch all parts of the initiate's body before administering the rite. Where the new converts have been women, this has created problems.

For some preachers in these informal meetings, to be obedient to God's truth in announcing the imminent return of Jesus Christ has meant specifically identifying certain nations to be associated with the anti-Christ at the time of great tribulation. Bible truth and human opinion have become so hopelessly entangled that the end result has been anything but orthodox Christian doctrine.

To point out what some regard as heresy or doctrinal deviation is not to demean the type of Christianity found in these meetings. Most are new Christians. They have experienced the power of the risen Christ. They lack much in the way of instruction. Having more bibles and listening to outside radio broadcasts will undoubtedly give some help in this process. Ultimately, however, these new converts are going to find most help in some type of closer relationship with the "magisterium" of the China Christian Council. "Liberal" elements may dominate this council, but the materials they have so far prepared for distribution to churches have been, in the words of one observer, "fundamentalistic." They have expounded the fundamentals of the faith necessary both for a firm doctrinal foundation and for nurturing life in Christ.

Whether in the open churches and the groups associated with them or in the free meeting places, the gospel is being contextualized in China. It is speaking to universal and transcendent human needs of sin, alienation, guilt, meaning, and hope. Less institutional than in the past, even within the open churches, it is relating well to Chinese culture by being diffused throughout society, by identifying with the people, by submitting to the government, and by participating in the current task of modernization and nation building. Existentially, it has contextualized itself to the needs of China in this stage of its history. Love, fellowship, reconciliation, and hope are being preached in Christ's name, and God has demonstrated the power to overcome sickness and the oppression of the demonic world. Most important of all, this is a Chinese gospel, with no taint of direct missionary influence and control. No longer can it be called foreign—a *yang jiao* with no claim on the allegiance of the Chinese people.

Obviously, this is not a mature church. Many years may be required for nurture to catch up with the tremendous numerical growth experienced since 1979. May we on the outside have faith that God, who has brought these churches into being, will, by one means or another, bring them to perfection as a "body without spot and blemish." Our Western efficiency makes us want to export our materials, methods, and personal help—and, possibly, to run ahead of God, who has done very well up to this point with almost no outside aid. Let us be wise masterbuilders and not do anything that will tear down the tremendous things that God has done in leading the Chinese Christian churches to this point in their spiritual pilgrimage.

CHAPTER TWELVE

Rejection of the Gospel in Chinese

Over a period of nearly 1,400 years, with the possible exception of the present, no key has been found to open the door of the Chinese heart to the gospel of Christ. As a "mission field" it has proved to be more frustrating than others. Christian emissaries to the world of Islam have never expected much in the way of results, and their estimates have been accurate. But China seemed different. Although the Chinese were a deeply ethical people and worshipped many gods in a show of piety, they held no deeply religious beliefs that would seem to prejudice them against the message of God's love. And so it was that missionaries, at least from the seventeenth century onward, always hoped that China would become a Christian nation. No obstacle or setback could ultimately quench this expectation.

THE FAILURE OF ALL EFFORTS

How can we explain the Chinese rejection of the Christian message? Glad to receive all the benefits dispensed in the name of Christ, even to the extent that some were called "rice Christians," they did not, in any significant number, wish to commit themselves to Christ. Nothing seemed to work—neither the Nestorian and Catholic attempts at accommodation with special emphasis on converting the emperor, the court, and the official class, nor the Protestant emphasis on reaching "the people" and generally affirming a gospel of no-compromise with Chinese culture. The Protestants, with many moralistic prohibitions, were antisocial, wanting largely to save individual "souls"; the Catholics, aiming at the community, seemed to many to be so tolerant that there was no point for the Chinese to believe their message. Joseph Levenson has commented on the gospel of accommodation:

> This tactic . . . was self-defeating; in effect, it authorized the potential convert to see in the foreign church organization, and in its foreign-composed Scriptures, at best vessels of the truth which must also exist in his own historical inheritance [*Confucian China,* I, 119].

Levenson's point is that whatever the gospel, whatever the method, whoever the messenger, it made little difference. Christianity and the missionaries, in his view, were caught up in historical processes and forces beyond their control. The destiny of China was unrelated to what Christians did or did not do. Latourette comments similarly:

> It must again be reiterated, however, that revolution would have come to China without the missionaries. Had never one of their number left his native soil, the family would have disintegrated, the Manchus have fallen, and Renaissance dawned and nationalism arisen [*History,* 841].

Likewise, Levenson affirms, the fate of Christianity was not dependent on what Christians did or did not do:

> In the seventeenth century, Chinese opposed Christianity as untraditional. In the twentieth century China, especially after the first World War, it was the principal anti-Christian cry that Christianity was unmodern. In the early instance, then, Christianity was criticized for not being Confucian; this was a criticism proper to Chinese civilization. In the later instance, Christianity was criticized for not being scientific; and this was a criticism from western civilization [*Confucian China,* I, 123].

If this seems to be a hopeless conundrum, a confusing missiological "Catch-22," it may only reflect an oft-repeated Chinese maxim: "Whatever you say about China is true somewhere and at some time; whatever you say about China is not true somewhere and at some time." Almost every gospel preached in China and every method has both worked and failed at some time and at some place. We always must ask specifically about the historical context. What was it that made a particular gospel in Chinese appropriate for a given situation?

Historically, as noted earlier, insufficient evidence precludes a determinative judgment on the reasons for the ultimate failure of Nestorian and early Catholic Christianity. In general, political factors—identification with those who lost power—would seem to have been more critical than theological factors. Here were historical processes beyond their power to control.

The failure of the Jesuits to be successful on the scale they had hoped surely was related to the tragic "rites controversy," which, with all its theological elements, was essentially political and cultural in nature. Who would prevail: the Jesuits or the more conservative Catholic orders; the emperor or the pope; missionaries *in situ* or the Vatican; Chinese culture or barbarian opinions?

AN ANTI-CHRISTIAN TRADITION

Not as apparent in the Jesuit era was the crystallization of what Cohen has called the "anti-Christian" tradition in China. Going back to as early as

Confucius, the Chinese had established a "cultural category which they used to label teachings and practices which deviated from a particular ideal or norm." From the Sung dynasty on, this norm was some form of Confucianism, and any set of beliefs—cultural, political, or social—that seemed to challenge this norm was considered to be heretical or heterodox. From the middle of the seventeenth century until the 1850s and 1860s, numerous publications labeled the Christian faith, together with Buddhism and Daoism, a sect that was, at worst, obscene, dangerous, foreign, and sinister and, at best, irrelevant to the Chinese who, in Confucian orthodoxy, possessed all that was needed. Cohen observes that an important element of these anti-Christian tracts was sex:

> On the more inflammatory side, Christians are accused of indulging in incestuous and homosexual relations, of fornicating freely with the members of the clergy, of glorifying and attaching special powers to the menstrual flow of women, of emasculating little boys, and of using black magic to accomplish their weird and unfathomable ends.[121]

From 1860 to 1900, earlier anti-Christian tracts and handbills were reprinted repeatedly and stirred the populace to a red-hot fever. Often promoted officially by local leaders, they could not help but incite numerous riots against both missionaries and Chinese Christians.[122]

In the late nineteenth and early twentieth centuries, Western science, pragmatism, and materialism intensified the impetus of the incipient anti-Christian tradition. As Chinese traveled abroad to many Western countries and as they read widely from Western authors, they realized that the West itself was hardly Christian, a fact adding to the formidable arguments they were able to muster at home.

THE GOSPEL OF POWER

The exact extent, strength, and influence that this "anti-Christian" tradition had on the masses of the Chinese might be debatable, but little doubt exists of its overall significance. Nor do many scholars question the impact of the gospel of power on China. This had not been a problem in the Nestorian period or when John of Montecorvino had been seeking to plant the church in China in the thirteenth century, at the time of the Mongol dynasty. External power was not a major difficulty during the Jesuit period, although Chinese officials were suspicious of the missionaries' relationship with the immediate sending base at Macao. The unwise attempt of the Vatican to impose its authority over the Chinese emperor smacked of political power but, without any show of force, it proved ineffective.

As already noted in chapter 4, the gospel of power had its greatest influence on China and on the image of Christianity in China at the beginning of the modern mission period. Without repeating what has already been said, the gospel of power entailed a number of elements: (1) British efforts to import opium into China; (2) a war between China and Great Britain; (3) treaties between China and Great Britain, and subsequently with the United States, France, and Russia; (4) provisions for "freedom of religion" and for many commercial and legal privileges for foreigners; (5) assertion of their rights by missionaries and Chinese Christians; (6) resistance by the gentry and Chinese populace to these "rights"; (7) use of gunboats and pressure on Chinese officials to enforce treaties; (8) state of uneasy and forced acceptance of missionaries.

Western missionaries with their "logic" were able to separate these strands one from the other, calling some religious, some political, and some commercial. To the Chinese masses, all that mattered was the overall impact—the gospel, opium, and gunboats. "Missionary incidents" were reactions not merely to "something foreign"—a favorite missionary cliché—but to a particular type of "religious foreignness" that had gained "rights" to give the Chinese something they had not asked for.

It was far too simple to assert, as was the missionary custom, that the gentry was manipulating the populace against the missionaries. Gilbert Reid, a missionary reformer who had organized The Mission Among the Higher Classes in China, commented on this point:

> An inter-action exists between the populace and the scholars or gentry. It may be that the latter head the opposition against the foreigner, knowing well that they will be promptly supported by the people, or it may be that the feeling or pressure is so strong from the populace that the gentry or scholars for the sake of popularity dare not remain inactive, and so intensify the hostility which already exists. The leader, then, must be one of the gentry, scholars, or headmen, or perhaps a bully, but he in turn can only succeed in instigating a disturbance when the populace are inclined to carry out a disturbance. Influence is interlinked, and the responsibility is mutual [*Sources,* 32].

A symbiotic relationship existed, then, between officials and the masses, the former responsible for collecting, producing, and distributing inflammatory literature that would create the climate in which the latter would be prepared to give support to antagonistic actions against missionaries.

Then, and possibly now, the gentry and the masses were not reacting solely, or even primarily, against the "religion" of the foreigner. More important was that these religious foreigners were perceived, very naturally, as subversive, fomenters of what would politically and socially undermine China. This viewpoint was buttressed by the fact that "Christianity often aroused the most interest precisely among those elements of the Chinese populace that were least loyal to the established order" [Fairbank, "Patterns," 493].

In their work in China, the missionaries were of most threat to the gentry, those scholar-officials who were the traditional elite of Chinese society and who served as its social glue.[123] Fairbank points out some of the dimensions of this conflict:

> Missionaries . . . though commoners in their lands of origin, were new rivals of the traditional elite in China. [They were] privileged characters protected by treaty rights of extraterritoriality and proselytism. These rights were exemplified in the missionaries' access to the mandarins, their capacity to demand offical attention and assistance, on a level comparable to that of the literati ["Patterns," 494–95].

The stage was set for a classic misunderstanding. The gentry, fearful for its own status and position, and challenged unwittingly by the missionaries, sought to keep them from the people. And the missionaries, seeking to avoid the gentry in the larger centers, developed what Fairbank has called the "agtropic [rural] tendency" by going to less populous locales where they would face less confrontation with the gentry [Fairbank, "Patterns," 492]. This only accentuated the problem and sparked an even wider distribution of anti-Christian literature, which in turn raised a crescendo of missionary protest and more appeals for protection.

Both groups were caught in a vicious circle, sending and receiving messages that were not intended and that only intensified the conflict. Conflict there was, but it was not what either side perceived it to be. Although both parties were culpable, the missionaries were in a better position to resolve the conflict: they followed a Leader whose principle of communication stipulated that one should begin with the context of one's hearers.

The gospel of power, then, produced a widescale resistance to the Christian message and helps to explain why Christianity was never espoused by more than 1 percent of the Chinese population at best. It was a "foreign" gospel, abetted in China by outside power, authority, and influence. In practical terms, missionaries, supported by the treaties, could do what they wanted: travel beyond treaty jurisdiction in the 1842–69 period; force reluctant landlords to sell or rent them property; protect Chinese converts in litigation matters; erect homes that violated local Chinese "superstitions"; preach the gospel in temple precincts; and many other activities that violated Chinese cultural and religious sensitivities. The main thing was to preach the gospel—God would take care of these other matters.

FUTURE PROSPECTS

Professor Lu Shiqiang, a scholar at the Academia Sinica, now located in Taiwan, comments:

> Investigations . . . tend to show that Christianity and the Confucian tradition are not necessarily incompatible; that Christian evangelism in

China, without political and military support, could have had a chance to survive and spread, through peaceful means and gradual and mutual understanding, granting at the same time that certain forms of conflict were to be expected before total harmony might be achieved between the two heritages. That so many unfortunate or tragic incidents [riots] had erupted was not due so much to a difference in dogmas as to such human weakness as selfishness and greed.[124]

Professor Lu may be overgenerous in his assessment of similarities between the Christian faith and the Confucian tradition. The Chinese did resist certain Christian doctrines: monotheism, the need for Christ's atonement, monogamy, abstention from all idolatrous practices. The Chinese tended to be very practical and were often apathetic about purely religious matters. The whole complex of activities related to ancestral rites has been a stumbling block to potential converts in every age of the Christian witness.

But let us not miss Lu's main point: all these differences would have been more amenable of solution in an atmosphere of freedom, unruffled by outside power and authority. Aggression and imperialism hung like the sword of Damocles over the entire ministry of Christian missions and Chinese churches until 1949. It had its impact on every other decision and activity of God's work in China—not always, possibly, upon the Christian community as such, but on multitudes of others who did not wish to become less Chinese by joining it. What has hurt the church the most, at least in the modern period, is not so much the unindigenized message—a "foreign" gospel—but a "foreign connection."

The critical factor, then, for the gospel in Chinese for Marxist China is a message and a community that relates itself well to the whole population and is radically independent from outside influence and help. This may seem to go against the universal element of the gospel—that Christians worldwide are mutually interdependent and that Christians everywhere are responsible for evangelizing the unevangelized. The churches in China, however, are in a period of transition. Their present need, unbalanced as it may seem to well-meaning outside observers, is to expunge the epithet "foreign" and work out its own identity in its new walk with God, the Lord of history.

God's faithful, if often bungling, servants brought the Christian faith to China. God has preserved it through periods of suffering and persecution. And now God's providential guidance has led to a situation in which it can finally escape the Damoclean sword of power. Is this the ultimate key to the explanation of why the gospel message is experiencing unparalleled receptivity in China today?

Notes

Works lacking full bibliographical details
are listed in Bibliography p. 263.

1. "People Groups of Mainland China" (Pasadena, Institute of Chinese Studies, 1982).

2. For most of this material I am indebted to H.G. Creel, *Chinese Thought*, 11–12.

3. Much of this analysis on the Chinese as a religious people comes from C.K. Yang, "Functional Relationship," 269–90.

4. In recent writings it has been used by writers as diverse as K.H. Ting, Choan-Seng Song, and Jonathan Zhao.

5. Lausanne Committee for World Evangelization, *The Willowbank Report* (Wheaton, Ill., 1978), 3ff.

6. The material in this section is taken from S. Ananda Kumar, "Culture," 49–57.

7. Bruce Waltke, *Creation and Chaos*, 13. In this work he quotes Ron Allen in an unpublished Th.M. thesis from Dallas Theological Seminary to the effect that "the problem is *not* one of borrowed theology but one of borrowed imagery."

8. Howard Marshall, "Culture and the New Testament," 32.

9. The material in this paragraph comes from Bruce Nicholls, "Towards a Theology of Gospel and Culture," in Stott and Coote, *The Gospel and Culture*, 74–5.

10. I have followed the general outline developed by Hesselgrave, *Communicating*, 134–39.

11. Throughout my discussion of the precise terminology of the tablet, I shall be using the translation of A.C. Moule, *Christians in China*, pp. 34–50. Frequently there are significant differences between this and the translation by P.Y. Saeki, *The Nestorian Monument in China*, 160–75.

12. For the Chinese text of the major Dunhuang documents listed here, see Lo Hsiang Lin, *Nestorianism*, 193–225, 57–69; and Jiang Wen-han, *Chinese Christianity*, 64–92.

13. Wylie, *Nestorian Tablet*, 67–68. Scholars differ as to the significance of the phrase "divided person." Moule indicates that some scholars (Havret) interpreted it to be used when a "spiritual being appears to two or more places at once or in human form" (*Christians in China*, 36). Others (Jiang Wen-han) interpret it to refer only to the second person of the Godhead in his role within the Trinity. Jiang renders it in colloquial Chinese *san wei i ti zhung fen chu lai*, i.e., "separated out from the Trinity (*Chinese Christianity*, 41). This leads him to conclude that the Nestorian documents reveal nothing of the Nestorian "heresy" p. 22. Saeki apparently is of the same opinion, translating the phrase in question as "whereupon one Person of our Trinity, the Messiah, who is the Luminous Lord of the Universe, veiling His true Majesty, appeared upon earth as a man" (*Nestorian Monument*, 163). Both Moule and Wylie seem to interpret the phrase as I have.

14. Others have felt that the "three" refers to faith, hope, and charity.

15. In these several instances, Saeki preserves the unique particularity of the Buddhist phraseology, whereas Moule universalizes the language, thus washing away its indigenous flavor.

16. This comes from the inscription, and I use it merely as a neat, short statement.

17. The situation was actually more complex. Very early (638 A.D.), the Nestorians also were referred to as *jing jiao*, "scripture religion," and a bit later as the *po si jing jiao*, "the Persian scripture religion." Another name common throughout its history in China was *da chin jiao*, "Syrian religion." See Jiang Wen-han, *Chinese Christianity*, 24.

18. Although the origin and meaning of this term is not perfectly certain, a good case may be made that it is related to the Arabic *a lo ha* and probably means "the God religion" or "those who worship God." See Jiang Wen-han, *Chinese Christianity*, 96.

19. Outerbridge notes that "the only relic of the Franciscan mission is a Latin Bible of the thirteenth century which was obtained at Ch'ang-chou by P. Philip Couplet of the Society of Jesus, toward the end of the seventeenth century. This Bible was in a stage of irreparable decay, but still wrapped in Chinese yellow silk. It is preserved in the Laurentian Library in Florence" (*Lost Churches*, 63).

20. For further elaboration of this point, see John D. Young, *Synthesis*, 19–21; Yan Lien-sheng, "The Concept of 'Pao' as a Basis for Social Relations in China," in John K. Fairbank (ed.), *Chinese Thought*, 291–309.

21. Matteo Ricci, *Opere storiche*, vol. 2, p. 343; also found in Young, *Synthesis*, 22.

22. Pope John Paul II, speaking at the Pontifical Gregorian University on October 25, 1982, referred to this work as "The Chinese translation of Cicero's 'De amicitia,' " a dubious contention ("Pope's Address on the Work of Father Ricci in China," *Tripod*, Hong Kong, Dec. 1982, p. 69).

23. Material taken from Paul Sih, "The Natural Law Philosophy of Mencius," in his *Chinese Culture*, 30–45.

24. Young (*Synthesis*, 54) calls Ricci's attempt the "first effort in East-West synthesis," an appraisal that neglects the Nestorian Chinese tradition.

25. Jean Charbonnier, "China-Christian Relations in the Spirit of Matteo Ricci," translated by Patrick Taveirne, *Tripod* (Hong Kong), Dec. 1982, p. 105.

26. For more elaboration on the varied reactions, see John Tong, "Ricci's Contribution," 112–21.

27. Preface in Xu Guangqi's geometry book *Ji-he-yuan-ben*; translation in John Tong, "Ricci's Contribution," 120.

28. Found in Xu's work *Epilogue of the Twenty-Five Theses*; translation in John Tong, "Ricci's Contribution," 120.

29. A reproduction of this tablet, and some of the translation quoted here, are found in Dunne, 292.

30. I am indebted to Wolfgang Franke for many of the insights in this concluding section.

31. Charles Gutzlaff, *Journals of Three Voyages Along the Coast of China* (Taibei, 1968) 197.

32. Most of the material on the missionary voyage comes from Walter Medhurst, "Voyage of the Huron," *Chinese Repository*, vol. 4, no. 7 (Nov. 1838) 308–30.

33. Even as Morrison was translating in Canton, two other scholars, a Mr. Lasser, an Armenian Christian raised in Macao, and Joshua Marshman, one of the Serampore trio, were making another Chinese translation in India. They completed the New Testament in 1811 and the entire Old Testament by 1823. This version never gained the popularity of Morrison's.

34. For an overview of this translation history, see John Wherry, "Historical Summary of the Different Versions of the Scriptures," *Records of the General Conference of the Protestant Missionaries of China* (Shanghai, 1890) 50–51.

35. One exception is a January 1851 article in *Spirit of Missions*, the official organ of the American Episcopal Mission—"Bishop Boone and the Shin Question" (pp. 40–53). Tastefully done, this piece does not convey the extreme seriousness with which the missionaries viewed this matter. It makes the debate look like a refined, academic discussion when, in reality, it involved the most complex question confronting them.

36. Arthur C. Moule, "A Manuscript Version of the New Testament," *Journal of the Royal Asiatic Society* (1949) 30.

37. The material in this section is taken largely from W.H. Medhurst, *An Inquiry into the Proper Mode of Rendering the Word God in Translating the Sacred Scriptures into the Chinese Language* (Shanghai, 1848) 12–13.

38. W.H. Medhurst, John Stronach, W.C. Milne, W. Lockhart, W. Muirhead, and J. Edkins.

39. "To the Protestant Missionaries Labouring at Hongkong and the Five Ports of China," from vol. 90 in a British and Foreign Bible Society compilation entitled *The Chinese Word for God* (London, n.d.) 8.

40. "A Confucian Tract, exhorting mankind always to preserve their celestial principles and their good hearts," *Chinese Repository*, vol. 4, no. 8 (Aug. 1846) 377–85. Daniel Bays points out that the convergency of sectarian literature in late 19th-century China with Christian tracts resulted in a larger number of converts to Christianity from the sectarians ("Christianity and Chinese Sects: The Role of Religious Tract Literature in the Late Nineteenth Century," in Fairbank and Barnett, *Christianity in China*).

41. This material is taken directly from Stronach's booklet found in the Oriental Manuscript Room of the British Museum, call number 15116.d.15.

42. My own translation from Gutzlaff's booklet found in the Oriental Manuscript Room of the British Library, call number 15116.e.35.

43. This quote is taken directly from Morrison's 17-leaf tract entitled "Miscellaneous Essays." It was examined in the Oriental Manuscript Room of the British Library.

44. This tract may be found in the Oriental Manuscript Room of the British Library, call number 15116.e.48.

45. The tract may be found in the Oriental Manuscript Room of the British Library, call number 15116.e.25. It is a translation of John A. James, *The Anxious Enquirer after Salvation Directed and Encouraged* (London, 1834).

46. The Chinese version used for this analysis was "Chia Yi Erh-yu Hsiang Lun," produced in Shanghai in 1858 (Oriental Manuscript Room of the British Library, call number 15116.3.38). For a detailed description of various versions, editions, and reprintings, see Wylie, *Memorials*, 16–17.

47. James Legge, *The Chinese Empire and Its Foreign Relations*.

48. The copy of *Tiandao Suyuan* used in this analysis is the revised edition of 1912 reprinted by Wen Chuan Publishing Co., Taibei, in 1966. The section on "natural theology" is on pp. 13–40.

49. "Chou-ban yi-wu shi-mu" ["management of barbarian affairs"], *Tung-zhi*, XVII, 25–26. Chinese officials here comment that Martin "wishes to imitate men like Ricci in making a name in China."

50. This material is taken from the *Shanghai Serial* (*Lu Ho Cong Tan*) in the Oriental Manuscript Room of the British Library, call number 15298 B1. Williamson's name in Chinese is Wei Lien-ch'en.

51. The specifically apologetic material found in *Tiandao Suyuan* is from pp. 37–73.

52. This brief analysis is made from a copy of Bridgman's book found in the Harvard-Yenching Library on the campus of Harvard University, Cambridge, Mass.

53. I am indebted to T.H. Tsien's article, "Impact on China through Translation" (*The Far Eastern Quarterly* [May 1954] 305–27) for much of the material in this paragraph.

54. *China Letters*, vol. 7, "Martin to his Board from Peking," letter #44, Oct. 1, 1863. Archives of the Presbyterian Historical Society, Philadelphia.

55. These magazines were in a line of succession with the publications of the Society for the Diffusion of Useful Knowledge in China and particularly Charles Gutzlaff's *Eastern Western Monthly Magazine* (Dong Xi Yang Gao meiyaeh Tangji Zhuan), which it absorbed in 1837.

56. The material in these two paragraphs comes from Wiley, *Memorials*, 120, and the *Chinese Serial* found in the Oriental Manuscript Room in the British Library, call number 15298.b.8.

57. The material in this paragraph comes from Wiley, *Memorials*, 133, and from the journal itself, found in the Oriental Manuscript Room in the British Library, call number 15298.b.5.

58. See Wiley, *Memorials*, and the journal itself, found in the Oriental Manuscript Room in the British Library, call number 15298.b.1.

59. Wiley, *Memorials*, 110, and British Library, 15298.a.38.

60. The Chinese name for *Peking Magazine* is *Zhongxi Wenjian Lu*. What I have analyzed is *Zhongxi Wenjian Lu Xuan Bian* ["selections from the *Zhongxi Wenjian Lu*"]. These were published in 1877 after the journal itself had ceased publication. Most of the articles in "Selections" were from Martin's pen.

61. Reported in James Broomhall, *Hudson Taylor and China's Open Century*, vol. 1 *Barbarians at the Gate* (London, 1981) 226.

62. Most of this material has been derived from Wiley, *Memorials*, 23–24. A cursory examination was made of the booklet itself in the Harvard-Yenching Library.

63. The material in these last few paragraphs comes from the *Baptist Missionary Magazine* ("Extracts from the Journal on the Native Assistant, Ching . . . Tsing." Vol. 26, no. 12 [Dec. 1846] 349–54).

64. This is the basic approach used by Justus Doolittle, missionary with the ABCFM, in his 18-page tract entitled *Disquisition on Filial Piety* (*Bian Xiao Lun*), written in the 1850s. See Wiley, *Memorials*, 203. The tract may be found in the Harvard-Yenching Library, call number TA1b82.5/19.

65. The material in the last several paragraphs comes from my own analysis of Martin's *Tiandao Suyuan*.

66. The material on Martin's views is taken from three of his books—*The Chinese, Their Education, Philosophy and Letters; Hanlin Papers*, Second Series (Shanghai, 1894); *The Lore of Cathay*—and from *Records of the General Conference of Protestant Missionaries in China, 1890* (Shanghai, 1891).

67. Remarks after the lecture by Joseph Edkins, "Buddhism and Tauism in Their Popular Aspects," *Records of the General Conference of the Protestant Missionaries of China* (Shanghai, 1878) 73.

68. "D.Z. Sheffield to Judson Smith," ABCFM Records, North China Mission, A.B.C.: 16.3.12, vol. 12, no. 201,3, May 29, 1889. Criticism of this type may explain why some of the material found in the earlier *Hanlin Papers* was deleted when the same lectures were incorporated in his later work *The Lore of Cathay*.

69. Most of the material on Martin's beliefs about Buddhism are found in *A Cycle of Cathay, Hanlin Papers* (Second Series), and *The Lore of Cathay*.

70. Even as friendly a critic as Reichelt referred to him as "that brilliant but often too audacious sinologue" (Reichelt, *Truth*, 36).

71. For a brief discussion of why Reichelt and the Christian Mission to Buddhists were not allowed to continue their affiliation with the Norwegian Missionary Society, see Jonas Jonson, *Lutheran Missions in a Time of Revolution: The China Experience 1944–51* (Uppsala, 1972) 124–31.

72. All this material on Reichelt's analysis of John's Prologue and other sections of the New Testament comes from his "The Johannine Approach," 90–101.

73. These examples are found in Karl Reichelt, "Indigenous Religious Phrases That May be Used to Interpret the Christian Message," *The Chinese Recorder* (Feb. 1927) 123–26. These are embodied in tracts and small booklets put out by Dao Feng Shan.

74. My analysis of China during the later Han dynasty draws upon Wright's *Buddhism*, 15–20.

75. For the origin, strengths, and weaknesses of this method, see Tang Yung-tung, "On 'Ko-yi,' the Earliest Method by which Indian Buddhism and Chinese Thought were Synthesized," in W.R. Inge et al., *Radha Krishnan Comparative Studies in Philosophy* (London, Allen & Unwin, 1951), 276–86.

76. I have drawn heavily on Kenneth D.S. Ch'en's work *The Chinese Transformation of Buddhism* for the material on the accommodation of Buddhism to Chinese life.

77. Paul Cohen, "Littoral and Hinterland in Nineteenth Century China: The 'Christian' Reformers," in Fairbank, *The Missionary Enterprise*, 198.

78. This description of a Taiping worship service is taken from Cornaby, *Peach Stones*, 246–48.

79. The specific contents of these tracts are analyzed in chap. 5, above, pp. 115–16.

80. For this analysis of the Taiping constitution I am indebted to Hsü, *Modern China*, 283–87.

81. The material on Hong Rengan comes largely from Jen Yu-wen, *Taiping Movement*, 351–76.

82. This section follows the broad outline and some of the content given in Boardman, *Christian Influence*, chap. 5, "The Christian Component: What the Taiping Took."

83. "Regarding Heavenly Principles." This tract, as well as Hong Xiuquan's *Annotations to The Old Testament and New Testament, Tian Wang's Comments on Edkin's Essay on God*, and the *Sanzijing* ["trimetrical classic"] are quoted in the English translation found in vol. 2 of Michael's *The Taiping Rebellion*.

84. The material from these several paragraphs has been taken from *Taiping Tianri* (Michael, II, 52–75).

85. This material on Confucius is quoted from *Taiping Tianri*; Michael, II, 56–57.

86. This material on the six sins comes from *Taiping Zhaoshu*; Michael, II, 26–30.

87. The role of the sovereign in effecting the salvation offered by heaven, particularly in defeating demons and in nurturing all his subjects, is described in detail in Michael, II, 237–50.

88. This and the following material on Yang and Xiao Chaoguei are from Jen Yu-wen, *Taiping Movement*, 50–51.

89. Michael, I, 23. See also P.M. Yap, "The Mental Illness of Hung Hsiu-ch'uan, Leader of the Taiping Rebellion," *Far Eastern Quarterly*, 13 (May 1954), 187–204. His illness may not have lasted forty days. This figure may have been used to be analogous to the forty days of Jesus' fasting mentioned in Liang Afa's tract.

90. Littell, 571. The following description utilizes Littell's outline, but the content comes from multiple sources.

91. *General Chronicle* (Oct. 1854) 223. This was in a July 21, 1854, letter from Legge to his board.

92. This article, dated June 22, 1862, in the *Daily Shipping and Commercial News* of February 6, 1863, was reproduced in the *North China Herald* of February 8, 1863. Found in Teng, *Taiping Rebellion*, 199. Other material in this section on Roberts is from Yuan Chung Teng, "Reverend I. Roberts."

93. Charles Kraft, *Christianity in Culture* (Maryknoll, N.Y., Orbis, 1978) 242–44. Paul Hiebert, "Sets and Structures," 117–27.

94. For this summary I am indebted to Deng Siyu and John Fairbank (eds.), *China's Response to the West* (New York, Atheneum, 1970) 195.

95. This material has been drawn from an unpublished paper by Jonathan Zhao, "The Chinese Indigenous Church Movement, 1911–1927," pp. 44–52, and Merwin, *Adventure*, 92–4.

96. I am here using the outline and some of the material proposed by Lee-Ming Ng in "Evaluation."

97. This material on Wu Leizhuan is a distillation of material found in Lee-Ming Ng, "Indigenization," 186–219.

98. For the argument of this paragraph I am indebted to Lee-Ming Ng, "Promise," 180.

99. This quotation and other material on Ni's view of trichotomous human nature are found in *The Spiritual Man*, I, 29ff.

100. For an analysis of the views of Witness Li, whose teaching can be traced in principle to Watchman Nee, see Duddy, *God-Men*.

101. For a balanced evaluation of Wang's theology, see Lam Wing-hung, *Wang Mingdao Yu Zhongquo Jiaohui* (Hong Kong, 1982) 126–243.

102. Mike Thornberry, "The Encounter of Christianity and Confucianism: How Modern Confucianism Views the Encounter," *South East Asia Journal of Theology*, vol. 10, no. 1 (July 1968) 47–62.

103. The material on this section comes from several articles on New Confucianism in *Ching Feng*, vol. 15, no. 3, 1972.

104. This quotation and other material on the fate of Confucianism in post–1949 China is taken from Julia Ching, "Confucius," 3–18.

105. This quotation and other material on Lee is found in Jung Young Lee, "The Yin-Yang Way of Thinking," *IRM*, vol. 60, no. 239 (July 1971) 363–70, and in Jung Young Lee, *A Theology of Change* (Maryknoll, N.Y., Orbis, 1977).

106. "Christian Faith and the Chinese Experience," Workshop Reports from an Ecumenical Colloquium in Louvain, Belgium, Sept. 9–14, 1974, pp. 22, 28. For lectures given at the Louvain conference and at another conference in Bastad, Sweden, Feb. 1974, see *Christianity and the New China* (S. Pasadena, Ecclesia Publications, 1976, 2 vols.).

107. Many of the emphases made by Zhao are also found in *Lausanne Occasional Papers* no. 6, Thailand Report, *Christian Witness to the Chinese People*. Zhao was one of the principal authors of this significant report.

108. The material in this paragraph is from Orr, *Religion*, 46–47.

109. Marcus Cheng's speech is recorded as Document 65 in MacInnis, *Religious Policy*, 201–7.

110. Ding Guangxun's message is found in Douglas J. Elwood (ed.), *Asian Christian Theology* (Philadelphia, 1980) 257–66.

111. "The Christian Conference of Asia (CCA) Consultation with Church Leaders from China," *China Notes*, vol. 19, no. 2–3 (Spring and Summer 1981) 161.

112. These statements are from David Adeney, *Pray for China Fellowship Prayer Bulletin* (Aug. 1981) 8.

113. Zao Senjie, "Christian Witness in New China," *China Notes*, vol. 19, no. 2–3 (Spring and Summer 1981) 167.

114. Sermon at Riverside Church, New York City, published in *Lutheran Information Bulletin*, Doc. No. 4.1.2.39, pp. 21–22.

115. Comments by Chen Zeming given at the Montreal Conference, Oct. 1981, sponsored by the Canada China Programme of the Canadian Council of Churches.

116. Christopher Lind, "China's Churches and the West," *The Ecumenist*, vol. 20, no. 3 (March–April 1982) 36–37. This board, seeking to use some of the money received as compensation for properties nationalized after 1949, sought to develop an educational project by working directly with the state, a paternalistic attitude in the view of Chinese church leaders.

117. From a paper relating to the Montreal Conference (Oct. 1981) sponsored by the China Programme of the Canadian Council of Churches.

118. "Religion and Feudal Superstitions," reprinted from *Renmin Ribao* ["the people's daily"], 1979, 3:15, and found in *China and Church Today* (May–June 1979) 4.

119. "C.S. Lewis's Contribution to a 'Missionary Theology': An Asia Perspective," *South East Asian Journal of Theology*, vol. 23, no. 1 (1982) 75–82.

120. "Case Studies from China," *International Review of Mission*, vol. 70, no. 278 (April 1981) 9.

121. The material on the anti-Christian tradition in China is from Paul Cohen, "The Anti-Christian Tradition in China," *The Journal of Asian Studies*, 20 (Feb. 1961) 160–79. The works to which Cohen refers are *P'o-hsieh-chi* (about 1640), *Pu-te-i* by Yang Kuang-hsien (1665), and *Pi-hsieh chi-shih* ["a record of facts to ward off heterodoxy"], written ca. 1860.

122. See Michael Stainton, "Sources of 19th Century Chinese Opposition to the Missionaries and Christianity," *Ching Feng*, vol. 20, no. 3. 1977, pp. 142–43. In addition to works mentioned by Cohen, he lists a Hunan tract, "The Human Call to Arms."

123. For a good understanding of the gentry, see Zhang Zhungli, *The Chinese Gentry*.

124. Lu Shih-ch'iang's English synopsis of *The Origin and Cause of the Anti-Christian Movement Among Chinese Officials and Gentry (1860–1874)* (Taibei, 1972) 43.

Bibliography

Adeney, David H. *China Christian Students Face the Revolution.* Downers Grove, Ill., Inter-Varsity Press, 1973.

Allen, Young J. "A Supreme Need for the Work in China," in his *Missionary Issues of the Twentieth Century,* 192.

Bennett, Adrian. "Missionary Journalism in Nineteenth Century China: Young J. Allen and the Early Wan-kuo kong-pao." Ph.D. thesis, University of California, 1971.

————, and Liu, Kwang-ching. "Christianity in the Chinese Idiom: Young J. Allen and the Early Chiao-hui hsin-pao, 1868–1870," in Fairbank, *Missionary Enterprise,* 191ff.

Bloodworth, Dennis. *The Chinese Looking Glass.* New York, Farrar, Straus and Giroux, 1967.

Boardman, Eugene. *Christian Influence Upon the Ideology of the Taiping Rebellion, 1851–64.* New York, Octagon, 1952.

Bohr, Paul Richard. "Religion in the People's Republic of China: The Limits of Toleration." *The China Council of the Asia Society* (June 1982).

————. "Liang Fa's Quest for Moral Power" in Barnett and Fairbanks (eds.). *Christianity in China.*

Bouquet, A. C. *The Christian Faith and Non-Christian Religions.* New York, Harper, 1958.

Burkholder, J. Lawrence. "Notes on the Theological Meaning of China," *Mission Focus,* 4:3 (Jan. 1967) 1–5.

Caldarola, Carlo. *Christianity the Japanese Way.* Leiden, Brill, 1979.

Chao, Jonathan. "The Gospel for Communist Society: A Preliminary Reflection on the Chinese Experience," *Gospel in Context,* 2:3 (July 1979) 32.

————. "Record of the Plenary Discussion," *Christianity and the New China,* 2:184 (1976) 184.

————, and Morris, Christopher. *Guidelines Toward a Christian Understanding of China.* Silver Spring, Md., China Graduate School of Theology, 1977.

Chao, T. C. *See* Zhao.

Charbonnier, Jean. "China-Christian Relations in the Spirit of Matteo Ricci," *Tripod* (Hong Kong) (Dec. 1982) 105.

————, and Triviere, Leon. "The New China and the History of Salvation," in *Christianity and the New China,* vol. 1, *Theological Implications of the New China.*

Ch'en, Jerome. *China and the West.* Indiana University Press, 1979.

Ch'en, Kenneth K. S. *The Chinese Transformation of Buddhism.* Princeton University Press, 1973.

Ching, Julia. *Confucianism and Christianity.* Tokyo, Kodansha International in cooperation with The Institute of Oriental Religions, 1977.

————. "Confucianism: A Philosophy of Man," in Whitehead, Shaw, and Girardot (eds.), *China and Christianity.*

————. "Confucius and His Modern Critics—1916 to Present," *Information Letter No. 7,* LWF Marxism and China Study (May 1974) 3–18.

————. "Hyphenated Christianity," *China Notes,* 16:3 (Summer 1978) 34.

Christianity and the New China. South Pasadena, Ecclesia Publications, 1976, 2 vols.

Chu, Michael (ed.). *The New China: A Catholic Response.* New York, Paulist, 1977.

Clasper, Paul. "C. S. Lewis's Contribution to a 'Missionary Theology': An Asian Perspective," *South East Asia Journal of Theology,* 23:1 (1982) 75–82.

Cohen, Paul. "The Anti-Christian Tradition in China," *The Journal of Asian Studies,* 20 (Feb. 1961) 160–79.

Colledge, T. R. "Suggestions with Regard to Employing Medical Practitioners in China," *Chinese Repository* (Dec. 1835) 388.

Cornaby, W. Arthur. *A String of Peach Stones.* London, Charles Kelly, 1895.

Covell, Ralph R. *W. A. P. Martin, Pioneer of Progress in China.* Washington, D.C., Christian University Press, 1978.

Craighead, James R. E. *Hunter Corbett: Fifty-Six Years a Missionary in China.* New York, Revell, 1921.

Creel, H. G. *Chinese Thought from Confucius to Mao Tse-tung.* Chicago, New American Library, 1960.

Cronin, Vincent. *The Wise Man from the West.* New York, Dutton, 1955.

D'Elia, Pascal M. *Catholic Native Episcopacy in China.* Shanghai, Tusewei Printing Press, 1927.

Ding, Guangxun. "Evangelism as a Chinese Christian Sees It," *Missiology: An International Review,* 11:3 (July 1983) 310–11.

————. "Religious Policy and Theological Reorientation in China," *China Notes,* 18:3 (Summer 1980) 121–24.

————. "Retrospect and Prospect," *International Review of Mission,* 70:278 (April 1981) 30.

Dodd, Charles H. "Hellenism and Christianity," in his *Independence.*

———— (ed.). *Independence, Convergence, and Borrowing.* Harvard Tercentenary Publications, Harvard University Press, 1937.

Dubose, Hampden C. *Preaching in Sinim or The Gospel to the Gentiles with Hints and Helps for Addressing a Heathen Audience.* Richmond, Presbyterian Committee of Publication, 1893.

Duddy, Neil T. *The God-Men.* Downers Grove, Ill., Inter-Varsity Press, 1981.

Dunne, George H. *Generation of Giants.* University of Notre Dame Press, 1962.

Edkins, Joseph. *Chinese Buddhism.* London, K. Paul, Tranch, Trübner and Co., 1893.

Ehrling, Bernard. "The Story of Watchman Nee," *Lutheran Quarterly,* 28:2 (May 1976) 150.

Eilert, Hakan. *Boundlessness: Studies in Karl Ludvig Reichelt's Missionary Thinking with Special Regard to the Buddhist-Christian Encounter.* Ringkobing, Aros; Eksp., DBK, 1974.

Eitel, E. J. *Buddhism, Its Historical, Theoretical and Practical Aspects.* Hong Kong, 1884.

Fairbank, John. *Chinese Thought and Institutions.* University of Chicago Press, 1957.

————. "Patterns Behind the Tientsin Massacre," *Harvard Journal of Asiatic Studies,* 20:3–4 (Dec. 1957) 493.

————. *Trade and Diplomacy on the China Coast: The Opening of the Treaty Ports, 1842–54.* Stanford University Press, 1953.

————— (ed.). *The Missionary Enterprise in China and America.* Harvard University Press, 1974.

—————, and Barnett, S. W. (eds.). *Christianity in China: Early Protestant Missionary Writings.* Harvard University Press, 1985.

Faricy, Robert. "Mao's Thought and Christian Belief," in Chu, *The New China,* 44–77.

Fay, Peter. *Opium War.* New York, Norton, 1976.

Feng Shangli. "The Contours of a Chinese Theology," *Ching Feng,* 13:1 (1970) 13–16.

Ferre, Frederick (ed.). *Natural Theology Selections: William Paley.* New York, Bobbs-Merrill, 1963.

Fleming, Daniel Johnson. *Christian Symbols in a World Community.* New York, Friendship Press, 1940.

—————. *Each With His Own Brush.* Friendship Press, 1938.

—————. *Heritage of Beauty.* Friendship Press, 1937.

Foster, John. *The Church of the T'ang Dynasty.* New York, Macmillan, 1939.

Franke, Wolfgang. *China and the West.* University of South Carolina Press, 1967.

Gernet, Jacques, *China and the Christian Impact: A Conflict of Cultures.* London, Cambridge University Press, 1985.

Giles, Herbert A. "The New Testament in Chinese," *The China Review,* 10 (Dec. 1881) 158.

Gluer, Winifred. "The Encounter Between Christianity and Chinese Buddhism During the Nineteenth Century and the First Half of the Twentieth Century," *Ching Feng,* 11:3 (1968) 50.

—————. "The Legacy of T. C. Chao," *International Bulletin of Missionary Research,* 6:4 (Oct. 1982) 168.

Goodrich, L. Carrington. *A Short History of the Chinese People.* New York, Harper and Row, 1963.

Grasso, Domenico. "The New China and God's Plan for Salvation," in Chu, *The New China.*

Grove, S. A. *The Scottish Philosophy of Common Sense.* Oxford, Clarendon, 1960.

Gulick, Edward. *Peter Parker and the Opening of China.* Harvard University Press, 1973.

Gutzlaff, Charles. *Journals of Three Voyages Along the Coast of China.* Taibei, Cheng Wen Publishing House, 1968.

Hamberg, Theodore. *The Visions of Hung-Siu-Tshuen and Origins of the Kwang-si Insurrection.* Hong Kong, China Mail, 1854.

Headland, Isaac T. "A Nation of Liars?", *The Chinese Recorder,* 28:4 (April 1897) 161–69.

Hesselgrave, David. *Communicating Christ Cross-Culturally.* Grand Rapids, Zondervan, 1978.

—————— (ed.). *New Horizons in World Mission.* Grand Rapids, Baker Book House, 1979.

Hiebert, Paul. "Sets and Structures: A Study of Church Patterns," in Hesselgrave, *New Horizons.*

Holth, Sverre. "Encounters of Christianity with Buddhism During the Nestorian Period," *Ching Feng,* no. 3 (1968) 26–27.

Hsü. *See* Xu.

Hu Shi (Shih). "The Indianization of China: A Case Study in Cultural Borrowing," in Dodd, *Independence,* 223–24.

Jen Yu-wen. *The Taiping Revolutionary Movement.* Yale University Press, 1973.

Jiang Wen-han. *Ancient Chinese Christianity and the Jews of Kai Feng.* Shanghai, Zhi Shi Press, 1982.

Jones, Francis P. *The Church in Communist China.* New York. Friendship Press, 1962.

Jonson, Jonas. *Lutheran Missions in a Time of Revolution: The China Experience 1944–51.* Uppsala, Tvavaga Forlags, 1972.

Kang, C. H. *Genesis and Chinese.* Hong Kong, Concordia, 1950.

———, and Nelson, Esther. *The Discovery of Genesis and Chinese.* St. Louis, Concordia, 1979.

Kinnear, Angus Ian. *Against the Tide.* Fort Washington, Pa., Christian Literature Crusade, 1973.

Koyama, Kosuke. *Three-Mile-An-Hour God: Biblical Reflections.* Maryknoll, N.Y., Orbis, 1980.

Kraemer, Hendrik. *Theology of the Laity.* Philadelphia, Westminster, 1958.

Kraft, Charles H. "Ideological Factors in Intercultural Borrowing," *Missiology* 2:3 (July 1974) 300.

Lam Wing-hung. *Wang Ming-tao and the Chinese Church.* Hong Kong, China Graduate School of Theology, 1982.

Latourette, Kenneth S. *The History of Christian Mission in China.* London, SPCK, 1929.

Lau, Maria Goretti. "Some Eschatological Thoughts in Matteo Ricci's *The True Idea of God,*" *Tripod* (Hong Kong) (Dec. 1982) 94.

Lazzarotto, Angelo S. *The Catholic Church in Post-Mao China.* Hong Kong, Holy Spirit Study Centre, 1982.

Lee, Peter. "Indigenous Theology—Overcropped Land or Under-Developed Field," *Ching Feng,* no. 1, 1974.

Lee, Shiu Keung. "Nestorian Christianity in the T'ang Dynasty," *Ching Feng,* no. 3–4 (1973) 121.

Leibniz, Gottfried Wilhelm. *Discourse on the Natural Theology of the Chinese,* Monograph no. 4 of the Society for Asian and Comparative Philosophy. University Press of Hawaii, 1977.

Levenson, Joseph R. *Confucian China and Its Modern Fate: A Trilogy.* University of California Press, 1968.

———. "Confucian and Taiping 'Heaven': The Political Implications of Clashing Religious Concepts," *Comparative Studies in Society and History,* 4 (July 1962) 450.

Li, Dun J. *The Ageless Chinese: A History.* New York, Scribner's, 3rd ed., 1978.

Lin, Lo Hsiang. *Nestorianism in the T'ang and Yuan Dynasties.* Hong Kong, University Press, 1966.

Lin, Robert H. J. *The Taiping Revolution: A Failure of Two Missions.* Washington, D.C., University Press of America, 1979.

Lin, Yu-tang. *My Country and My People.* New York, John Day Press, 1935.

Lin-Le (Lieut. Lindley, R.N.) *Ti-Ping Tien-Kwoh: The History of the Ti-Ping Revolution.* London, Day, 1866, 2 vols.

Littell, John. "Missionaries and Politics in China—The Taiping Rebellion," *Political Science Quarterly,* 43:4 (Dec. 1928) 571.

Lu, Siqiang. English synopsis of *The Origin and Cause of the Anti-Christian Movement Among Chinese Officials and Gentry 1860–1874.* Taibei, Institute of Modern History Academia Sinica, 1972.

———. *Zhongguo Guanshen Fanjiaodi Yuanyin* ["the origin and cause of the anti-Christian movement among Chinese officials and gentry 1860–1874"]. Taibei, Institute of Modern History Academia Sinica, 1966.

Lyall, Leslie. *Three of China's Mighty Men.* London, Overseas Missionary Fellowship Books, 1973.

MacInnis, Donald E. "Theological and Missiological Implications of China's Revolution," *Missiology: An International Review,* 1:4 (Oct. 1973) 443–44.

——— (ed.) *Religious Policy and Practice in Communist China.* New York, Macmillan, 1972.

Malatesta, Edward. "Matteo Ricci, Friend of China," *Tripod* (Hong Kong), 12, Special Issue on Matteo Ricci (Dec. 1982).

Martin, Mary Louise. "East Meets West: The Jesuits in China (1582–1773). A Report on a Symposium," *Tripod* (Hong Kong), 12 (Dec. 1982).

Martin, William A.P. *The Chinese, Their Education, Philosophy and Letters.* New York, Harper and Brothers, 1881.

———. *A Cycle of Cathay.* New York, 3rd ed., 1900.

———. *The Lore of Cathay.* New York, Fleming H. Revell, 1912.

———. "The Metric System for China," *The Chinese Recorder,* 5 (March-Apr. 1874) 58–59.

———. "Two Embassies," I, 119–20. Manuscript, 1860, Presbyterian Historical Society, Philadelphia.

——— (ed.). *Hanlin Papers,* Second Series. Shanghai, Kelly and Walsh, 1894.

McCartee, D. B. *Xiaojing Fumu.* ["obedience to parents."] Ningbo, 1848.

Meadows, Thomas. *The Chinese and Their Rebellions.* London, Academic Reprints, 1856.

Medhurst, Walter Henry. *China: Its State and Prospects.* Boston, 1838.

———. "Critical Review of Books of the Insurgents." Pamphlet 13, China Sundries, at the library of The Institute of African and Oriental Studies, London, call number CCWM N6/18.

———. *An Inquiry into the Proper Mode of Rendering the Word God in Translating the Sacred Scriptures into the Chinese Language.* Shanghai, 1848.

———. "Reply to the Essay of Dr. Boone on the Proper Rendering of the Words Elohim and Theos into the Chinese Language," *Chinese Repository,* 17:10–12 (Oct.-Dec. 1848) 552–53.

Merwin, Wallace. *Adventure in Unity.* Grand Rapids, Eerdmans, 1974.

Michael, Franz H. *The Taiping Rebellion: History and Documents.* Seattle, University of Washington Press, 1966.

Miller, Perry. *American Thought,* vol. 1, *Civil War to World War I.* San Francisco, Rinehart, 1954.

Moule, A. C. *Christians in China Before the Year 1500.* London, 1930.

Nee. *See* Ni.

Neill, Stephen. *History of Christian Missions.* Baltimore, Penguin, 1964.

Nevius, John. *Demon Possession.* Grand Rapids, Kregel Publications, 8th ed., 1968.

Ng, Lee-Ming. "An Evaluation of T. C. Chao's Thought," *Ching Feng,* vol. 14, no. 1-2. (1971) 5–59.

———. "From Indigenization to Revolution," *Ching Feng,* no. 4, 186–219.

———. "The Promise and Limitations of Chinese Protestant Theologians, 1920–50" *Ching Feng,* vol. 21, no. 4, vol. 22, no. 1.

Ni Duosheng (Watchman Nee). *Love Not the World.* Eastbourne, Christian Literature Crusade, 1976.

———. *Sit, Walk, Stand.* London, Victory Press, 1963; Fort Washington, Pa., Christian Literature Crusade, 1972.

———. *The Spiritual Man.* New York, Christian Fellowship Publications, 1968.

Noren, Loren. "The Life and Work of Karl Ludvig Reichelt," *Ching Feng,* no. 3 (1967) 14.

Ogden, Schubert. *The Reality of God.* New York, Harper and Row, 1966.

Orr, Robert G. *Religion in China.* New York, Friendship Press, 1980.

Outerbridge, Leonard M. *The Lost Churches of China.* Philadelphia, Westminster, 1952.

Paton, David. *Christian Missions and the Judgment of God.* London, SCM, 1953.

Patterson, George N. *Christianity in Communist China.* Waco, Word Books, 1969.

Peterson, Willard J. "Western Natural Philosophy Published in the Late Ming China," *Proceedings of the American Philosophical Society,* 117:4 (Aug. 15, 1973) 316.

Pollak, Michael. *Mandarins, Jews and Missionaries: The Jewish Experience in the Chinese Empire.* Philadelphia, Jewish Publication Society of America, 1980.

Pro Mundi Vita. Statement on "China and the Churches in the Making of the World," in *Christianity and the New China,* vol. 2.

Reichelt, Karl. "Buddhism in China at the Present Time and the New Challenge to the Christian Church," *International Review of Missions,* vol. 26 (April 1937) 162.

——. "The Johannine Approach," in *The Authority of the Faith.* Tambaram Series, vol. 1 (London, 1939) 90–101.

——. *Meditation and Piety in the Far East.* New York, Aros; Harper, 1954.

——. *Truth and Tradition in Chinese Buddhism.* Shanghai, Commercial Press, 1934.

Reid, Gilbert. *The Sources of the Anti-Foreign Disturbances in China.* Shanghai, 1903.

Ricci, Matteo. *China in the Sixteenth Century: The Journals of Matthew Ricci, 1583–1610,* translated by Louis Gallagher. New York, Random House, 1953.

——. *Opere Storiche* (Macerata, Giorgetti, 1911–1913), in Young, *East-West Synthesis,* 22.

——. *Tianzhu Shiyi.* Taichung, Taiwan, 1966.

Richard, Timothy. *An Epistle to All Buddhists.* Shanghai, 1916.

——. *The New Testament of Higher Buddhism.* Edinburgh, Clark, 1910.

Rowbotham, Arnold. *Missionary and Mandarin.* New York, Russell and Russell, 1966.

Rule, Paul. "Is Maoism Open to the Transcendent?" in Chu, *The New China.*

Saeki, P.Y. *The Nestorian Monument in China.* London, SPCK, 1916.

Shi (Shih). *See* Hu Shi.

Shih, Vincent. *The Taiping Ideology: Its Sources, Interpretations, and Influences.* Seattle, University of Washington Press, 1972.

Sih, Paul. *Chinese Culture and Christianity.* Taibei, China Culture Publication Foundation, 1957.

Song, Choan-Seng. "An Analysis of Contemporary Chinese Culture and Its Implications for the Task of Theology," *South East Asia Journal of Theology* (April 1963) 21–22.

——. *Christian Mission in Reconstruction.* Maryknoll, N.Y., Orbis, 1977.

——. "New China and Salvation History: A Methodological Enquiry," *South East Asia Journal of Theology,* no. 2 (1974) 57.

——. *The Tears of Lady Meng.* Maryknoll, N.Y., Orbis, 1982.

——. *Third-Eye Theology.* Orbis, 1979.

Soothill, William E. *Timothy Richard of China.* London, Seeley, Service and Company, 1924.

Spelman, Douglas G. E.C. Liu (ed.), "Christianity in Chinese: The Protestant Term Question," in *Papers on China Seminars at Harvard.* Harvard University Press, 1969.

Stainton, Michael. "Sources of 19th Century Chinese Opposition to the Missionaries and Christianity," *Ching Feng,* no. 3 (1977) 142–43.

Stewart, Dugald. *Outlines of Moral Philosophy.* Edinburgh, W. Creech, 1793.

Stott, John, and Coote, Robert (eds.) *The Gospel and Culture.* Pasadena, William Carey Library, 1979.

Sullivan, Francis A. "Theological Implications of the New China," in Chu, *New China.*

Syrdal, Rolf. *To the End of the Earth.* Minneapolis, Augsburg, 1967.

Tang, C. K. *Religion in Chinese Society.* University of California Press, 1967.

Teng, S.Y. *The Taiping Rebellion and the Western Powers.* Oxford, Clarendon, 1971.

————, and Fairbank, John (eds.) *China's Response to the West.* New York, Atheneum, 1970.

Thompson, R.W. *Griffith John.* London, The Religious Tract Society, 1908.

Thornberry, Mike. "The Encounter of Christianity and Confucianism: How Modern Confucianism Views the Encounter," *South East Asia Journal of Theology,* 10:1 (July 1968) 47–62.

Tong, John. "Ricci's Contribution to China," *Tripod* (Hong Kong) (Dec. 1982).

Tsien, T. H. "Impact on China through Translation," *Far Eastern Quarterly,* vol. 13 (May 1954) 305–27.

Visser 't Hooft, W. A. "Accommodation—True and False," *South East Asia Journal of Theology,* 8:3 (Jan. 1967) 13–14.

Walls, Andrew F. "The Gospel as the Prisoner and Liberator of Culture," *Faith and Thought,* 108:1–2 (Oct. 1981) 39–43.

Waltke, Bruce. *Creation and Chaos.* Portland, Western Conservative Baptist Seminary, 1974.

Walton, Alan H. (ed.) *The Awakening of Faith by Ashvagosha.* New York, University Books, 1960.

Wardlaw, Thomas. *Griffith John: The Story of Fifty Years in China.* London, 1908.

Wayland, Francis. "Report of Dr. Wayland to Board of American Baptist Union," *Baptist Missionary Magazine* (July 1854) 220.

West, Charles. "Some Theological Reflections on China," *China Notes,* 14:4 (Fall 1976) 39.

Wherry, John. "Historical Summary of the Different Versions of the Scriptures," *Records of the General Conference of the Protestant Missionaries of China,* Shanghai, May 7–20, 1890. Shanghai, American Presbyterian Mission Press, 1890.

Whitehead, Raymond. "Christ, Salvation, and Maoism." Address given at the American Society of Missiology, North Park Seminary, Chicago, June 1977.

————, Shaw, Yu-ming, and Girardot, N.J. (eds.) *China and Christianity.* University of Notre Dame Press, 1979.

Williamson, Henry R. *British Baptists in China 1845–1952.* London, Carey Kingsgate Press, 1957.

The Willowbank Report. Lausanne Committee on World Evangelization, Wheaton, Ill., 1978.

Witek, John W. *Controversial Ideas in China and in Europe: A Biography of Jean-Francis Fucquet, S.J. (1665–1741).* Rome, Institutum Historicum S.I., 1982.

Woo, Franklin J. "God's Call to a New Beginning—A Report, Montreal, Canada—October 2–9, 1981" *China Notes,* 19:4 (Fall 1981) 186.

Workman, George Bell. "The Chinese Mind and Missionary Approach." Th.M. Thesis, Union Theological Seminary, 1939.

Wright, Arthur. *Buddhism in Chinese History.* Stanford University Press, 1959.

Wu Pei-yi. "Self-Examination and Confession of Sins in Traditional China," *Harvard Journal of Asiatic Studies,* vol. 39 (June 1979) 6.

Wylie, Alexander. *Memorials of Protestant Missionaries*. Shanghai, American Presbyterian Mission Press, 1867.

———. "The Nestorian Tablet in Si-ngan Foo," in *Chinese Researches*. Shanghai, 1897.

Xu (Hsü), Immanuel. *The Rise of Modern China*. New York, Oxford University Press, 1970.

———. "The Secret Mission of the Lord Amherst on the China Coast, 1832," *Harvard Journal of Asiatic Studies*, 17, pp. 251–52.

Xu (Hsü), Paul, "Apology in Behalf of the Jesuits," *Chinese Repository* (March 1850) 118–26.

Yang, C. K. "The Functional Relationship between Confucian Thought and Chinese Religion," in Fairbank, *Chinese Thought*.

———. *Religion in Chinese Society*. University of California Press, 1967.

Young, John D. *East-West Synthesis: Matteo Ricci and Confucianism*. Hong Kong, Centre of Asian Studies, University of Hong Kong, 1980.

Yuan Chung Teng. "Reverend Issachar Jocox Roberts and the Taiping Rebellion," *The Journal of Asian Studies*, 23:1 (Nov. 1963).

Yu-pin, Paul. *Eyes East*. Patterson, N.J., St. Anthony Guild Press, 1945.

Zhang Zhungli. *The Chinese Gentry: Studies on Their Role in Nineteenth Century Chinese Society*. Seattle, University of Washington Press, 1955.

Zhao, Jonathan. *See* Chao.

Zhao Zichen (T.C. Chao). "Christianity and Confucianism," *International Review of Missions* (1928) 596–97.

———. "The Possibility of the Development of Christian Theology in China in the Next Forty Years," *Nanking Theological Review*, 26:1–2, pp. 14–21.

Zurcher, E. *The Buddhist Conquest of China: The Spread and Adaptation of Buddhism in Early Medieval China*. Leiden, Brill, 1959; reprint, 1972.

INDEX

Abeel, David, 71, 75, 80, 82
Abraham, 30, 169
Academia Sinica, 184, 252
Acceptance of, new ideas, 134
Accommodation, 15, 66, 104, 119, 140-45, 222, 248
Accusation meetings, 225-26
Activism, Confucian, 187-95
Adam, 26, 28, 34
Adams, John Quincy, 83
Adorer, 114
Adultery, 162
Africa, 2, 39, 112
Aleni, Giulio, 60
Allen, Roland, 3
Allen, Young J., 109-10, 184
Aloah, 89
Alohe, 26
Alopa, 86
Alopen, 22-23, 25
Altaic people, 4
America, 75, 97
American(s), xiv, 72, 83, 96, 98, 105, 176
American Bible Society, 90
American Board of Commissioners for Foreign Missions, 72, 155, 178
American Seaman's Friend Society, 76
Amherst, Lord, 73, 75
Amitabha, 89, 139, 145
Amitofu, 89, 139
Amoy, 82-83, 123
An Shigao, 138
Ancestral rites, 9, 50, 56, 62-63, 66, 94, 117-21, 142, 152, 167, 222, 253
Ancestral tablet, 62-63, 118
Andrew, Brother, 237
Angel, 62, 163, 173
Anglican, 196
Anglo-Chinese college, 72

Anglo-Chinese Concord Almanac, 109
Anhui, 137
Animal world, 101-2
Animism, 157, 243
Ankoy tea hills, 73, 79
Anlushan, 30
Annam, 183
Anti-Christian: movement, 185-88, 249, 252; tradition, 249-50
Anti-communist, 234
Anti-foreign, 65
Anti-missionary riots, 184
Anxious Inquirer, 96
Apologetic, 45, 50, 94, 98-99, 102-6, 114, 129, 227, 231
Apostolic legitimacy, 231
Appropriation, 135, 145-47
A–Q, 185
Aquinas, Thomas, 49, 56
Arghun Khan, 37
Arhat, 140
Aristotelian theory, 12, 43, 192, 212
Art forms, Buddhistic, 145
Asia, 2
Assembly hall churches, 196
Assistant king, 170
Astronomy, 42-43, 136
Asvagosha, 31, 126-28
Atheism, 227, 235-36
Athens, 129
Attitudes: Jesuit, 83-84; Protestant, 78, 81, 83
Augustine, 50, 63, 129, 191
Austin-Sparks, J., 197
Avalokitesvara, 145
Awakening of Faith, 31, 125-28
Babel, 207
Babylon, 105, 127
Babylonian epic, 15-16

Baghdad, 37

Baldus, Jean-Henri, 81

Bangkok, 70

Baptism, 29, 60, 70, 114, 118, 152, 166, 178, 230, 246

Baptist, 91; American, 90, 107; English, 120, 125; Southern, 177

Baptizing, 56, 152

Barbarians, 44, 65, 74, 79, 133, 162, 173

Barber, Margaret, 197

Bassett, Jean, 85

Bastad, 240

Batavia, 70, 72, 75, 158

Bates, M. Searle, 179

Beijing (Peking), 39-40, 42, 44, 49, 51, 54, 59, 65, 68, 99, 114, 123, 153, 184-85, 200, 219, 225, 227, 231

Benevolence (*ren*), 10, 14, 189, 194

Bernard of Clairvaux, 132

Bible, 90-91, 95, 103, 105, 116, 118, 155, 157, 180, 188, 211, 226, 230, 236, 240, 244; Protestant, 85-90; Roman Catholic, 85

Black Sea, 37

Bloodworth, Dennis, 13

Bo Juyi, 144

Boardman, Eugene, 174

Bodhisattva, 20, 29, 31, 89, 97, 124, 126, 141, 221

Body, of God, 158-59

Bohea hills, 73

Bonham, George, 171

Book of Changes (*Yi Ching*), 146, 212

Book of the Will, 25

Boone, William, 88

Borneo, 72

Borrowing, mass, 135-40

Bouquet, A.D., 221

Bourgeois ideology, 228

Bow, ceremonial, 178

Boxers, 184

Braaten, Carl, 218

Brainerd, David, 197

Brazil, 112

Brethren movement, 196-97

Bridgman, Elijah, 71, 106, 156

Brief Geographical History of the U.S. of America, 106-7

British, 71-72, 83-84, 86, 96, 98, 176

British and Foreign Bible Society, 76, 86, 90

British East India Company, 69, 73, 85

British Museum, 20, 85-86

Brown, Thomas, 97

Buddha(s), 29-31, 54, 55, 124, 126, 137-39, 141, 147, 149, 209, 220-21

Buddhism, 7, 9, 12, 14, 22-26, 28-34, 36, 38, 47, 49, 52, 55, 57-58, 62, 65, 73, 89, 94-97, 104-5, 108, 122-49, 152, 167, 173-75, 188, 191, 206, 220-21, 229, 233, 237, 250; attempted accommodation, 140-41; attitude to filial piety, 141-42; contrast in north and south China, 138; economic life, 143-44; educational efforts, 144-45; entrance into China, 136; imagery and beauty, 140; imperial patronage, 137-38; Indian, 133; missionaries, 138, 140; political submission, 142-43; preferred by Huns, 138; Protestant missionary attitudes toward, 122-32; reinterpretation of Indian Buddhism, 145-47; resistance to and persecution, 141-43; spread among gentry, 137; spread among masses, 136-40; use of Daoist terminology, 138, 140-41; why not viewed as foreign, 147-48; works of mercy, 138, 144-45

Burial customs, 56

Burkholder, J. Lawrence, 213-14

Caesaro-papism, 138

Cai Yongpei, 185

Caldarola, Carlo, 204

Calendar, 42-43, 136

Cambaluc, 37-38. *See also* Beijing

Cannon, 43

Canton, 39-40, 68-71, 73, 76, 79-80, 82, 85-86, 91, 111, 116, 151, 155-56, 177-78, 182

Capitalism, 193-94, 204, 227, 234, 237

Carpini, Giovanni de Piano, 37

Carter, Jimmy, 229

Cartography, 42

Catechism, 94-95, 154

Catechist, 59, 114, 170

Cathay, 37

Catholic: Chinese, 230-31; Roman, 231. *See also* Roman Catholic

Catholic National Administrative Commission, 230
Celibacy, 53-54, 60, 133
Ceylon, 138
Chan, 142, 145-46
Changan, 3, 22, 25, 137-38
Chang-tzu, 139
Character analysis, 206-8
Charbonnier, Jean, 216
Chen, Jianfu, 209
Ch'en, Kenneth, 133, 135
Chen, Zeming, 238-39
Cheng, Jingyi, 187, 204
Cheng, Marcus, 227
Chile, 112
China: Buddhist faith in, 122-32; changes in, 213-14, 224-25; churches in Marxist, 225-31; contextualization of Buddhism, 133-49; cultural unity, 6-7; gospel of power, 68-84; gospel under Communism, 231-47; Jesuits in, 39-67; mind, 7-14, 39; modern Christian expressions, 203-13; national identity, 206; Nestorians, 35; peoples, 4-7; religions, 14; resistance to gospel, 4, 248-53; socio-economic groups, 5-6; Taiping civil war, 150-81; theological meaning of new, 213-23; use of Chinese characters, 206-07
China Centenary Conference, 99
China Christian Council, 230, 236, 247
China Continuation Committee, 186-87
China Inland Mission, 200
China: Its State and Prospects, 72
Chinese and Foreign Gazette, 109
Chinese Catholic Culture Movement, 203
Chinese Christian Union, 156
Chinese Communist Party, 185
Chinese Repository, 71, 75
Chinese Serial, 108-9
Chinese, Their Education, Philosophy and Letters, The, 119
Chinese United League, 184
Ching, Julia, 14, 209-11
Chiutaiso, 41
Christ, 115, 122, 128-31, 158, 168, 171-72, 180, 190, 209, 217, 220, 233-34
Christ and Culture, 198
Christian Literature Society, 99

Christian Manifesto, 202, 225
Christian Mission to Buddhists, 128-32
Christianity: African, 2-3; anonymous, 217, 221; British, 2; Celtic, 3, 31; Franciscan, 36-39; hyphenated, 209-11; Irish, 1; Jewish, 1; Mongol dynasty, 36-39; Nestorian, 6; Nigerian, 2; spread of, 103-5; Taiping, 150-81; Western, xiii; Yuan dynasty, 36-39;
Christianity and Chinese Culture, 194
Christianity the Japanese Way, 204
Chu Hsi. 55. *See also* Zhu Xi
Chung Chi College, 243
Church-centric, 187
Church Missionary Society, 69, 75, 197
Church News, 110
Church of Christ in China, 192
Churches: assembly hall, 196-97; independent, 196; local, 197
Civil service examinations, 41, 61, 151, 162, 173, 184
Civilization, western, 110-14
Clasper, Paul, 243
Clement of Alexandria, 129
Clocks, 42
Cohen, Paul, 249-50
Common Sense Philosophy, 12, 97-98
Communism, 154, 188, 193, 233
Communists, 188, 202, 216, 221, 227, 239
Community, 245, 248
Concubinage, 56
Confessions, 61, 114
Confucian activism, 187-95
Confucian teaching, 9, 12, 23, 25-26, 29, 32, 36, 41, 50, 55, 58, 66, 93, 95, 102, 123, 136, 138, 140-42, 155, 157, 165, 173, 177, 183, 188, 191, 194-95, 201, 203-4, 206, 209-10, 221, 137, 149-50, 252
Confucianism, 6-7, 9-12, 14, 21, 32, 48, 54-55, 65, 96, 105-6, 123-24, 129, 131, 137, 146, 173-74, 183, 189-90, 193, 195, 209-11, 250
Confucius, 7-8, 41-42, 46-47, 57, 60-61, 63, 95, 103, 106, 116-18, 136, 139, 141, 151, 157, 163-65, 183, 189, 203-4, 209-10, 212, 250

Congregation for the Propagation of the Faith, 203, 216

Conscience, 53

Constantine, 32, 118, 175

Constantinople, 37

Constitution, 225, 235

Constitution, Taiping, 154-55

Constitutionism, 183-84

Contextualization, 4, 15, 43, 133-49, 190, 194, 208, 213, 223, 243, 247

Contradiction, 227, 231, 238

Conversion, Buddhist terms for, 130–31

Conversions, 70, 72, 120, 198, 201, 221

Converts, Chinese: Jesuit, 57-61, 85, 114; Protestant, 115-17, 129

Coolie trade, 112

Copernicus, 43

Corbett, Hunter, 108

Covenant, 16, 161

Craighead, James, 108

Creel, H.G., 47, 146

Cronin, Vincent, 55

Cross, 27-28, 58, 114, 122, 200, 216, 220, 241

Crucifix, 59-60

Crucifixion, 54, 56, 59-60

Cuba, 112

Cultural identity, 13, 39, 206

Cyrus, 214

Dainichi, 62

Daiso, 31

Dao, 19, 29, 50, 54, 99, 102, 106, 112-13, 122, 128-32, 139-40, 145, 162, 195, 206, 209, 211

Dao Feng Shan, 122, 129, 207

Dao you, 128

Dao-de, 191, 201

Daode Jing, 139

Daoism, 7, 9, 10-12, 14, 22-25, 29-30, 48-49, 53, 55, 57-58, 60, 62, 65, 96, 105, 123-24, 129, 131, 137, 140, 146-47, 161, 173-74, 191, 198, 204, 229, 250

Daoistic pietism, 195-205

Da-Qing Jing-Jiao Xuan-Yuan zhi-ben Jing, 25

Darwin, Charles, 106

Datong, 157

Death, 28, 51, 62, 120, 121

Delegates' Version, 90

Democracy, 208-9, 224

Demons, 51, 125, 150-52, 161-64, 166-67, 228, 242-43, 247

Deng, Xiaoping, 229

Deus, 31, 62

Devil, 28, 124, 207

Dewey, John, 185

Di, 87-89

Dialogue Between Two Friends, 97

Dialogues with a Temple Keeper, 95

Diamond Sutra, 126

Ding Guangxun, 218, 231-40

Dinghai, 83

Discovery of Genesis and Chinese, 206

Dissertation on the Theology of the Chinese, 86

Divination, 8, 62, 242

Dodd, C.H., 17

Domestic and Foreign Mission Society for the Protestant Episcopal Church, 72

Domestication, 135, 145-47

Dominicans, 40, 47-48, 59, 62, 64, 68, 86-87, 118

Dong Wang, 169

Douglas, Carstairs, 123

Dowager, Empress, 183-84

Dubose, Hampden, 99

Dung Zhongshu, 8, 103

Dunhuang, 25, 31, 137

Dutch, 72

Dyer, Samuel, 115

Earth, age, 105

Eastern Prince (King), 158, 166, 169, 171

Eckhart, Meister, 132

Eclipses, 43

Eddy, Sherwood, 192

Eden, 105, 192

Edessa, 20

Edict of Religious Toleration, 176

Edinburgh 1910, 186

Edinburgh, University of, 97

Edkins, Joseph, 123, 125, 156, 159, 176

Education, 70, 72, 107, 115, 144, 184-85, 208

Edwards, Jonathan, 197

Egypt, 105, 112, 127, 217-18

Eilert, Hakan, 131

Eitel, Ernst J., 123

Elder brother of Jesus, 150-52
Elements, 56, 107
Elite, 41-42, 136, 146, 148, 228, 237, 248, 252; scholarly, 41, 58, 252
Elohim, 87-88
Elvira, Council of, 64
Emperor, Chinese, 39-40, 46, 54, 56, 66, 77, 79, 88, 111, 117, 136-37, 139, 142-44, 183, 248-50; Chien Lung, 111; Dao Guang, 74; Jade, 88; Kangxi, 44-45, 65, 118; Wan Li, 42, 57, 60, 64
Emptiness, 49
Engels, Frederich, 227
England, 72, 81, 85, 96, 111-12, 171
English, xiv, 83
Episcopalians, 75, 88
Eschatology, 52, 82, 97, 125, 199, 239-49
Eternal fate, 60
Ethical issues, 141-42
Euclid, 56-57, 107
Europe, 37, 40, 48, 59, 64, 66, 75, 97, 124, 180, 213
European, 86, 104-5
Evangelical Missionary Society of Basel, 123
Evangelism, 70, 72, 85, 91, 178, 197, 252-53
Eve, 163, 207
Evidences of Christianity, 99-106, 114, 118
Evolution, 105-6, 132
Exercises, 56, 59
Exhortation to Learning, 183
Exorcism, 228, 242-43
Extraterritoriality, 82, 84, 252
Eyes East, 203
Fairbank, John, 182, 252
Faith, Christian, 94, 103-05, 201, 217, 231, 235
Faith healing, 242-43
Fan Yung tai, 99
Faricy, Robert, 216
Fasting, 52, 60, 102
Feastdays, 60
Feng Guifen, 183
Feng Shangli, 211-12
Feng Yingjing, 45
Feng Yunshan, 152-53
Feng-shui (geomancy), 9

Festivals, religious, 115, 144, 228
Feudalism, 6-7, 12, 136, 185, 193, 210, 214, 228, 234, 237, 242
Figurism, 48
Filial piety, 30, 53, 62-63, 95, 104, 117, 120, 133, 141-42, 164, 167, 190, 222, 224
Finney, Charles, 197
Five classics, 155, 157, 173
Five don'ts, 226
Five elements, 8, 56, 98, 100, 141
Five excellencies, 227
Five loves, 227
Five musts, 226
Five precepts, 140
Five relationships, 10, 95, 105, 107, 140
Five virtues, 10, 95
Five Year Movement, 192
Forgiveness, 174, 232, 241
Form, 17-18
Formosa, 111
Foster, John, 34
Foucquet, Jean-Francis, 48
Four books, 155
Four elements, 141
France, 64, 111, 183
Franciscans, 38-40, 47-48, 59-60, 62, 64, 68, 86, 118
Franke, Wolfgang, 39, 58, 66
Free meeting places, 242-47
Freedom, human, 219
Freedom of religion, 225, 242, 246, 251
French, 183, 197
Friendship, 44-45
Fryer, John, 111
Fujian (Fukien), 69, 77, 80
Functional substitute, 120, 224
Funerals, 62, 245
Furtado, Francisco, 60
Future life, 124, 142, 175, 177
Fuzhou, 79, 82-83
Gambling, 74, 94, 154, 156, 162, 164
Gan Wang, 170
Gao Zung, 24
Genahr, Ferdinand, 95
Genesis and Chinese, 206
Genghis Khan, 3
Gentry, 6, 63, 65, 69, 78, 118, 136, 139, 251-52

Geomancy, 62, 242
German, 185
Germany, 64, 183
Glasgow, Univeristy of, 97
Globe Magazine, 110
Gloria in Excelsis Deo, 25, 29
Gnosticism, 16-17
God: creative power, 26, 51, 100, 116, 219, 220; existence, 48-49, 98, 100-101, 232; in Buddhism, 126-27; names, 61-62, 87-90, 178; nature, 41-42, 59, 94, 101-3, 107, 132, 156, 158, 209, 213, 219, 238-40, 243; providence, 104, 124, 175, 214; source of life, 118; Taiping doctrine of, 158-62
Go-i, 140
Golden Mean, 95, 99, 222
Gongyang, zhuan, 157
Good Words Exhorting the Age, 115-16, 155
Goodrich, Carrington, 138
Gordon, Charles (Chinese), 154
Gordon, G. J., 79
Goshen College, 213
Gospel, under Communism: apologetic, 231-33; community, 245; family-centered, 244; incarnate, 238; lay-centered, 244; nature, 242; non-traditional features, 246-47; political, 220, 233-39; prayer, 244; spiritual power, 242-43; suffering, 245-46
Gozhi huibian, 111
Grasso, Domenico, 215
Great Britain, 81, 183
Greece, 127
Greek, 17, 19, 38, 86, 122, 131, 191, 208
Gregorian University, 216
Guang Xuehui, 184
Guangdong, 40, 152-53, 169
Guangxi, 40, 152-53, 169
Guanyin, 125, 145
Gulangsu, 83
Gunboats, 251
Guomindang, 185, 234
Gutzlaff, Charles (Karl), 69, 73-77, 79-80, 95, 155-56, 158
Guyon, Madame, 197, 199
Hakka, 151-52
Hamburg, 156

Han dynasty, 21, 103, 112, 136-37, 151
Han people, 4, 148
Hankow, 176
Happer, Dr., 178
Healing, 28, 242-43
Heart, 93-94
Heaven, 7, 24, 31, 46, 51-53, 56, 58, 93-95, 99, 101, 103, 105, 112, 118, 124-25, 136, 151, 153, 156, 162-66, 168, 173, 189, 208
Heaven, mandate, 7-8, 173, 211
Heavenly: bodies, 100; brother, 160; elder brother, 150-52, 160, 163, 165, 167-69; family, 160-61, 171; father, 160-61, 163, 165-66, 169; King, 153, 156, 161, 166; Lord, 36, 49, 53-54, 62-63, 87, 117; mother, 150, 160; sister-in-law, 160
Hebrew, 131
Hell, 31, 52-53, 60, 94, 97, 103, 105, 124-25, 142, 153-54, 162, 168, 240
Heresies, 27, 57, 78, 174, 197, 247, 250, 255
Hermeneutics, 199-200
Herschel, John F.W., 107
Hiebert, Paul, 180
Hillier, C.B., 109
Hinayana, 31, 126-27, 137
Hodgson, John, Jr., 85
Holmes, E.J., 177-78
Holy Spirit, 56, 90, 95, 150, 169, 171, 177, 194, 211, 217, 237, 244
Home-house meetings, 196, 199, 228-29, 234, 236-37, 242
Homer, 109
Hong Kong, 82-83, 108, 111, 129, 151, 207-8, 243
Hong Rengan, 152, 156, 170-72, 176-78
Hong Xiuquan: contact with Roberts, 152, 155-56; insanity, 172; view of himself, 152, 168; visions, 151-52
Hospitals, 70
Hsu, Immanuel, 211, 224
Huangdi, 88
Hubei, 183
Hui people, 148
Huiyuan, 139
Human: body, 101-2; destiny, 60; nature, 26, 41, 53-54, 94, 101, 103, 166, 208

Humanism, 7, 10, 214
Hume, David, 98
Hunan, 183
Hunanghui, 49
Huns, 138
Huron, 76-77, 79-81
Hymn to the Holy Trinity, 25
I Jing, 8, 26, 103, 146, 212
I Wang, 170
Idealism, 98, 231
Identification, 91, 237
Idolatry, 56, 62, 64, 66, 74, 94-95, 100,
    105, 116, 118-20, 156, 161-62, 171,
    175, 217, 253
Idols, 152, 154
Ignatius, St., 59
Ili, 183
Imitation of Christ, 56
Imperialism, 185, 193, 196, 202, 214,
    225-26, 228, 234, 236-37, 253
Incarnation, 15, 40, 220, 222-223, 237
Independent churches, 196
India, 3, 13, 31, 40, 52, 74, 105, 112, 114,
    127, 133, 138, 142-43
Indian, 72, 105, 135, 142, 145
Indianization, 134
Indigeneity: structural, xiv, 188, 192,
    196, 244; theological, xiv, 189, 197
Indigenization, 14-15, 56, 143, 147-48,
    187-89, 195, 204, 220; of Buddhism,
    133-49; New Testament, 16-17; Old
    Testament, 15-16; principles for, 17-
    19
Indigenous, xiv, 4, 187, 225
Inter-Varsity, 233
Introduction to Messiah, 25, 28
Intuition, 198-99
Ireland, 1, 3
Islam, 34, 38, 96, 148, 233, 248
Israel, 165-66, 171, 217-18
Italy, 64, 111
James, John Angell, 96
Japan, 3, 19, 31, 40, 60, 62, 73, 104, 112,
    114, 125-26, 183-85, 193, 199, 202,
    204, 213, 221
Japanese, 62
Java, 72
Jehovah, 61, 89, 124
Jen Yu-wen, 157, 169, 173-74

Jesuits, 3, 6, 36, 38-68, 76, 86-87, 94, 97,
    107, 118, 122, 249-50
Jesus, 16-17, 96-97, 104; birthplace, 106;
    center of Gospel, 106; compared to
    Pusa and Confucius, 116-17; death
    of, 27-28; essence of Christianity, 188,
    209, 221; example of, 194; miracles,
    54, 104; model, 194, 209; nature, 27,
    104; resurrection, 28, 104; science,
    108; second advent, 198, 202, 244, 246
Jewish, 16–17, 47
Jews, 23, 99, 106, 127, 149
Jiang Jieshi (Chiang Kai Shek), 201, 234
Jiang Peifan, 240
Jiangsu, 137-38
Jiangsu Christian Council, 240
Jiaohui Xinbao, 108, 110
Jiaozhou, 137
Jin Dan Jiao, 24, 36
Jing Feng Shan, 128
Jing Jiao, 30
Jing Tianying, 225
John, Griffith, 108, 156, 176
John, the Gospel of, 129
John of Montecorvino, 38, 250
Jones, Francis, 235
Judaism, 233
Judgment, 97, 116, 177, 226
Judson, Adoniram, 107-08
Jupiter, 88
Justin Martyr, 129
Kaifeng, 149
Kang, C.H., 206
Kang Yuwei, 183-84
Karakorum, 37
Karma, 139, 142
Keraits, 36-37
Keswick conferences, 197
Key of faith, 4
Khotan, 138
Khubilai Khan, 38
Kingdom of God (heaven), 17, 126, 132,
    167, 174, 190, 192-94, 201, 242
Kitamori, Kazoh, 19, 221
Knowledge, 10; western, 109
Knox, John, 197
Koran, 18, 91
Korea, 31, 125-26, 183, 234
Kowtow, 83

Koyama, Kosuke, 26
Kraemer, Hendrik, 129
Kraft, Charles, 135, 180
Kumar, S. Ananda, 15-16
Kumarajiva, 138, 141
Kung Fu Zi (Confucius), 21
Kushan Empire, 136
Lao-tzu, 139, 191
Latin, 31, 38, 61-62
Latourette, K.S., 31-33, 64, 72, 115, 173, 249
Law(s): biblical, 17; ecclesiastical, 60; exclusive, 74-75,77, 80; moral, 14
Lay activities, 243
Lazarist, 69, 81
Lee, Jung Young, 212-13
Lee, Peter, 207-08
Legge, James, 25, 98, 109, 128, 156, 175
Leibniz, Gottfried, 48
Levenson, Joseph, 172-73, 248-49
Lewis, C.S., 243
Li (reason, principle, truth), 49, 93, 95, 100, 102, 110, 142, 166
Li, Witness, 196
Li Chih-tsao, 55
Li Hongzhang, 154
Li Ma-tou, 44
Li Zhizao, 62. See also Li Chih-tsao
Li Zhowu, 42
Liang A-fa, 70-71, 115, 151, 158, 171
Liang Qichao, 183
Liberation theology, 15, 218, 221, 235, 239-40
Licentiousness, 164
Lin, Robert, 179
Lin Yu-tang, 11
Lindsay, Hugh Hamilton, 73, 75
Linghun, 62, 101
Literary efforts: Jesuits, 44-59, 94, 114-15; Protestants, 70, 73, 91-114
Literati, 55, 58, 77, 107
Literature, 77; Confucian references, 94-96; nature of, 106-8; Roman Catholic missionaries, 114-115; secular, 106-14
Littell, John, 174
Little flock, 196-226
Liturgy, 38, 61
Liu Shaoqi, 210
Livingston, David, 112

Locke, John, 98
Logos, 17-19, 122, 128-29, 132, 221
Logos spermatikos, 129
London, 2, 96, 196, 223
London Missionary Society, 72, 74-76, 86, 95-97, 102, 108, 115, 123, 151, 159, 170, 175-76, 201
Longobardi, Nicolo, 47-48, 62
Lotus, 122, 220
Lotus Scripture, 125
Louvain, 215, 240
Love, 171, 174, 190, 192, 220, 239, 247
Loyal King, 176
Loyang, 137-38
Loyola, 56
Lu Siqiang, 184, 252
Lu Xiangshan, 47
Lu Xun, 185
Lucifer, 51
Luther, Martin, 156, 197
Lying, 94, 156
Macao, 40, 56, 59, 65, 68-72, 76, 80, 91, 112, 151, 250
MacGowan, Daniel, 107, 109
MacInnes, Donald, 215
Madras Missionary Conference 1938, 129
Magic, 137, 144, 157, 161
Mahayana, 31, 126-27, 131, 145
Maitreya, 145
Malacca, 70, 72, 97, 151
Malays, 72
Manchus, 43, 151, 153-54, 182-84, 196, 249; anti-Manchus, 153-54
Mandate of heaven. See Heaven, mandate
Manichaeism, 23, 30, 149
Manifesto to the World on Behalf of Chinese Culture, 208
Mao Zedong, 214-15, 227-28
Maoism, 210, 214, 216-17, 222-23
Marie, Fr. Ste., 47
Mark, 37
Marriage practices, 56
Martin, Mary Louise, 58
Martin, Samuel, 178
Martin, W.A.P., 99-106, 110-14, 118-19, 123-24, 132, 175, 177-78, 181, 183
Martyrdom, 245-46

Marxism, 148, 170, 172, 185, 188, 193, 210, 216, 231, 235, 239, 253
Mary, 27, 115, 150, 227
Mass conversion, 148
Masses for dead, 30-31
Masses of people, 59, 195, 251
Materialism, 231, 233
Mathematics, 57
May 4 Movement, 185
Meadows, Thomas, 155, 158, 170, 172-73
Meaning, 17-18
Medhurst, Walter, 72-73, 75-77, 79, 86, 88, 109, 156, 158, 178
Medicine, 73, 77, 243
Meeting points, 242
Melchizedek, 129, 168-69
Mencius, 7-8, 46-47, 53-54, 95, 102-3, 157, 189, 212
Mercy, boat of, 28-29
Mercy, works of, 29
Mesopotamia, 20
Messiah, 1-2, 7, 28, 106, 126
Metempsychosis, 52, 124
Methodist, 109
Meyer, F.B., 197
Miao tribespeople, 4, 152
Michael, Franz, 172, 174
Middle way, 11-12
Milne, William, 97, 115-16, 151
Min river, 73, 79
Mind, Chinese, 7-14, 39
Ming dynasty, 39, 43, 45, 49, 52, 57, 61, 63, 65, 68, 102, 154, 157, 203
Mingdi, 136
Minority groups, 4
Miracles, 103-4, 242-43
Mission Among the Higher Classes in China, 251
Missionary Conference Shanghai (1877), 119; (1890) 119, 186; (1907) 120, 186
Missionary Herald, 75
Missionary incidents, 184, 251, 253
Mission-centric, 187
Modernization, 170, 183-84, 208, 247
Modernizations, four, 229
Mohammedanism, 91. *See also* Muslims
Monastic, 133, 142-43, 180
Mongoloid, 4
Mongols, 4, 6, 28, 37-39, 86, 250

Monism, 51
Mon-khmer, 5
Monotheistim, 106, 158, 206, 253
Montreal Conference, 239-41
Moral tracts, 93
de Morales, Juan Bautista, 61
Morality, 53, 94, 104, 201, 223, 232
Morrison, Robert, 69, 71, 76, 85-86, 96, 115, 158, 171
Morrison Education Society, 71, 109
Moseley, William, 85-86
Moses, 206
Moti, 189
Moule, A.C., 28
Muirhead, William, 96, 156, 176
Mukyokai, 204
Mulien, 141
Murder, 164
Murray, Andrew, 197
Muslims, 18, 23-24, 36-37, 43, 148, 221, 229
Mysticism, 195-97, 199
Nan Wango, 170
Nanchang, 40-42
Nanjing, 40, 42, 49, 65, 69, 126, 128-29, 153, 156, 159, 166, 170, 176-77, 182, 203
Nanjing Union Theological College, 190, 230-31, 239
Nanking, 55
Naples, 37, 112
National Beijing University, 185
National Christian Conference, 186
Nationalism, 185, 197, 200, 237
Nationalist Party (Guomindang), 185
Natural law, theology, reason, 46, 48, 52, 55, 71, 86, 94, 97-103, 109-10
Natural Philosphy, 107
Natural Theology, 98, 100
Nature, 8, 10, 12, 110-12; human, 14, 26, 41, 52-54, 199
Needham, Joseph, 43
Neill, Stephen, 40
Neo-Confucian, 46-47, 55, 57, 63, 146, 208-09
Nerchinsk, treaty of, 43
Nestorian, 37-38, 65, 58, 86, 147, 199, 248-50; degree of syncretism, 33-34; early translations, 25-26; evaluation

of, 32-35; filial piety, 30; foreign nature, 33; gospel, 25-29; growth in Persia, 20-21; impact on Roman Empire, 32; imperial patronage, 22-24; influence on Buddhism, 30-31; monument, 24, 28, 34; names of their religion, 30; patriotism, 30; persecution, 24; priests, 30; relation to Buddhists, 30-31; relation to political power, 32-33; translation efforts, 24-25, 31; use of Dao, 29
Nestorius, 20, 27
Netherlands Missionary Society, 69, 73
Nevius, John, 3
New Confucian, The, 209
New Life Movement, 201
New Testament, 38, 104, 116, 125, 155, 167, 175, 177, 201, 228, 242
Newton, John, 107
Ng, Lee-ming, 259
Ni, Watchman (Ni Duosheng), 196-202, 204, 225, 242
Nicea, 1-2
Nicholls, Bruce, 18
Niebuhr, Richard, 198, 203
Nigeria, 2
Ningbo, 82-83, 99, 107, 109
Nirvana, 31, 133, 140
Nisibis, 20
Nixon, Richard, 229
Noah, 47
North American, 196
North China Tract Society, 99
Northeastern Theological Seminary, 230
Northern China United Christian Promotion Association, 202
Northern King, 170
Norwegian Missionary Society, 128
O'Collins, Gerald, 216
Odes for Youth, 155
Odorico de Pordenone, 38
Offerings, food, 63
Ogden, Schubert, 219
Old Testament, 104, 116, 155, 160, 165, 167-68, 171, 177, 189, 214, 228, 239
Olyphant, David, 76
Onguts, 36
Ontological necessity, 18
Opium, 73, 76-77, 80, 82-83, 94, 112, 117, 153-54, 156, 251

Opium war, 81-83, 153
Opthalmic hospital, 70
Oral communication, 90-91
Origen, 129, 191-92
Origin of Species, 106
Outerbridge, Leonard, 21, 64
Outlines of Astronomy, 107
Outline of Moral Philosophy, 101
Pacific, islands of, 105
Pagoda, 145
Pain of God, 19, 221
Palestine, 104, 106
Paley, William, 98, 100-102
Pan Gu, 105, 161-62
Pannenberg, Wolfhart, 218
Pantheism, 41, 51, 233
Papal delegation, 59
Paris, 37
Parker, Peter, 70-71
Parthia, 138
Patriotic Association of Chinese Catholics, 229-30
Paul, St., 78, 129
Pax tatarica, 37
Pearl River, 39
Pei Wang, 170
Peking (Beijing), 45
Peking Magazine, 111-14
Penang, 70, 72, 115
Penn-Lewis, Jesse, 197, 199
People movement, 180
People's Political Consultative Conference, 227, 231
People's Republic of China, 170, 185, 192, 210, 217, 229
Perboyre, 69
Perfect Man's Model, 95
Persecution, 65, 68-69, 135, 141-43, 229, 237, 245-46
Persia, 20, 27, 32, 34, 37, 39, 127, 214
Persian religions, 149
Philippi, 78
Pietists, 195-97, 201, 204
Points of contact, 131
Politeness, 11
Political, 225-26, 231, 234-35; theory, Chinese, 39
Polo, Marco, 38, 213
Polo, Nicolo and Maffeo, 38
Polygyny, 7, 56, 66, 154

Pompei, 112
Poor Joseph, 96
Pope, 40, 56, 64, 66, 68-69, 230-31, 249
Portugal, 64
Portuguese, 39-40, 56, 59, 68, 71-72, 112
Power, in missions, 65, 68-84, 104, 106, 147-48, 195, 249-50
Power of God, 18
Praeparatio evangelica, 125, 221
Prayer(s), 30, 114, 167-68, 198, 241, 244
Prayer meeting, 230
Preevangelism, 54-55
Presbyterian: American, 108; English, 123
Prester, John, 37
Priesthood, 60
Princeton Seminary, 97
Principia, 107
Prophecy, fulfilled, 103-4
Propriety, 10, 14
Protectorate, French, 82
Protestants, 6, 33, 44, 67-68, 70, 81-82, 94, 97, 107, 117, 119, 122, 136, 139, 147-48, 156, 170, 186, 204, 217-22, 225, 229, 231, 248
Psalter, 38
Ptolemaic theory, 43
Pure Land Buddhism, 31, 125-26, 139, 145
Pusa, 89, 104. *See also* Bodhisattva
Pythagoras, 52
Qi Xin Lun, 125-28. *See also Awakening of Faith*
Qing dynasty, 45, 49, 52, 63, 65, 68, 137, 153, 203
Quanshi Liangyan, 115-16, 155
Questions About Christianity, 95
Questions Concerning the Faith, 233
Reality, cognitive approaches to, 12-13
Reason, 46, 48, 52, 98, 146
Rebirth, 145
Reciprocity (*bao*), 44
Reconciliation, 19, 238, 247
Red Guards, 245
Redeemer, 234
Redeemer of sickness, 169
Reform, 111-14, 199
Reformation, Protestant, 40, 85
Reformers, 113, 148, 183-84
Reichelt, Karl, 31, 122, 128-32

Reid, Gilbert, 119, 184, 251
Reid, Thomas, 97
Reincarnation, 95, 97
Relationships, 10, 19, 95, 238, 240
Religion: diffused and specialized, 9; foreign, xiii, 124, 133, 142, 188, 194, 237-38, 241, 247, 251-53; freedom of, 225, 236, 242-43, 246, 251; need for, 214, 225
Religions, Chinese, 229
Religious Affairs Bureau, 225-26, 229, 246
Religious conflicts, 236
Ren, 10, 14, 109, 189-90, 194, 211. *See also* Benevolence
Repentance, 124, 166, 232
Republicanism, 183-84
Results, early Protestant, 72, 186
Resurrection, 54, 95, 97, 104, 202, 216, 220
Retribution, 124
Revelation, 90, 98, 235; direct, 100-101, 103, 129, 156, 218; general, 100-101, 127, 129, 207, 218
Revival, religious, 192, 198
Revolution, 187; cultural, 210; 228-29, 237, 240, 242, 245; literary, 185; permanent, 216; Wuchang, 184
Revolutionary, 184, 193
Rhenish Mission Society, 95
Ricci, Matteo, 13, 36, 40-42, 44, 45-67, 102, 203
Richard, Timothy, 24, 31, 120, 125-28, 132, 183, 184
Righteousness, 10, 14, 208, 211
Rites controversy, 61-67, 118, 249
River trips, 79-81
Riverside Church, 239
Robbery, 164
Roberts, Evan, 197
Roberts, Issacher, 152, 155-56, 177-78
Roman Catholic Church, 38, 39, 53-54, 62, 120, 124, 136-37, 139, 147, 186, 204, 216, 229, 231, 245, 248-49; attitudes of Protestants, 69; attitude to Protestants, 81; disunity, 65; interpretations of new China, 215-17; literature work, 44-59, 94, 114-15; protected by French, 82; response to new context, 186-87, 202-5; sacrifi-

cial spirit, 69; Taiping rebellion, 174-81

Roman empire, 99, 112, 124, 138

Rome, 31, 37-38

Rowbotham, Arnold, 41, 64

Royal Society, 85

Ruggieri, Nichole, 36, 40-41, 59

Rulai, 127

Rule, Paul, 216

Russia, 43, 183, 185

Sabbath, 94, 156, 167, 178

Sabellianism, 200

Sacred Explanation of the Life of Christ Illustrated with Pictures, 60

Sacrifices, 8-9, 62-63, 102, 105, 118, 142, 167, 171

Saeki, P.Y., 23-24, 26, 30

Sakyamoni, 29, 52

Salvation, 29, 94-97, 114-25, 125, 130, 132, 140, 165-66, 188, 190, 195, 201-2, 215-19, 232

Salvation Army, 226

Salvation by grace, 31

Sangha, 142-44, 146

Sanhui, 49

Sanskirt, 105, 127-28, 138, 141, 145

Satan, 26, 199, 234-44

Sauma, 37

Scholasticism, 55

Science, 42, 57, 59, 69, 105-14

Scottish realism, 97-98, 106. *See also* Common Sense Philosophy

Script, unified, 6

Scriptures, 29, 94, 102, 115, 155, 171, 175, 202, 218

Seamen, ministry to, 71

Self-propagation, 231

Self-strengthening, 182

Seminaries, 230

Seneca, 45

Sermon on Mount, 94, 96

Seventh Day Adventists, 226

Sex, 250

Shang period, 158

Shangdi, 61-62, 87-88, 90, 95, 99, 102, 157-58

Shandong, 77, 108, 137, 184-85, 210

Shanghai, 57, 77, 82-83, 111, 119, 176, 180, 184, 226

Shanghai Serial, 102, 109

Shanxi, 184, 226

Shanzi, 141

Shaw, Yuming, 66

Sheffield, D.Z., 124

Shen, 62, 87-90, 99

Shen ye, 158

Shenyang, 230

Shenyehohua, 158

Shi, Hu, 134-35, 139, 145-46, 185

Shield King, 170, 176

Shih, Vincent, 166

Shouters, 246

Shujing, 87

Shun, 60, 105, 183, 212

Shusaku, Endo, 221

Sichuan, 4, 85, 137

Signs and wonders, 242-43

Sih, Paul, 46

Silence, 221

Silk trade, 136

Sin, 26, 93, 96-97, 103, 124, 143, 162-65, 188, 193-94, 201, 208, 212, 232, 240

Sincerity, 10

Singapore, 70, 72, 81

Sinicization, 135, 138, 139, 145, 148

Sinim, 175

Sinkiang, 183

Sino-Japanese conflict, 14, 183

Sit, Walk, Stand, 198

Slave trade, 2, 89, 112

Sloane, Sir Hans, 85

Smith, Adam, 97

Smith, F.H., 12

Social Reconstruction, 192

Socialism, 194

Society for the Diffusion of Christian and General Knowledge Among the Chinese, 184

Society for the Diffusion of Useful Knowledge, 71, 110

Society for the Study of National Strengthening, 183

Society of Jesus (Jesuits), 6, 39, 40, 102; attitudes, 41, 43-44; literature, use of, 44-59; natural theology, 46, 48, 52, 55; power, use of, 59; problems, 59-67; Protestant view of, 69, 102; rites controversy, 61-67; science, use of, 42, 57-59, 69; "term question," 61

Socrates, 101

Sodalities, 59
Sogdiana, 138
Son of God, 17-18, 168-69, 171-72, 175, 228, 234
Son of heaven, 39, 66, 74, 136
Son of man, 17-18
Song, C.S., 218-21
Soochow, 176-77
Soothill, W.E., 128
Sorcery, 9
Soul(s), 31, 49-50, 52, 62, 89, 95, 101, 103, 106, 124, 139, 142, 144, 146, 198
Southern King, 170
Spain, 64
Spirit(s), 88, 198
Spiritual Food, 201
Spiritual Man, 198
Spirituality, 198, 204, 220, 246
Spring and Autumn Annals, 157
Squire, E.B., 69
State-church relationships, 30, 199, 202, 223, 233
Stevens, E.B., 73, 76-77, 79-80, 155
Stewart, Dugald, 97, 101-2
Stronach, John, 95
Student Christian Movement, 192
Stupa, 145
Suffering church, 216, 229, 245
Sullivan, F.A., 216-17
Summa Theologie, 56
Sun Yat-sen, 184-85, 224
Sung dynasty, 47, 95, 102, 141, 146, 157, 175, 250
Sunyata, 131
Superior person, 10, 50-52, 95, 194, 212
Superstitions, 111, 242-43
Swatow, 196
Swedenborgianism, 173
Sylph, 73
Syncretism, 16-17, 56, 147
Syrian, 23
Ta Ch'in, 23, 27
Ta Ch'in Illustrius Book, 25
Tadzhiks, 5
Tai people, 4
Tai Zung, 22-25, 33
Taiji, 8, 26, 49, 100, 102, 105
Taipei, 184
Taiping, 115, 150-82; attitude of Roman Catholic missionaries to, 180; capital at Nanjing, 153; Chinese content of Gospel, 173-74; church attendance, 154; civil service examination, 155; conditions producing, 151-53; constitution, 154-55; documents, 158; eschatology, 167-68; evaluation of Gospel, 170-73; example of "people movement," 180; expanded organization, 153; founder, 151-53; God worshippers, 152-53; land policy, 154; military battles, 153; military organization, 154; missionary evaluation of, 174-81; moral requirements, 154-55; name, 153; prayers, 167-68; reasons for failure, 153, 180-81; religious ceremonies, 166-67; religious standards, 166; salvation, 165-66; sin, 162-65; sources of ideology, 116, 155-57; Taiping Gospel, 157-68; views toward Confucius, 163; views toward Jesus, 168-69; weaknesses of Christianity, 168-70
Taiwan, 196, 208-9, 231, 252
Taiyuan, 226
Tan Sitong, 183
Tang dynasty, 3, 6, 20-21, 24, 142-44, 146
Taoism. *See* Daoism
Tathagata, 127-28
Taylor, Hudson, 120
Tears of Lady Meng, 220
Ten Commandments, 94, 114, 116, 162, 165
"Term question," Protestant, 86-90
Tertullian, 99, 191-92
Theism, 106, 227, 231
Theological thinking, 14, 190-91
Theos, 87-88
Thomas, St., 127
Thomas a Kempis, 132
Thomistic, 97, 203
Three Character Classic, 154
Three-self movement, 188, 192, 196, 200, 202, 225, 228-30, 234-35, 242, 245-46
Three selves, xiv
Thucydides, 109
Tian, 61-62, 88, 158
Tian Feng, 230
Tian Wang, 153, 167
Tiandao. *See* Dao
Tiandao Suyuan, 99-106

Tianfu, 158
Tianjin, 73-74, 99
Tianli, 110
Tianli Yaolun, 158
Tianshen, 62
Tianzhu, 62, 87, 99
Tibeto-Burmese, 4
Tien Tai, 125
Timur, Emperor, 38
Tract, Confucian, 92-93
Trade, 39, 73
Translation, of classics, 56
Transmigration, 94, 103. *See also* Metempsychosis
Treaty ports, 82-83, 148
Treaties, 82, 84, 182, 188, 234, 237, 251-52
Triad society, 153
Tribute system, 82
Trimetrical classic, 161
Trinity, 49, 157, 170-71, 177, 200, 239-40
Trinity College, 197
Triviere, Leon, 216
True Idea of God (Tianzhu Shiyi), 45; demons and human souls, 51; false religions, 49; God's existence, 48-49; God's nature, 49, 51; human destiny, 52-53; human nature, 53; human soul, 49-50; Jesus, 54; priestly celibacy, 53-54; similarity to *Evidences of Christianity*, 102; state of death, 51
Truth, 11
Tung Wen Guan, 99
Tungusic groups, 4
Turkic peoples, 4
Tushita heaven, 145
Uettong Baptist Church, 156
Uighur, 36-37
Unc Khan. *See* Prester, John
Union Bible, 90
United Board for Christian Higher Education in China, 238
United front, 227, 229
Unity: church, 226; race, 105
Urban VIII, Pope, 60
Utopia, 183
Vairocana, 30
Valignano, 3, 60
Vatican, 40, 62, 64, 67, 86, 114, 216, 229-31, 249-50

Vatican II, 216, 231
Venus, 111
Verbiest, Ferdinand, 43
Versailles treaty, 185
Vihnanavada, 145
Virtues, five, 10
Visser't Hooft, W.A., 19
Von Ball, Adam Schall, 43, 56, 60
Vulgate, 86
"Wall of light," 70-73
Wallace, Anthony, 135
Walton, Alan, 127
Wang Mingdao, 200-02, 204, 225-26, 242
Wang Yang-ming, 157
Wang Zhuanshan, 57
Wanguo Gongbao, 110. *See Globe Magazine*
War, 82
Way, 23, 29. *See also* Dao
Wayland, Francis, 90
Wei, Isaac, 225
West, Charles, 217
Western Prince (King), 158, 166, 169
Westernization, 109, 182, 246
Whampoa, 76
Whitehead, Raymond, 214, 217-19
Whitfield, George, 197
Wife of God, 150
William of Rubruk, 37
Williams, Samuel Wells, 71
Williamson, Alexander, 102
Willowbank Consultation, 15-16
Wisdom of God, 18
Witchcraft, 164
Witherspoon, John, 97
Word of God, 18
Worship, 156, 162, 165, 222, 228, 236, 242
Worship God Society, 152, 174
Wright, Arthur, 137
Wu, 105
Wu Hou, 24, 30
Wu Leizhuan, 194-95, 204
Wu Yaozong, 192-94, 202, 204
Wu Yungzhuan, 233
Wu Zung, 24, 32
Wuchang, 137
Wylie, Alexander, 25, 102
Xavier, Francis, 3, 31, 40, 62
Xi Wang, 169

Xian, 25
Xiao Chaoguei, 158, 166, 169-70, 172
Xinjiang, 5
Xiongnu, 138
Xu Guangqi, 45, 54, 57-58, 62
Xuan Zhuang, 23
Xun, Lu, 185
Xun Zi, 103
Yang, C.K., 8, 9
Yang, Tingyun, 62
Yang Xiuqing, 158, 166, 169-72
Yangtze river, 4, 153
Yao, 60, 105, 183, 212
Yates, Matthew, 119
Yelikowen, 38
Yellow turban revolt, 138
Yenjing University, 187, 194, 195
Yi people, 4
Yin-yang, 8, 26, 51, 89, 100, 105, 146, 212-13
Yi-shen lun, 25
Y.M.C.A.-Y.W.C.A., 192, 230
Yuan dynasty, 3, 24, 86
Yuan Shikai, 185
Yueh-zhi, 136
Yu-huang, 88
Yulanpen, 142
Yulanpen Jing, 142
Yunnan, 4, 183

Yu-pin, Paul, 203
Zaitun, 38
Zen, 204, 209
Zeng Guofan, 154
Zengmi, 142
Zeus, 17, 88
Zhang Junmai, 208
Zhang Zidong, 183
Zhao, Zichen, 187-92, 204, 231
Zhao Tianen (*see* Jonathan Chao), 222-223, 246
Zhaoqing, 40-42
Zheng, 166
Zhenru, 127-28
Zhi-xuan an-lo Jing, 25
Zhong Wang, 176-77
Zhong Yong, 95
Zhongzi Wenjian Lu (Peking Magazine), 111-14
Zhou, 149, 158
Zhou, rites of, 154
Zhou Enlai, 225
Zhu Changlo, 49
Zhuang Zi, 191
Zhuxi (Chu Hsi), 47, 95, 102, 211
Zili, 184
Zoroastrians, 23, 30, 130
Zurcher, E., 139, 145